EMOTIONAL COMMUNITIES IN THE EARLY MIDDLE AGES

EMOTIONAL COMMUNITIES *in the* EARLY MIDDLE AGES

Barbara H. Rosenwein

CORNELL UNIVERSITY PRESS

Ithaca & London

Copyright © 2006 by Cornell University

All rights reserved. Except for brief quotations in a review, this book, or parts thereof, must not be reproduced in any form without permission in writing from the publisher. For information, address Cornell University Press, Sage House, 512 East State Street, Ithaca, New York 14850.

First published 2006 by Cornell University Press
First printing, Cornell paperbacks, 2007

Printed in the United States of America

Library of Congress Cataloging-in-Publication Data
Rosenwein, Barbara H.
  Emotional communities in the early Middle Ages / Barbara H. Rosenwein.
    p. cm.
  Includes bibliographical references and index.
  ISBN-13: 978-0-8014-4478-4 (cloth : alk. paper)
  ISBN-13: 978-0-8014-7416-3 (pbk. : alk. paper)
    1. Emotions—History. 2. Social history—Medieval, 500-1500.
  I. Title.
  BF531.R68 2006
  152.4094'09021—dc22
                                              2006001767

Cornell University Press strives to use environmentally responsible suppliers and materials to the fullest extent possible in the publishing of its books. Such materials include vegetable-based, low-VOC inks and acid-free papers that are recycled, totally chlorine-free, or partly composed of nonwood fibers. For further information, visit our website at www.cornellpress.cornell.edu.

Cloth printing   10 9 8 7 6 5 4 3 2 1
Paperback printing   10 9 8 7 6 5 4 3 2 1

TO TOM, AS ALWAYS

This warrior irascibility of yours;
when it has come back home, what is it like
with your wife, children, and slaves?
Do you think that it's useful there, too?
CICERO, *Tusculan Disputations*

CONTENTS

List of Tables and Map x

Prefatory Note xi

Acknowledgments xiii

Abbreviations xvii

Introduction 1

1. The Ancient Legacy 32
2. Confronting Death 57
3. Passions and Power 79
4. The Poet and the Bishop 100
5. Courtly Discipline 130
6. Reveling in Rancor 163

Conclusion 191

Selected Bibliography 205

Index 221

TABLES AND MAP

TABLES

1. The Stoic Emotional Grid 39
2. Cicero's List of Stoic Emotions and Approximate English Equivalents 40
3. Partial Latin Emotion Word List and Approximate English Equivalents 52
4. Emotion Words at Trier and Clermont Compared 70
5. Emotion Words in Vienne Inscriptions 74
6. Emotion Words in Non-Episcopal Vienne Inscriptions 76
7. The Merovingians 104

MAP

The Early Medieval West 58

PREFATORY NOTE

I have regularized the use of *i/j* and *u/v* in accordance with the rules given by H. A. Kelly, "Uniformity and Sense in Editing and Citing Medieval Texts," in *Medieval Academy News* (Spring 2004), p. 8: I use the *i* and *u* for the vowel sound and *j* and *v* for the consonant sound. However, I have not regularized other orthography, so that when quoting from a source that "misspells" a word, I give the word in its original form, without either emendation or the cautionary *sic*. Nor have I changed the punctuation of the editions that I have used, however dubious they may be. All translations are my own unless otherwise noted, but I have consulted—and acknowledge with gratitude—the various translations that have been made of many of the sources used herein.

ACKNOWLEDGMENTS

I am grateful to Damien Boquet, Monique Bourin, Michel Bourin, Karl Brunner, Nancy Gauthier, Mayke de Jong, Daniela Romagnoli, Robert E. Rosenwein, Julia M. H. Smith, Daniel Smail, and my Loyola colleagues Leslie Dossey, Allen Frantzen, and Theresa Gross-Diaz for illuminating discussions. I offer special thanks to Tom Rosenwein and Esther Cohen, both of whom, in effect, suggested I write this book. Riccardo Cristiani, Albrecht Diem, and Piroska Nagy were nearly constant e-mail companions.

John Ackerman, Damien Boquet, Riccardo Cristiani, Mayke de Jong, Maureen C. Miller, Alexander C. Murray, Piroska Nagy, Tom Rosenwein, Julia Smith, and Ian Wood generously read the first draft and offered extraordinarily helpful comments and suggestions. Graham Robert Edwards and Danuta Shanzer gave illuminating advice on the second draft. Nancy Gauthier read and commented on chapter 2; Catherine Mardikes and Jacqueline Long reviewed chapter 1. The errors and infelicities that remain are mine.

Invitations to speak on the topic of this book made it possible for me to discuss and refine my ideas. Jinty Nelson, Walter Pohl, and Mary Carruthers (at London, Vienna, and New York, respectively, in 1999 and 2000) give me my first opportunities to speak on the subject. A talk at the Sorbonne in 2001, at the welcome invitation of Monique Bourin and Claude Gauvard, allowed me to consider emotions in politics. My colleagues at the Loyola Medieval Studies Center—Leslie Dossey, Blake Dutton, Allen Frantzen, Theresa Gross-Diaz, Jacqueline Long, Dennis Martin, the late Michael Masi, Sally Metzler—were kind enough to adopt the topic "Emotions and Gestures" for our 2001 lecture series at my request, giving us all the occasion to explore the subject with our students and me the chance to sum up my thoughts in a lecture that eventually became an article, "Worrying about Emotions in History."

I thank Richard Abels, Ann Astell, François Bougard, Karl Brunner, Robert Bucholz, Isabelle Cochelin, Mayke de Jong, Sharon Farmer, Rachel Fulton, Mary Garrison, Claude Gauvard, Hans-Werner Goetz, Andrea Griesebner, Lynn Hunt, Paul Hyams, Robert Jacobs, Gerhard Jaritz, Jörg Jarnut, C. Stephen Jaeger, Ingrid Kasten, Richard Kieckhefer, Carol Lansing, Régine Le Jan, Maureen Miller, Piroska Nagy, Barbara Newman, Susie Phillips, Walter Pohl, Ann Roberts, Alan Thacker, Anna Trumbore, and Marta VanLandingham for further opportunities to present my work at venues ranging from Vienna to Santa Barbara during the period 2002 to 2005.

In April 2001 I spent a memorable day at the invitation of Stephen D. White and Elizabeth Pastan teaching "Emotions" to their joint seminar at Emory University (Atlanta). In November 2001 through January 2002, I had a magical experience as Scholar in Residence at the American Academy of Rome, thanks to the kind invitation of Lester K. Little. There I worked on the materials that would become chapters 3, 5, and 6 of this book, and I was able to present some of my work to that diverse and learned audience, which I warmly thank. I should in particular like to record my gratitude to Carmela Franklin, a marvelous and generous guide to Rome's archives. Daniela Romagnoli's invitation to write for the catalogue *Il Medioevo Europeo di Jacques Le Goff* in 2003 as well as speak about emotions in Parma gave me my first experience lecturing in Italian, a heady moment for which I am enormously grateful.

I am indebted to the National Endowment for the Humanities for a Fellowship in 1999–2000 that allowed me to launch the research for this book. I thank Loyola University Chicago for supporting this project in numerous ways: a subvention during 1999–2000; a leave of absence so that I might go to Rome in 2001; a fellowship (2002) to attend Loyola's Center for Ethics, where I studied (under David Ozar) the connection between ethical theories and notions of emotion; the constant support of my department, colleagues, and chairs Anthony Cardoza and Susan Hirsch; the interest of my graduate students Will Cavert, Kirsten DeVries, Andrew Donnelly, Thomas Greene, Vance Martin, Frances Mitilineos, Daniel O'Gorman, Jilana Ordman, and Alan Zola; and the efficient, unstinting, and knowledgeable help of History Subject librarian Michael Napora and Interlibrary Loan librarians Ursula Scholz and Jennifer Stegen.

I must also mention two extraordinary visiting professorships. In May 2004, at the invitation of François Menant, Régine Le Jan, and Monique Bourin, I had the honor and pleasure to be Professeur invité at the École Normale Supérieure, where I gave three papers in the seminars (respectively) of François Menant, Régine Le Jan, and Antoine Lilti. After each lecture, as soon as the discussion began, the first question to be posed was invariably: "Are you really talking about emotions?" And so I learned, if rather late, that "emotions" is in many ways an Anglophone category. I am indebted to the questions and comments of those seminar audiences, and should like to mention Dominique Iogna-Prat in particular, who in addition to participating at the lectures was also their translator!

I had the equally keen honor and pleasure to be invited to the University of Utrecht in June 2005, where I taught a course on the history of emotions and gave a lecture series on, in effect, what would become this book. Mayke de Jong was my kind, generous, and tireless host; I am deeply grateful to her. Symke Haverkamp was my outstanding teaching assistant. I am grateful to the students and auditors in both classes and lectures and should like to single out for particular thanks Giselle de Nie, Rob Meens, and Otto Vervaart.

I now turn with love and affection to my family—my husband, Tom; my children, Jess and Frank; my mother, Roz; my sister, Oms. They know, and I am grateful for it, that "emotional support" for a medievalist often means leaving her alone for very long periods of time in the company of a computer and a great many books.

ABBREVIATIONS

AASS	*Acta Sanctorum quotquot toto orbe coluntur,* ed. Joannus Bollandus et al., 67 vols. (1640–1940)
AHR	*American Historical Review*
ChLA	*Chartae Latinae Antiquiores*
CCSL	Corpus christianorum. Series Latina
CSEL	Corpus scriptorum ecclesiasticorum latinorum
Greg. Tur.	Gregory of Tours
GC	*Liber in gloria confessorum*
GM	*Liber in gloria martyrum*
Histories	*Historiarum libri X*
VJ	*Liber de passione et virtutibus sancti Juliani martyris*
VM	*Libri I–IV de virtutibus beati Martini episcopi*
VP	*Liber Vitae Patrum*
Gregory I	Gregory I the Great
MGH	Monumenta Germaniae Historica
AA	Auctores Antiquissimi
D Merov	Diplomata regum francorum e stirpe Merovingica
SRM	Scriptores rerum merovingicarum
PL	Patrologia Latina, ed. Migne
RICG	*Recueil des inscriptions chrétiennes de la Gaule antérieures à la Renaissance carolingienne*
I	*Première Belgique,* ed. Nancy Gauthier
VIII	*Aquitaine première,* ed. Françoise Prévot
XV	*Viennoise du Nord,* ed. Henri I. Marrou and Françoise Descombes
SC	*Sources chrétiennes*
TCCG	*Topographie chrétienne des cités de la Gaule des origines au milieu du VIIIe siècle,* ed. Nancy Gauthier and J.-Ch. Picard
Clermont	*TCCG 6: Province ecclésiastique de Bourges (Aquitania Prima)*
Trier	*TCCG 1: Province ecclésiastique de Trèves (Belgica Prima)*
Vienne	*TCCG 3: Provinces ecclésiastiques de Vienne et d'Arles*

EMOTIONAL COMMUNITIES IN THE EARLY MIDDLE AGES

INTRODUCTION

This is a book about the history of emotions. The topic is paradoxically very old—historians have *always* talked about emotions—and almost entirely unexplored, since for the most part such talk has been either unfocused or misguided. For the unfocused variety, consider Tacitus, who, when describing the condition of Rome at Nero's death, said that the senators were "joyous" (*laeti*); the commoners "roused to hope" (*in spem erecti*); and the lowest classes "mournful" (*maesti*).[1] He did not intend thereby a serious discussion of emotions but rather a lively evocation of the different classes at Rome and their disparate interests.[2] Historians continue to write in this way when they wish to be colorful. Thus David Fromkin tells us that on the eve of the First World War the German chancellor and senior officers "awaited events with different hopes, fears, and expectations."[3] These are perfectly ordinary and innocent examples of "unfocused" historical emotion talk. I shall leave until later in this chapter the discussion of focused studies, for they are a relatively recent development to which this book must pay considerable attention. Suffice to say that for the most part they have been inspired by a particularly simplistic notion of the emotions that makes passions not so much different from age to age as either "on" (impulsive and violent) or "off" (restrained).

The fact that there is a history of emotions but that it has been studied (for the most part) wrongly or badly is one reason that I have written this book. There is another reason as well: I am convinced that, as sociologists already know very well, "the source of emotion, its governing laws, and its consequences are an inseparable part of the social process."[4] Historians need to take emotions as seriously as they have lately taken other "invisible" top-

---

1. Tacitus, *The Histories* 1.4, trans. Clifford H. Moore, Loeb Classical Library (London, 1925), p. 8.

2. Ramsay MacMullen, however, argues in *Feelings in History, Ancient and Modern* (Claremont, Calif., 2003) that writers like Tacitus did their history exactly right and that modern historians too should learn to tuck passions into their bloodless prose. But this they do, as David Fromkin in note 3 below exemplifies.

3. David Fromkin, *Europe's Last Summer: Who Started the Great War in 1914?* (New York, 2004), p. 180.

4. David D. Franks, "The Bias against Emotions in Western Civilization," in *Sociology of*

ics, such as ecology and gender. I use as my starting point the Early Middle Ages because the Middle Ages remains, despite caveats, a direct ancestor of modern Western civilization, and the Early Middle Ages is its link to the ancient world and thus to the Greek and Roman legacy of ideas and words having to do with emotions. The Early Middle Ages is thus a natural starting point. Focused studies of emotions have treated the Middle Ages as one emotional period. I challenge this view. Even very short time spans, such as the sixth to late seventh centuries, which are the ones covered in this book, saw vast changes in the uses of emotional vocabulary and expressive repertories. But arriving at this conclusion requires considering contexts far more precise than "medieval" or "modern."

I postulate the existence of "emotional communities": groups in which people adhere to the same norms of emotional expression and value—or devalue—the same or related emotions. More than one emotional community may exist—indeed normally does exist—contemporaneously, and these communities may change over time. Some come to the fore to dominate our sources, then recede in importance. Others are almost entirely hidden from us, though we may imagine they exist and may even see some of their effects on more visible groups. In this book I trace a number of emotional communities, and in several instances I show how one displaced another, at least from the point of view of the production of texts. I do not claim to have found *all* the emotional communities of even the sixth and seventh centuries; if this book's title were to be glossed, it would be as *Some* Emotional Communities, not *The* Emotional Communities in the Early Middle Ages.[5]

Emotions: Syllabi and Instructional Materials, ed. Catherine G. Valentine, Steve Derné, and Beverley Cuthbertson Johnson (New York, 1999), p. 29.

5. Ripe for exploration are the emotional communities of St. Augustine (d. 430) and St. Jerome (d. 420), which perhaps overlapped rather little. Similarly begging for study are the emotional communities of the southern Gallic elite, whether represented by the generation of Paulinus of Nola (d. 431) or that of Sidonius Apollinaris (d. ca. 484) and Ruricius of Limoges (d. 510). I, however, have chosen to begin my study later, with the "two Gregories," one at Rome, the other in Gaul, ca. 600. They call for quite different methodological strategies, which makes them useful for an exploratory essay such as this. Further, since they lived around the same time, they may be fruitfully compared. Presumably every social group that wrote enough could be a "test case" for an emotional community. Augustine, Jerome, and the circle of Ruricius clearly are worth the trouble for themselves. Also worth the trouble, but for very different reasons, would be a study of *all* the emotional communities contemporaneous with one another in some defined space. I have tried to give a hint of the sort of pic-

Thus far I have spoken of emotions in history and emotional communities as if the meaning of the word "emotions" were self-evident. It is not, even though as recently as 2001 Martha Nussbaum declared that "emotions" was a universal "sub-category of thought."[6] In fact, the use of the catch-all term "emotions" to refer to "joy, love, anger, fear, happiness, guilt, sadness, embarrassment [and] hope" is quite recent even in the Anglophone world.[7] The *Oxford English Dictionary* records that the earliest meaning of the term (dating from 1579) was "a social agitation"; "emotion" gained the significance of mental agitation only about a century later. Nevertheless, as Thomas Dixon has shown, it was not the favored word for psychological turmoil until about 1800.[8] Before then, people spoke more often—and more precisely—of passions, affections, and sentiments. All of these referred to fairly clear subsets of the words and ideas that today come under the umbrella of emotions. It was the scientific community that privileged the term "emotions" and gave it the portmanteau meaning that it now has. Otniel Dror has demonstrated the advantages that this offered to white-coated professionals in their laboratories.[9]

Many European languages have more than one word for the phenomena that Anglophones call "emotions," and often these terms are not interchangeable. In France, love is not an *émotion;* it is a *sentiment.* Anger, however, is an *émotion,* for an *émotion* is short term and violent, while a *sentiment* is more subtle and of longer duration. German has *Gefühle,* a broad term that is used when feelings are strong and irrational, rather like *les émotions* in

---

ture that might emerge from the latter project in my study of epitaphs in three cities; see chapter 2.

6. Martha C. Nussbaum, *Upheavals of Thought: The Intelligence of Emotions* (Cambridge, 2001), esp. p. 24 and n. 3. But Benedicte Grima, *The Performance of Emotion among Paxtun Women: "The Misfortunes Which Have Befallen Me"* (Austin, 1992), pp. 34–39, points out that there is no word that tracks "emotion" in Paxto, and she provides bibliography on the topic for other cultural groups.

7. The list of words is taken from Randolph R. Cornelius, *The Science of Emotion: Research and Tradition in the Psychology of Emotion* (Upper Saddle River, N.J., 1996), p. 1.

8. Thomas Dixon, *From Passions to Emotions: The Creation of a Secular Psychological Category* (Cambridge, 2003). See also Dylan Evans, *Emotion: The Science of Sentiment* (Oxford, 2001), and Robert Dimit, "European 'Emotion' before the Invention of Emotions: The Passions of the Mind." I thank Professor Dimit for allowing me to read his article before publication.

9. Otniel E. Dror, "The Scientific Image of Emotion: Experience and Technologies of Inscription," *Configurations* 7 (1999): 355–401; idem, "Techniques of the Brain and the Paradox of Emotions, 1880–1930," *Science in Context* 14 (2001): 643–60.

French, while *Empfindungen* are more contemplative and inward, rather closer to *les sentiments*. Italians speak of *emozioni* and *sentimenti;* the two words sometimes have the same implications as their counterparts in French, while at other times they are virtually equivalent, much as the English word "feelings" tracks approximately the same lexical field as "emotions."[10]

How important should these distinctions be for our inquiry into the "emotional communities" of the early Middle Ages? If they constituted watertight definitions, it would be necessary to rethink the title as well as the very terms of this book. But they are nothing of the sort. Consider the category "passions," which in the mid-eighteenth century was a term in active use. In Samuel Johnson's dictionary (1755) it was defined by one authority as "the receiving of any action in a large philosophical sense; in a more limited philosophical sense, it signifies any of the affections of human nature; as love, fear, joy, sorrow: but the common people confine it only to anger."[11] Thus, although "passions" had a distinct connotation (powerful feelings such as anger), it also might compass the same terms that were signified by "affections." Similarly, my *Petit Robert*, published in 1985, defines both *sentiment* and *émotion* as a *réaction affective*, an "affective reaction," though (generally) of different intensities and durations. Clearly there is a continuum, not a decisive break, between *émotion* and *sentiment,* passion and affection.[12]

The ancient world had many emotion words, as we shall see in chapter 1, and it also had generic terms that were about equivalent to the term "emotions," though never precisely so. I use the term emotions in this book with full knowledge that it is a convenience: a constructed term that refers to affective reactions of all sorts, intensities, and durations. We shall see that, despite its drawbacks, it is serviceable, even for the medieval world where, in-

---

10. I am grateful to Riccardo Cristiani, Dominique Iogna-Prat, Régine Le Jan, Walter Pohl, and the audiences of my 2004 lectures in Paris for enlightening discussions on these points. Note that a recent survey of the emotions in (mainly modern) history in Italian is titled *Storia delle passione (History of the Passions)*. The editor says, presumably with a wink, that she chose the term to contrast it with the "dispassionate" (*spassionata*) present. More seriously, she sees a difference between "*passioni*" and "*emozioni*": passions are inseparable from their forms of expression (*rappresentazione*). See *Storia delle Passioni,* ed. Silvia Vegetti Finzi (Rome, 1995), pp. v–vi.

11. Samuel Johnson, *A Dictionary of the English Language* (1755; repr., New York, 1967), s.v. "passions"; quoted in Dixon, *From Passions to Emotions,* p. 62.

12. I am grateful to Damien Boquet for discussions on this point.

deed, it had some distant ancestors—in the Latin phrase *motus animi* (motions of the soul) and in the Latin adjective *commotus* (moved). To vary my prose, I also make use of "passions," "feelings," and, to a lesser extent, "affects" as equivalents of "emotions."

THE "CHILDHOOD OF MAN"

This is not the first book to trace the history of emotions. But the topic—as a focus rather than as a colorful aside—is relatively recent, having effectively begun less than a century ago with the work of Johan Huizinga. In his perennially popular book on the Late Middle Ages, Huizinga likened the emotional tenor of the period to that of modern childhood: "Every experience," he wrote, "had that degree of directness and absoluteness that joy and sadness still have in the mind of a child."[13] It was a "fairy tale" world where feelings were "sharper" and "unmediated." "We have to transpose ourselves into this impressionability of mind, into this sensitivity to tears and spiritual repentance, into this susceptibility, before we can judge how colorful and intensive life was then."[14] Passions of every sort held sway; the medieval city was filled with "vacillating moods of unrefined exuberance, sudden cruelty, and tender emotions," while "daily life offered unlimited range for acts of flaming passion and childish imagination."[15] Huizinga's Middle Ages was the childhood of man.

Childhood, however, never lasts. The Late Middle Ages was, for Huizinga, its last gasp. The modern world—the busy, dull, dispassionate world of adults—was on its way. This was clear from Huizinga's repeated use of the word "still" (*nog* in Dutch). Thus he noted that "a conflict between royal princes over a chessboard was *still* as plausible as a motive in the fifteenth century as in Carolingian romance"; and "during the fifteenth century the immediate emotional affect is *still* directly expressed in ways that frequently break through the veneer of utility and calculation."[16] Again, putting the same point another way, medieval "politics are *not yet* completely in the grip of bureaucracy and protocol."[17] Adulthood was the world of "util-

---

13. *Herfsttij der Middeleeuwen* (Haarlem, 1919). I quote here from Johan Huizinga, *The Autumn of the Middle Ages*, trans. Rodney J. Payton and Ulrich Mammitzsch (Chicago, 1996), p. 1.
14. Huizinga, *Autumn of the Middle Ages*, pp. 7–8.
15. Ibid., pp. 2, 8.
16. Ibid., pp. 8, 15 (emphasis mine). I thank Mayke de Jong for helping me with the Dutch.
17. Ibid., p. 12 (emphasis mine).

ity and calculation," of "bureaucracy and protocol"; it was Huizinga's own era.

Huizinga's words, by now nearly a century old, ought to be the instructive relic of an earlier historical sensibility. In fact his view of the Middle Ages remains foundational today, especially for the history of emotions, violence, impulsivity, behavior, and crime (all of which tend to be seen as related or even identical).[18] While the ontogenic theory of history—the theory that traces a trajectory from infancy to adulthood—is today out of fashion, it persists "undercover" in the history of human behavior and feeling. In the 1930s the *Annales* school adopted it in the guise of the "structure" of "mentalities."[19] A certain historiographical strand continues this tradition today. Jean Delumeau in France and Peter Dinzelbacher in Austria, for example, treat fear as a built-in structure of the medieval mind. In *Rassurer et protéger* Delumeau speaks of a *sentiment de sécurité*,[20] deriving the idea from John Bowlby's studies of infantile needs.[21] By terming benedictions, processions, indulgences, and so on "mechanisms of reassurance," Delumeau reinforces Huizinga's vision of medieval people as childlike in their goals and behaviors.[22]

Elsewhere the paradigm of Huizinga persists under the cloak of "emo-

---

18. See, for example, Thomas W. Gallant, "Honor, Masculinity, and Ritual Knife Fighting in Nineteenth-Century Greece," *AHR* 105 (2000): 358–82, with further bibliography.

19. See Marc Bloch, *Feudal Society,* trans. L. A. Manyon (Chicago, 1961), p. 73: the Middle Ages was "a civilization in which moral or social convention did *not yet* require well-bred people to repress their tears and their raptures" (emphasis mine). For further discussion of this aspect of the *Annales* school, see Barbara H. Rosenwein, "Worrying about Emotions in History," *AHR* 107 (2002): 921–45, esp. 832–34.

20. Jean Delumeau, *Rassurer et protéger. Le sentiment de sécurité dans l'Occident d'autrefois* (Paris, 1989). The idea was already anticipated in Jean Delumeau, *La Peur en Occident, XIVe–XVIIIe siècle. Une cité assiégée* (Paris, 1978), pp. 149–56, a section entitled "Le sentiment d'insécurité." See also Peter Dinzelbacher, *Angst im Mittelalter. Teufels-, Todes- und Gotteserfahrung; Mentalitätsgeschichte und Ikonographie* (Paderborn, 1996). More recently, Dinzelbacher, "La donna, il figlio e l'amore. La nuova emozionalità del XII secolo," in *Il secolo XII: la «renovatio» dell'Europa cristiana,* ed. Giles Constable et al. (Bologna, 2003), pp. 207–52, has argued that affectionate love, a sign of maturity, was lacking in the Early Middle Ages because the conditions of life were too primitive and punishing for it to thrive.

21. John Bowlby, *Attachment and Loss,* vol. 1, *Attachment* (New York, 1969), pp. 200–203.

22. Delumeau, *La Peur,* p. 17, speaks of the importance of "attachment" between the directing classes and the commonality. When the directing classes refuse the love from below, *peur et haine* (fear and hate) are the results.

tionology" or its close relation, "the civilizing process." In 1985 Peter and Carol Stearns created the term "emotionology" to describe "the standards that a society, or a definable group within a society, maintains toward basic emotions and their appropriate expression."[23] Before the days of emotionology—that is, before the mid-eighteenth century—there was no internalized self-restraint. The Stearnses claimed that "public temper tantrums, along with frequent weeping and boisterous joy, were far more common in premodern society than they were to become in the nineteenth and twentieth centuries. Adults were in many ways, by modern standards, childlike in their indulgence in temper, which is one reason that they so readily played games with children."[24]

Powerfully bolstering this "up from childhood" history was the theory of the "civilizing process" elaborated by Norbert Elias in the 1930s, but which began to make inroads in historical circles only in the 1970s, when it was translated into English, French, and Italian. Elias's book was a grand synthesis, perhaps the last such of the twentieth century. It embraced history, sociology, and psychology in two dazzling—and extremely entertaining—volumes. Like Max Weber, Elias was interested in rationalization, bureaucratization, and the juggernaut of the modern state, with its "monopoly of force." Like Freud, however, he was keen to understand the individual psyche. He faulted the sociologists for separating ideas and ideology from what he, adopting Freud, called "the structure of drives, the direction and form of human affects and passions."[25] At the same time, he thought that the Freudians separated the psyche from society. Lamenting the narrow vision of psychologists, Elias pointed out that they made "no distinction . . . between the natural raw material of drives, which indeed perhaps changes little throughout the whole history of mankind, and the increasingly more firmly wrought structures of control."[26] Elias's focus was thus on the historicity of the superego; in his view, the process of civilizing set up more and more controls over the drives (or affects, impulses, emotions—Elias

---

23. Peter N. Stearns with Carol Z. Stearns, "Emotionology: Clarifying the History of Emotions and Emotional Standards," *AHR* 90 (1985): 813.

24. Carol Zisowitz Stearns and Peter N. Stearns, *Anger: The Struggle for Emotional Control in America's History* (Chicago, 1986), p. 25.

25. Norbert Elias, *The Civilizing Process,* trans. Edmund Jephcott, rev. ed. (Oxford, 2000), p. 408.

26. Ibid., p. 409.

used such words interchangeably). The energies of the Western psyche became progressively compartmentalized, so that eventually cognition and reason became fairly impermeable to emotions.

Thus the importance of history to Elias. He insisted that what he was tracing in the "civilizing process" was empirical, not theoretical. He had made "a scrutiny of documents of historical experience."[27] Above all he looked at books of etiquette, because he saw a direct link between behavior, emotion, and impulse control. He quoted the *Disticha Catonis* (written in the third or fourth century and popular thereafter), which he called the "code of behavior encountered throughout the Middle Ages." Its maxims, such as "You should follow honorable men and vent your wrath on the wicked," were for Elias evidence of medieval "simplicity, its naïveté." Painting the by then familiar Huizingan picture, Elias continued: "There are [in the Middle Ages], as in all societies where the emotions are expressed more violently and directly, fewer psychological nuances and complexities in the general stock of ideas. There are friend and foe, desire and aversion, good and bad people."[28]

The lack of a strong overriding power meant that medieval knights—for Elias, they were the key to the whole discussion—could give in to their violent impulses: "The release of the affects in battle in the Middle Ages was no longer, perhaps, quite so uninhibited as in the early period of the Great Migrations. But it was open and uninhibited enough."[29]

This situation changed gradually. At the courts of the most powerful medieval princes the gentling influence of the "lady" and the tyranny of the lord combined to make "more peaceful conduct obligatory."[30] Later, in the sixteenth century, the process took hold permanently. At the courts of absolute rulers who monopolized all power, men were forced by circumstance to control themselves. Eventually external requirements effected intrapsychic transformations: "As the individual was now embedded in the human network quite differently from before and moulded by the web of his dependencies, so too did the structure of individual consciousness and affects change."[31] And, looking at the matter psychodynamically, Elias argued that "wars and feuds diminish. . . . But at the same time the battlefield is, in a

---

27. Ibid., p. x.
28. Ibid., p. 55.
29. Ibid., p. 162.
30. Ibid., pp. 245–46.
31. Ibid., p. 397.

sense, moved within. . . . An individualized pattern of near-automatic habits is established and consolidated within [the human being], a specific 'super-ego,' which endeavours to control, transform, or suppress his affects in keeping with the social structure."[32] As society became more complex, the state more powerful, and individuals more interdependent, the controls only increased, so that modern man's psyche today is hedged about in every way.[33]

Despite the fact that almost every element of this argument has problems, Elias's theory remains triumphant today.[34] When I first began to write this very paragraph, the *New York Times* was telling us that "Elias has posthumously become [a] theoretical guru." Barbara Hanawalt, a prominent contemporary medievalist, was quoted in the same article as saying, "Elias is onto something: people begin to change their notions of how people should behave. In the 14th century people are concerned with whether someone is of good or ill repute; it's a collective, community judgment. When you get into the 15th century, the question is about someone's 'governance.' There is a shift from community reputation to an emphasis on internal control."[35]

---

32. Ibid., p. 375.

33. Norbert Elias attempts to explain why the restraints were less durable in Germany—that is, why Eichmann existed and the Holocaust took place; Elias, *The Germans: Power Struggles and the Development of Habitus in the Nineteenth and Twentieth Centuries,* ed. Michael Schröter, trans. Eric Dunning and Stephen Mennell (New York, 1996).

34. The reception of Elias's work is assessed in Gerd Schwerhoff, "Zivilisationsprozeß und Geschichtswissenschaft. Norbert Elias' Forschungsparadigma in historischer Sicht," *Historische Zeitschrift* 266 (1998): 561–606. Elias's historical accuracy regarding the early modern court and its culture is critiqued in Jeroen Duindam, *Myths of Power: Norbert Elias and the Early Modern European Court* (Amsterdam, [1994]). The Freudian theory of drives, on which Elias's theory fundamentally depends, has been repudiated by most psychologists (see below) and even many psychoanalysts, e.g., John Bowlby (*Attachment and Loss,* vol. 1, chap. 7). Daniela Romagnoli has shown that comportment books were already produced in the sixth century and became abundant by the twelfth, not only at the courts and the monasteries of Europe but above all in the cities; see her "La courtoisie dans la ville: un modèle complexe," in *La ville et la cour. Des bonnes et des mauvaises manières,* ed. Daniela Romagnoli (Paris, 1995), chap. 1. See also *Medieval Conduct,* ed. Kathleen Ashley and Robert L. A. Clark (Minneapolis, 2001). Finally, a recent collection of articles thoroughly critiques Elias's use, abuse, and ignorance of sources: *Zivilisationsprozesse. Zu Erziehungsschriften in der Vormoderne,* ed. Rüdiger Schnell (Cologne, 2004).

35. Alexander Stille, "Did Knives and Forks Cut Murders? Counting Backward, Historians Resurrect Crime Statistics and Find the Middle Ages More Violent Than Now," *New York Times,* May 3, 2003, pp. A21–23.

Emotionology and the civilizing process are convenient theories for historians. For those studying the postmedieval period they provide a virtual tabula rasa—a Middle Ages of childish (read: unmediated) emotionality and impulsivity—on which the early modern period can build its edifices of autonomy and reason.[36] But "early modern" itself is a historical construct whose validity must come from a sound understanding of the Middle Ages. Was the Middle Ages emotionally childish, impulsive, and unrestrained? Some medievalists have already found the contrary to be the case. Moreover, current theories of the emotions challenge the very possibility.

UPENDING OLD MODELS

Even Elias admitted restraints at the medieval princely courts, so the fact that literary scholars discovered that troubadour poetry celebrated love—delicate, temperate, and deeply felt—hardly rattled the paradigm. But in the 1950s such love was discovered in the monasteries as well. Jean Leclercq, for example, praised monastic love—the love that Cistercian brethren delighted to explore both in relation to themselves and to God—as sublime self-expression.[37] Soon John C. Moore's *Love in Twelfth-Century France* found love not only in the monasteries and the courts but also in the cities, among the "schoolmen."[38]

Further eroding the model was C. Stephen Jaeger, who, in a series of writings that began in the 1980s, found the "civilizing process" taking place at the courts of tenth- and eleventh-century German imperial rulers.[39] In

---

36. But scholars of the ancient world can adopt Elias as well: William V. Harris, *Restraining Rage: The Ideology of Anger Control in Classical Antiquity* (Cambridge, Mass., 2001), p. 150, thinks that the "civilizing process" occurred for "the first time" in the ancient world. Thus Harris continues the bracketing off of the Middle Ages first "achieved" by the Renaissance.

37. Jean Leclercq, *L'amour des lettres et le désir de Dieu. Initiation aux auteurs monastiques du Moyen Age* (Paris, 1957); translated by Catherine Misrahi as *The Love of Learning and the Desire for God* (New York, 1961); see also idem, *Monks and Love in Twelfth-Century France* (Oxford, 1979).

38. Moore, *Love in Twelfth-Century France* (Philadelphia, 1972). See now as well John W. Baldwin, *The Language of Sex: Five Voices from Northern France around 1200* (Chicago, 1994).

39. C. Stephen Jaeger, *The Origins of Courtliness: Civilizing Trends and the Formation of Courtly Ideals, 939–1210* (Philadelphia, 1985); idem, *The Envy of Angels: Cathedral Schools and Social Ideals in Medieval Europe, 950–1200* (Philadelphia, 1994). Janet L. Nelson argues that courtliness "was made in the earlier Middle Ages, in the courts of so-called barbarian kings"; Nelson, "Gendering Courts in the Early Medieval West," in *Gender in the Early Medieval World: East and West, 300–900*, ed. Leslie Brubaker and Julia M. H. Smith (Cambridge, 2004), p. 186.

the late 90s, he went further, putting aristocratic love at center stage. This was a highly restrained love that was understood at the time as "the source of a morality and a heroism of self-control and self-mastery."[40] Yet this love flourished as early as the sixth century, and it experienced a real blossoming among the members of the Carolingian court in the ninth century.

The largely literary approaches of Leclercq, Moore, and Jaeger were complemented by the work of some legal historians. J.E.A. Jolliffe, pioneer of a legal school that saw functionality (rather than pure impulsivity) in medieval emotional expression, argued that the medieval English king's anger was an effective political tool.[41] Because the royal public and private personae could not be separated, Jolliffe argued, "the ruler's personal hates and fears were released as efficient forces to play about the political world."[42] Royal anger—*ira* or *malevolentia*—placed disfavored persons in a sort of "limbo"; they were not quite outlaws, but neither were they under the law's protection.[43] Royal wrath brought men and institutions to heel. The study of the king's emotions was, for Jolliffe, essential for understanding the twelfth-century polity.

W. H. Auden had written "Law Like Love" a decade before Jolliffe wrote about his twelfth-century kings.[44] In the late 1960s, Fredric Cheyette used Auden's poem to drive home the points of his pioneering essay on pre-thirteenth-century French law. Arbiters out of court—normally *amici* (friends, cronies) of both sides—not remote judges *en banc*, made informal legal systems work precisely by recognizing the emotional components of disputing. As Cheyette put it, the arbiters "must assuage anger, soothe wounded pride, find the solution that will bring peace."[45] Just as Cheyette was writing, a few English and American anthropologists were adopting a processual model of dispute resolution.[46] Their colleagues in medieval his-

---

40. C. Stephen Jaeger, *Ennobling Love: In Search of a Lost Sensibility* (Philadelphia, 1999), ix.

41. J. E. A. Jolliffe, *Angevin Kingship*, 2d ed. (London, 1963), chap. 4. The first edition of this book appeared in 1955.

42. Ibid., 95.

43. Ibid., p. 97.

44. W. H. Auden, "Law Like Love," in *The Collected Poetry of W. H. Auden* (New York, 1945), pp. 74–76.

45. Fredric L. Cheyette, "Giving Each His Due," in *Debating the Middle Ages: Issues and Readings*, ed. Lester K. Little and Barbara H. Rosenwein (Oxford 1998), pp. 170–79, quote on p. 176; originally published as "Suum cuique tribuere," *French Historical Studies* 6 (1969/70): 287–99.

46. Key readings for this group: *The Ethnography of Law*, ed. Laura Nader (Menasha,

tory soon joined them.[47] This confluence of interests need not necessarily have led to emotions history, but in fact it did so, as historians recognized the key role of emotions in moments of crisis and dispute. In the early 1980s, Michael Clanchy was quoting the *Leges Henrici Primi*—where *amor* (love) triumphs over *judicium* (justice)—and citing anthropological literature on law in acephalous societies in a paper that broadened out from the English village "loveday" to the whole question of law as "the extension and reinforcement of bonds of affection beyond the immediate family."[48]

By the nineties, a number of Anglo-American scholars of medieval law considered emotions to be as normal and central a topic in their field as "felony" and "trespass" had been for Pollock and Maitland.[49] These emotions were understood not as the products of "vacillating moods" but rather as tied to dearly held goals and values. Thus William Ian Miller wrote on affect and honor, Stephen D. White looked at anger and the exercise of lordship, and Paul Hyams and Daniel Smail explored the role of rancor and hatred in the development of law.[50] In Germany Gerd Althoff, approaching similar legal and political materials from an interest in nonverbal gesture

---

Wisc., 1965); *The Disputing Process: Law in Ten Societies,* ed. Laura Nader and Harry F. Todd (New York, 1978); Simon Roberts, *Order and Dispute: An Introduction to Legal Anthropology* (Harmondsworth, England, 1979).

47. See for example, the essays in *Disputes and Settlements: Law and Human Relations in the West,* ed. John Bossy (Cambridge, 1983).

48. Michael Clanchy, "Law and Love in the Middle Ages," in *Disputes and Settlements,* ed. Bossy, p. 50.

49. Nevertheless, their contribution was (and is) not widely noted. It is telling that Michael Toch claims to be drawing upon *mentalités* methodology in discussing the emotions evident in the records of a Bavarian manorial court, whereas in fact the author is more clearly following the path of the Anglo-American legal historians delineated here; Toch, "Ethics, Emotion and Self-interest: Rural Bavaria in the Later Middle Ages," *Journal of Medieval History* 17 (1991): 135–47.

50. William Ian Miller, *Humiliation: And Other Essays on Honor, Social Discomfort, and Violence* (Ithaca, N.Y., 1993), chap. 3; Stephen D. White, "The Politics of Anger," in *Anger's Past: The Social Uses of an Emotion in the Middle Ages,* ed. Barbara H. Rosenwein (Ithaca, N.Y., 1998), chap. 6; Paul Hyams, *Rancor and Reconciliation in Medieval England* (Ithaca, N.Y. 2003), chap. 2; Daniel Lord Smail, "Hatred as a Social Institution in Late-Medieval Society," *Speculum* 76 (2001): 90–126. Further essential studies along these lines: Richard E. Barton, "'Zealous Anger' and the Renegotiation of Aristocratic Relationships in Eleventh- and Twelfth-Century France," in *Anger's Past,* ed. Rosenwein, chap. 7; Claude Gauvard, *"De Grace Especial." Crime, état et société en France à la fin du Moyen Age,* 2 vols. (Paris, 1991).

rather than law, argued that emotions were "staged"—as all emotions are packaged—to relay important information about power and authority. Both rulers and their subjects followed "rules of the game": ritual acts, including emotional displays, that followed clear models and signaled clear messages to all concerned.[51]

It is thus evident that many medievalists have moved beyond the paradigm of an emotionally childlike and impulsive Middle Ages. They have carved out arenas—love in the monastery, love in the courts, staged anger in ceremonies of lordship and kingship, love in the twelfth century—where the model does not apply. Since the 1970s they have found strong theoretical ground for their assertions, as a number of them explicitly recognize, because of the revolution in the way in which emotions came to be conceptualized by psychologists, anthropologists, and sociologists.

The "old" theory of the emotions was hydraulic. Whether Darwinian or Freudian, psychologists assumed that passions were "drives" or forms of energy that would surge forth toward "discharge" unless they were controlled, tamped down, or channeled.[52] The theories of the 1960s and 1970s, however, were free of instincts, drives, and energies. Thus for Magda Arnold, an early leader in the field of cognitive psychology, emotions were the result of a certain type of perception, a *relational* perception that appraised an object

---

51. The key studies are Gerd Althoff, "Empörung, Tränen, Zerknirschung. 'Emotionen' in der öffentlichen Kommunikation des Mittelalters," *Frühmittelalterliche Studien* 30 (1996): 60–79; idem, "*Ira Regis:* Prolegomena to a History of Royal Anger," in *Anger's Past*, ed. Rosenwein, chap. 3; idem, "Demonstration und Inszenierung. Spielregeln der Kommunikation in mittelalterlicher Öffentlichkeit," *Frühmittelalterliche Studien* 27 (1993): 27–50. See also idem, *Otto III,* trans. Phyllis G. Jestice (University Park, Pa., 2003). For others working within this historiographical tradition, see Ruth Schmidt-Wiegand, "Gebärdensprache im mittelalterlichen Recht," *Frühmittelalterliche Studien* 16 (1982): 363–79; Martin J. Schubert, *Zur Theorie des Gebarens im Mittelalter. Analyse von nichtsprachlicher Äußerung in mittelhochdeutscher Epik: Rolandslied, Eneasroman, Tristan* (Cologne, 1991); Matthias Becher, "'*Cum lacrimis et gemitu*': Vom Weinen der Sieger und der Besiegten im frühen und hohen Mittelalter," in *Formen und Funktionen öffentlicher Kommunikation im Mittelalter,* ed. Gerd Althoff and Verena Epp (Stuttgart, 2001), pp. 25–52.

52. Charles Darwin postulated a "nerve-force" that was liberated in intense sensations, some of them emotions; Darwin, *The Expression of the Emotions in Man and Animals,* 3d ed., ed. Paul Ekman (New York, 1998), p. 74. For Freud's theory of instinctual energy see, most conveniently, Sigmund Freud, *The Complete Introductory Lectures on Psychoanalysis,* trans. and ed. James Strachey (New York, 1966), chap. 31.

(or person or situation or fantasy) as "desirable or undesirable, valuable or harmful *for me*."[53] Such appraisals depended on a person's notion of what was good or bad; they were judgments based on past experience and present values and goals. Emotional sequences were not, then, impulses leading to intermediate moderating controls (or not), followed by behavior. That was the old school. The new school argued a sequence that began with perception followed by appraisal, leading in turn to emotion, which was followed by action readiness. There were no impulses to tamp down and control, only appraisals—automatic, quick, and nonreflective.

Recent work in cognitive psychology puts great stress on goals. When events or objects are "congruent" or "incongruent" with plans (as Craig Smith and Richard Lazarus put it), when they "interrupt" expectations and goals (as George Mandler would have it), or when they disrupt and/or fulfill our "best laid schemes" (as Keith Oatley describes it), emotions are the result.[54] Oatley's theory in particular opens out from the individual realm to the social precisely because of its connection to goals; for him "emotions manage transitions between plans," while "social emotions help manage transitions to new joint plans and help to maintain them."[55] The close connection between emotions and goals aligns them with conscious, well-considered thought; there is no need—indeed, it is incorrect—to separate emotions from ideas: the assessment of what is valuable or harmful has everything to do with what individuals, groups, and societies want for themselves.

Further undermining the grip of the hydraulic model is social constructionism, an important offshoot of cognitive theory.[56] For the most part

---

53. Magda B. Arnold, *Emotion and Personality*, 2 vols. (New York, 1960), 1:171 (emphasis mine). For an excellent guide to many current psychological theories of the emotions, see Cornelius, *Science of Emotion*. For the evolutionary approach see, e.g., Steven Pinker, *How the Mind Works*, 2d ed. (New York, 1999); for the view from the brain, see, e.g., Antonio R. Damasio, *The Feeling of What Happens: Body and Emotion in the Making of Consciousness* (New York, 1999), and Joseph LeDoux, *The Emotional Brain: The Mysterious Underpinnings of Emotional Life* (New York, 1996).

54. Craig A. Smith and Richard S. Lazarus, "Appraisal Components, Core Relational Themes, and the Emotions," *Cognition and Emotion* 7 (1993): 233–69; George Mandler, *Mind and Emotion* (New York, 1975), chap. 7; Keith Oatley, *Best Laid Schemes: The Psychology of Emotions* (Cambridge, 1992).

55. Oatley, *Best Laid Schemes*, p. 178.

56. Cornelius, *Science of Emotion*, p. 155, points out that social constructionism is "an outgrowth of the cognitive revolution." But for cognitivists, "appraisals represent innate re-

agreeing that at least some emotions are "hardwired" in the human (and animal) psyche, social constructionists point out that emotional expression takes as many forms as there are cultures. Thus romantic love is privileged in one place, reviled in another, and unknown in still a third.[57] Anger is expressed by bodily swelling, reddening, or whitening in one culture, while in another it leads to wordy insults.[58] In Japan there is a feeling, *amae*, of contented dependence on another; but in English there is nothing comparable and presumably no feeling that corresponds to it.[59] No one is born knowing appropriate modes of expression, or whether to imagine emotions as internal or external, or whether to privilege or disregard an emotion. These things make up the "feeling rules" that societies impart.[60] Putting social constructionism and the cognitive view together, we may say that if emotions are assessments based on experience and goals, the norms of the individual's social context provide the framework in which such evaluations take place and derive their meaning. There is nothing whatever "hydraulic"—nothing demanding release—in this cognitivist/social constructionist view.

The psychologist Randolph Cornelius says that Americans would consider *amae* "embarrassingly childish."[61] But the cognitive and social constructionist theories of emotion suggest that no emotion is childish. Even for children, emotions are not "pure" or unmediated; all are the products of experience, and experience itself is shaped by the practices and norms of a person's household, neighborhood, and larger society. Even the most "impulsive" of behaviors is judged so within a particular context. If an emotional display seems "extreme," that is itself a perception from within a set of emotional norms that is socially determined.

---

sponses to evolutionarily significant events," while for social constructionists they are socially shaped responses to events that are socially defined as significant.

57. William M. Reddy, "European Ways of Love: The Historical Specificity of Romantic Love," paper presented for the workshop "Love, Religion, and Europeanness," Kulturwissenschaftliches Institut, Essen, Germany, February 21–22, 2003. I am very grateful to Professor Reddy for sending me a copy of this paper.

58. Miller, *Humiliation*, chap. 3.

59. On *amae*, see Takeo Doi, *The Anatomy of Dependence*, trans. John Bester (Tokyo, 1973); H. Morsbach and W. J. Tyler, "A Japanese Emotion: *Amae*," in *The Social Construction of Emotions*, ed. Rom Harré (Oxford, 1986), chap. 15. Dylan Evans, who is presumably British, claims that he has felt it (*Emotion*, pp. 1–3).

60. For "feeling rules" see Arlie Russell Hochschild, *The Managed Heart: Commercialization of Human Feeling* (Berkeley, 1983), p. 76.

61. Cornelius, *Science of Emotion*, p. 172.

RELATIVISM AND ITS DISCONTENTS

The historian William Reddy and the philosopher Martha Nussbaum, the two most important recent commentators on the emotions, dislike the relativism that social constructionism implies.[62] If one cannot make judgments about emotions, if all emotions are created equal, then there is no room for advocacy. Without right or wrong, there can be no ethics, no basis for change, and no critique. Reddy's and Nussbaum's objections are significant for the history of medieval emotions, but for two opposing reasons. Nussbaum, a moral philosopher, largely skips the Middle Ages in her quest for a socially ameliorative form of love: she seeks an emotional life that goes beyond the self and leads to altruism, and here she finds the Middle Ages wanting. Reddy is not interested in the Middle Ages per se. But because he proposes a theory of social transformation based on the nature of emotions, he points the way toward a new emotions history in which the Middle Ages may potentially be integrated. Let us explore their briefs in turn.

Nussbaum, who does not hesitate to call emotions "thoughts"—"upheavals of thoughts"—not only accepts but adds muscle to the cognitive view by finding it both cogent and potentially therapeutic.[63] If assessments are based on past experiences, then a childhood full of imaginative play and an adulthood full of art provide an incomparable repertoire of objects, images, and responses for individuals to work with. Nevertheless, Nussbaum wishes to move beyond the cognitive stance. Recognizing that the new psychology does not lead to "normative questions," she insists that "it is right to ask" these anyway, and she spends fully two-thirds of her book exploring whether "there is anything about emotions that makes them subversive of morality (or, in other ways, of human flourishing)."[64] In fact, she finds the contrary: the right emotions are good. And because emotions are based on assessments, they can be altered (and made better) by "altering our perceptions of objects."[65]

There are many "right" emotions, but love is the one for which Nuss-

---

62. I am not the first to compare these two thinkers: see Jeremy D. Popkin's review of Reddy's *Navigation of Feeling* in *H-France Review* 2 (November 2002), no. 118, www3.uakron.edu/hfrance/vol2reviews/popkin4.html.

63. Nussbaum, *Upheavals of Thought;* on cognitivism's therapeutic potential, also see eadem, *The Therapy of Desire: Theory and Practice in Hellenistic Ethics* (Princeton, 1994).

64. Nussbaum, *Upheavals of Thought,* pp. 11–12.

65. Ibid., p. 15.

baum cares to find a history. Here the Middle Ages falls short, for it contributes little to the "ladder of love tradition" that interests Nussbaum—a tradition that attempts "to reform or educate erotic love so as to keep its creative force while purifying it of ambivalence and excess, and making it more friendly to general social aims." (Here Nussbaum has unfortunately not read the work of C. Stephen Jaeger.) Thus, while claiming that "one could write an illuminating history of moral thought from Plato to Nietzsche using that motif [of love's ladder] alone," in fact Nussbaum brackets off and omits the Middle Ages.[66] She sees the origins of "love's education" in the ancient world and finds it again in the early modern period.

With the exception of courtly love and the neo-Aristotelian philosophy of St. Thomas, the Middle Ages fail, for Nussbaum, to provide a notion of love that appreciates individuality, is respectful of human agency, and leads to compassion for the hungry, the grieving, and the persecuted.[67] In Nussbaum's hands, St. Augustine becomes responsible for this blinkered view; although (unlike the Stoics) he accepted—even celebrated—emotions, he also mistrusted them except insofar as their object was God. Dante, by contrast, liberated love. Nussbaum's cutting-edge views of emotions are in this way incorporated into a traditional view of history in which the Italian Renaissance is the dividing line between inadequate and full human awareness.

William Reddy echoes Nussbaum in judging certain emotional stances as better than others.[68] But he has a different agenda: he seeks not emotional desiderata but emotional liberation. Unhappy with both the moral relativism of social constructionism, which argues that all societies are "created equal" because there is no universal or essential truth, Reddy postulates that emotions "are the real world-anchor of signs."[69] By that he means, first, that they exist; and second, that they take the form that we know them in the context of the signs—which depend on the cultures—that elicit them. For Reddy, emotions have protean potential. But they are not expressed in protean ways because, already in their expression, they have been shaped, molded, and channeled rather thoroughly. Nevertheless—and this is the key point—that molding is never entirely successful. Reddy makes this argu-

---

66. Ibid., p. 469.
67. Nussbaum sums up the emotional desiderata as well as the importance of courtly love and Thomism; ibid., pp. 563–64; see also pp. 580–90.
68. I see no evidence that either scholar has read the other.
69. William M. Reddy, "Against Constructionism: The Historical Ethnography of Emotions," *Current Anthropology* 38 (1997): 331.

ment by coining the word "emotives." These are "emotion talk and emotional gestures," which "alter the states of the speakers from whom they derive."[70] Emotional expressions are, for Reddy, analogous to "performatives," statements which, in certain contexts, have the ability to transform things or statuses. In the case of emotions, people's statements (e.g., "I am angry") are attempts to describe feelings. At the same time, the words themselves change those feelings. "I am angry" is, as it were, a "first draft," trying out an expression. It is necessarily inadequate, calling forth either its reinforcement ("Yes, I am furious") or its contradiction ("No, I am hurt, not angry") or something in between. Even while revising the drafts, however, emotives blank out the other possible interpretations of feelings; emotives are choices—automatic choices, for the most part—made from a huge repertory of possibilities. Most of those possibilities will never be explored because most are not recognized, or hardly recognized, by the society in which an individual lives and feels.

Reddy's view gets theoretical ballast from a particular variant of cognitive theory pursued by Alice Isen and Gregory Andrade Diamond. Isen and Diamond stress emotions' automaticity. They argue that affect "can be understood as a deeply ingrained, overlearned habit."[71] For Reddy (as for Isen and Diamond) this means that people can learn and unlearn feelings, although, as with any habit, such change is difficult. It also means that while the habit remains comfortable, it crowds out other, nonautomatic responses, which are possible but require "cognitive capacity," an effort of will or at least of attention.[72]

This explains, for Reddy, why "conventional emotives authorized in a given community" have "extensive power."[73] But such power is often dangerous because it stifles the experimental nature of emotional expression. When emotives are forced to follow a few narrow channels—when, to put it another way, emotional conventions allow for only a few overlearned

---

70. Ibid., p. 327. This is Reddy's most capacious definition of emotives; at other times he does not mention gestures at all. See, for example, William M. Reddy, *The Navigation of Feeling: A Framework for the History of Emotions* (Cambridge, 2001), p. 105: "Emotives are translations *into words* about . . . the ongoing translation tasks that currently occupy attention" (emphasis mine).

71. Alice M. Isen and Gregory Andrade Diamond, "Affect and Automaticity," in *Unintended Thought,* ed. James S. Uleman and John A. Bargh (New York, 1989), p. 144.

72. Ibid., p. 126.

73. Reddy, "Against Constructionism," p. 333.

habits—people suffer. Emotives are first drafts that press for reformulation, but all too often second drafts are not permitted. Emotives are meant to allow people to navigate through life, following their goals, changing their goals, if necessary. Indeed, "emotional liberty" is precisely the liberty to allow emotives free enough expression for the individual "to undergo conversion experiences and life-course changes involving numerous contrasting, often incommensurable factors."[74] "Emotional suffering" follows from this; one suffers as one sorts out the "incommensurable factors" that make two dearly held goals incompatible. Some of this suffering is inevitable. Some of it, however, is induced by conventional emotives that are made mandatory by a given "emotional regime."

Because emotives are engines of conversion, they become important sources for historical change. Thus Reddy's book has a bipartite form, with the first section a discussion of the psychological literature on emotions, the second a discussion of the causes and results of the French Revolution. While the "emotional regime" of the eighteenth century was highly constricted, a *politesse* of the court in which emotions mattered not at all, there were also "emotional refuges" in which the court's emotional values were jettisoned. In the salons and popular novels, on the stage, and within affectionate family circles, a new set of normative emotives was born, "sentimentalism," which held that emotions were the purest and highest of human expressions.[75] Once the royal court was dismantled by the French Revolution, the emotional norms of the refuges became the new "regime." Every act had to be justified by "real feeling." Policies had to come from natural passion, which was understood to be equivalent to natural morality. Anyone who opposed such policies was, therefore, evil. The Terror was unleashed to deal with the wicked, those whose hearts were insincere. But since (as we know from the theory of emotives) no emotion is pure and unchanging, the very premises and goals of sentimentalism were bound at every moment to show

---

74. Reddy, *Navigation of Feeling*, p. 123. See also William M. Reddy, "Emotional Liberty: Politics and History in the Anthropology of Emotions," *Cultural Anthropology* 14 (1999): 256–88.

75. It is as if Reddy has turned Habermas's notion of the bourgeois public sphere—the *salons*, theaters, and clubs in which private people exercised their reason and criticized public authority— into a realm of emotional experimentation. See Jürgen Habermas, *The Structural Transformation of the Public Sphere: An Inquiry into a Category of Bourgeois Society*, trans. Thomas Burger (Cambridge, Mass., 1989), esp. chaps. 2 and 3.

their weaknesses. People felt guilty about disagreeing with the Terror, and they felt guilty about their guilt. They felt fear for themselves and grief at the execution of friends. In short, they experienced acute emotional suffering.

Under the pressures of this extreme discomfort, "Jacobin-style emotives" were duly rejected, a reaction set in with the Directory, and sentimentalism ceased to define the emotional regime.[76] The new political regime rejected emotionality, elevating "masculine reason" in its place, while a variant of sentimentalism found a role in art, literature, and intimate family life. But, unlike the emotional refuges of the past, the new ones allowed emotions to be associated with weakness as well as strength. Released from the constraints of high-mindedness and moral goodness, emotives now had freer play in people's lives. The liberty wrought by the French Revolution was emotional.

EMOTIONAL REGIMES / EMOTIONAL COMMUNITIES

Thus Reddy gives a scheme for historical change that does not rely on an ontogenic argument. It is not progressive restraint that leads to the modern world for Reddy but rather emotives and the emotional suffering that they entailed in the eighteenth century. Admittedly the emotional regime at the royal court was highly restrained and controlling. But this did not create—as Elias would have it—internalized superegos. Rather it led men and women to seek emotional relief in refuges which, while imposing their own norms and restraints, allowed for alternative forms of emotional expression. Reddy suggests that this double-sided emotional life could not last because the refuges pressed to remake the world in their image. "The Revolution . . . began as an effort to transform all of France, by means of benevolent gestures of reform, into a kind of emotional refuge."[77] Hence one emotional regime was replaced by another. But the new one turned out to be even more painful than the first. Rejecting its constraints, the Directory and the Napoleonic era created a new, more open emotional regime even as it demoted emotions by opposing them to Reason. For Reddy, all emotional regimes are constraining, and people must search for the regime most open to alternatives, experiment, failure, and deviance.

Reddy is entirely straightforward in preferring some emotional regimes

---

76. Reddy, *Navigation of Feeling*, p. 207.
77. Ibid., p. 147.

to others.[78] What he does not say—but is nevertheless implicit in his work—is that the trajectory of Western history (at least the recent trajectory) is in the right direction. We begin with the court of Louis XIV, where emotional life was entirely stifled. We continue with the emotional refuges of the salons and Masonic lodges, where emotives were appreciated and cultivated. Nevertheless, these refuges harbored a fatal flaw, which became evident once they themselves attained the status of an "emotional regime": the erroneous assumption that policies and morality could be based on "true" emotions. The emotional suffering produced by this new regime gave way in turn to the romantic passions of the nineteenth century, which was also "wrong" in its separation of emotion from reason, but was, in any event, less painful and more open. This regime has more or less persisted until the present.

Making emotional suffering the agent for historical change is a hypothesis full of hope, but it is problematic as a general theory. It discounts the fundamental comfort of "deeply ingrained, overlearned habits." One of the reasons that anthropologists have been reluctant to judge the emotional tenor of the cultures that they study is because, on the whole, people adjust to the cultural constraints that surround them and feel, if not happy, then at least "at ease." Some suffer, to be sure. In the world of the Bedouins studied by Lila Abu-Lughod, for example, a man named Rashīd made a fool of himself by falling in love with his wife. But his very foolhardiness became a way to reinforce the general norms among the members of his family: "his mother, brothers, and cousins criticized him as lacking in *'agl* [social good sense], and even the children, his nephews and nieces, all told me that they no longer feared him."[79] The children were not suffering; they were relieved. One man's suffering can be (and often is) another's delight.

Thus at the court of Louis XIV in 1692 the king wanted to arrange an ignominious marriage for his nephew the duc de Chartres with one of his illegitimate daughters. The young duc, weak and speechless in front of the king, consented. His parents were humiliated; his mother burst into tears.

---

78. Ibid., p. 146: "If the theory of emotives is right, then sentimentalism's view of human nature was wrong in interesting ways. (And in saying it was 'wrong' I am purposefully breaking with a relativist stance vis-à-vis the subject matter of my research.)"

79. Lila Abu-Lughod, *Veiled Sentiments: Honor and Poetry in a Bedouin Society* (Berkeley, 1986), p. 97. For Reddy's comments on Rashīd and his wife, see *Navigation of Feeling*, pp. 39–40, 134–37, where he emphasizes the wife's suffering; she did not love Rashīd and ran away from him.

At dinner the young man's red eyes and his mother's welling tears did not discomfit the king at all.[80] "Far from disquieting the king," Reddy observes, "[the mother's] behavior appeared to suit him perfectly. He did not seek mastery over her emotions. Submission of the will, displayed through a minimal compliance with etiquette, was quite sufficient."[81] Thus is the courtly "emotional regime" summed up in Reddy's scheme. But it may not be amiss to point out that some people—namely the king—got satisfaction from this anti-emotional regime. And what of the other courtiers standing about?[82] The anthropologist Renato Rosaldo described the agonized anguish that the Ilongots of the Philippines felt when in 1972 martial law declared a ban on their beloved practice of headhunting.[83] But presumably Ferdinand Marcos and the local Protestant ministers long opposed to the practice were very pleased that the Ilongots generally complied.[84] Who suffers, who delights, has a great deal to do with who is in power. An emotional regime that induces suffering in some does not induce it in all.

Reddy's theory, too, may not take into sufficient account the pride and honor that is associated, in some cultures, with suffering. The Paxtun women whom Benedicte Grima studied in Pakistan during the 1980s were honored and admired precisely because they suffered, expressed their suffering, and were known by others to suffer. For them, "crying is the appropriate response to most events."[85] At her wedding, for example, the bride arrives with "downcast" eyes, in tears; she is called "beautiful" as she "performs" her sadness with exquisite grace.[86] For many medieval Christian writers, suffering was the *imitatio Christi*, the imitation of Christ's life on

---

80. Louis de Saint-Simon, *Mémoires complets et authentiques de Louis de Saint-Simon*, ed. Adolphe Chéruel (Paris, 1965), 1:17–25.

81. Reddy, *Navigation of Feeling*, p. 141.

82. In fact, even the king pretended that the young man felt "passion" for the bride in question (Saint-Simon, *Mémoires complets*, p. 22), and Saint-Simon himself was interested precisely in the emotions at court.

83. Renato Rosaldo, *Culture and Truth: The Remaking of Social Analysis*, 2d ed. (Boston, 1993), pp. 4–6. See also idem, *Ilongot Headhunting: A Social History, 1883–1974* (Stanford, 1980), pp. 285–89.

84. Rosaldo shows that conversion to Christianity was one way the Ilongots assuaged their pain. Headhunting had been an outlet for grief, and now Christianity became grief's refuge (*Ilongot Headhunting*, pp. 285–89).

85. Benedicte Grima, *The Performance of Emotion: "The Misfortunes Which Have Befallen Me"* (Austin, 1992), p. 49.

86. Ibid., p. 56.

earth; it was highly valued. And this literary theme had a lived counterpart, at least if the hairshirts and ascetic devotions in the lives of saints had any basis at all in practice.[87]

There are further difficulties, especially for medievalists. Reddy's scheme postulates overarching "regimes" that are quite clearly tied to state formation and hegemony. He recognizes one set of emotives for the royal court and another set—a very different one—for emotional refuges. But the refuges' emotives grew out of—and in this sense were created by—the court's own emotive inadequacies. Although the venues for such refuges were legion—at theaters and clubs as well as in novels, to name a few—the new emotives within these refuges were all of one type: sentimentalism. Reddy has taken an important step by recognizing the possibility of emotional refuges. In much anthropological literature, there is *one* culture, *one* emotional style for every society studied, though individuals are recognized to adapt to it in various ways. But Reddy's refuges leave us with a bipartite society: either one is at court *or* one is in a sentimental refuge. It is possible, though doubtful, that modern mass society yields just such limited alternatives.

Certainly there is no reason to imagine that the Middle Ages—or even particular periods within the Middle Ages—was divided between just two possible emotional stances. Admittedly, we shall see in the course of this book some early medieval royal courts that fostered and privileged certain emotional styles. But it would be wrong to call them "regimes." Rather, they seem to have represented the particular emotional styles of a momentarily powerful fraction of the population, an elite faction. Although difficult to glimpse, especially in the Early Middle Ages (when our sources are so meager), other sets of emotional norms no doubt coexisted with those that were dominant. This is why I argue in this book that there were (and are) various "emotional communities" at any given time. Arlie Hochschild's discussion of the "managed heart" of airline stewardesses is pertinent here.[88] The "hostesses" were trained, by order of the airlines, to deny their anger and

---

87. This critique of Reddy was already raised in brief in Popkin's review of *Navigation of Feeling* (p. 4). For Reddy's reply, see *H-France Review* 2 (November 2002), no. 119, www3.uakron.edu/hfrance/vol2reviews/reddy2.html (p. 1): "I define 'emotional suffering' as something unwanted. I would therefore exclude from this category suffering that is embraced by the sufferer." On different valuations of suffering, see Esther Cohen, "The Animated Pain of the Body," *AHR* 105 (2000): 36–68.

88. Hochschild, *Managed Heart*.

disgust, instead behaving—and feeling—benevolently toward recalcitrant and drunken passengers. Alienated from their "true" emotions, these women could hardly "reenter" the world of their friends and family without a sense of phoniness or disgust at their "commercial" selves. Yet the world of friends and family also managed emotions, which were shaped for purposes of "social exchange" if not for financial profit. Thus one sees in airline stewardesses an artificial but nevertheless perfectly coherent emotional community that coexisted side by side with others.

For Hochschild, it is wrenching to go from one emotional community to another.[89] But this cannot be true for everyone. Anthropologists do it all the time, presumably enjoying the experience, which is indeed part of the very call of their profession. Renato Rosaldo described his initial perplexity at headhunters who claimed that culling heads assuaged their sadness. Later he understood and felt their complex intermingling of "bereavement, rage, and headhunting"; he entered their emotional community.[90] Abu-Lughod wrote that she would "miss" the emotional community afforded by her bedouin hosts, "the joys of a sociable world in which people hug and talk and shout and laugh without fear of losing one another."[91] Clearly Abu-Lughod's normal emotional surroundings were rather different.

Imagine, then, a large circle within which are smaller circles, none entirely concentric but rather distributed unevenly within the given space. The large circle is the overarching emotional community, tied together by fundamental assumptions, values, goals, feeling rules, and accepted modes of expression. The smaller circles represent subordinate emotional communities, partaking in the larger one and revealing its possibilities and its limitations. They too may be subdivided. At the same time, other large circles may exist, either entirely isolated from or intersecting with the first at one or more points.

Whether overarching or subordinate, emotional communities are not coterminous with just any group. A crowded street does not constitute an emotional community. An emotional community is a group in which people have a common stake, interests, values, and goals. Thus it is often a

---

89. But this is an assumption not borne out by much data. See the review of Hochschild's book by Theodore D. Kemper in *American Journal of Sociology* 90 (1985): 1368–71: "Although emotional estrangement is proposed often enough, there are few data to support such a conclusion" (p. 1370).

90. Rosaldo, *Culture and Truth*, p. 11.

91. Abu-Lughod, *Veiled Sentiments*, p. xiii.

social community. But it is also possibly a "textual community," created and reinforced by ideologies, teachings, and common presuppositions.[92] With their very vocabulary, texts offer exemplars of emotions belittled and valorized.[93] In the Middle Ages, texts were memorized, made part of the self, and "lived with" in a way analogous to communing with a friend.[94] Hagiography (the lives of saints) was written so that men and women would have models of behavior and attitude.[95] The readers of these lives took that purpose seriously.

Thus emotional communities are in some ways what Foucault called a common "discourse": shared vocabularies and ways of thinking that have a controlling function, a disciplining function. Emotional communities are similar as well to Bourdieu's notion of "habitus": internalized norms that determine how we think and act and that may be different in different groups. Some sociologists speak of "group styles," in which "implicit, culturally patterned styles of membership filter collective representations" that may include "vocabularies, symbols, or codes."[96] I use the term "communities" in order to stress the social and relational nature of emotions; to allow room for Reddy's very useful notion of "emotives," which change the discourse and the habitus by their very existence; and to emphasize some people's adaptability to different sorts of emotional conventions as they move from one group to another.[97]

---

92. For textual communities, see Brian Stock, *The Implications of Literacy: Written Language and Models of Interpretation in the Eleventh and Twelfth Centuries* (Princeton, N.J., 1983).

93. In the modern world, films and mass media do this as well. Thus Nussbaum finds it useful to analyze a popular American film, *Terms of Endearment,* because it "appealed to a mass audience in its own culture and elicited strong emotions from it" (*Upheavals of Thought,* p. 165).

94. Reading partook of the process of "meditative imaging" discussed in Giselle de Nie, "Images of Invisible Dynamics: Self and Non-Self in Sixth-Century Saints' Lives," *Studia Patristica* 35 (2001): 52–64.

95. There was little "emotionology" as such in the Middle Ages—there were few advice books (though exceptions, such as "mirrors of princes," existed) and nothing written for a broad "middle class" until the very end of the period. But the normative value of texts such as saints' lives, penitentials, and liturgical readings must not be overlooked as sources that shaped emotional conventions and norms as surely as family and neighborhood.

96. Nina Eliasoph and Paul Lichterman, "Culture in Interaction," *American Journal of Sociology* 108 (2003): 735.

97. On the importance of early medieval communities—monks, laity and clergy, the imagined community of the living and dead, and so on—the bibliography is enormous. I cite here

METHODS AND SOLUTIONS

Emotional communities are not constituted by one or two emotions but rather by constellations—or sets—of emotions. Their characteristic styles depend not only on the emotions that they emphasize—and how and in what contexts they do so—but also by the ones that they demote to the tangential or do not recognize at all. To discover and analyze these communities I read related texts, noting all the words, gestures, and cries that signify feelings—or the absence of feelings. I am interested in who is feeling what (or is imagined to feel what), when, and why. Are there differences between men and women? I look for narratives within which feelings have a place, and I try to find common patterns within and across texts. I also seek implicit theories—insofar as possible—of emotions, virtues, and vices (all of which are related in the Western tradition, as will become clear in the next chapter).

Thus an important part of my method is to gather a dossier of materials (almost always written sources) that belong together because they point to an identifiable group, whether tied together by personal friendships, shared texts, or institutional affiliations. When I can find them—and when they are relevant to my group—I welcome on equal footing conciliar legislation, charters, hagiography, letters, histories, and chronicles. I set aside any isolated work, however interesting it may otherwise be. Always I miss what historians would look at first in the modern period—diaries, memoirs, interviews—though it may well be that we wrongly think of these as accessing emotion better than other sources: it is our own emotional community that values them for conveying intimate and sincere emotional expression. More serious is the lack of materials reflecting the lower classes. The extant writings of the Early Middle Ages echo only the voices of the elites—and the clerical elites at that.

Written texts present numerous problems. To be sure, many may be solved by the new and old auxiliary sciences of the historian—paleography, codicology, textual criticism, philology. But the historian of emotion is immediately confronted with somewhat different and as yet largely unmet challenges. Already long ago we realized that our sources are "interested," often "insincere." What should we make of them when they purport to tell us about emotions? Further, as composed texts, are they not very far from

---

one excellent recent synthesis: Régine Le Jan, *La société du haut Moyen Âge, VIe–IXe siècle* (Paris, 2003).

"real" emotions, communicating them (at best) via a distorting "second hand"? Then, too, do not genres dictate the "emotional tenor" that a text will have, quite independently from any supposed community? Finally, are texts not full of *topoi,* repeated commonplaces derived from other places, sources, and eras? What can *topoi* tell us about real feeling?

These are serious matters, but they are not insurmountable. Emotions are always delivered "secondhand," whether one adopts Reddy's notion of emotives or thinks simply of the ways in which one knows about feelings in ordinary life: via gestures, bodily changes, words, exclamations, tears. None of these things *are* the emotion; they are symptoms that must be interpreted—both by the person feeling them and by observers.[98] Texts provide one set of interpretations; the reader (or historian) studying them supplies others. The psychoanalyst with a patient on the couch is not in a much different position, though of course she can interrogate the patient in ways that historians can do only less directly with texts. Nevertheless, both historian and analyst depend on self-reportage, words, and silences.

The constraints of genre admittedly pose a problem. Might not the well-meaning historian mistake a particular genre, with its rules of expression, for an "emotional community"? I have tried to overcome this potential pitfall by drawing together different kinds of sources. Nevertheless, it is true that some of the dossiers that I have been able to gather are rather heavily weighted toward a particular genre. This is no doubt largely the result of chance survival rather than the favoring by a community of one genre over the other. (But *if* one genre were in fact privileged over others by a community, this would strengthen my case, since it would suggest that emotional communities choose the genres most compatible with their styles.) The rules of genre were not, however, ironclad. They themselves were "social products"—elaborated by people under certain conditions and with certain goals in mind—and they could be drawn upon and manipulated with some freedom. Like Isen and Diamond's "automatic habits," they shaped emotional expression even as they themselves were used and bent so as to be emotionally expressive. Thus, for example, we will see that what was a banal epitaph in one region was quite exceptional in another, that saints' lives

---

98. It is true that the James-Lange theory and its variants argue that the bodily change *is* the emotion. But bodily changes still need to be interpreted, a process that relies on cognition and thus is subject to social shaping, misapprehension, denial, and all the other mechanisms that mediate between an "emotion" and its naming. On the James-Lange theory see most conveniently Cornelius, *Science of Emotion,* chap. 3.

written in the first half of the seventh century were markedly less emotional than those written later in the century, and that charters—the early medieval equivalent of legal documents—were not entirely determined by boilerplate.[99]

It is true that genres tend to have different uses for emotions. Presumably letters best reveal how a person "really" feels. Saints' lives tell us how people were supposed to behave, emphasizing emotional ideals. Sermons, too, emphasize "oughts." Histories and chronicles, it would seem at first glance, must be driven by their subject matter and thus pose special problems: if someone or some event is emotional, the historian has no choice but to portray it thus. This, however, cannot be right, for the choice of subject and the way in which it is portrayed has everything to do with a historian's emotional community and the ways in which he or she imagines her audience. But surely biblical exegesis is utterly subject driven; an exegete must deal with emotional passages because they come up, willy-nilly, in books of the bible. To be sure, we cannot then say that *those passages* express the exegete's emotional community. But if a hagiographer, homilist, or letter writer quotes an emotional passage from the bible, then that is grist for our mill, though it is important not just to "count" it as "emotional" but to know whether the passage is quoted with approval or censure and in what context.

That texts may be insincere, make things up, mislead, and even lie is precisely what the historian's craft is meant to confront. We no longer think that texts are transparent windows onto "reality." We would be wrong to drop this stance when it comes to emotions. In one of his saints' lives, the sixth-century bishop Gregory of Tours described a joyful baby.[100] But no one knows how a baby "really" feels; and besides, this baby's joy was part of a miracle that Gregory was promoting. There is much to doubt in the account. But that Gregory *imagined* a child laughing with joy, that he found this a convincing image, that he expected his audience to find it so as well: *this* we may say is probably true. Even if Gregory were deliberately lying, his lie would betray a truth, namely that in his day it was possible to imagine happy babies.

But perhaps happy babies were *not* part of Gregory's world but constituted merely a *topos* that he knew about from his writing and education.

---

99. See chapter 2 for epitaphs, compare the emotional tenor of hagiography in chapters 5 and 6, and consider the discussion of charters in chapter 6 below.

100. Greg. Tur., *VP* 2.4, ed. Bruno Krusch, MGH SRM 1/2, p. 221.

Like the "Dear" that we use today in formal letter salutations, even to people we do not know—"Dear Sir or Madam"—*topoi* are conventions that have largely lost their meaning. Or so they appear. Medieval writings are full of these expressions, which in part were meant to show off the writer's literary background and mastery of certain conventions. The sixth-century panegyrist Venantius Fortunatus used the metaphor of sweetness (*dulcedo*) continually in his writings. To Ernst Curtius, writing half a century ago, this was seen as proof of his artificiality.[101] But what would be the use of the metaphor if it had no meaning? [102] Fortunatus employed the phrase because it helped him win favor; when he wrote of the "sweetness" of one of his patrons, he was drawing "attention to a characteristic which he had ulterior motives to applaud."[103] Artificial sentiments—even the mollifying "Dear Sir"—tell us about conventions and habits; these have everything to do with emotion, as Isen and Diamond have been at pains to point out. And even if Isen and Diamond are wrong, insincerity tells us about how people are supposed to feel. Fortunatus's patron was presumably made happy by the epithet "sweet." (That few men would be happy with it today tells us that our own emotional community is quite different from Fortunatus's.) Today we send Hallmark cards. Is this an act of sincere emotion? It is hard to know; but one thing is certain: it tells us about prevailing emotional norms. For the historian, this is precious enough.

THE SHAPE OF THIS BOOK

This deliberately short book is in effect an extended essay and an invitation to others to add to the picture that it sketches. Each chapter raises a different methodological problem in connection with studying emotional communities. It should be said at the outset that statistics is not among the methods used. Though there are plenty of numbers and much counting of

---

101. Ernst Robert Curtius, *European Literature and the Latin Middle Ages,* trans. Willard R. Trask (New York, 1953), p. 412. The high value placed on sincerity in the modern world is in fact a historical phenomenon; Reddy argues persuasively that "sincerity must be considered a specialized skill . . . that develops only in certain historical and political settings" (*Navigation of Feeling,* p. 109).

102. Indeed, Massimo Montanari denies that *topoi* exist, for once they are properly contextualized, they take on various meanings; Montanari, "Uomini e orsi nelle fonti agiografiche dell'alto Medioevo," in *Il Bosco nel medioevo,* ed. Bruno Andreolli and Massimo Montanari (Bologna, 1988), p. 57. I thank Professor Montanari for sending me a copy of his article.

103. Peter Godman, *Poets and Emperors: Frankish Politics and Carolingian Poetry* (Oxford, 1987), p. 16.

emotion words in this book, they are meant to serve as rough-and-ready snapshots, not as proofs. Chapter 1 begins with the Western tradition of emotion thought and emotion words, sketching the Latin legacy that would be transmitted directly to the Early Middle Ages. This chapter does not take up any emotional communities as such; indeed, it flattens out the ancient world as if it were merely a repository of *topoi,* words, and ideas about emotions ready to be drawn upon by future generations. No one in the Early Middle Ages would embrace the entire legacy, which itself was the product of many different emotional communities. Rather, succeeding generations carefully, though no doubt unconsciously, drew upon various parts of the ancient legacy—those most readily available and most consonant with their values and goals.

Chapter 2 takes up the possibility of studying coexisting emotional communities in different regions, suggesting that they might be connected to local traditions. Thus it looks at the funerary inscriptions of three different Gallic cities and suggests that quite different emotional communities were involved in each. Chapter 3 explores an emotional community through the writings of one person, Pope Gregory the Great (590–604). The methodological problem here is to take one man's writings as reflection of a larger community: I consider Gregory's work to represent the assumptions and norms of the clerical/monastic community for which he wrote and in which he spent his days.

Chapters 4, 5, and 6 turn to Francia; the triptych is meant to illustrate how and why different emotional communities may come to the fore and then fade away. Again, each chapter poses a different methodological problem. Chapter 4 seeks to discover an emotional community from the writings of two friends, Gregory of Tours and Venantius Fortunatus (whom we have just met). They were contemporaries of Gregory the Great, and their community of feeling had much in common with the pope's. But, working with the scheme of circles suggested above, we may say that their emotional community intersected with but did not entirely track the boundaries of the affective group in which Gregory lived. I argue that the emotional community of the two friends was characteristic of the court at Metz, about which, however, we know very little else. Chapter 5 finds a later, and very different, emotional community at the Neustrian court of Clothar II and his heirs, for which we have considerable evidence from a relatively wide variety of sources. Here the methodological issue is to see commonalities across many different genres by many different people, as well as to be sensitive to some telling differences. Chapter 6 raises perhaps the most harrowing methodological questions, for it draws mainly on anonymous writings. How can such writers constitute a social group, let alone an emotional community? I argue that in this case they can and do, and that their emotional community, that of the late seventh century, was quite different from any we had seen before.

I end my study here, in the late seventh century. The eighth century was a "new world," increasingly marked by Carolingian hegemony. The "epigraphic habit," which commemorated the dead and with which we begin the study of emotional communities in chapter 2, originated in its Christian form at the end of the fourth century and petered out at the close of the seventh century.[104] I take my cue from this rough-and-ready barometer. The next period—surely the eighth through early tenth centuries—deserves its own book. The book's conclusion, then, reviews the arguments of the previous chapters, confronts some caveats, and proposes a theory of emotional communities as agents of change. It is commonplace to see the modern period as one of dramatic transformations, while the Middle Ages—especially the Early Middle Ages—is thought to have changed with glacial slowness. But we shall see that, at least in the history of emotions, startling shifts took place within one or two generations. The history of emotions helps us to see new dynamism in a historical period that seems otherwise largely stagnant.

104. Mark A. Handley, *Death, Society and Culture: Inscriptions and Epitaphs in Gaul and Spain, AD 300–750,* BAR International Series 1135 (Oxford, 2003), p. 12. Bonnie Effros, *Caring for Body and Soul: Burial and the Afterlife in the Merovingian World* (University Park, Pa., 2002), chap. 3, points out that, while rare, epigraphs nevertheless continued to be composed and engraved during the late seventh to mid-eighth century.

I

THE ANCIENT LEGACY

Far from being utterly different from our own, the emotions of the ancient and early medieval worlds were recognizable antecedents of the modern variety. The capacious category "emotions" that exists today in both popular and learned thought in the Anglophone world had recognizable counterparts in the ancient and late antique worlds. Then too, the *contents* of our idea of the emotions—words such as fear, love, hate, and gestures such as weeping—had their parallels in the Greek and Roman past. The two principal ways in which we conceive of emotions—as impulses needing to be tamped down or as rational assessments—are of extraordinarily long standing. And the modern disjunctive valuation of emotions—as inimical or as essential to the good life—was also rehearsed in the ancient world.

This world was filled with its own emotional communities, but this chapter is not concerned with them. Its purpose, rather, is to suggest in outline the legacy of emotion concepts and words that antiquity offered to the medieval world. Its main points may be summarized briefly: Aristotle considered emotions useful, but the Stoics determined to extirpate them. Certain groups of Christians adhered to the Stoic view, incorporating emotions into a notion of "vices." Chief among these groups was the Desert Fathers, a subset of patristic writers who fled normal human society; spent their days in prayer, fasting, and penance; and taught their disciples to follow their lead. More mainstream Christian Fathers, such as Saint Augustine, were enormously influenced by these ascetics. While welcoming some emotions under some circumstances, and certainly unable to do without them when describing human beings and their foibles, patristic writers nevertheless often identified emotions with sins. Later emotional communities drawing upon these ideas had to deal with the resulting ambivalence.

"CLASSICAL" EMOTIONS

In Homer, places in the mind and body were said to contain the sorts of things that we associate with emotions. The "inner wind" of *thumos*—often located in the chest—was the site of "grief, fear, anxiety, hope, desire, love, anger, joy, delight, and so on."[1] (Later on, however, *thumos* would be associated almost exclusively with anger.) The *kardia* (heart), too, was "involved in anger, courage, fear, joy, pain, and patience." In later poets the heart was explicitly treated as the locus of hope and love.[2] For Homer *psuchē* was a "shade," not part of a living person at all, but later poets understood it as an interior entity. In Aeschylus (d. 456 B.C.E.) it was linked to pleasure, *hēdonē*.[3] In the plays of Sophocles (d. 406 B.C.E.), *psuchē*, the "soul," was where anger, courage, grief, joy, and other emotions rose and ebbed.[4]

None of this was systematized. Shirley Darcus Sullivan, a modern commentator trying to make sense of Greek psychology as it emerges from the literary sources, uses terms like "sharing" and "partaking" to talk about the relationship between *thumos* and emotions. Nor was there a "theory" of emotions as yet, though implicitly the poets linked emotions to madness and thus to a hydraulic scheme; emotions were forces out of rational control.[5]

This idea was made explicit in Plato (d.? 347 B.C.E.). He spoke of *pathos*, which meant for him more or less what "emotion" means to an Anglophone.[6] Plato did not like emotions very much: in the *Phaedo* Socrates dismisses his wife, Xanthippe, when she bursts into tears at the prospect of his execution, and he chides Apollodorus, who weeps as well, for his "woman-

---

1. Caroline P. Caswell, *A Study of "Thumos" in Early Greek Epic* (Leiden, 1990), p. 34. For further studies of Homeric emotions, see Robert Zaborowski, *La crainte et le courage dans l'Iliade et l'Odyssée. Contribution lexicographique à la psychologie homérique des sentiments* (Warsaw, 2002), with further bibliography on pp. 35–38. See also Shirley Darcus Sullivan, *Psychological and Ethical Ideas: What Early Greeks Say* (Leiden, 1995), p. 38; eadem, *Sophocles' Use of Psychological Terminology: Old and New* (Ottawa, 1999), pp. 29–35. I thank Catherine Mardikes and Richard Kraut for help in gathering a bibliography on emotions in the Greek world.

2. Sullivan, *Sophocles' Use*, p. 144. On both *kardia* and *thumos* see Hayden Pelliccia, *Mind, Body, and Speech in Homer and Pindar* (Göttingen, 1995), with extensive bibliography. Pelliccia's work (esp. pp. 15–27) suggests that scholarly approaches to Greek psychology have until recently been affected by the same "evolutionary" assumptions as those of medieval historians.

3. Shirley Darcus Sullivan, *Aeschylus' Use of Psychological Terminology: Traditional and New* (Montreal, 1997), p. 149.

4. Sullivan, *Sophocles' Use*, pp. 172–75.

5. Ibid., p. 211.

6. Harris, *Restraining Rage*, pp. 84–85, says that *pathos* means "something close to 'emotion'" first in Plato's *Phaedrus*; Aristotle's use of the plural, *pathē*, may have been itself innovative.

ish" behavior.⁷ But Plato's distaste for the display of emotions did not prevent his talking about them, most notably in the *Philebus* and the *Timaeus* (two late dialogues) as well as the *Republic* and the *Phaedrus*.⁸

The *Philebus* provides the briefest account and may serve to introduce most of Plato's key terms. Here Socrates makes an unusual appearance (he is rare in the late dialogues) to debate the role of pleasure in the life of the mind.⁹ He observes that pleasure (*hēdonē*) and pain (*lupē*) are usually mixed together. When the soul (*psuchē*) feels anger, fear, yearning, mourning, love, jealousy and envy, it feels sweet pleasure even as it suffers pains. "You remember," says Socrates, "how people enjoy weeping at tragedies." Let us note that Plato here brings up weeping, quite unselfconsciously, as part of his theory of the emotions. Our connection of that gesture/bodily sign to feelings is not just a modern construct.

The argument is brief in the *Philebus*, for Socrates refuses to stay up late to explain how each of the emotions is an admixture of pain and pleasure.¹⁰ He wants to get on to the really important issue: how contemplation of the forms is wholly pleasurable. Again, in the *Timaeus* Plato makes very clear that the emotions are problematic.¹¹ Here he presents a creation story in which God's children heedlessly gave "dread and inevitable" emotions (*pathēmata*) to morals. Here Plato assimilates the emotions to what will later be called the vices. He damns pleasure as "the strongest allurement of evil," while pain frightens "good things away." We are in a keenly moral universe now. In the soul, all the emotions—anger, fear, confidence, hope, and love—mingle together in "reasonless sensation."¹²

The immortal part of the soul, for Plato, is in the head; the mortal part,

---

7. Plato, *Phaedo* 60a and 117d, trans. Harold N. Fowler, Loeb Classical Library (Cambridge, Mass., 1966), pp. 208–9, 400–401. Hélène Monsacré points out that the association between women and tears found in Plato was a late development in the Greek world; Monsacré, *Les larmes d'Achille. Le héros, la femme et la souffrance dans la poésie d'Homère* (Paris, 1984), esp. pp. 137–38. In the *Iliad* the heroes wept regularly—above all from grief and fear.

8. Plato devalues emotions and looks to reason to conquer them; *Republic* 3.6 (604b–606e), trans. Paul Shorey, Loeb Classical Library (Cambridge, Mass., 1963), pp. 454–63.

9. Plato, *Philebus* 47d–48d, trans. Harold N. Fowler, Loeb Classical Library (Cambridge, Mass., 1942), pp. 330–33.

10. Ibid., 50d, pp. 340–41.

11. Plato, *Timaeus* 69c–71b, in *The Timaeus of Plato*, ed. and trans. R. D. Archer-Hind (London, 1888), pp. 257–65.

12. Harris, *Restraining Rage*, pp. 170–71 dates the opposition between reason and anger to the period around the start of the Peloponnesian war.

replete with the emotions, is below the neck. This mortal soul is bipartite: nearest the head is the "better part," the heart, filled with the emotions of manliness (*andreia*) and anger (*thumos*). Its emotions are warlike and, unlike other emotions, are potential allies of reason. Below the heart is the second, lesser part, the liver, full of the desires (*epithumiai*) and appetites. This anatomy has a specificity lacking in the poets. Plato is drawing on medical literature.[13] (Later the scheme would be expressed as an unholy trinity: the liver as the container for the concupiscent or desiderative part of the soul; the heart as the irascible or spirited part; the brain as the site of reason.)

Plato's theory was dynamic and confrontational. The appetites were wild beasts; reason, the lion tamer. Reason's whip was anger, which rose at its behest to restrain the other emotions. Despite its role as the container of the baser passions, the liver, thick and smooth, was also reason's ally. When it learned what was going on in the mind, it struck "terror into the appetitive part," inducing nausea and pain. There was thus a close connection for Plato between "soulful" desires like jealousy (*zēlos*) and bodily appetites such as hunger and thirst: his example of self-restraint giving way to excess was the desire (*epithumia*) for food: "if [that desire] prevails over the higher reason and the other desires, it is called gluttony [*gastrimargia*]."[14]

Aristotle (d. 322 B.C.E.) proposed a fundamentally different theory of emotions. For him the *pathē* (he used the plural form of *pathos*) were rational. They depended on conviction and resulted from judgments about *phantasia*, things hoped for or remembered.[15] Emotions were cognitive responses to lived experience in the world. Indeed, modern cognitive psychologists admit their debt to Aristotle.[16] The topic of *pathē* came up for Aristotle largely in the context of his work on rhetoric rather than ethics: he wanted to explain to the advocate how to play on the emotions of a jury. It

---

13. As noted by Galen, *On the Doctrines of Hippocrates and Plato*, ed. and trans. Phillip de Lacy (Berlin, 1980–84), p. 361. In the view of Mario Vegetti, *La medicina in Platone* (Venice, 1995), p. xiii, the *Timaeus* drew above all on Italian and Sicilian medical teaching.

14. Plato, *Phaedrus* 238a–b, trans. Harold N. Fowler, Loeb Classical Library (Cambridge, Mass., 1982), p. 447.

15. On things hoped for or remembered, Aristotle, *The "Art" of Rhetoric* 1.11.6 (1370a), trans. John Henry Freese, Loeb Classical Library (London, 1926), pp. 116–17. For *thumos* as the source of many emotions (e.g., anger, courage, affection) in Aristotle, see Cristina Viano, "Competitive Emotions and *Thumos* in Aristotle's *Rhetoric*," in *Envy, Spite and Jealousy: The Rivalrous Emotions in Ancient Greece*, ed. David Konstan and N. Keith Rutter, Edinburgh Leventis Studies 2 (Edinburgh, 2003), pp. 85–97.

16. Cornelius, *Science of Emotions*, p. 115.

was necessary to take stock of the emotions that might get in the way of—or be conducive to—a favorable judgment. Aristotle named fourteen pertinent emotions: anger (*orgē*) and its opposite, mildness (*praotēs*); love (*philia*) and hate (*misos*); fear (*phobos*) and its opposite, confidence (*tharrein*); shame (*aischunē*) and shamelessness (*anaischuntia*); benevolence (*charis*) and lack of benevolence (*acharistia*); pity (*eleos*) and indignation (*nemesan*); and lastly, envy (*phthonos*) and desire to emulate (*zēlos*).[17]

While admitting, like Plato, that emotions were amalgams of pleasure and pain, Aristotle tended to put the emphasis on pain (*lupē*). Pity, for example was "a kind of pain excited by the sight of evil, deadly or painful, which befalls one who does not deserve it."[18] Envy was "a kind of pain at the sight of [someone else's] good fortune,"[19] while the desire to emulate (*zēlos*) was a "pain not due to the fact that another possesses [highly valued goods] but to the fact that we ourselves do not."[20] The exception was anger, which was "always accompanied by a certain pleasure [*hēdonē*], due to the hope of revenge to come."[21]

Far more important to Aristotle than feelings, whether pleasurable or painful, were the people who were feeling and the social situations that provoked them. Indeed, Aristotle was interested in a sociology of emotion, played out in the context of a highly competitive and abrasive society in which men were acutely aware of their status and honor.[22] This explains his long discourse on the many slights, dishonors, and insults to a man's superior rank that might evoke wrath.[23] The goodness or badness of an emo-

---

17. Aristotle, *Rhetoric* 2.3.1–2.11.7 (1380a–88b), pp. 184–247.
18. Ibid., 2.8.2 (1385b), p. 225.
19. Ibid., 2.10.1 (1387b), p. 239.
20. Ibid., 2.11.1 (1388a), p. 243.
21. Ibid., 2.2.2 (1378b), p. 173.
22. For a thorough discussion of Aristotle's terms and their significance in the Greek world, see David Konstan, *The Emotions of the Ancient Greeks: Studies in Aristotle and Classical Literature* (Toronto, forthcoming). I am very grateful to Professor Konstan for sending me the typescript of this study before publication.
23. Aristotle, *Rhetoric* 2.2.3–2.2.7 (1378b–79a), pp. 174–77. On the relationship between the "rough-and-tumble context of Aristotle's Athens" and the emotions he discusses, see David Konstan, "Aristotle on Anger and the Emotions: The Strategies of Status," in *Ancient Anger: Perspectives from Homer to Galen,* ed. Susanna Braund and Glenn W. Most, Yale Classical Studies, vol. 32 (Cambridge, 2003), 99–120, with "rough-and-tumble" at p. 117. Nevertheless, a man's disposition, age, and condition determined when and to what extent he was moved by the *pathē*. The importance of disposition was Aristotle's main point in the *Nicomachean Ethics,*

tion—its ethical valence—had to do with how socially appropriate it was. The more normative, the better.[24]

Let us sum up. The ancient Greek world recognized emotions, and the words that Greek writers used for specific emotions are not entirely unfamiliar to us today in their modern vernacular equivalents.[25] Already by Plato's day the word *pathos* meant more or less what we mean by an emotion. (And it is important to realize that there is no firm consensus even today about what we mean, as will become clear by the end of this chapter.) Both Plato and Aristotle had theories of emotions that were not entirely dissimilar from modern notions. Plato's theory resembled the hydraulic model; Aristotle's the cognitive. Finally, both mentioned examples of *pathos/pathē* that figure (in English equivalents) on modern psychologists' lists of emotions. To be sure, what Plato and Aristotle meant by "orgē" in their slave-owning, male-dominated society was quite different from what we mean by "anger" in our society of mass consumers and special interest groups. But nothing of the past is the same today. That's why we have historians.

THE STOICS

The Stoics, whose school of philosophy was at its height around the time of Chrysippus (d. ca. 206 B.C.E.), put together the theoretical legacies of Plato

---

where he surveyed the *pathē* only to dismiss them as largely irrelevant to virtue (*aretē*); see Aristotle, *The Nicomachean Ethics* 2.5 (1106a), trans. H. Rackham, Loeb Classical Library (Cambridge, Mass., 1932), pp. 88–89. Here, Aristotle's list of emotions, admittedly open-ended, consisted of eleven words, some different from those in the *Rhetoric*, since the needs of the forensic orator were no longer at issue: desire (*epithumia*), anger (*orgē*), fear (*phobos*), confidence (*thrasos*), envy (*phthonos*), joy (*chara*), love (*philia*), hate (*misos*), yearning (*pothos*), jealousy/desire to emulate (*zēlos*), and pity (*eleos*).

24. Aristotle, *Nicomachean Ethics* 2.6.10–12 (1106b), p. 93: "one can be frightened or bold, feel desire or anger or pity, and experience pleasure and pain in general, either too much or too little, and in both cases wrongly; whereas to feel these feelings at the right time, on the right occasion, towards the right people, for the right purpose and in the right manner, is to feel the best amount of them, which is the mean amount—and the best amount is of course the mark of virtue." The thrust of this statement is not that moderate emotions are best but rather "that emotions (whether weak or strong) should be ethically appropriate to the specific situation," as noted in *The Passions in Roman Thought and Literature*, ed. Susanna Morton Braund and Christopher Gill (Cambridge, 1997), p. 7.

25. On this point for rancorous words in particular, see Harris, *Restraining Rage*, chap. 3 and Konstan, *Emotions of the Ancient Greeks*.

and Aristotle. They agreed with Aristotle that emotions were judgments. But in their view, they were bad judgments. In this way, they agreed with Plato: emotions were inimical to the virtuous life.

It is wrong to assume a unanimous Stoic position on the emotions. Nevertheless, their views may be fairly pulled together for our purposes here. They conceived of emotions as consisting of two judgments: an appraisal of something as being good or bad, and an assessment of the appropriate way to react.[26] They argued that all emotions fell within four categories on a grid that considered both the present and the future. The two emotions of the present were pleasure and pain; those of the future were desire and fear (see table 1). Pleasure (*hēdonē* in Greek; *laetitia* and *voluptas* in Latin) was a judgment that something good was present and that it was appropriate to feel (in reaction) a kind of bodily expansion. Pain (*lupē; aegritudo*) was a judgment that something bad was present and that it was appropriate to feel a sort of sinking. Fear (*phobos; metus*) was the judgment that something bad was imminent and that it was appropriate to avoid it. Desire (*epithumia; libido, appetitus,* or *cupiditas*) was the assessment that something good was imminent and that it was appropriate to reach for it.[27]

Within this grid fell every sort of emotion. Expounding on the Stoic *pathē* (which he translated into Latin as *perturbationes*) in his *Tusculan Disputations,* the Roman writer and politician Cicero (d. 43 B.C.E) named many of them, though his list was meant to be open-ended.[28] Because these Latin terms constituted a major part of the repertory of emotion words that Cicero himself knew, and because they remained an important subset of the possible emotion words that medieval people might use, I present them here in alphabetical order in table 2.

---

26. For what follows I have consulted, among other studies, Marcia L. Colish, *The Stoic Tradition from Antiquity to the Early Middle Ages,* vol. 1: *Stoicism in Classical Latin Literature,* rev. ed. (Leiden, 1990); Nussbaum, *Therapy of Desire;* Richard Newhauser, *The Treatise on Vices and Virtues in Latin and the Vernacular* (Turnhout, 1993); Simo Knuuttila, "Medieval Theories of the Passions of the Soul," in *Emotions and Choice from Boethius to Descartes,* ed. Henrik Lagerlund and Mikko Yrjönsuuri (Dordrecht, 2002), pp. 49–83; and especially Richard Sorabji, *Emotion and Peace of Mind: From Stoic Agitation to Christian Temptation. The Gifford Lectures* (Oxford, 2000).

27. See Sorabji, *Emotion and Peace of Mind,* pp. 29–30; I have added *voluptas* to Sorabji's list of Latin terms for pleasure because it is used in place of *laetitia* in Cicero, *Tusculan Disputations* 4.7.16, trans. J. E. King, Loeb Classical Library (Cambridge, Mass., 1945), p. 344.

28. Ibid., 4.7.16–4.9.22, pp. 344–50 makes clear that Cicero is not naming every emotion but rather pertinent examples.

TABLE 1. *The Stoic Emotional Grid*

	Assessed as a good	Assessed as an evil
Present	pleasure (*hēdonē, laetitia, voluptas*)	pain (*lupē, aegritudo*)
Future	desire (*epithumia, libido, appetitus, cupiditas*)	fear (*phobos, metus*)

The Stoics were convinced that the wise man (or woman) was unswayed by passion, and therefore they considered such lists of emotion words important tools for reason to wield as it convinced judgment not to assent to emotion. The process began with a pre-emotion, which intimated that an emotion was on its way. These were the "first movements," manifesting themselves as pallor, weeping, shuddering, or an expansion or contraction of the chest. For the Stoics these were not emotions themselves but rather signals that something had the appearance of being good or bad. You should then exercise your judgment to realize that the appearance was false, avoiding the emotion itself. In this way, you circumvented *both* judgments involved in emotion: the assent to anything external being good or bad as well as the assent to the bodily reactions that were appropriate to the emotions.

Thus in the ancient world the Stoics proposed a coherent theory of the emotions, a plan for their management, and an open-ended list of words that alerted reason to vigilant action.

LATE ANTIQUE WORDS AND THEORIES

Cicero presented himself primarily as a translator and admiring critic of the Stoic position.[29] About a century later the Roman philosopher and statesman Seneca (d. 65 C.E.) modified the theory by elaborating on the idea of "first movements." He introduced the will (*voluntas*) into the psychological mix, making it the part of reason that assented to the "movement" and transformed it into an emotion.[30] Seneca used *affectus* as his term of art for the emotions. He was particularly interested in anger (*ira*), which he termed not only an emotion but a vice (*vitium*). Other *affectus* that he men-

---

29. On the context for Cicero's writing on the topic, see *Cicero on the Emotions: Tusculan Disputations 3 and 4*, trans. Margaret Graver (Chicago, 2002), pp. xii–xv.

30. See Brad Inwood, "Seneca and Psychological Dualism," in *Passions and Perceptions: Studies in Hellenistic Philosophy of Mind. Proceedings of the Fifth Symposium Hellenisticum*, ed. Jacques Brunschwig and Martha C. Nussbaum (Cambridge, 1993), esp. pp. 173–81; Sorabji, *Emotion and Peace of Mind*, pp. 69–70.

TABLE 2. *Cicero's List of Stoic Emotions and Approximate English Equivalents*

adflictatio, affliction
  adflictari, to be miserable or afflicted
aegritudo, pain, distress
aemulatio, rivalry
  aemulari, to rival
aerumna, weariness
angor, anxiety
  angi, to be vexed
commotio animi, strong emotion
conturbatio, agitation
cupiditas, desire
delectatio, pleasure
desiderium, desire, longing
desperatio, despair
  desperare, to despair
discordia, discord
dolor, sorrow
  dolere, to sorrow
elatio animi, elated emotion
exanimatio, paralyzing terror
excandescentia, heatedness (of anger)
formido, dread
gaudium, joy
indigentia, need, greed
inimicitia, enmity
invidentia, envying
  invidere, to envy
invidia, envy; spite
ira, anger
jactatio, ostentation
laetitia, happiness

lamentatio, lamenting, mourning
  lamentari, to lament
libido, desire
luctus, grief
  lugere, to grieve
maeror, sorrow
  maerere, to sorrow
malevolentia, malice, spite
metus, fear, dread
misericordia, pity
  misereri, to pity
molestia, annoyance
obtrectatio, jealousy
  obtrectare, to be jealous
odium, hatred
pavor, panic
perturbatio, emotion
pigritia, indolence, sloth
pudor, shame
sollicitudo, worry
  sollicitari, to worry
spes, hope
terror, terror
timor, fright
voluptas, pleasure

[emotion markers:
dentium crepitus, chattering of teeth from fear
pallor, whitening from fear
rubor, blushing from shame
tremor, trembling from fear]

Note: I provide here generic and simple English equivalents, taking into account the translations in *Cicero on the Emotions: Tusculan Disputations 3 and 4*, trans. and with commentary by Margaret Graver (Chicago, 2002). Noun terms are from Cicero, *Tusculan Disputations* 4.5.10–4.9.22 and 4.37.80 (for *spes* [hope]); verbs are from 3:34.83–84; emotion markers are ibid., 4.8.19. Cicero found nouns more comfortable than verbs to refer to emotions, and it is striking that nouns are today the most characteristic way in which English speakers think theoretically of emotion words. See Phillip Shaver et al., "Emotion Knowledge: Further Exploration of a Prototype Approach," *Journal of Personality and Social Psychology* 52 (1987): 1061–86.

tioned in passing included *libido* (lust or desire), *metus* (fear), *audacia* (recklessness), *amor* (love), and *odium* (hate).[31] He thought that some people— "hotter" people—were more liable to anger than others; this was playing on the medical humoral theories of the day.[32] But even Galen (d. ca. 200 C.E.), himself a doctor, sought the remedy for emotions less in physical therapy than through education and exercises in mental self-control with a good tutor.[33]

None of these philosophers made up emotion words; they found them in the popular and learned vocabulary of their day. Like modern psychologists (as we shall see), they were concerned to schematize them, and, again like modern psychologists, they were particularly interested in a few key emotions: anger seems to have been—and to some extent remains—a sort of benchmark for all the others.[34]

The triumph of Christianity did not change the words used for emotions, but it altered their meanings. Christian values and goals overturned old norms: bold acts became the practices of ascetics, not martial heroes; the moral elite became the "converted," not the well educated; virtue became a matter of humility, not manliness. Or, rather, the ascetics became the "athletes of God"; the converted knew the only truth; and manliness was redefined in Christian terms. Consider St. Augustine's jaundiced view of his father's "old-fashioned" values: when the older man scrimped to pay for his boy's education, Augustine complained: "Yet this very same father didn't care how I grew with regard to You or how chaste I was."[35] And when the

---

31. Seneca, *On Anger* 1.1.1, 1.1.5, 1.3.6, 1.7.1, trans. John W. Basore, Loeb Classical Library (Cambridge, Mass., 1963), pp. 106, 108, 114, 124. For a penetrating study of *affectus*, to which my own work is beholden, see Damien Boquet, *L'ordre de l'affect au Moyen Âge. Autour de l'anthropologie affective d'Aelred de Rievaulx* (Caen, 2005), with a discussion of Seneca on pp. 43–46.

32. Seneca, *On Anger* 2.19.2–5, pp. 204–6.

33. Galen, *On the Passions and Errors of the Soul*, trans. Paul W. Harkins ([Columbus, Ohio], 1963).

34. See Janine Fillion-Lahille, *Le De ira de Sénèque et la philosophie stoïcienne des passions* (Paris, 1984); Julia Annas, "Epicurean Emotions," *Greek, Roman, and Byzantine Studies* 30 (1989): 145–64; Nussbaum, *Therapy of Desire*, p. 404 n. 1; Galen's *On the Passions* is largely about anger; for Lactantius, see below at note 38. Modern studies include Stearns and Stearns, *Anger;* Carol Tavris, *Anger: The Misunderstood Emotion* (rev. ed.; New York, 1989).

35. Augustine, *Confessions* 2.3.5, ed. Pierre de Labriolle, Les Belles Lettres, 2 vols. (Paris, 1969, 1977), 1:33: "cum interea non satageret idem pater, qualis crescerem tibi aut quam castus essem."

father, viewing his pubescent son at the baths, thought about grandchildren, Augustine accused him of reveling in self-will, "loving your creature in place of You."[36]

As Christians deliberately turned pagan definitions of good and evil upside down, old emotional habits had to change. Parenting, education, and the availability of hallowed models—first of the martyrs and later of the saints—helped make this transformation possible. Christ's kingdom was not of this world: that essential fact was absorbed in different ways by different groups. But one thing is certain: Christianity had the potential to effect seismic shifts in the emotions that were valued or disdained as well as the norms of their expression.

Within this changed landscape, the outlines of two different tendencies may be seen: on the one hand were Christians who tentatively welcomed the ancient world's rich emotional vocabulary and its implications for feeling; on the other hand were those who rejected a great many emotions. (No one could reject emotions entirely. Even the Stoics had countenanced *eupatheiai*—a very few "good" emotions which, however, only the "wise man" experienced.)[37] Lactantius and Jerome may serve here as representatives of the first group, the Desert Fathers of the second.

Lactantius (d. ca. 330), a Christian rhetorician and tutor to the son of Emperor Constantine I, argued the usefulness of emotions, making the point by taking on the tricky topic of the emotions of God. God gets angry (*irascitur*) and hates (*odit*) the wicked, Lactantius argued. It is true that God is free of emotions such as lust (*libido*), fear (*timor*), covetousness (*avaritia*), grief (*maeror*), and envy (*invidia*).[38] But, Lactantius argued, He is full of joy and love, hate and anger. Thus we find in Lactantius the verbs *diligo* and *amo* (both meaning to love) and the nouns *caritas* (love) and *laetitia* (happiness) pared with *odi* (to hate), because God's happiness and love for the good turned on hating and being angry at the wicked.[39]

---

36. Augustine, *Confessions* 2.3.6, 1:33: "creaturam tuam pro te amavit."

37. See Sorabji, *Emotion and Peace of Mind*, pp. 47–51.

38. Lactantius, *On the Anger of God* 16.7, in *Lactance, La colère de dieu,* ed. Christiane Ingremeau, SC 289 (Paris, 1982), p. 170.

39. Lactantius, *On the Anger of God* 4.10–11, p. 106: "Ita qui bonos diligit, et malos odit, et qui malos non odit, nec bonos diligit, quia et diligere bonos ex odio malorum venit et malos odisse ex bonorum caritate discendit. Nemo est qui amet vitam sine odio mortis." (For he who loves the good also hates the bad, and he who does not hate the bad also does not love the good. For loving the good comes from hating the bad, and hating the bad derives from love of the good. There is no one who loves life without hating death.) For God's joy, see

Jerome (d. ca. 420) was an ascetic close to the Desert Fathers. But when he set about to translate the bible into Latin—the so-called Vulgate—he had perforce to describe the behaviors of numerous people who clung to "the world" because that was how he found them in the Hebrew and Greek texts. Thus he drew on the vocabulary at hand. He never intended to provide an inventory of emotion words, but we shall use him for that purpose here, in order to supplement the list from Cicero and thus to give a partial sense of the vocabulary that was available to the Early Middle Ages. A systematic survey would include far more than Jerome's Vulgate: it would, at the least, incorporate the emotion words of other biblical translations of the time, the so-called *Vetus Latina*. It would look, too, at the words incorporated into Christian liturgical rites and the vocabularies of homilies, which referred, perforce, to the daily lives, values, and feelings of people in the world.

Here Jerome must suffice. It is telling that he employed only forty-six of Cicero's sixty emotion words.[40] Jerome, like Cicero, belonged to—and wrote for—an emotional community, privileging certain emotions over others. He also added to Cicero's list. How do we know that such "new words" connoted emotions? Because they come up as pairs with—or transformations of—the terms of affect that we already know to have been considered as such.

Thus in Jerome's rendition of the bible, Elcana was sad (*tristis*) because he loved (*diligebat*) his barren wife Anna, while she, who was bitter in heart (*amaro animo*), prayed to the Lord with many tears (*flens largiter*) (1 Sam. 1:5–10). Here love—which, as we saw with Lactantius, was associated with the emotions—was linked to sorrow, and Anna's unhappiness was proved by tears. Similarly associated with weeping is *lamentatio:* "Let them hasten and take up a lamentation for us; let our eyes shed tears [*lacrimas*]" (Jer.

---

ibid., 15.6, p. 166. For more discussion of Lactantius's contribution to incorporating the emotions into the Christian life and world view, see David Konstan, *Pity Transformed* (London, 2001), pp. 121–24.

40. The words not included in the Vulgate are *adflictatio/adflictari; aegritudo; angor/angi* (though *anxius* is much used); *conturbatio* as mental agitation; *exanimatio; excandescentia* (a word, in any case, made up by Cicero to mean "nascent anger"; see Harris, *Restraining Rage*, pp. 68–69); *invidentia; malevolentia; obtrectatio/obtrectare; dentium crepitus;* and *rubor* (in the sense of blushing). To do these word searches, I used the on-line searchable Douay-Rheims Vulgate text at http://www.lib.uchicago.edu/efts/ARTFL/public/bibles/vulgate.search.html, verifying the passages in the critical edition *Biblia Sacra iuxta vulgatam versionem*, ed. Robert Weber, 2 vols. (Stuttgart, 1969).

9:18).⁴¹ And "a voice was heard on high of lamentation [*lamentationis*], of weeping [*fletus*], and mourning [*luctus*], of Rachel wailing [*plorantis*] for her children" (Jer. 31:15). When Moses died, "the children of Israel wept for [*fleverunt*] him in the plains of Moab thirty days: and the days of their mourning [*planctus*] in which they mourned [*lugentium*] for Moses were ended" (Deut. 34:8). Tears, however, are multivalent. When Joseph saw his brother Benjamin after many years, "he embraced [*amplexatus*] him and wept [*flevit*]: and Benjamin in like manner wept [*flente*] also on his neck. And Joseph kissed [*osculatus*] all his brethren, and wept [*ploravit*] upon every one of them" (Gen. 45:14–15). Here family feeling was expressed not by a particular word but rather by the gestures that signified it: embracing, weeping, and kissing. Similarly, sorrow was sometimes indicated by groans: "For my life is wasted with grief [*maerore; dolore*]: and my years in groans [*gemitu; gemitibus*]" (Ps. 30:11).⁴² And fear might be indicated by trembling, as when Jesus confronted the woman with the issue of blood: she fell at his feet "fearing and trembling [*timens et tremens*]" (Mark 5:33).

Emotions are labile and subject to revision.⁴³ Thus sorrow may turn into joy, as when Mardochai announces new holy days to the Jews because "on those days the Jews revenged themselves, and their mourning [*luctus*] and sorrow [*tristitia*] were turned into mirth [*hilaritatem*] and joy [*gaudium*], and . . . these should be days of feasting and gladness [*laetitiae*]" (Esther 9:22). Or joy may come to an end: "Laughter [*risus*] shall be mingled with sorrow [*dolore*], and mourning [*luctus*] taketh hold of the end of joy [*gaudii*]" (Prov. 14:13).⁴⁴

Anger, too, is associated with other feelings, but not ordinarily its opposite. Above all it is paired with fury (*furor*). In Deuteronomy, Moses warns the Israelites that those who serve another God will not be forgiven, but

---

41. I ordinarily follow the Douay translation, modifying where necessary. I follow the text of the Vulgate given in *Biblia Sacra iuxta vulgata versionem*.

42. For the Psalms, Jerome gave two versions, one according to the Septuagint (the Greek bible) and one based on the Hebrew version. Hence the different words in parentheses.

43. Recall the observations of Reddy, *Navigation of Feeling*, as discussed above in the introduction, at note 73.

44. See also James 4:9: "Be afflicted, and mourn [*lugete*], and weep [*plorate*]: let your laughter [*risus*] be turned into mourning [*luctum*], and your joy [*gaudium*] into sorrow [*moerorem*]." Joy (*gaudium*) was one of the few Stoic *eupatheiae*, that is, movements of the soul based on true judgments, and was thus distinguished, in their scheme, from *laetitia*. For the Latin terms, see Cicero, *Tusculan Disputations* 4.6.13, p. 340.

rather that God's fury (*furor*) and jealousy (*zelus*) will be ignited. After all, God destroyed Sodom and Gomorrah, Adama and Seboim, in anger (*ira*) and fury (*furor*). Indeed, the "anger of his fury" (*ira furoris*) is "immense" (Deut. 29:20–24).[45] Hatred, however, is never brought together with fury; rather it is often linked to its opposite, love. After Amnon raped his half-sister, he "hated her [*exosam habuit*] with an exceeding great hatred [*odio*]: so that the hatred [*odium*] wherewith he hated [*oderat*] her was greater than the love [*amore*] with which he had loved [*dilexerat*] her before" (2 Sam. 13:15). When Samson's wife wanted to know the answer to his riddle, she wept and complained: "Thou hatest [*odisti*] me and dost not love [*diligis*] me" (Judg. 14:16).

Love was a particularly difficult term for any Christian translator because of its associations to both high virtue (love of God and neighbor) and low vice (love of self). When Jerome translated Ecclesiastes 9:5–6, "For the living know that they shall die, but the dead know nothing more, neither have they a reward any more: for the memory of them is forgotten. Their love also, and their hatred, and their envy are all perished," he used the Latin term *amor* for love. But when he came to translate 1 John 4:8 and 4:16, "God is love" he used the word *caritas* for the Greek *agapē*. Later Augustine would explain the connection between *amor* and *caritas*: "For if it is someone's purpose to love [*amare*] God and to love [*amare*] his neighbor as himself, not according to man but according to God, . . . this is usually called *caritas* in holy scripture. But it is also termed *amor* in those same holy writings."[46] *Caritas*, which was God's love, was thus equivalent to *amor*. But was *amor* equivalent to *caritas*? Often enough, even the Fathers were willing to let the lines blur.[47]

---

45. For further associations of the terms *ira* and *furor* see 1 Sam. 20:34; 1 Sam. 28:18; Ps. 68:25; Ps. 84:5.

46. Augustine, *City of God* 14.7, ed. Bernardus Dombart and Alphonsus Kalb, CCSL 47–48 (Turnhout, 1955), p. 421: "Nam cuius propositum est amare Deum et non secundum hominem, sed secundum Deum amare proximum, sicut etiam se ipsum . . . quae usitatius in scripturis sanctis caritas appellatur; sed amor quoque secundum easdem sacras litteras dicitur." See also Augustine's translation of "God is love" with *dilectio* in his *Tractatus in epistola Johannis ad Parthos*: "Deus dilectio est," quoted and discussed in Anita Guerreau-Jalabert, "*Caritas* y don en la sociedad medieval occidental," *Hispania* 60 (2000): 30.

47. See Hélène Pétré, *Caritas. Étude sur le vocabulaire latin de la charité chrétienne* (Louvain, 1948), chap. 1, for the meanings of *diligo* and *amo*, *caritas* and *amor* in the classical period; *amor* implicated the body; *caritas* often implied "esteem"; *diligo* often suggested "affection." But all three terms might also simply be used as synonyms. In the Christianized Roman em-

Jerome also transmitted in his translation a theory of the emotions that grew out of the Stoic view. When Christ explained his parable of "the things come from a man that defile a man," he commented: "For from within, out of the heart of men, proceed evil thoughts [*cogitationes malae*], adulteries [*adulteria*], fornications [*fornicationes*], murders *[homicidia]*, thefts [*furta*], covetousness [*avaritiae*], wickedness [*nequitiae*], deceit [*dolus*], lasciviousness [*impudicitiae*], an evil eye [*oculus malus*], blasphemy [*blasphemia]*, pride [*superbia*], foolishness [*stultitia*]. All these evil things come from within, and defile a man" (Mark 7:15, 21–23). We have seen that one of these words — *avaritia* — was classed as an emotion by Lactantius. And the idea of "evil thoughts" was already in the time of Jerome being assimilated to the Stoic "first movements," with important results.

The view that evil thoughts were closely tied to emotions was the contribution of the Desert Fathers, and it led to a repudiation of many — though not all — emotions in those who adopted it. This development is clearly seen in the work of Evagrius (d. 399), a hermit for the last decade or so of his life in the Nitrian desert in Egypt.[48] A hermit, to be sure; but he was also a teacher with a group of disciples. He left a number of writings, of which his *Practical Treatise* is a characteristic example. Here he spoke of "eight thoughts": gluttony (*gastrimargia*), lust (*porneia*), avarice (*philarguria*), distress (*lupē*), anger (*orgē*), acedia, vanity (*kenodoxia*), pride (*huperphania*).

---

pire, as Pétré argues in chaps. 2 and 3, *caritas* was used less often than *dilectio,* but when it was employed, in her view, it normally meant spiritual love, though there might be exceptions. Emile Schmitt points out that even St. Augustine saw marriage as a locus of *caritas;* Schmitt, *Le mariage chrétien dans l'oeuvre de Saint Augustin. Une théologie baptismale de la vie conjugale* (Paris, 1983), pp. 280–87. Guerreau-Jalabert, "*Caritas* y don," reveals the many ways in which *caritas* was used to represent a variety of social relations throughout the Middle Ages. See also eadem, "*Spiritus* et *caritas.* Le baptême dans la société médiévale," in *La parenté spirituelle. Textes rassemblés et présentés,* ed. Françoise Héritier-Augé and Elisabeth Copet-Rougier (Paris, 1995), pp. 133–203. Verena Epp argues that *caritas, dilectio* and *amor* were synonymous for many writers in the early Middle Ages; Epp, *Amicitia. Zur Geschichte personaler, sozialer, politischer und geistlicher Beziehungen im frühen Mittelalter* (Stuttgart, 1999), pp. 37–42. Isabelle Réal notes that in the Merovingian world *amor* tended to be used for physical, passionate love, while *dilectio* and *caritas* referred to the licit love of married couples; Réal, *Vies de saints, vie de famille. Représentation et système de la parenté dans le Royaume mérovingien (481–751) d'après les sources hagiographiques* (Turnhout, 2001), pp. 350–51.

48. Nevertheless, the first to make the association between pre-emotions and "bad thoughts" was Origen (d. ca. 254); see Sorabji, *Emotion and Peace of Mind,* p. 346.

They were not emotions but rather their first prickings and tinglings—the Stoic first movements, but in Evagrius's view sent by the demons.[49] If you assented to them and let them linger, they would stir up emotions proper: "It is up to us whether they linger or not, or whether they stir up emotions [*pathē*] or not."[50] Assent to the "pleasure of the thought" is sin.[51] You refuse such assent by opposing one thought against another in a kind of psychomachy, a battle of thoughts. Thus, "the demon of vainglory is opposed to the demon of fornication and the two cannot assail the soul at the same time, for the first promises honors while the other leads to dishonor. If, therefore, one of the two approaches and presses you closely, then elicit in yourself the thoughts of the opposing demon and if you can, drive out one nail (as they say) with another."[52]

John Cassian (d. 435), one of Evagrius's disciples and founder and abbot of Saint-Victor at Marseille, latinized and slightly rearranged Evagrius's list of "thoughts": gluttony (*gastrimargia; ventris ingluvies*), lust (*fornicatio*), avarice (*filargyria; avaritia; amor pecuniae*), anger (*ira*), sadness (*tristitia*), anxiety (*acedia; anxietas; taedium cordis*), ostentation (*cenodoxia; jactantia; vana gloria*), and pride (*superbia*). But, unlike Evagrius, he did not treat them as prior to sin; they *were* sins, indeed they were the chief vices (*principalia vitia*).[53] They were also emotions (for which Cassian used the term *passiones*). Thus Jesus was tempted by *fornicatio* but was "free of the contagion of this passion."[54]

---

49. Evagrius of Pontus, *Practical Treatise* 6, in *Évagre de Pontique, Traité pratique ou Le moine,* ed. and trans. Antoine Guillaumont and Claire Guillaumont, 2 vols., SC 170-71 (Paris, 1971), 2:506-9. The editors provide an excellent background to Evagrius's scheme; ibid., 1:38-84. Origen had said that the demons introduced these thoughts, and Evagrius largely—but not entirely—adopted this idea; see the discussion below in chap. 6 at note 83, and see Sorabji, *Emotion and Peace of Mind,* p. 359.

50. Evagrius of Pontus, *Practical Treatise* 6, 2:508-9.

51. Sorabji, *Emotion and Peace of Mind,* p. 360.

52. Evagrius, *Practical Treatise* 58, 2:636-37.

53. John Cassian, *Conlationes XXIIII* 5.2, ed. Michael Petschenig, CSEL 13, pt. 2 (Vienna, 1886), p. 121. I am grateful to Columba Stewart for discussions concerning Cassian's notion of the emotions.

54. Cassian, *Conlationes* 5.5, p. 124: "absque huius passionis contagio"; see also ibid., 5.7.1, p. 127, where Cassian interrupts himself to talk about the vices—here called passions—beyond gluttony and fornication: "Et ut de efficientiis ceterarum quoque passionum, quarum narrationem intercidere nos expositio . . . conpulit . . . disseramus." (Now to talk about the

In this way, under the aegis of the Desert Fathers, the "deadly sins" originated in theories of emotion. In effect the Fathers were simply hardening ancient views—chiefly those of Plato and the Stoics—that disapproved of the emotions and founded whole ethical schemes on their extirpation or control. The best-known list of sins, the one by Pope Gregory the Great (d. 604), separated pride (*superbia*) from the others as the "root" (*radix*) of all the rest, leaving seven: vanity (*inanis gloria*), envy (*invidia*), anger (*ira*), sadness (*tristitia*), avarice (*avaritia*), gluttony (*ventris ingluvies*), and lust (*luxuria*).[55] Of these, only gluttony was not directly part of the emotions tradition of the past. But in fact no thinker had ever entirely dissociated bodily appetites from mental desires. Plato had located *gastrimargia* at the lower depths of the mortal soul, along with the other *epithumiai*. Aristotle sometimes included thirst and hunger among the *pathē*.[56] The Stoic "first movements" and their second judgment about "appropriate reactions" were as much distress of the body as of the soul. The medical model of Galen and others considered the physiological states that lay behind psychological ones.[57] Already Evagrius considered *gastrimargia* one of the "eight thoughts," a prelude to emotions, so that when Cassian turned it into a vice and a passion, he was not taking a big step.

The "organic" metaphor of a root (pride) with branches (the sins) was also a natural outgrowth of the emotions tradition. The ancient philosophers had long recognized the interrelatedness of emotional states. Cicero reported that the Stoics called intemperance (*intemperantia*) the "fountain-

---

effects of the other passions, which the exposition on Christ compelled us to interrupt.) Augustine conveniently sums up all the Latin equivalents of the Greek *pathē*: "Duae sunt sententiae philosophorum de his animi motibus, quae Graeci *pathē*, nostri autem quidam, sicut Cicero, perturbationes, quidam affectiones vel affectus, quidam vero, sicut iste, de Graeco expressius passiones vocant." (Among the philosophers there are two views of these motions of the soul [*animi motibus*], which the Greeks call *pathē* but which some of us, like Cicero, call *perturbationes* and which others call *affectiones* or *affectus,* and still others, like [Apuleius], call *passiones,* which is closer to the Greek.) Augustine, *City of God* 9.4, ed. Bernard Dombart and Alfons Kalb, CCSL 47 (Turnhout, 1955), p. 251.

55. Gregory the Great, *Moralia in Job* 31.45.87, ed. Marcus Adriaen, CCSL 143, 143A, 143B (Turnhout, 1979, 1985), p. 1610.

56. Stephen R. Leighton, "Aristotle and the Emotions," in *Essays on Aristotle's Rhetoric*, ed. Amélie Oksenberg Rorty (Berkeley, 1996), p. 220.

57. James Hankinson, "Actions and Passions: Affection, Emotion and Moral Self-Management in Galen's Philosophical Psychology," in *Passions and Perceptions*, ed. Brunschwig and Nussbaum, pp. 220–21.

head" (*fons*) of all the emotions.[58] He himself noted that a man in distress will give in to fear and depression as well.[59] For Galen, "insatiate desire" was "a kind of foundation for covetousness, love of glory, ambition, lust for power, and love of strife. . . . And yet I would not hesitate to say that greed [*pleonexia*] is the foundation [*krēpis*] of all these vices."[60]

Yet long traditions cannot obviate the very real changes introduced by Evagrius, Cassian, and the other Desert Fathers. They turned some emotions into sins and thus freighted them with meanings not explicitly given other emotions.[61] Sin, in the view of the post-Nicaean church, was tied to the flesh.[62] When emotions became sins, they ceased to be cognitive appraisals (as they had been for the Stoics) and became, instead, part of man's corrupt and fallible nature.[63] One consequence of this was that some emotion words could do double duty, expressing both feelings and moral states. In like fashion, virtue was now sometimes conceptualized as contrary to emotion: "Because the vices are motions and perturbations of the soul, virtue is, by contrast, calmness and tranquility of soul," wrote Lactantius.[64]

At the same time, however, while stopping up the parade of emotion words, the Desert Fathers let loose the wordless signs of emotional outpouring. For Cassian, compunction made itself known by shouts (*clamores*), groans (*gemitus*), and tears.[65] Indeed, Cassian parsed the causes of weeping: some tears came of compunction, others of joy, or of terror, or of pity.[66] "I

---

58. Cicero, *Tusculan Disputations* 4.9.22, p. 348.

59. Ibid., 3.7.14, p. 242.

60. Galen, *De propriorum animi cuiuslibet affectuum dignotione et curatione* 10, ed. Wilko de Boer (Leipzig, 1937), p. 35; Galen, *On the Passions,* pp. 65–66. I thank my colleague James Keenan for helping me with Galen's Greek.

61. But, on another view, we might say that "the part stands for the whole" and that the Seven Deadly Sins are prototypes for *all* the sins, as is argued in George Lakoff, *Women, Fire, and Dangerous Things: What Categories Reveal about the Mind* (Chicago, 1986), p. 89.

62. On the change, see the suggestive remarks of Susanna Elm, *"Virgins of God": The Making of Asceticism in Late Antiquity* (Oxford, 1994), pp. 379–81.

63. To some extent, cognitive psychologists are still battling this development. See Phoebe C. Ellsworth, "Some Implications of Cognitive Appraisal Theories of Emotion," in *International Review of Studies on Emotion,* vol. 1, ed. Ken T. Strongman (Chichester, 1991), 143–44.

64. Lactantius, *Divinae institutiones* 7.10, PL 6, col. 768: "Quia vitia commotiones et perturbationes animi sunt, virtus e contrario lenitudo et tranquillitas animi est."

65. Cassian, *Conlationes* 9.27, p. 274.

66. Ibid., 9.29–30, pp. 274–76.

can't think of a state more sublime," said Germanus, Cassian's genial interlocutor, as he recalled the joy of one episode of weeping.[67]

Greatly admiring the Desert Fathers but not one himself, St. Augustine (d. 430), bishop of Hippo and arguably the most influential Christian thinker during the Early Middle Ages, gave a new direction to the emotions tradition that in effect reconciled the two attitudes (welcoming versus hostile) discussed here. Augustine accepted most emotions as good if rightly ordered, bad if wrongly directed.[68] Conjoining "first movements" with the emotions, he subjected all "motions" to the will:[69]

> The important factor . . . is the character of a man's will [*voluntas*]. If the will is wrongly directed, the emotions [*motus*] will be wrong; if the will is right the emotions will be not only blameless, but praiseworthy. The will is engaged in all of them; in fact they are all essentially acts of will. For what is desire [*cupiditas*] or happiness [*laetitia*] but an act of will [*voluntas*] in agreement [*consensione*] with what we wish for? And what is fear [*metus*] or sadness [*tristitia*] but an act of will in disagreement with what we reject?[70]

Corrupted by the Fall, the human will ordinarily assented to the wrong things. But with God's grace, a person could rightly be "angry [*irasci*] at a sinner to correct him, feel sorrow [*contristari*] for the afflicted to free him, fear [*timere*] that a person in danger might perish."[71] Oriented toward God,

---

67. Ibid., 9.28, p. 274: "quo statu reor nihil esse sublimius."

68. The exception was lust; see Sorabji, *Emotion and Peace of Mind*, chap. 26.

69. Augustine was ambivalent about the importance of first movements. In *City of God* 14.19 he "fail[ed] to distinguish first movements from emotions;" see Sorabji, *Emotion and Peace of Mind*, p. 384. But in his sermons he elaborated on the "cognitive cause of 'preliminary passions,'" namely doubt; see Sarah C. Byers, "Augustine and the Cognitive Cause of Stoic 'Preliminary Passions' (*Propatheiai*)," *Journal of the History of Philosophy* 41 (2003): 433.

70. Augustine, *City of God* 14.6, p. 421: "Interest autem qualis sit voluntas hominis; quia si perversa est, perversos habebit hoc motus; si autem recta est, non solum inculpabiles, verum etiam laudabiles erunt. Voluntas est quippe in omnibus; immo omnes nihil aliud quam voluntates sunt. Nam quid est cupiditas et laetitia nisi voluntas in eorum consensione quae volumus? Et quid est metus atque tristitia nisi voluntas in dissensione ab his quae nolumus?" The translation here is taken from Augustine, *City of God,* ed. David Knowles, trans. Henry Bettenson (Harmondsworth, England, 1972), p. 555, slightly modified.

71. Augustine, *City of God* 9.5, p. 254: "Irasci enim peccanti ut corrigatur, contristari pro adflicto ut liberetur, timere periclitanti ne pereat."

the emotions were good; oriented toward the world, they were evil. And thus for Augustine, as for Lactantius, it was perfectly possible for God himself to be full of feelings: "You love [*amas*] but you don't burn [*aestuas*], you are jealous [*zelas*] but untroubled [*securus*], you repent [*paenitet*] without sorrowing [*doles*], you get angry [*irasceris*] yet you are tranquil."[72]

A book could (and should) be written about Augustine's emotional vocabulary. Here, however, I merely wish to explore briefly an aspect of his emotional expression that few of the writings we have thus far seen had cause to bring up: terms of endearment.[73] In Augustine's writings there are three chief words of affection: *dulcis* (sweet) and its superlative, *dulcissimus* (sweetest); *dilectus* (beloved) and its superlative, *dilectissimus* (related to the verb *diligere,* to love); and *carus* (dear) and its superlative, *carissimus* (related to *caritas*). In the *Confessions,* for example, God is "most sweet" (*dulcissimus*), as is Nebridius, the "sweetest and kindest of friends" (*amicus dulcissimus et mitissimus*).[74] Indeed, Nebridius is "dearest" (*carissimus*).[75] In the *City of God* Marcellinus, the chaste imperial commissioner who asks Augustine to write the book, is his "dearest son" (*filius carissimus*).[76] Isaac is, in Augustine's view, Abraham's "most beloved" (*dilectissimus*) son.[77]

We have now a real thesaurus of words: nouns, verbs, adjectives. Nor should we forget that almost all verbs can become adjectives: *iratus* (angered) is as much an emotion word as *ira* (anger). Table 3 summarizes the word hoard gathered here. It is entirely open-ended since it cannot pretend to be exhaustive. Nevertheless, it is a fair sampling. We shall see that some early emotional communities drew almost exclusively from this list, for its terms, after all, came from the normative vocabulary of the bible, among other sources. Other communities discovered some different modes of expression. The vernacular languages added new possibilities. Nevertheless, it may be said that even today our theories of emotions and our modes of expressing them—through words, gestures, and terms of endearment—are

---

72. Augustine, *Confessions* 1.4.4, ed. Labriolle, 1:5: "Amas nec aestuas, zelas et securus es, paenitet te et non doles, irasceris et tranquillus es."

73. The exception is the bible, where, for example, Paul calls Timothy "filius meus charissimus" (my dearest son) (1 Cor 4:17).

74. Augustine, *Confessions* 7.3.5, 1:149; ibid., 8.6.13, 1:186.

75. Ibid., 4.3.6, 1:70.

76. Augustine, *City of God* praef., p. 1.

77. Ibid., 16.32, p. 536, elaborating on the bible's "Tolle filium . . . quem diligis" (Take your son, whom you love) (Gen 22:2).

TABLE 3. *Partial Latin Emotion Word List and Approximate English Equivalents*

adflictio/adflictatio, pain
   adflictari, to be miserable or afflicted
aegritudo, pain, distress
aemulatio, rivalry
   aemulari, to be envious
aerumna, weariness
affectus, emotion
amor, love
   amare, to love
amplexor, to embrace
angor/anxietas, anxiety
   angi, to be vexed
audacia, recklessness
avaritia, covetousness, avarice
caritas, love
   carus/carissimus, dear/dearest
clamor, shout
commotio animi, (strong) emotion
contristari, feel sympathy for
conturbatio, agitation
cupiditas, desire
delectatio, pleasure
dentium crepitus, chattering of teeth from fear
desiderium, desire, longing
desperatio, despair
   desperare, to despair
dilectus/dilectissimus, beloved/most beloved
   diligere, to love
discordia, discord
dolor, sorrow
   dolere, to sorrow
dulcis/dulcissimus, sweet/sweetest
elatio animi, emotion

exanimatio, paralyzing terror
excandescentia, heatedness (of anger)
exosus, hated
fletus, weeping
   flere, to weep
formido, dread
fornicatio, lust
furor, fury
gastrimargia, gluttony
gaudium, joy
gemitus, sigh
hilaritas, cheerfulness
inanis gloria, vainglory
indigentia, need, greed
inimicitia, enmity
invidentia, envying
invidia, envy, spite
   invidere, to envy
ira, anger
   irasci, to get angry
jactatio, ostentation
lacrimae, tears
laetitia, happiness
lamentatio, lamenting, mourning
   lamentari, to lament
libido, desire
luctus, grief
   lugere, to grieve
maeror, sorrow
   maerere, to sorrow
malevolentia, malice, spite
metus, fear, dread
misericordia, pity
   misereri, to pity
molestia, annoyance
motus, emotion

obtrectatio, jealousy
   obtrectare, to be jealous
odium, hatred
   odisse, to hate
osculor, to kiss
paenitere, to repent
pallor, whitening from fear
passio, emotion
pavor, panic
perturbatio, emotion
pigritia, indolence, sloth
planctus, mourning
plorare, to weep and wail
pudor, shame
risus, laughter
rubor, blushing from shame

sollicitudo, worry
   sollicitari, to worry
spes, hope
superbia, pride
terror, terror
timor, fright
   timere, to fear
tremor, trembling from fear
   tremere, to shudder
tristitia, sorrow
   tristis, sad
ventris ingluvies, gluttony
voluptas, pleasure
zelus, jealousy, rivalry
   zelare, to be jealous

Note: I provide here the list from Cicero (table 2) intermingled with emotion words drawn from other ancient writers surveyed in this chapter. The words here are a small sample of the available vocabulary. Emotion markers are not separated from other emotion words here.

not cut off from their corresponding elements in the ancient world. Just how closely our own lists track the old ones is my next and final point.

MODERN LISTS

Modern scientists and scholars often speak with uncanny authority on which words belong in the category of "emotions." Rom Harré observes: "One well known textbook [on emotions] mentions only depression, anxiety, lust and anger, but lust and depression are not emotions. Depression is a mood and lust a bodily agitation."[78] In fact, however, not all psychologists agree that depression is not an emotion; Ken Strongman, for one, calls it just that.[79] The same may be said for lust, which figures in the list of emo-

---

78. *Social Construction of Emotions*, ed. Harré, p. 5.
79. Ken T. Strongman, *The Psychology of Emotion* (3d ed., Chichester, 1987), pp. 208–12.

tion words under "love" in an article on the emotions published by Phillip Shaver in the same year as Harré was writing.[80]

Thus, despite the authoritative tone of scholars on the topic, there is no agreement about precisely what terms belong in the category of emotion. Each theory perforce generates its own list.[81] The most famous of these inventories is Paul Ekman and Wallace Friesen's, who claimed to have isolated six universal emotions: happiness, sadness, fear, disgust, anger, and surprise.[82] The two psychologists showed pictures of people whose facial expressions "corresponded" to each emotion. Even people outside of Western cultures could (more or less) correctly name the emotion that corresponded to the grimace. But more recently Ekman has become interested in autonomic nervous system patterns, and this has led him to postulate seventeen basic emotions. These are "amusement, anger, awe, contempt, contentment, disgust, embarrassment, excitement, fear, guilt, interest, pride in achievement, relief, sadness, satisfaction, sensory pleasure, and shame."[83]

Both of Ekman's lists are grounded in the Darwinian notion that emotions (and their bodily concomitants) are products of evolution and thus species related. Other lists depend on different theories. Robert Plutchik is also a Darwinian, but he is interested in translating the subjective language of emotions into behavioral and functional terms common to both human beings and animals. Consider the behavioral words "withdrawing" and "escaping" or the functional term that corresponds to those behaviors, "protection." "Withdrawing," "escaping," and "protection" are,

---

80. Phillip Shaver et al., "Emotion Knowledge: Further Exploration of a Prototype Approach," *Journal of Personality and Social Psychology* 52 (1987): 1066, table 1, where lust shows high "prototypicality" ratings. See also Sandra Metts, Susan Sprecher, and Pamela C. Regan, "Communication and Sexual Desire," in *Handbook of Communication and Emotion: Research, Theory, Applications, and Contexts,* ed. Peter A. Andersen and Laura K. Guerrero (San Diego, 1998), pp. 353–77.

81. The study of emotion by psychologists is relatively new. Consider *Approaches to Emotion,* ed. Klaus R. Scherer and Paul Ekman (Hillsdale, N.J., 1984), p. xi: "After many years of neglect during which time only a few scholars were concerned with emotion . . . emotion has become a vital, almost fashionable topic in the social and behavioral sciences."

82. Paul Ekman and Wallace V. Friesen, "Constants across Cultures in the Face and Emotion," *Journal of Personality and Social Psychology* 17 (1971): 124–29.

83. Paul Ekman, "All Emotions Are Basic," in *The Nature of Emotion: Fundamental Questions,* ed. Paul Ekman and Richard J. Davidson (New York, 1994), p. 18.

for Plutchik, translations of "fear." Or, rather, since "fear" is of lower intensity than "terror," Plutchik pairs the two. Thus "fear/terror" corresponds to "withdrawing/escaping," and both in turn correspond to "protection." Plutchik has eight such emotions: fear/terror, anger/rage; joy/ecstasy; sadness/grief; acceptance/trust; disgust/loathing; expectancy/anticipation; surprise/astonishment.[84] Like the Stoics, he arranges these as a grid—but *his* grid is shaped like a top. He has the eight most vehement subjective emotions on the crown of the top, with grief opposite ecstasy and so on. Again, as with the Stoics, other emotions then are classed under this topmost grid, with "pensiveness," for example, going down one side of the top, ranked under "grief/sadness."[85] Elaborating on Plutchik's scheme, Phillip Shaver and his associates argue that emotion categories such as "fear" are "fuzzy sets," in and around which many other "emotion names" may cluster. They identify 135 words that arguably signify an emotion.[86] But Keith Oatley, a cognitivist who hypothesizes that emotions manage changes in plans or goals, suggests five basic emotions: happiness, sadness, fear, anger, and disgust. Each accomplishes a different transition.[87]

There is, then, both enormous disagreement and considerable overlap within modern scholarly definitions. As we have seen, this was equally characteristic of the ancient world's view of emotions. In addition many emotion words inventoried in modern lists were (in their Greek or Latin equivalents) part of the repertory that ancient writers considered to be *pathē* or *perturbationes*. The top ten of Shaver's "prototypical" emotions, that is, the emotion words that his respondents—all psychology students at the University of Denver—most frequently identified as "an emotion" were (in order of most prototypical to least): love, anger, hate, depression, fear, jealousy, happiness, passion, affection, and sadness. If we translated these words into Latin, all would fit nicely into table 3. There is, then, no reason to worry that studying the emotions of the Western Middle Ages

---

84. Robert Plutchik, "Emotions: A General Psychoevolutionary Theory," in *Approaches to Emotion*, ed. Scherer and Ekman, p. 200, table 8.1.

85. Ibid., p. 203, fig. 8.1.

86. See Shaver et al., "Emotion Knowledge," p. 1066, table. 1, where the emotion words are listed.

87. Oatley, *Best Laid Schemes*, p. 55, table 3, for the basic emotions.

is any more anachronistic than studying its universities, ideas, or political institutions. To be sure, all were different from their manifestations today,[88] but in every case the historian can have fair hopes of entering sympathetically into a mind-set that is not entirely foreign to her own. Western emotions have persisted over the long haul.

88. The differences between ancient Greek emotions and our own are made clear in Konstan, *Emotions of the Ancient Greeks*.

2
CONFRONTING DEATH

The ancient world offered a large repertory of ideas about emotions and words to express them, as chapter 1 has suggested. But subsequent groups drew on this treasury only selectively. For one thing, they had other repertories—sub-Latin and perhaps vernacular ideas and words—to work with. For another, different groups used certain modes of expression—but not others—because the norms and habits of their particular emotional community made some forms of expression more comfortable and automatic than others.

We may be able to glimpse different contemporaneous emotional communities of the Early Middle Ages—groups that drew upon the traditional vocabulary in different ways—via the funerary epitaph. This was generally inscribed on a small marble plaque placed in a niche in the cover of a tomb. We know of about fifteen hundred Christian funerary inscriptions from Gaul, dating from circa 350 to 750.[1] Although often scattered, important clusters exist in a few places, allowing us to associate types of epitaphs—and the sentiments they express—with places and settlements. The cities with the greatest number of funerary inscriptions are, in order, Trier, Vienne, and Lyon. In this chapter, we shall consider the inscriptions from Trier, Vienne, and Clermont (see map of the Early Medieval West), for the very practical reason that they exist in excellent critical editions. We shall see enough differences to suggest that funerary inscriptions may be one revealing element of emotional communities in the Early Middle Ages. They must al-

---

1. See Yitzhak Hen, *Culture and Religion in Merovingian Gaul, A.D. 481–751* (Leiden, 1995), p. 146. In e-mail conversations with me, Nancy Gauthier seconded this estimate; I wish to thank Prof. Gauthier for her help with all aspects of this chapter. A much higher estimate—2,657 inscriptions—has been given in Handley, *Death, Society and Culture*, p. 5. But this is because he counts fragments, some as small as a single letter or decorative motif. See also idem, "Beyond Hagiography: Epigraphic Commemoration and the Cult of Saints in Late Antique Trier," in *Society and Culture in Late Antique Gaul: Revisiting the Sources*, ed. Ralph W. Mathisen and Danuta Shanzer (Aldershot, 2001), p. 188, where Handley gives the number "more than 2500."

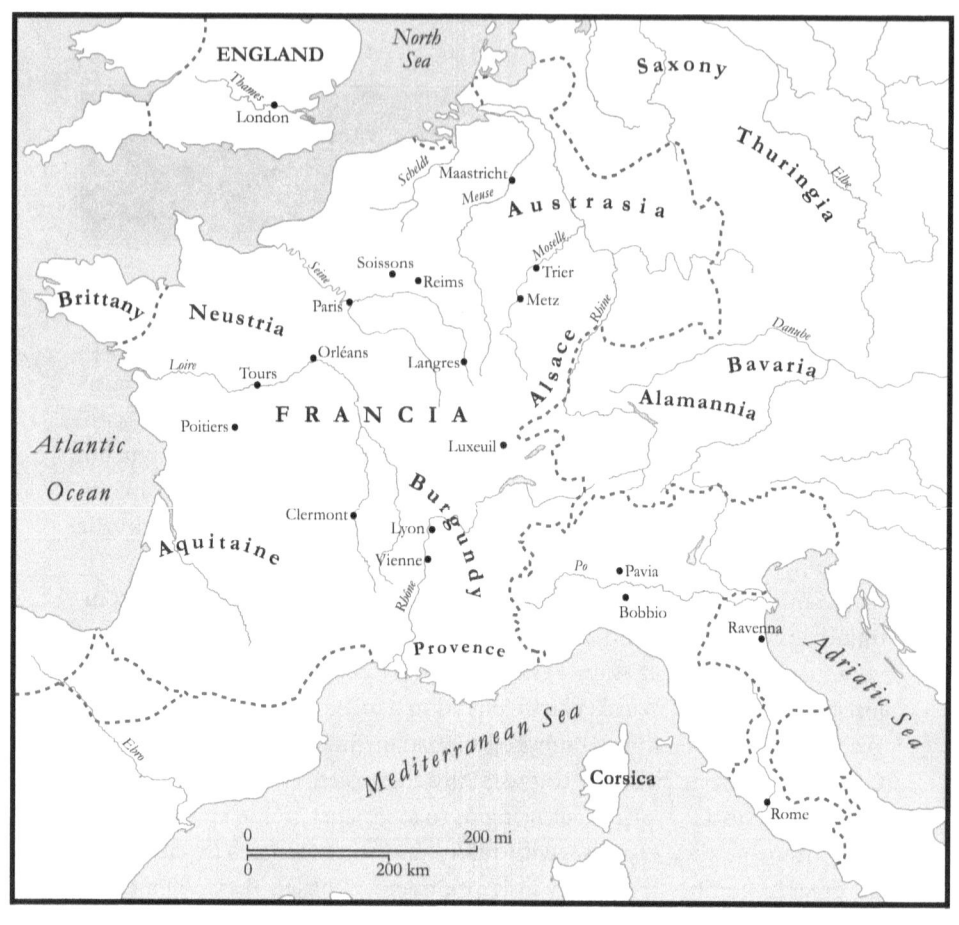

MAP OF THE EARLY MEDIEVAL WEST

ways be considered partial indicators because, while they can hint at norms about expressing grief, affection, and other emotions connected with death, they cannot tell us about the emotions invoked in other aspects of life. Furthermore, they are rare. Although these materials demand to be counted—and the next few pages are filled with numbers and even some percentages—I do not claim to be using statistics. The numbers are meant simply to be suggestive. Supplemented by the evidence brought together in the ensuing chapters, they may help to elucidate the notion of emotional communities and their vicissitudes.

People at Trier, Clermont, and Vienne privileged different ways of expressing their feelings about death and dead ones.[2] At Trier, they had a repertory of eleven emotion words; at Clermont they used only seven, not all overlapping with the Trier vocabulary. At Vienne, twenty-four words expressed feeling. This comparatively high number had little to do with the number of inscriptions there. A rough-and-ready estimate would put the number of inscriptions from Vienne at about half those of Trier.[3]

We cannot attribute the repertory of emotion words simply to the ateliers that carved the inscriptions. Mark Handley has recently argued that inscriptions were mainly borrowed from model books—though perhaps different ones for each cemetery workshop—and that some "boilerplate" may already have been carved before inscriptions were commissioned.[4] But this does not obviate the important role of the client. Individual choices by commemorators were involved at every step. First, they had to decide

---

2. Margaret King outlines the reasons for scholarly opposition to using epitaphs to recover emotions: the sentiments expressed are conventional rather than "genuine"; King, "Commemoration of Infants on Roman Funerary Inscriptions," in *The Epigraphy of Death: Studies in the History and Society of Greece and Rome,* ed. G. J. Oliver (Liverpool, 2000), pp. 119–21. But we have seen that emotions are indeed expressed through conventions and for conventional, habitual, and "automatic" purposes. It is only the hydraulic view that demands that emotions "well up" spontaneously; the social constructionist view recognizes that the welling up itself—however personal it may feel—is highly scripted by social norms. On pp. 131–34 King makes much the same point.

3. Where possible, I have considered only inscriptions that can be contextualized within particular cemeteries: at Trier, I consider only the inscriptions from the cemeteries of Saint-Eucherius (to the south) and Saint-Paulin and Saint-Maximin to the north; at Vienne, I consider the inscriptions from the cemeteries of Saint-Gervais, Saint-Sévère, and Saint-Pierre. There are too few inscriptions at Clermont to allow for such contextualization.

4. Handley, *Death, Society and Culture,* pp. 28–29.

whether or not to commission an epitaph for the deceased. This may well have been, in part, an economic issue. Inscriptions cost money. Then the words had to be chosen. If an emotion word was added, that meant additional costs. In some instances, it looks as if the cutter could not read the text supplied to him by the patron of the stone, which means that at least in those cases the patron, not the carver, made the decision about which words to use.[5]

A letter from Sidonius Apollinaris (d. ca. 484), bishop of Clermont during the last decade of his life, suggests how natural it was for an aristocrat from southern Gaul to write and put up an epitaph to honor the dead. In this instance the deceased was Claudianus Mamertus, a priest at Vienne and brother of a bishop there, who had written a book on the nature of the soul and dedicated it to Sidonius. Claudianus had averred that he was Sidonius's "special and intimate" (*specialis atque intumus*) friend, and Sidonius had replied with effusive praise. When he learned of Claudianus's death, Sidonius wrote to the dead man's great-nephew, mingling words of grief with reminiscences and homage, and including a poem which he reports "having inscribed over the bones" (*super . . . ossa conscripsi*) of his "like-minded brother" (*unanimi fratris*).[6]

To be sure, few people composed long original poems. There were formulae, and most of the epitaphs adhered to them. However, these formulae could—and did—change. For example, in the region around Trier the phrase *pro caritate* (for love) was replaced after circa 500 by equivalent—but different—expressions, such as *propter caritate* (on account of love), *pro amore* (for love), and *pro dilectione* (for love).[7] Sometimes changes followed waves of fashion emanating from Rome. Trier was especially prone to follow the styles of the Eternal City, no doubt because it had been an imperial residence itself, with long-distance connections and high-flown preten-

---

5. E.g., *Recueil des inscriptions chrétiennes de la Gaule antérieures à la Renaissance carolingienne* (hereafter *RICG*), vol. 1, *Première Belgique*, ed. Nancy Gauthier (Paris, 1975) (hereafter *RICG I*), no. 194A; see Gauthier's remarks on p. 484.

6. Sidonius, *Letters, Books III–IX*, 4.2, trans. W. B. Anderson, Loeb Classical Library (Cambridge, 1965), pp. 64–68, for Claudianus's letter to Sidonius (quote on p. 66), and ibid., 4.3, pp. 68–78, for Sidonius's reply. For the epitaph itself, see ibid., 4.11, pp. 106–8. About a century later, Venantius Fortunatus, an Italian who ingratiated himself with the Gallic elite (see below, chap. 4) busied himself by writing epitaphs as well: see the entire fourth book of Venantius Fortunatus, *Poems* in *Venance Fortunat Poèmes*, ed. and trans. Marc Reydellet, Les Belles Lettres, 2 vols. (Paris, 1994, 1998), 1:130–63.

7. *RICG I*, p. 100.

sions.⁸ These small changes tell us that no formula book ruled for all time. Even workshops were social products; they took their cues, however slowly and with however much inertia, from those who made use of them.

"Banal," is the word that the inscriptions' modern editors use for the most routine of the formulae. But what was banal at Trier was not so at Vienne. At Vienne most people commissioning epitaphs were careful to specify dates; at Trier people almost never added dates to their inscriptions. At Trier the ages of the deceased were specified with an accuracy (even to the day) that was rare at either Clermont or Vienne.⁹ Banality, as we have seen, is useful to the historian of emotions, telling us what sentiments—or non-sentiments—are socially normative under particular circumstances. If the banalities of early medieval Christian epigraphs in Gaul were different in different places, that should alert us to the possibility that we are dealing with different emotional communities.

To be sure, all of these inscriptions belonged to one overarching community, since the fact that the inscriptions were Christian implies that those who paid for the plaques, and those who lay beneath them, belonged to the universal community of believers. Sharing a common religious affiliation, they agreed on spiritual aspirations and therefore, again in a general sort of way, on the emotions appropriate to the Christian life.¹⁰ However distinctive the clusters of such words were for each community, nevertheless nearly all of the emotional vocabulary they used is either included in table 3 or is related to a word therein.¹¹ We know that some people moved about and

---

8. Consider, for example, the adoption of the formula *plus minus* to indicate approximate age. The phrase was first used at Rome and appropriated at Trier before it was taken up at any other place in Gaul. See Gauthier's remarks, *RICG I*, p. 42.

9. On the norms for reporting age, see Gauthier's introductory comments in *RICG I*, pp. 40–42.

10. See Oatley, *Best Laid Schemes*, on goals and emotions.

11. Indeed, only two words in the emotional vocabulary of the inscriptions from Trier, Clermont, and Vienne are not derived from words on table 3: *levamen* and *solamen*, both of which mean "solace" or "comfort." Nevertheless they have an analog in the Vulgate: *solacium*. This term, a less poetic equivalent for *solamen*, is there associated with feelings, as in Phil. 2:2, where it is linked to love (*solacium caritatis*). It is, of course, possible that I wrongly include *solamen* and *levamen* as emotion words; the English word "relief," which I take to be the feeling of one who has been "comforted," is number 63 in Shaver's list of 213 emotion words (Shaver et al., "Emotion Knowledge," table 1). But Shaver does not include "solace" in his list at all. Naturally the Vulgate is not the only source for Latin emotion words of Late Antiquity, as I have already remarked in chapter 1.

yet were comfortable with the epigraphic formulae of their adopted homes. Optata and her husband, for example, who put up an epitaph for their son Numidius at Trier, were probably from North Africa (Optata was a common name in Africa, and Numidius recalls the Roman province of Numidia). Yet they chose an inscription for their son's stone that would have pleased just about any native at Trier.[12] Thus, the different emotional communities at Trier, Clermont, and Vienne were what I have called "subordinate": they were subsets of the same Christian emotional community that existed in Gaul (and elsewhere) from the fifth through the seventh centuries.[13]

"THE SWEETEST LITTLE GIRL": FAMILY AFFECTION AT TRIER

The city of Trier, strategically situated on the Moselle river between Mainz and Metz, was a major commercial center in the Roman period. Under the emperors Diocletian (d. 316) and Constantine (d. 337) it became an imperial residence. In its heyday, the fourth century, its population may have been as high as sixty thousand souls. In the fifth century the city was buffeted by the wars between the "Romans" and the "barbarians," or, at any rate, by the army leaders who claimed to represent those sides. Around 475 Trier came under Frankish rule, and in the ensuing two centuries its population shrank dramatically.[14] Under the Merovingians, Frankish rulers from circa 480 to 751, Trier was part of the kingdom or subkingdom of Austrasia, but it was not a capital city: Metz, to its south, had that honor.

---

12. *RICG I*, no. 45. For more on the formulaic quality of the inscription Optata and her husband commissioned, see note 18 below.

13. Lisa Bailey, "Building Urban Christian Communities: Sermons on Local Saints in the Eusebius Gallicanus Collection," *Early Medieval Europe* 12 (2003): 1–24 shows that Christian "tradition" was "not a monolith, uniformly applied, but . . . a vocabulary upon which [local] preachers could choose to draw and which they could shape to their own ends" (p. 2). We see the same selective recourse to the thesaurus of Christian emotional vocabulary in local inscriptions. Compare Peter Brown's notion of "micro-Christendoms" in *The Rise of Western Christendom: Triumph and Diversity A.D. 200–1000* (Oxford, 1996), and see also Éric Rebillard, "*In hora mortis.*" *Évolution de la pastorale chrétienne de la mort aux IVe et Ve siècles dans l'occident Latin* (Rome, 1994), in which very different Christian attitudes toward death are parsed.

14. For the historical background, see Nancy Gauthier, *L'Évangélisation des pays de la Moselle. La province romaine de Première Belgique entre Antiquité et Moyen âge, IIIe–VIIIe siècles* (Paris, 1980); *Topographie chrétienne des cités de la Gaule des origines au milieu du VIIIe siècle*, ed. Nancy Gauthier and J.-Ch. Picard (hereafter *TCCG*), vol. 1: *Province ecclésiastique de Trèves (Belgica Prima)*, ed. Nancy Gauthier (Paris, 1986) (hereafter *TCCG: Trier*); and Eugen Ewig, *Trier im Merowingerreich. Civitas, Stadt, Bistum* (Trier, 1954).

Even before the Constantinian revolution, which made Christianity the favored religion of the empire, Trier had had some Christian inhabitants. Possibly the earliest of these were Greek in origin, finding their way to Trier via the Mediterranean trading emporium of Marseille. In the third century Trier had a bishop, and in the fourth century it boasted a grand episcopal complex, with two churches, a baptistery, and building annexes.[15] Around the same time several funerary churches were built outside the walls of the city. Here is where Christians were buried and where most of the inscriptions on behalf of the dead at Trier are found. Although most burials in these cemeteries, as elsewhere, were not marked by funerary inscriptions, a significant number of epitaphs have been found at Trier.[16]

Just outside the city's southern wall was the church of Saint Eucharius (today Saint-Mathias) surrounded by its cemetery; just beyond Trier's northern gate was the cemetery of the churches of Saint-Paulin and Saint-Maximin. These are the sources of the inscriptions to be considered here, since these cemeteries formed real communities of the dead and the living, who were associated with one another not only by commemoration but also by the saint near to whose church the burials were located. At Trier each cemetery had an identity; as Handley has pointed out, "the devotees of a particular saint's cult were marked out not only by the location of their burials, but also by the decoration, layout, and style of their epitaphs. . . . A corporate and unified image was being presented."[17]

The common, indeed stereotypical formula for both cemeteries is exemplified by the inscription for Numidius, to which we have already made reference: "Here lies in peace Numidius, who lived 7 years; Valerius and Op-

---

15. *TCCG: Trier*, pp. 22–23.

16. The number depends on how one assesses the fragments. *Katalog der frühchristlichen Inschriften in Trier*, ed. Erich Gose (Berlin, 1958) (hereafter Gose) inventories almost every piece, for a total of 845, plus several double-sided stones. *RICG I*, rather than repeating all the fragments taken up by Gose, counts only those sufficiently complete to merit comment, plus some not accounted for by Gose (see p. 37), for a total of 242 (plus some two-sided stones). *Katalog der frühchristlichen Inschriften des bischöflichen Dom- und Diözesanmuseums Trier*, ed. Hiltrud Merten (Trier, 1990) (hereafter Merten), which contains 127 items, repeats many of the entries in Gose and *RICG I* while adding a few more hitherto unpublished.

17. See Handley, "Beyond Hagiography," pp. 195, 196–97, including note 58, for discussion of the fact that it "mattered [to people] where they were buried." For more on the ways that epitaphs were used to express identity, see idem, "Inscribing Time and Identity in the Kingdom of Burgundy," in *Ethnicity and Culture in Late Antiquity*, ed. Stephen Mitchell and Geoffrey Greatrex (London, 2000), pp. 83–102.

tata, his parents, put up this epitaph."[18] The great majority of inscriptions at Trier are factual, much like this one. However, slightly more than one hundred epitaphs express emotion.[19] At Saint-Eucharius, which Handley has shown was the more popular cemetery during the late fourth and early fifth centuries, with a falling off in the fifth, seven emotion words were employed on fifty-eight stones, the most common by far being the endearments *carissimus* (dearest), which appears fourteen times, and *dulcissimus* (sweetest), which occurs twelve times.[20] In addition seven stones very likely once had one or the other word but are now so fragmentary as to render the reading uncertain.[21] Next most frequent is *caritas*, here clearly meaning love since it is invoked by relatives of the deceased as their motive for putting up the epitaph; it appears nine times, while *amor*, the twin of *caritas*, appears twice.[22] *Felix* (happy) is used once, and *gaudium* (joy) comes up either once or twice, depending on whether one reads the word "GAUDI" on a very

---

18. *RICG I*, no. 45. The editor comments (p. 195) that the formula "conforme au schéma stéréotypé de Saint-Mathias II," i.e., of one of its cemetery's engraving workshops. In this and subsequent quotations of epitaphs, I shall not normally signal editorial indications of ellipses, conjectural additions, etc.

19. The number cannot be specified completely, not only because new epitaphs are constantly being discovered but also because the fragmentary condition of the inscriptions and the ambiguity of their words sometimes make the reconstruction of the text a matter of guesswork. As an example of the latter, Gose, no. 422, interprets the epitaph for Elpidia as "Hic requiescit in pace Elpidia, qui vixit plus menus annus XL. carus conjux suus titulum posuit" (Here Elpidia rests in peace, who lived more or less 40 years; her dear husband put up her epitaph), but *RICG I*, no. 119, takes Carus to be the name of the husband. Fragments are extremely difficult to interpret: is Gose, no. 514, right to reconstruct ". . . MA SOROR" as "dulcissi/MA SOROR" (i.e., *dulcissima soror*, "very sweet sister," the majuscules here indicating the letters that are certain)? *Dulcissimus* is very common in these epitaphs, as we shall see, but "carissi/MA SOROR" is also a possible reconstruction (see *RICG I*, no. 139, which has *conjux carissima*), and another possibility is a proper name, such as "Euony/MA SOROR," as in *RICG I*, no. 94.

20. *Carissimus* (in various forms and spellings, including *karus*) appears in *RICG I*, nos. 4, 24, 28, 32a, 46, 49, 53, 59, 64, 71, 75; Gose, nos. 75, 309, 327. *Dulcissimus* (variously spelled) appears in *RICG I*, nos. 13b, 26, 27, 30, 35, 39, 40, 55, 83, 91; Gose, nos. 87, 132.

21. The fragmentary stones are *RICG I*, no. 6; Gose 8, 134, 169, 170, 171, 172. Consider the latter, for example, which reads ". . . SIME . . ." Gose suggests "caris/SIME," but "dulcis/SIME" seems possible as well.

22. *Caritas* is in *RICG I*, nos. 1, 30, 47, 55, 57, 62, 67, 68; Gose no. 59; *amor* is in *RICG I*, no. 87, and in Gose, no. 28.

fragmentary stone to be the name of a person or a reference to the joys of the life to come.[23] Finally the opposite of joy, *dolor* (sorrow), appears twice.[24]

The northern cemetery, centered on the churches of Saint-Paulin and Saint-Maximin, grew in popularity as the cult at the south end of the city waned.[25] The emotion words on the northern epitaphs were shaded just slightly differently from their southern counterparts. Here the number of stones employing emotional vocabulary was a bit smaller (fifty epitaphs) but the number of emotion words was somewhat larger: nine words all told. The most striking differences between the cemeteries, however, have to do with frequency of word usage. *Dulcissimus* (sweetest) was by far the favored epithet, both for the deceased and (as we shall see) for the commemorators; it appeared twenty times.[26] *Carissimus* (dearest), by contrast, came up only three times.[27] *Caritas* (love) was used very much as in the south end of the city, with nine appearances, seconded by *amor* (love), which came up twice.[28] Quite new was the northern cemetery's emphasis on *dolor* (sorrow) and other words of mourning—while eliminating all words of joy. Sorrow (*dolor* and its variants, especially its verbal forms) itself occurred eight times, while one particularly feeling (if fragmentary) epitaph evoked lamentation (*planctis non plangat*) and the tears wrung by death (*mors flenda*).[29] Two epitaphs in this cemetery referred to consolation (*solamen*), while one saw Hell "raging" (*Tartarus furens*).[30]

Were there two emotional communities at Trier, one using the northern cemetery, the other the southern? It seems unlikely. As we shall see, in both places the epitaphs emphasized family relationships, whether or not they ex-

---

23. *Felix* is in Gose, no. 19; *gaudium* (or variants) is in *RICG I*, nos. 19, 89 (where it may refer to the name Gaudi/Gaudilla).

24. *RICG I*, nos. 58, 74.

25. Handley, "Beyond Hagiography," p. 197.

26. *Dulcissimus* appears in *RICG I*, nos. 103, 111, 118, 120, 138, 143, 156, 159, 164, 169, 170, 176, 178 (twice), 182, 189; Gose, nos. 415, 533, 544, 600b.

27. *Carissimus* appears in *RICG I*, nos. 139, 142, 144. Either *carissimus* or *dulcissimus* is possible to fill out the letters that remain in Gose, nos. 485, 503.

28. *Caritas* is in *RICG I*, nos. 94, 149, 151, 162, 183, 187; Gose, nos. 434, 451, 452; for *amor* see *RICG I*, nos. 135, 147.

29. For *dolor* (and its variants) see *RICG I*, nos. 115, 122, 133, 140, 167, 193; Merten, no. 39; Gose, no. 438. The epitaph that evokes plangent feelings is *RICG I*, no. 194A.

30. For *solamen*, see *RICG I*, nos. 192, 196 (probably); for *Tartarus furens*, see no. 170.

plicitly expressed feelings. The differences between the "emotional styles" of the cemeteries seem best explained by changes over time: the more plangent epitaphs were largely from a later period. Dating the Trier epitaphs must always be a "best guess" because no dating clauses were used. That said, at the northern cemetery eighteen inscriptions using emotion words that *can* be dated precisely enough are from the period before 500, while eleven are from the sixth century and later.[31] Three of the epitaphs using *dolor* come from the first period, three from the second, which also saw the epitaph about mourning (*planctis non plangat*). Thus, before 500, 17 percent of the epitaphs evoked sorrow, while after that date 36 percent did so. Compare these numbers with those from the southern cemetery of Saint Eucharius, where twenty-seven epitaphs came from the earlier period, but only six from after 500.[32] Handley has shown that people were moving their allegiance to the northern cemetery; now we see that a subtle transformation in emotional tenor—more intense, more plangent—was part of that change. I suggest that this is one reason why *dulcissimus* came to be used more frequently than *carissimus:* although the words are essentially synonymous, the newly intense emotional style in the north favored the more sentimental word, based on the adjective *dulcis* (sweet).[33] In chapter 4 we shall see more evidence of the popularity of *dulcedo* (sweetness) in the sixth century. I suggest that the Trier epitaphs from both northern and southern cemeteries were the product of one community that underwent gradual transformation over time in tandem with changes in cultic practices.

Who paid for cutting the extra letters of *dulcissimus* or *carissimus,* by far the most frequent emotion terms? The short answer is that close relatives did so. But greater precision is possible. Of the fifty-six epitaphs using *carissimus/dulcissimus* in the two cemeteries, at least nineteen (34 percent) were

---

31. From before the year 500: *RICG I,* nos. 94, 103, 111, 118, 120, 133, 139, 140, 142, 143, 149, 151, 159, 162, 167, 176, 192, 196; from after 500: nos. 115, 122, 135, 138, 147, 156, 170, 178, 183, 193, 194.

32. From before the year 500: *RICG I,* nos. 4, 6, 13b, 19, 24, 26, 28, 30, 32a, 35, 39, 40, 46, 47, 49, 53, 55, 57, 58, 59, 62, 64, 67, 68, 74, 83, 87; from after 500: nos. 1, 27, 71, 75, 89, 91.

33. Hanne Sigismund Nielsen suggests that in ancient Rome *carissimus* was a general term of endearment that could be applied to spouses as well as children, while *dulcissimus* was most often used for a child; Nielsen, "Interpreting Epithets in Roman Epitaphs," in *The Roman Family in Italy: Status, Sentiment, Space,* ed. Beryl Rawson and Paul Weaver (Canberra, 1997), pp. 169–204, esp. pp. 190–93. Because these terms were also used at Trier to describe the commemorators themselves (see the discussion at note 39 below) comparisons with Rome are problematic. Certainly it is clear that *dulcissimus* was at least sometimes applied to spouses, as in *RICG I,* nos. 26, 32a, 39, 111, 138, 170, 189, 544.

put up by parents on behalf of a child.[34] "Here lies in peace the sweetest child [*infas dulcissima*], Arablia, his daughter, who lived 7 years, . . . months and 10 days; Posidonius, her father, put up this epitaph, in peace," reads one relatively typical inscription.[35] Or: "Leo lies here in peace; he lived for one year and 40 days; for their very dear son [*filio charissimo*], his parents put up [this epitaph]."[36] Sometimes these sentiments were reinforced by a word for love: "Here rests the very sweet child [*infans dulcissima*] Lupantia, in peace [and] faithful [*fidelis*], who lived 3 years, 5 months, 18 days. Treverius, her father, for love [*pro caritatem*] put up this epitaph for his daughter."[37]

Mark Handley has pointed out that child commemoration at Trier was "far higher than elsewhere in Gaul."[38] We now know that the Treveri not only put up epitaphs for their children but sometimes paid for an extra word or two to indicate nearness, dearness, and feeling. But if it was normative among certain parents to express affection for their children, husbands and wives were only slightly less demonstrative. Of the fifty-six epitaphs using *carissimus/dulcissimus,* fifteen (or 27 percent) were put up by spouses.

Endearments were also typically applied to the bereaved, as though the feelings of the deceased were known and needed to be acknowledged: "Here rests Merabaudis in peace, who lived 1 year and 11 months; her very sweet parents [*patris dulcissimi*] put up this epitaph."[39] Or again, this time in the instance of children honoring their mother: "Here Concordia lies in peace, who lived more or less 65 years; Concordius and Concordialis, her very sweet children [*filii dulcissimi*] put up this epitaph."[40] The wife of Scottus, the deceased, was "very sweet" to him: "To the one who reposes well here, Scottus, who lived 65 years, his very sweet spouse [*cojux dulcissima*] put up this epitaph for love [*pro caritatem*]; Scottus, peace be with you!"[41] The wife of the dead Vitalis was "very dear": "Here rests Vitalis, who lived

---

34. I say "at least nineteen" because some of the inscriptions are too fragmentary to determine who has died and who has put up the stone. See the observations of Gauthier in *RICG I*, pp. 47–48. King, "Commemoration of Infants," p. 141, finds, by contrast, that *dulcissimus* alone "forms 46.1 percent of the total" of Roman inscriptions put up for infants, with *benemerens* (well-deserving) following at 23% and *carissimus* at 13.4%.

35. *RICG I*, no. 103.
36. *RICG I*, no. 28.
37. *RICG I*, no. 30.
38. Handley, *Death, Society and Culture*, p. 71.
39. *RICG I*, no. 40.
40. *RICG I*, no. 13b.
41. *RICG I*, no. 55.

85 years; he served in the *Joviani Seniores* [a military corps] for 40 years; his very dear wife [*conjux karissima*] put up this epitaph."[42] The dead Perses's husband was equally dear: "Perses rests here in peace, who lived 45 years; her very dear husband [*conjux karissimus*] put up this epitaph."[43]

At Trier, the affections of both the departed and the living were acknowledged. To be sure, some emotion words were associated with forces outside the family: it was Tartarus that raged (*furens*) rather than the deceased or the bereaved, and *gaudium* referred to heaven, not earthly life.[44] But in other cases people's feelings were very much at center stage. "Here is buried a woman of senatorial rank, who merited, by the mercy of God, not to know about the death of her daughter which soon followed [her own] in peace; this consolation [*solamen*] was accorded to her."[45]

Thus affection was a privileged emotion at Trier, above all the affection between children and parents and, to a slightly lesser extent, between husbands and wives.[46] That affection, as the inscriptions make very clear, went in both directions. Even the dead could still feel the dearness and the sweetness of those left behind. The stones at Trier reveal to us, first, a certain kind of affectionate sensibility and, second, subtle changes in that sensibility over time.

"OH, GREEDY DEATH": IMPERSONAL EMOTIONS AT CLERMONT

Clermont, the capital city of the Auvergne in what is today south central France, came under Visigothic rule in 475. Although the Visigoths were Arian—a heretical form of Christianity that held that Christ was not equal to

---

42. *RICG I*, no. 71.

43. *RICG I*, no. 49.

44. For *Tartarus furens*, see *RICG I*, no. 170. Note that, although this is part of a line derived largely from a sermon of Maximus of Turin (d. ca. 415), the author of the epitaph added the word *furens*; see Gauthier's remarks, p. 429. *RICG I*, no. 19, does speak of the donor of the stone as *gaudens* (rejoicing). But he is a bishop, the epitaph is for the first two bishops of Trier (thus put up long after their deaths), and he is rejoicing because he has given their bodies a resting place for the promised resurrection.

45. *RICG I*, no. 192.

46. It should go without saying that this flies in the face of the thesis of Philippe Ariès, *Centuries of Childhood*, trans. Robert Baldick (New York, 1962), to the effect that medieval people did not love their children. It is only one final nail in that thesis's coffin, since recent studies have all shown its inadequacies. For good recent reviews of the issue, see Pauline Stafford, "Parents and Children in the Early Middle Ages," *Early Medieval Europe* 10 (2001): 257–71, and Barbara A. Hanawalt, "Medievalists and the Study of Childhood," *Speculum* 77 (2002): 440–60.

nor coeternal with the Father—Clermont, like other Catholic cities, was allowed to pursue its own religious agenda.[47] After Clovis (d. 511), king of the Franks, conquered the Visigoths in 507, he sent his oldest son, Theuderic (d. 533), to take Clermont along with Albi and Rodez. Under Theuderic, Clermont became part of the northeastern Frankish kingdom (eventually called Austrasia), which also embraced Trier. Thus Trier and Clermont, despite their distance from each other, were "sister" cities. They were also sometimes competitive. Theuderic, who became king upon the death of Clovis, "reformed" Trier's clergy by sending in replacements from Clermont.[48] Bishop Gregory of Tours (d. ca. 594), for his part, contributed to Trier's fame by claiming that its bishop Nicetius had been the savior of a man from Clermont.[49] In the seventh century, Clermont became part of the unified kingdom of Clothar II (d. 629), which embraced Austrasia, Neustria, and Burgundy. But because it was traditionally part of Austrasia alone, when Clothar's son Dagobert became king of Austrasia, Clermont once again was tied to that particular kingdom.[50] (For all of these kings, see table 7.)

The evidence from the Christian funeral inscriptions, scant as it is, suggests an emotional community at Clermont quite different from the one at Trier. This is true of both the emotional repertory and the contexts in which the words were used (see table 4). Admittedly only six epitaphs at Clermont used any emotion word whatever.[51] Nevertheless, some observations may

47. On Clermont under the Arians, see Ian Wood, *The Merovingian Kingdoms, 450–751* (London, 1994), pp. 16–19. On the topography of Clermont, see *TCCG: Clermont*, pp. 27–40, and P.-F. Fournier, "Clermont-Ferrand au VIe siècle. Recherches sur la topographie de la ville," *Bibliothèque de l'École des Chartes* 128 (1970): 273–344.

48. Gregory of Tours *Liber Vitae Patrum* 6.2, MGH SRM 1/2 (rev. ed., Hannover, 1969) (hereafter Greg. Tur., *VP*), p. 231.

49. Ibid., 17.5, pp. 282–83.

50. See the remarks on Clermont's position vis-à-vis Austrasia in *Late Merovingian France: History and Hagiography, 640–720,* ed. and trans. Paul Fouracre and Richard A. Gerberding (Manchester, 1996), pp. 268–70. For an overview of the church and the cult of saints at Clermont see Ian Wood, "Constructing Cults in Early Medieval France: Local Saints and Churches in Burgundy and the Auvergne 400–1000," in *Local Saints and Local Churches in the Early Medieval West,* ed. Alan Thacker and Richard Sharpe (Oxford, 2002), pp. 155–87, and idem, "The Ecclesiastical Politics of Merovingian Clermont," in *Ideal and Reality in Frankish and Anglo-Saxon Society: Studies Presented to J. M. Wallace-Hadrill,* ed. Patrick Wormald, Donald Bullough, and Roger Collins (Oxford, 1983), pp. 34–57.

51. *RICG,* vol. VIII, *Aquitaine première,* ed. Françoise Prévot (Paris, 1997) (hereafter *RICG VIII*), nos 16, 17, 21, 23, 34, 35. The extant repertory of Clermont's epitaphs is in *RICG VIII,* nos. 15–36. I eliminate nos. 20 and 22 because they are known only as literary epitaphs and

TABLE 4. *Emotion Words at Trier and Clermont Compared*

Trier	Clermont
amor (love)	*amator* (lover)
carus/carissimus (dear/dearest)	—
caritas (love)	—
—	*cupidus* (greedy)
dolere/dolor (sorrow)	*dolor* (sorrow)
dulcissimus (sweetest)	—
felix (happy)	*felix* (happy)
flere (to weep)	—
furere (to rage)	*furor* (rage)
gaudere/gaudium (to rejoice/joy)	—
—	*ha! hem! ho!* (ha, ah, oh)
—	*invidus* (envious)
—	*lacrimae* (tears)
planctus (lamentation)	—
solamen (solace)	—

be made. Terms of endearment never appeared. There were no "very sweet" children, no "dearest" spouses. Indeed, there were very few epitaphs altogether. Gregory of Tours, a native of the region, reported that the tombs in the church of St. Venerandus at Clermont were covered with sculpted scenes from the New Testament, but he had seen only one with an inscription: "To Galla of blessed memory."[52] Having spent part of his boyhood in Lyon, where epitaphs were far more common, Gregory consoled himself with the thought that the names must be known in heaven.[53]

---

may not have been inscribed and placed in a cemetery. Because there are so few epitaphs *in toto* from Clermont, I could not restrict the sample to specific cemeteries.

52. Gregory of Tours, *Liber in gloria confessorum* 34–35, MGH SRM 1/2 (hereafter Greg. Tur., *GC*), p. 319. The inscription for Galla is *RICG VIII*, no. 15. She may have been Gregory's relation, since he had an uncle named Gallus, a relatively rare name.

53. Greg. Tur., *GC* 35, p. 320. For the inscriptions of Lyon, it is still necessary to consult *Inscriptions chrétiennes de la Gaule antérieures au VIIIe siècle,* ed. Edmond Le Blant, 2 vols. (Paris, 1856, 1865), vol. 1, nos. 15–86A, vol. 2, nos. 663–69, and *Nouveau receuil des inscriptions chrétiennes de la Gaule antérieures au VIIIe siècle,* ed. Edmond Le Blant (Paris, 1892), nos. 3–18. *RICG XVI* on the Lyonnais is being prepared by Marie-Hélène Soulet; see her preliminary article on the subject of conjugal feeling in these epitaphs in "L'image de l'amour conjugal et

The emotion words used at Clermont were highly charged. There were even some exclamations: *ha!*, *hem!*, *ho!*, suggesting a bursting heart (the actual meanings of the words being vague, but their expressivity without question). Thus, while "the damp earth consumes the perishable body, nevertheless he does not occupy the hollows of the sepulcher but, *ha!*, [rather] the heavens, he whom Justice made happy [*felicem*] [though] buried in this tomb. Levite of the Lord, oh [*hem!*] Innocentius—his name comes from his grandfather—is blessed in his way of life [*morebus*]."[54] Or, in another epitaph: "Oh [*ho*] greedy death, . . . sorrow [*dolur*] to the family."[55]

Though the parents of a child probably put up this latter epitaph, at Clermont, the commemorators never said who they were, nor did they say how they related to the deceased. Instead the emotions in the cemeteries of Clermont were largely impersonal or even nonhuman. To be sure, we have just seen that Innocentius was happy in heaven. And there was one "lover," Vincomalus. Probably a cleric, his stone is very mutilated, but the editor of the inscription, Françoise Prévot, guesses that he was a "lover of the poor" (AMATU/r pauperum)—the material in lowercase represents her conjecture—and, more certainly ("lover" is used twice on this one stone), a "lover of the church" (AMATUR ECL/esiae).[56] But, as we have seen, on the inscription for the child the entity that was "greedy" was not a person but rather Death and the source of parental sorrow: "Oh, greedy Death, who snatches life from little ones, . . . sorrow to the family."[57] Nor did greed exhaust the emotional life of Death, for in the epitaph for a deacon named

---

de l'épouse dans l'épigraphie chrétienne lyonnaise aux VIe et VIIe siècles," in *La Femme au Moyen Âge,* ed. Michel Rouche and Jean Heuclin (Maubeuge, 1990), pp. 139–45. On Gregory of Tours's childhood first at Clermont and later at Lyon, see Raymond van Dam, *Saints and Their Miracles in Late Antique Gaul* (Princeton, 1993), pp. 52–55, though recently the length of his residence at Lyon has been brought into question by Martin Heinzelmann, *Gregory of Tours: History and Society in the Sixth Century,* trans. Christopher Carroll (Cambridge, 2001), p. 32.

54. *RICG VIII*, no. 16: "[Corpus?] fragele umeda terra sumit, non tenit ad [tamen?] hic antra sepulcri sed ha! celos quem justa [fecerunt?] felicem, condetum hoc tomolo. Levita domini [?] hem Innocencius—illi nomen ad avo protra[ctum?] beatus in morebus." The editor remarks that "justa" "is employed not in the sense of 'just works' but rather of Justice in general" (p. 102).

55. *RICG VIII,* no. 35. For the text see note 57 below.

56. *RICG VIII,* no. 34.

57. *RICG VIII,* no. 35: "Ho mors cupeta [abstu?]let parvolis vita[m?] [. . .]gis parentibus dolu[r? . . . o?]lenus in Christi no[mine]." Probably "-lenus" is the fragment of a name.

Emellio, Death was "envious" (*inveda*) and therefore stole his life away.[58] The epitaph for the "devout" Georgia claimed that she could have selected from many suitors, but instead she chose God "in a happier marriage" (*feliciore toro*).[59] Human, but nevertheless impersonal are the emotions in the epitaph for Sidonius Apollinaris himself. He gave laws to soften "barbarian fury" (*barbarico furori*) and did much else to bring public peace. Thus "whoever comes here to implore God with tears [*cum lacrimis*]" should pour out prayers at his tomb.[60]

Many of these conceits—such as the personification of death—are classical.[61] That does not make them the less telling. Conceits have to make some sense to be used. The "normal" epitaph at Clermont—if "normal" may be said of a place that rarely put up an epitaph!—was one like that for Cerva: "In this tomb rests Cerva of good memory, who lived in peace 35 years. She departed the day before the kalends of July."[62]

Most of the epitaphs at Clermont that may be dated appear to come from the seventh century.[63] Four of the six "emotional" epitaphs are from that century. Were it not for the epitaph for Sidonius, there would be nothing for the fifth century, while Georgia's "happier marriage" is our only sample for the sixth. We may say, then, that at Clermont people on the whole were taciturn when confronting death, at least publicly. They cared about the dead: why else would they have entombed them in sculpted stone? But they were wary of words. In the seventh century, when they found a voice, the emotions they expressed were, by comparison with those at Trier, less personal and affectionate. They imagined death as greedy and envious, the bringer of sorrow.

"FEARING PROSPERITY, LAUGHING AT ADVERSITY": HEAVENLY EMOTIONS AT VIENNE

Under Rome's rule in the fourth century, Vienne, a city on the Rhône River in what is today southeastern France, was the capital city of a Gallic

---

58. *RICG VIII*, no. 23.

59. *RICG VIII*, no. 17. She is here called "Christi . . . divota" (dedicated to Christ). Greg. Tur., *GC* 33, p. 318, speaks of a "puella . . . devota Deo" (girl dedicated to God) at Clermont named Georgia; when she died, her funeral cortege was miraculously accompanied by a flock of doves.

60. *RICG VIII*, no. 21.

61. See the remarks of the editor, *RICG VIII*, pp. 63–65.

62. *RICG VIII*, no. 32.

63. That is, ten epitaphs out of sixteen.

province.⁶⁴ In the 430s it came under the control of the Burgundians, who acted on the whole as defenders of the empire. When emperors ceased to exist in the West (476), Gundobad (d. 516) stayed on as king of the Burgundians. He had been an emperor-maker and had important relations with Italy and Byzantium, but, unlike the Romans, he did not use Vienne as his capital, favoring instead Lyon and Chalon-sur-Saône.⁶⁵ However, Vienne remained important as a Catholic religious center. Avitus, bishop of Vienne (ca. 494–ca. 518), was an advisor to the Burgundian kings and an important leader of the episcopal community.⁶⁶ Although the king himself was an Arian Christian, he fully tolerated Catholicism, and many members of his family, including his son Sigismund, who succeeded him in 516, were Catholic. Thus Vienne flourished as a Catholic city under the Burgundians, and when Burgundy was conquered by the Franks in 534 it continued to thrive. It was a key center of monasticism in the late sixth century and remained an important producer of ecclesiastical manuscripts in the seventh.⁶⁷

There were three important Christian cemeteries at Vienne, The one at Saint-Gervais was just south of the city; that near the church of Saint-Sévère was to the north; and the most important of the cemeteries, in the shadow of the church of Saint-Pierre, was southwest of the city's walls.⁶⁸ All told, we have about a hundred inscriptions from these cemeteries.⁶⁹

There is a lushness to the emotions repertory at Vienne that we have not

---

64. On its provincial status, see André Pelletier, "Vienne et la réorganisation provinciale de la Gaule au Bas-Empire," *Latomus* 26 (1967): 491–99.

65. For background on Vienne, see *Avitus of Vienne: Letters and Selected Prose*, ed., and trans. Danuta Shanzer and Ian Wood (Liverpool, 2002), esp. pp. 13–27; *TCCG*, vol. 3: *Provinces ecclésiastiques de Vienne et d'Arles*, ed. Jacques Biarne (Paris, 1986), pp. 13–15, 17–35 (hereafter *TCCG: Vienne*); Jean-François Reynaud, "'Vienne la Sainte' au moyen-âge," *Archeologia* 88 (1975): 44–54.

66. His was the "dominant voice" at the Council of Epaon (517), for example: see *Avitus of Vienne*, ed. and trans. Shanzer and Wood, p. 10.

67. Wood, *Merovingian Kingdoms*, p. 252.

68. For a summary of the *status quaestionis* regarding Saint-Pierre, see Monique Jannet-Vallat, "L'organisation spatiale des cimetières Saint-Pierre et Saint-Georges de Vienne (IVe–XVIIIe siècle)," in *Archéologie du cimetière chrétien,* Actes du 2e colloque A.R.C.H.E.A. (Association en Région Centre pour l'Histoire et l'Archéologie), ed. Henri Galinié and Elisabeth Zadora-Rio (Tours, 1996), pp. 125–37.

69. Those for the cemetery of Saint-Gervais are *RICG*, vol. 15: *Viennoise du Nord,* ed. Henri I. Marrou and Françoise Descombes (Paris, 1985) (hereafter *RICG XV*), nos. 39–63 (a total of twenty-four inscriptions); for the cemetery of Saint-Sévère, ibid., nos. 64–74 (ten inscriptions); for the cemetery of Saint-Pierre, ibid., nos. 75–141, of which no. 98 has two faces, a

TABLE 5. *Emotion Words in Vienne Inscriptions*

Emotion word	*RICG XV*, no.
amare/amor (to love; love)	73, 81, 99
carus (dear)	41
caritas (love)	69, 72, 112, 121
diligere (to love)	112, 121, 140
dolere/dolor (to sorrow; sorrow)	42, 99, 118
felix (happy)	81, 95
flere/deflere/fletus (to weep; weeping)	81, 99, 118
furor (rage)	97
gaudere/gaudium (to rejoice; joy)	92, 99, 101, 118
gemere (to groan)	97, 101
ingemere (to bewail)	99
invidus (envious)	104
lacrimae (tears)	92, 97, 101
laetus (joyful)	99
levamen (consolation)	97
metuere (to fear)	82, 96
maeror/maestus/maestificare (mourning; sad; to make sad)	81, 99
planctus (lamentation)	101
ridere (to laugh)	82, 96
solamen (consolation)	81, 99
terrere (to frighten)	81
timere (to fear)	91, 120
tremere (to tremble)	99
tristis (sad)	81

seen elsewhere. The full panoply may be seen in table 5. However, let us not allow this emotional exuberance to mislead us into thinking that people at Vienne reveled in emotional outpourings. Only twenty of the epitaphs there contain emotion words. As at Clermont and Trier, nonemotional inscriptions were favored—if inscriptions were wanted at all: "In this tomb Fluri-

and b, and thus must be considered twice, while no. 87 is probably not a funeral epitaph at all and should thus not be counted (resulting in a total of sixty-six inscriptions).

nus of good memory reposes in peace, who lived around 40 years. He died in peace the 3ᵈ day of the Kalends of August, the 17th year after the consulate of Basil, a man of senatorial rank, and the [numbers missing] year of the indiction."[70] As at Clermont, many burials went without written commemoration altogether.

But when an epitaph did include emotions at Vienne, it often indulged in more than one. The inscription for Bishop Avitus, for example, had seven emotion words covering the gamut of feeling from sorrow to love and fear: "whoever you may be who sees the sad [*mestificum*] honor of this tomb . . . will weep [*deflebis*]. . . . He terrifies by loving [*amando terret*]."[71] Burial place of bishops, the church of Saint-Pierre boasted four episcopal epitaphs, most of them full of emotional content.[72] Do these skew our results? Would Vienne seem dry and emotionless without its passionate bishops and their emotive followers? Table 6 lists the emotion words that result when the episcopal inscriptions are omitted.

This is still a rich haul. At Trier the stonecutters had a repertory of eleven emotion words; at Clermont it was down to seven (not counting the exclamations). At Vienne, however, a paltry sixteen non-episcopal tombs yield a total of fourteen emotion words. The episcopal sepulchers may have magnified the pattern, but they did not distort it: if an epitaph at Vienne talked about feelings, then it might well (37.5 percent of the time) do so more than once. The metrical inscription for Sylvia is the lushest of these instances. Although, as was normal at Vienne, there is no indication of who put up the epitaph, nevertheless the emotional focus of the inscription is her feelings about her children and theirs about her. Sylvia "rejoiced [*gaudebat*] to have recovered her ancestors in her children." One had become a priest, another achieved the title of *patricius*. These children were not indifferent to their mother. The epitaph concludes: "Let her children cease to be troubled by tears and lamentation [*lacrimis planctusque*]. It is not right to groan [*gemere*] about that which ought to be celebrated."[73] In this way, the emotions of the moment were at one and the same time recognized and downgraded as they were absorbed into the Augustinian world view; they were redirected from

---

70. *RICG XV*, no. 68.

71. *RICG XV*, no. 81.

72. *RICG XV*, nos. 81 (for Avitus), 95 (for Pantagathus), 97 (for Hesychius), 99 (for Namatius). No. 95 is the exception, as it contains only one emotion word, *felix*, to describe Pantagathus's happiness in his descendants.

73. *RICG XV*, no. 101.

TABLE 6. *Emotion Words in Non-Episcopal Vienne Inscriptions*

Emotion word	*RICG VIII*, no.
amare (to love)	73
caritas (love)	69, 72, 112, 121
carus (dear)	41
diligere (to love)	112, 140
dolere/dolor (to sorrow; sorrow)	42, 118
flere (to weep)	118
gaudere/gaudium (to rejoice; joy)	92, 101, 118
gemere (to groan)	101
invidus (envious)	104
lacrimae (tears)	92, 101
metuere (to fear)	82, 96
planctus (lamentation)	101
ridere (to laugh)	82, 96
timere (to fear)	91, 120

worldly things to celestial, and death was transformed from a sad to a happy event.

Thus, in the few epitaphs at Vienne where emotions came into play, Christian goals predominated. Even in the simplest case, where only the anodyne *carus* appeared, the word was used to reinforce a picture of Christian virtue: "[The deceased], dear [*cara*] to all, dutiful [*pia*] to the poor, kind [*benigna*] to slaves."[74] While at Trier the word "love" (*caritas, amor*) referred to the family member's motive for putting up an epitaph, at Vienne love meant Christian charity: "In this tomb rests in peace the servant of God Dulcitia of good memory, a consecrated virgin [*sanctimonialis*], of excellent morals, profuse good will, enormous love [*charitate largissima*]."[75] When an epitaph at Vienne used the verb "to laugh," it was not for joy but to ridicule the world: "[Celsa] repudiated worldly things and subjected her flesh to the cross, and fearing [*maetuens*] prosperity, she always laughed at [*ridens*] adversity."[76]

74. *RICG XV*, no. 41.
75. *RICG XV*, no. 69.
76. *RICG XV*, no. 82. Cf. also no. 96. On love of the world and fear of death, see Rebillard, "In hora mortis," chap. 3.

Was this emotional community—one that rejected emotions unless directed heavenward—the product of a siege mentality? Has too little been made of the pressures Catholics may have felt in a kingdom where the king was Arian? It is unlikely. Almost all of the epitaphs that contain emotion words date from the sixth century, when Vienne was firmly under Catholic kings.[77] At Vienne, if people recognized emotions in connection with death—or, at least, were willing to publicize them—it was in the sixth century. And if they did so, they had a colorful palette of emotion words from which to choose, including seven words for sorrow, tears, and lamentation. They recognized death's pain, but they deflected it, to speak of the resurrection: "Father, don't be sorrowful [*ne doleas*]; mother, you too stop weeping [*flere desiste*]: your child has the joys [*gaudia*] of eternal life."[78] They acknowledged the force of love, and they turned it into a virtue rather than a feeling: "In this tomb rests [the deceased], a priest, . . . pure in faith, . . . kind . . . beloved [*amatus*]."[79]

The epitaphs for the dead suggest that there were at least three different emotional communities in Gaul before the eighth century. Although the people who commissioned the gravestones were all Christians (hence at least professedly despising the world and all positive feelings for it) and shared the same basic emotional vocabulary, they drew upon, used, and put together in different ways the potential repertory of emotional responses to death that the cultural constraints of religion and word supplies permitted.

At Trier the emphasis was on words of affection in the context (we can see from Clermont and Vienne how rare it was!) of family membership: mothers, fathers, husbands, wives, and children named themselves right on the tombstone. The inscriptions at Trier in effect recreated family circles, and this fact did not change over the course of three centuries. But the emotion words at Trier became more intense, a transformation comparable to one at Vienne, where emotion words were virtually absent from epitaphs until the sixth century. At Vienne emotions were then immediately tied to otherworldly values, whereas at Trier they remained (insofar as our small sample allows us to make any generalization at all) connected to family feel-

---

77. *RICG XV*, no. 72, is fifth century; nos. 41, 42, 69, 73, 81, 82, 91, 92, 95, 96, 97, 99, 101, 112, 118, 120, 121, and 140 are sixth century; no. 104 is seventh century.
78. *RICG XV*, no. 118.
79. *RICG XV*, no. 73.

ing. Clermont shows us that personification and depersonalization was still another mode of managing and expressing feeling.

Gallic epitaphs may thus provide a glimpse into the variety of ways in which ancient and early Christian religious and emotive traditions meshed, at least around the issue of death. But death is only one potentially emotional moment in life. To see others, to see a whole panoply of issues and the ways in which one extraordinarily sensitive observer thought and felt about them, again drawing upon the religious and emotive traditions of antiquity, we turn now to Rome and to its perhaps most famous early medieval pope: Gregory the Great.

3

PASSIONS AND POWER

Born in Rome of a prominent family with strong links to the church and a tradition of ascetic piety, Pope Gregory the Great (590–604) first threw himself into civic duties and then retired, still at Rome, to a monastery dedicated to St. Andrew on the Caelian Hill, one of seven monastic houses that he founded on his family property at Rome and Palermo.[1] When recalled from the monastic life to become papal ambassador to the imperial court at Constantinople, Gregory began the first of his voluminous exegetical writings, the *Moralia in Job*. After becoming pope in 590, against his will (or so he protested), he turned energetically to the practical tasks at hand. We learn from his extant letters (over eight hundred have survived, only a small fraction of the original number) that he was keen to manage the papal patrimonies, oversee the church hierarchy in Italy, and oil the lines of communication between himself and other ruling courts.[2] In the very first months of his papacy he wrote a handbook for bishops, the *Pastoral Rule*. Meanwhile, he continued his *Moralia*, which he finished in 591. He wrote forty *Homilies on the Gospels* around the same time and worked assiduously on twenty-two *Homilies on the Book of Ezechiel*, completed at last in 601.[3] In between, amidst other exegetical writings that today exist only in fragments, he completed four books of *Dialogues* for "those who," as he put it, "are fired up with love for the heavenly fatherland more by concrete

---

1. On the basic facts of Gregory's life, thought, times, and policies, see Robert A. Markus, *Gregory the Great and His World* (Cambridge, 1997); Carole Straw, *Gregory the Great*, Authors of the Middle Ages, Historical and Religious Writers of the Latin West, vol. 4, no. 12 (Aldershot, 1996), pp. 1–72; and Sofia Boesch Gajano, *Gregorio Magno. Alle origini del Medioevo* (Rome, 2004). I am grateful to Elisabeth Zadora-Rio and Bruno Judic for providing me with a preliminary bibliography on (respectively) the site of Gregory's monastery and Gregory's writings.

2. Gregory I, *Registrum Epistularum*, ed. Dag Norberg, CCSL 140 and 140A (Turnhout, 1982). On the fraction of letters that this represents, see Markus, *Gregory*, pp. 206–8.

3. Paul Meyvaert, "The Date of Gregory the Great's Commentaries on the Canticle of Canticles and on 1 Kings," *Sacris Erudiri* 23 (1979): 201 n. 25.

examples than by sermons."⁴ In the *Dialogues* he painted an *Italia sacra,* a landscape of raging plague, marauding armies, and errant souls, all calmed by serene, wonder-working monks.⁵

Gregory was the most prolific writer of his age. This in itself makes him irresistible for a historian of emotion. Did Gregory recognize emotions? What did he think of them? How did he express them (if he did)? The answers to these questions will occupy us throughout this chapter. But first it is necessary to deal with a possible objection: that an analysis of Gregory deflects us from our task of exploring emotional communities. With epitaphs we were able to look at collective responses to death in different venues. What can we say of one man?

I maintain that Gregory allows us to see *his* emotional community. I intend to explore Gregory not as a subject of psychohistory but rather as a member of a community, even though we know about that community from him alone. No individual is isolated from his or her social context—or contexts. This is very clear in Gregory's case, as he was a gregarious and social person. Whatever he wrote he addressed to others; and in those writings he evoked a whole universe of human behavior, obligations, ideals, follies, relations—and, at times, feelings. Should we treat Gregory's evocations of the world as purely imaginary? Only in part. All texts create their own universes. But we nevertheless have learned to use those texts to get at, if not reality, then perceptions of reality. This is what I ask of Gregory's writings. I do not wish to argue that he was a "man of his times"; recent work on Gregory has shown that his great popularity came after his lifetime, not during it.⁶ On the other hand, he was not a madman, spinning his wheels

---

4. Gregory I, *Dialogues* 1, prol. 9, in *Gregoire le Grand, Dialogues,* ed. Adalbert de Vogüé, trans. Paul Antin, 3 vols., SC 251, 260, 265 (Paris, 1978–80), 2:16: "Et sunt nonnulli quos ad amorem patriae caelestis plus exempla quam praedicamenta succendunt." On the corpus of Gregory's writings and the authenticity of those that have been disputed, see the convenient summaries in Markus, *Gregory,* pp. 14–16; Conrad Leyser, *Authority and Asceticism from Augustine to Gregory the Great* (Oxford, 2000), pp. 135–43; and, for the latest word on the authenticity of the *Dialogues,* Adalbert de Vogüé, "Gregoire le Grand est-il l'auteur des *Dialogues?*" *Revue d'histoire ecclésiastique* 99 (2004): 158–61.

5. Sofia Boesch Gajano almost single-handedly rescued the *Dialogues* from scholarly ridicule; Gajano, "La proposta agiografica dei 'Dialogi' di Gregorio Magno," *Studi Medievali,* ser. terza, 21 (1980): 623–64. See now as well eadem, *Gregorio Magno,* esp. pt. 2.

6. Alan Thacker, "Memorializing Gregory the Great: The Origin and Transmission of a Papal Cult in the Seventh and Early Eighth Centuries," *Early Medieval Europe* 7 (1998): 59–84. I am grateful to Tom Noble for this reference.

without effect. He commanded the recognition of certain people in his own day—ordinarily male, clerical, and Roman—and they were also, in large part, the audience for his writings. It was a rarified group, no doubt; but it was not, for all that, any more unique than the mourning parents of Trier.

Unlike those parents, however, Gregory had a mission. He spoke to his own community—the men with whom he surrounded himself—and he also attempted to speak to others. His homilies, for example, were addressed to worshipers at Roman churches. His letters were written to far-flung recipients. Gregory was not one to enter into other emotional worlds—those apart from his clerical colleagues—except to change and reform them; his emotional involvement was pastoral. It was the role of the churchman—of Gregory—to recognize and work with others. But unlike an anthropologist who joins communities to observe and understand them, Gregory joined to uplift and transform.

EMOTIONS AS VICES

We have already seen that Gregory drew on the "bad thoughts" and "vices" elaborated by the desert Fathers and turned them into the battalion of the Seven Deadly Sins. His list—vainglory (*inanis gloria*), envy (*invidia*), anger (*ira*), sadness (*tristitia*), avarice (*avaritia*), gluttony (*ventris ingluvies*), and lust (*luxuria*), all rooted in pride (*superbia*)—dominated church thinking for centuries.[7] The words need to be contextualized. When they appear—in the *Moralia in Job*—they are not singled out for historical stardom; they are simply invoked to illustrate, as Gregory often did, the "thoughts"—that is, in Stoic terms, the "emotions"—that assail people. When explaining the passage "And his possession was . . . a family exceeding great" in Job 1:3, Gregory took "family" to mean the innumerable thoughts (*cogitationes innumeras*) that we must control under the domination of the mind (*sub mentis dominatione*). If they are out of our control, then they behave like the slaves of a household when the mistress is away, "neglecting their duties," and "confounding the right order of living" (*ordinem vivendi confundunt*).[8]

Building on Cassian's and Augustine's ideas about emotions, Gregory elaborated on the theory of consent. Cogitations are first suggested to the mind by the devil; if allowed to remain, they become a delight (*delectatio*) to the flesh. Then the spirit consents to them and ultimately "hardens" around

---

7. Gregory I, *Moralia in Job* 31.45.87, CCSL 143B, p. 1610.
8. Ibid., 1.30.42, CCSL 143, p. 47.

them out of pride, so that what was once a suggestion becomes a habit (*consuetudo*).⁹

It is not easy to put a stop to this process. The mind is difficult to control. It begins by wishing to do justice, for example, but then, sneaking in "from the side" (*ex latere*), anger (*ira*) arrives; or the mind intends to be serious, but, again "from the side" sadness (*tristitia*) takes over, "and all the work that the mind begins with good intention is clouded over by a veil of sorrow [*velamine maeroris*]." Similarly, a good deed, which should be accompanied by a "weight of gravity" (*pondus gravitatis*), brings "immoderate joy" (*laetitia immoderata*) instead.¹⁰ At other times the "unclean spirits," envious (*invidunt*) of our heavenward gaze, "inflame the pure [*mundas*] thoughts of our mind with the burning of sexual desire [*mentis nostrae cogitationes ardore libidinis*]."¹¹ In this way, even virtues bring vices in their train.¹²

Drawing on the tradition of the psychomachy, a mental battle that pitted the virtues against the vices, Gregory saw the human mind at war. But rather than celebrate the triumph of the virtues, as others writers were wont to do, Gregory emphasized impassivity.¹³ The "raging enemy" thought he could "move" Job (*eum moveri credidit*) by bodily torments, but he was unable to touch the emotions of Job's mind (*passionem mentis*).¹⁴ Job is a Christian version of the Stoic, unperturbed by the pre-emotions (which, as we have seen, had been by Gregory's day turned into the emotions themselves) that buffet ordinary people. Job is in the mode of Christ, whose

---

9. Ibid., 4.27.49, CCSL 143, p. 193. The last part is not far from Isen and Andrade's notion of affect's automaticity. See introduction, note 71.

10. Ibid., 1.36.53, CCSL 143, pp. 53–54: "atque omne opus quod mens bona intentione incohat, haec velamine maeroris obumbrat. . . . Saepe se bono operi laetitia immoderata subiungit cumque plus mentem quam decet, hilarescere exigit, ab actione bona omne pondus gravitatis repellit."

11. Ibid., 2.47.74, CCSL 143, p. 103: "Saepe enim mundas mentis nostrae cogitationes ardore libidinis accendunt."

12. See ibid., 2.49.76, CCSL 143, pp. 105–6, where each virtue is paired with its own vice. Here the vice that goes with justice (*justitia*) is self-love (*amor suus*), but compare ibid., 3.33.65, p. 155, where it is immoderate anger (*immoderata ira*) that hides behind and pretends to be justice.

13. For the decisive triumph of the virtues, see Prudentius, *Psychomachia* ll. 629–30, trans. H. J. Thomson, Loeb Classical Library (London, 1949), p. 322.

14. Gregory I, *Moralia* praef. 4.9, CCSL 143, p. 15.

mind, however subject to temptation, was never shaken.[15] When Job curses the day he was born, Gregory says that his words are not those of someone "moved by anger" (*ira commoti*) but rather of one "tranquil in doctrine" (*doctrina tranquilli*). Job is not being emotional—or, more precisely, he has not succumbed to the "vice of emotion" (*perturbationis vitio*); he is simply and correctly disseminating Christian teachings, whereby this world is dung and birth into it is rightly cursed.[16]

From this perspective, no emotion is good. Even love is suspect. When Job's wife tells him to "bless God and die," Gregory points out that the "ancient adversary" uses "those who are attached to us" (*qui nobis adhaerent*) to make his case. This is why the bible warns, "Beware of thy own children" (Ecclus. 32:26), and "Let every man take heed of his neighbor, and let him not trust in any brother of his" (Jer. 9:4). Expelled from the "hearts of the good," the devil uses those who are "very much loved" (*valde diliguntur*) as his proxies; he speaks eloquently through the "alluring words" of those who are loved (*amantur*).[17]

Even penance is problematic. It reminds us of bad deeds, and the resulting "confusion fogs the mind with stirred-up thoughts [*perturbatis cogitationibus*]." We are confounded by "heavy sorrow [*gravi maerore*]." Indeed, "a crowd of thoughts clamors in our mind [*animo*]: sorrow [*maeror*] grinds us down, anxiety [*anxietas*] wastes us, and our mind [*mens*] is turned into tribulation [*aerumna*]." Any pleasure we might take in the perverted act (*pravae delectationis gaudium*) is short lived, since the negative emotions that come in its train make it a source of bitterness (*amaritudine*) and sharp tears (*asperis fletibus*).[18]

---

15. Ibid., 3.16.30, CCSL 143, pp. 134–35: "mentem tamen mediatoris Dei et hominum tentatione quassare non valuit" (even so, [the Devil] could not shake the mind of the mediator between God and man by temptation).

16. Ibid., 4.1.3, CCSL 143, p. 165.

17. Ibid., 3.8,13, CCSL 143, p. 122. See also ibid., 3.20.38, p. 139, where sinners draw others in "as if loving" (*quasi diligentes*).

18. Ibid., 4.17.32–18.33, CCSL 143, pp. 184–85: "ita confusio perturbatis cogitationibus obnubilat mentem.... Cum enim ad mentem male gesta paenitendo reducimus, gravi mox maerore confundimur; perstrepit in animo turba cogitationum, maeror conterit, anxietas devastat, in aerumna mens vertitur et quasi quodam nubilo caliginis obscuratur... Diem amaritudine involvimus cum pravae delectationis gaudium, quae supplicia sequantur aspicimus, et asperis hoc fletibus circumdamus."

VIRTUOUS EMOTIONS

The last point, however, casts a different light on emotions. They cannot be entirely bad, since the tears that we shed out of the misery of penance "expiate whatever sin the mind [*animus*] has committed by negligence."[19] The deadly sin of *tristitia* can be a virtue as well as a vice: a person "cleanses the wantonness [*lasciviam*] of his [or her] pleasure [*voluptatis suae*] by lamentations of sorrow [*tristitiae lamentis*]."[20]

"Fear" can be good as well, for it is the proper response to the tumult of unwanted thoughts. Commenting on Job 20:2, "Therefore various thoughts succeed one another in me, and my mind is hurried away to different things," Gregory explains: "[It is as if Job] were saying in plain words: 'Because I am contemplating the terror of the last judgment, therefore I am confounded in fear [*in timore*] by the tumults of my thoughts.'" The mind, according to Gregory, is "hurried away" because it is thinking "in agitated fear" (*sollicito pavore*) of all it should have done but did not, all it did do but should not have done.[21] The penitent soul is rightly "terrified by fear" (*pavore terretur*), trembling between hope (*spem*) and dread (*formidinem*). Even if the sin has been remitted by God, the "afflicted mind" (*mens afflicta*) continues to be fearful (*trepidat*).[22] This is all to the good. Yet by itself, unsupported by virtue, fear is a liability, paralyzing the mind into inaction.[23] Gregory even calls fear (*timor*) a "temptation" (*temptatio*) sent by "the multitude of impure spirits"; it "insinuates itself in our heart and disturbs the powers of our fortitude."[24] Thus there are "carnal members of the church" whose fear (*metus*) and audacity (*audacia*) cause them to persuade others to wickedness.[25]

---

19. Ibid., 4.18.34, CCSL 143, p. 185: "ut videlicet circumdantes fletus expient quicquid delectatus per neglegentiam animus delinquit."

20. Ibid., 4.18.33, CCSL 143, p. 185: "voluptatis suae lasciviam tristitiae lamentis tergat."

21. Ibid., 15.1.1, CCSL 143A, p. 749: "Ac si apertis vocibus dicat: Quia extremi iudicii terrorem considero, idcirco cogitationum tumultibus in timore confundor. Tanto se quippe animus amplius in cogitatione dilaniat, quanto illud esse terribile quod imminet, pensat. Et in diversa mens rapitur, quando modo mala quae egit, modo bona quae agere neglexit."

22. Ibid., 4.36.71, CCSL 143, p. 215.

23. Ibid., 1.32.45, CCSL 143, p. 49.

24. Ibid., 2.49.76, CCSL 143, p. 105: "Nonnumquam se timor cordi insinuat et vires nostrae fortitudinis turbat."

25. Ibid., 3.20.38, CCSL 143, p. 139.

In this way for Gregory, as for Augustine, emotions were potentially good, but only if they were properly directed. For Augustine that direction was upward, toward God. For Gregory, without discounting this point, the direction was most importantly downward, from the holy man (who had already achieved inner peace) to weaker brethren. When Job's friends showed their love (*caritas*) for him by weeping, tearing their garments, and sprinkling dust on their heads, Gregory approved. He explained that consolation consists in becoming emotionally like the one you are comforting: "for the process [*ordo*] of consolation is that when we want to stop an afflicted person from grieving [*maerore*], we first try to empathize [*concordare*] with his sorrow [*luctui*] by grieving [*maerendo*]."[26] The comforter must conform his mind to the sufferer's or be alienated from him (*separatur*). It is a matter of "softening" your mind, rendering it "congruent" (*congruens*) to that of another. By congruency, the comforter "inheres" (*inhaeret*), and by inhering, he draws (*trahat*) the sufferer to him. Gregory likened the process to joining a piece of iron to iron—both parts must first be heated up and softened. "We do not raise up the fallen unless we bend from our inflexible standing posture."[27]

This is the "condescension of emotion" (*condescensio passionis*), the lowering of the self emotionally to participate in the emotional life of another.[28] Only very special people can do it properly. Though Job's friends had the right idea, they went too far; their grief on his behalf knew no limits. Consolation must soothe rather than "sink the mind of the afflicted into the heaviness of despair."[29] Only holy men (*sancti viri*) know how to do this. They banish all the annoying thoughts (*cogitationum insolentias*) that assail everyone else; they "sigh out of love for inward quiet [*in amorem intimae quietis*]"; and yet they "do not leave off giving counsel to others out of love [*caritatem*]."[30]

---

26. Ibid., 3.12.20, CCSL 143, p. 127: "Ordo quippe consolationis est ut cum volumus afflictum quempiam a maerore suspendere, studeamus prius maerendo eius luctui concordare."

27. Ibid., 3.12.20, CCSL 143, p. 127: "nec iacentes erigimus, nisi a rigore nostri status inclinemur."

28. Ibid., praef. 3.7, CCSL 143, p. 13; see also ibid., 19.25.45, CCSL 143A, p. 991: "caritatis condescensio" (the condescension of love).

29. Ibid., 3.12.21, CCSL 143, p. 127: "afflicti animum ad pondus desperationis premat."

30. Ibid., 4.30.58–59, CCSL 143, pp. 203–4. See Carole Straw, *Gregory the Great: Perfection in Imperfection* (Berkeley, 1988), chap. 4.

EMOTIONS OF AUTHORITY

Who were these holy men? They were the rulers of the holy church (*sanctae Ecclesiae rectores*).[31] Gregory was one of them. Like Saint Paul inhabiting the "third heaven," Gregory nevertheless cast his eyes down to earth "out of compassion" (*per compassionem*).[32] As Conrad Leyser has observed, "Gregory was prepared to take the risk of claiming to be morally qualified to lead, to shoulder all the burdens of the faithful."[33] One of his moral qualifications consisted in longing for the "inward quiet" yet agreeing to enter into the emotional lives of others.[34] The introduction to Gregory's *Dialogues* should be understood in this light. He was "pressed down [*depressus*] by the tumults of the worldly . . . and sought a secret place, the friend of sorrow [*amicum moerori*]."[35] Not much before this time, Cassiodorus (d. 583) had written about "the holy congregation of the just, which is heir of the Lord, pressed down [*depressa*] by worldly evils."[36] It was consonant with Gregory's view of himself. From his secret vantage point, he could survey "everything that is wont to inflict sorrow [*dolorem*]."[37] When his friend Peter found him in this "secret place," Gregory immediately began to tell the stories that made up the *Dialogues*.[38]

The emotions of others were burdens, to be sure, but they were also the major hooks on which to anchor any salvific message. Compassion—emotion shared—was the way in which the churchman "inhered" in his flock and "drew" it out. Had not Paul said, "Who is weak and I am not weak? Who is tempted to evil and I am not burned?" (2 Cor. 11:29).

Gregory had a keen apocalyptic sense. The last judgment was imminent;

---

31. Gregory I, *Moralia* 4.31.61, CCSL 143, p. 205.

32. Gregory I, *Dialogues* 3.12.11, SC 260, p. 342. See 2 Cor. 12:2–3. On *compassio* and *compatior*, terms created by Christian writers, see Konstan, *Pity Transformed*, chap. 4.

33. Leyser, *Authority and Asceticism*, p. 162.

34. On such identification with others, see ibid., pp. 172–77; Markus, *Gregory*, pp. 26–31; and Straw, *Gregory: Perfection*, pp. 201–2.

35. Gregory I, *Dialogues* 1.1, SC 260, p. 10: "Quadam die, nimiis quorumdam saecularium tumultibus depressus . . . secretum locum petii amicum moerori."

36. Cassiodorus, *Expositio in psalterium* 60, PL 70, col. 425: "Congregatio sancta justorum, quae est haereditas Domini, depressa malis saeculi."

37. Gregory I, *Dialogues* 1.1, SC 260, p. 10: "cuncta quae infligere dolorem consueverant."

38. Boesch Gajano, *Gregorio Magno*, pp. 262–64, argues that one of the purposes of the *Dialogues* was to furnish Roman clerics with a large number of saints, doctrines, and miracles that they might use flexibly in their pastoral work.

human beings had but a brief "time out" on earth.[39] The pastor—someone like Gregory!—"preached the right ways," his words shining like silver.[40] But they did not always fall on willing ears. People had to be made receptive. One solution was to use force: this was the role of the secular ruler, the "rhinoceros" who "broke up the clods of the valley," softening the hearts of the wicked by compulsion.[41] The other was to use what modern psychologists would call "emotion management." This was the job of the rectors of the church, Gregory included.

Consider Gregory's admiring account of a "man of God" who came down "from the mountain"—much like Paul from his third heaven.[42] Each year this *vir Dei* visited Quadragesimus, the subdeacon of a church and Gregory's informant. On one such visit the man of God noticed a poor little woman (*paupercula*) sitting in evident distress next to the body of her recently deceased husband. All the proper rites had been performed for the dead man—the washing, clothing, wrapping in linen—but it was by now too late for the burial. Here is how Gregory described the scene:

> The widow thus sat next to the body of the dead man, spending the whole night weeping a great deal [*in magnis fletibus*]. She satisfied her sorrow by continual cries of lamentation. And when this had continued for a rather long time [*diutius*], and the woman did not cease weeping in any way, the man of God . . . was much moved [*conpunctus*] and said to Quadragesimus, "My soul suffers [*conpatitur*] along with the sorrow of this woman. Rise, I beg you, and let us pray."[43]

The two went into a nearby church and prayed for a long time (*diutius*). Then the man collected some dust from the base of the altar, returned to the corpse with Quadragesimus, and gave himself over to more prayer. But this time, after he had prayed (again *diutius*), he rose and pulled off the linen

---

39. On Gregory's apocalypticism, see Markus, *Gregory,* chap. 4; for Gregory's notion of the brief "space of life," see Barbara H. Rosenwein, "Emotional Space," in *Codierungen von Emotionen im Mittelalter,* ed. C. Stephen Jaeger and Ingrid Kasten (Berlin, 2003), pp. 289–93.

40. Gregory I, *Moralia* 4.31.62, CCSL 143, p. 206: "rectores . . . qui et sapienter vivendo aurum possideant et aliis recta praedicando, argento sacrae locutionis enitescant."

41. Ibid., 31.5.7, CCSL 143B, p. 1554.

42. Gregory I, *Dialogues* 3.17.2–5, SC 260, pp. 336–40.

43. Ibid., 3.17.2–3, SC 260, p. 338: "Juxta defuncti igitur corpus viduata mulier sedit, quae in magnis fletibus noctem ducens, continuis lamentorum vocibus satisfaciebat dolori. Cumque hoc diutius fieret et flere mulier nullo modo cessaret, vir Dei . . . Quadragesimo subdiacono conpunctus ait: 'Dolori huius mulieris anima mea conpatitur. Rogo, surge et oremus.'"

cover from the face of the corpse. "When the woman saw this being done," Gregory continued, "she began to protest vigorously, astonished [*mirari*] at what he wanted to do."⁴⁴ Without replying, the man rubbed the corpse's face with the dust. "And the dead man, as he was being rubbed for a very long time [still another *diutius*]," Gregory said, "received his soul" and returned to life. Now it was the wife's turn. Gregory continued: "When the woman, worn out by lamenting, saw this, she began to weep even more from joy [*ex gaudio*] and to shout out. Then the man of God restrained her with a mild injunction, 'Hush, hush; but if anyone asks you how this was done, say simply that the Lord Jesus Christ did these things.'"⁴⁵

The story unfolds as if in slow motion, with very long periods of intense activity—weeping, praying, rubbing. Emotions power the action. They take the narrative from the death of the husband to his resurrection. They are natural feelings born, in Gregory's view, out of the situation itself and the proper human responses to it. The widow is in pain and anguish; the man of God is struck, in turn, with compunction arising from compassion;⁴⁶ his seeming act of defilement horrifies the widow; then the miracle turns her sorrow into joy We see here a broad spectrum of feelings—sorrow, compunction, compassion, wonder, and joy—and the fluid transformation of one emotion into another.

What gave the *vir Dei* the right to intervene in the poor woman's life? Consider for a moment the fact that he intruded by befouling a beloved dead husband, washed and ready for burial. It was the ancient equivalent of "shock treatment"; today it would be considered a perfect example of psychiatric abuse of power. But it "worked." And it did so not just because the meddler was godly but because, as such, he was willing to come down from the mountain, lower himself to the dust, and share in the *paupercula*'s sorrow, even if she did not understand that to be the case at first. Without his compassion, the man of God would have had neither the will nor the right to act. He would not have been able to turn the woman's thoughts from her

---

44. Ibid., 3.17.4, *SC* 260, p. 338: "Quod cum mulier fieri cerneret, contradicere vehementer coepit et mirari quid vellet facere."

45. Ibid., 3.17.5, *SC* 260, p. 340: "Quod dum mulier lamentis fatigata conspiceret, coepit ex gaudio magis flere et voces amplius edere. Quam vir Domini modesta prohibitione conpescuit, dicens: 'Tace, tace, sed si quis vos requisierit qualiter factum sit, hoc solummodo dicite, quia Dominus Jesus Christus opera sua fecit.'"

46. For the relationship of compunction to tears, see ibid., 3.33.10–34.6, *SC* 260, pp. 398–404.

husband to God; he would not have been able to demonstrate the power of Christ. Emotions were powerful tools in the pastor's arsenal.

Gregory used them himself, justifying his religious authority through the manipulation of feeling. Let us consider a particular case in which, like the anonymous *vir Dei*, Gregory discovered someone in distress, knew just what to do about it, and imposed his solution on others—to their initial horror—in order to get it accomplished.

The person in distress in this instance was Justus, a monk at Gregory's monastery, who on his deathbed admitted to having secretly held on to three gold coins.[47] When Gregory learned of this he was extremely disturbed: "I could not bear it calmly [*aequanimiter*]," for it broke the monastery's rule against private property. Thus, "struck with overwhelming grief [*nimio moerore*], I began to think about what I should do both to purge the dying man and to provide an example for the monks still living."[48] Here grief took the place of the *vir Dei*'s feeling of compunction. Gregory's horrifying solution—his counterpart, as it were, to uncovering and rubbing dust over the dead man—was to have the monastery's prior order all the monks not to associate with the dying man or, indeed, utter one word to console him. Only when Justus was at death's door was he to learn—from someone outside the monastery—that he was abominated (*abominatus sit*) by all the monks because of his three coins. Moreover his body was to be thrown into a pit dug out of human excrement, the coins hurled atop the corpse. His fellow monks were to chant the clamor, "Let your money be with you in Hell."[49]

All this happened. The dying monk bewailed his guilt and died in sorrow (*tristitia*), which, as Gregory points out, was a very good thing for his soul. Thirty days passed, and then the counterpart to the resurrection of the *paupercula*'s husband began, initiated by an emotion, Gregory's compassion (*conpati*). He began, as he says "to think of [Justus's] punishments with heavy sorrow [*dolore gravi*]" and to seek a remedy. Sadly (*tristis*) calling the

---

47. The story is found in ibid., 4.57.9–15, *SC* 265, pp. 188–92.

48. Ibid., 4.57.10, *SC* 265, p. 188: "aequanimiter ferre non valui . . . Tunc nimio moerore percussus cogitare coepi, vel quid ad purgationem morientis facerem, vel quid in exemplum viventibus fratribus providerem."

49. Ibid., 4.57.11, *SC* 265, pp. 190: "simul omnes clamantes: 'Pecunia tua tecum sit in perditione.'" For liturgical clamors and curses, see Lester K. Little, *Benedictine Maledictions: Liturgical Cursing in Romanesque France* (Ithaca, N.Y., 1993).

prior before him, he said, "The brother who died has long been tormented by fire. We ought therefore to do something out of love [*aliquid caritatis*] for him and help as much as we can so that he may be freed."[50] Gregory ordered daily masses on behalf of Justus for thirty days, at the end of which period the dead man appeared in a vision saying, "I'm fine now" (*Jam modo bene sum*).

Here, as in the instance of the *vir Dei*, the pastor condescended to feel. But we can see from these two examples that his feelings were not exactly "congruent" with those of the sufferer. Rather they anticipated the emotions that the sufferer *should* have, "drawing out" new emotions from old. We are not told why Justus confessed to having three coins, but Gregory's response, born of his unhappiness at the news, had a major impact on Justus's state of mind. The dying man asked anxiously (*anxie*) to commend himself to the brethren, and when told he was an abomination to all, he groaned bitterly (*vehementer ingemuit*) over his guilt and died "in sadness itself" (*in ipsa tristitia*). Moreover, Gregory transformed the very emotional life of the monastery. When the monks learned that they had been forbidden to associate with Justus, not to give him even one word of consolation, they were *perturbati*, stirred up with all sorts of feelings. They began guiltily to bring out *their* little bits of private property so that they'd not meet Justus's fate.

Gregory was not the abbot of his monastery.[51] Nevertheless he had the "right" to order the punishment for Justus. Whatever the actual power relations within the monastery may have been, Gregory justified his authority not by position but by sentiment. Both his punishment for Justus and his work to reprieve him were motivated by sorrow.

In another case of "emotional condescension," when Gregory was already pope, he wrote to Venantius, *patricius Italiae*.[52] Venantius had taken

---

50. Gregory I, *Dialogues* 4.57.14, *SC* 265, p. 192: "coepit animus meus defuncto fratri conpati eiusque cum dolore gravi supplicia pensare, et si quod esset ereptionis eius remedium quaerere. Tunc evocato ad me eodem Pretioso monasterii nostri praeposito tristis dixi: 'Diu est quod frater ille, qui defunctus est, igne cruciatur. Debemus ei aliquid caritatis inpendere, et eum in quantum possumus ut eripiatur adiuvare.'"

51. Jeffrey Richards decisively rebuts the view that Gregory was abbot at St. Andrew's; Richards, *Consul of God: The Life and Times of Gregory the Great* (London, 1980), pp. 32–33.

52. Gregory I, *Registrum* 1.33, CCSL 140, pp. 39–41. In identifying this Venantius as the husband of Italica and father of Antonina and Barbara, as opposed to another Venantius who also appears in the corpus of Gregory's letters, I am following *The Prosopography of the Later*

up the monastic life, changed his mind, and abandoned it. "You recall the habit that you have worn," Gregory wrote, more out of hope than conviction.[53] "I confess," Gregory continued, "I speak in sorrow [*maerens*]; overcome by the unhappiness [*tristitia*] of your deed, I can hardly bring forth any words."[54] Then Gregory proceeded to pledge his love and claim its precedence over all others. He predicted that everyone would come to Venantius with a different message, pretending to care about him. But "they love not you but your property [*non te, sed res tuas diligunt*]." Gregory, by contrast, loved Venantius himself. "May Almighty God show to your heart with how much love [*amore*], how much charity [*caritate*] my heart embraces you."[55] And he continued in this vein, with words of love, for several more lines. In this case, however, descending from the mountain had no effect. Five years later we find Gregory writing to "ex-monk" Venantius.[56]

FEELINGS VALORIZED AND DEVALUED

Gregory did not ordinarily talk about emotions. The "inward quiet" was the ideal. The most emotional passages in Gregory's writings ironically had to do with his unhappiness at being assailed by emotions, the "fruitless tumults of his thoughts" (*vanis cogitationum tumultibus*).[57] To the Byzantine princess Theoctista he wrote, "I have lost the profound joys [*gaudia*] of my quiet . . . and therefore I bitterly bewail [*deploro*] my expulsion far from the face of my Creator."[58] There was a time, he continued, when he desired (*appetens*) nothing, feared (*pertimescens*) nothing, and seemed "to stand on the summit of things."[59] But then, attacked by temptation, he fell "into fears and terrors [*ad timores pavoresque*], for even if I feel no fear [*nil timeo*] for myself, I dread [*formido*] much for those who have been committed to

---

Roman Empire, vol. 3, A.D. *527–641*, ed. John Robert Martindale (Cambridge, 1992), pp. 1367–68.

53. Gregory I, *Registrum* 1.33, CCSL 140, p. 40: "In quo enim habitu fueris recolis."

54. Ibid., p. 41: "Ecce, fateor, maerens loquor et facti tui tristitia addictus edere verba vix valeo."

55. Ibid.: "Omnipotens Deus cordi tuo indicet cor meum quanto amore, quanta te caritate complectitur."

56. Ibid., 6.42, CCSL 140, pp. 414–15.

57. Ibid., 1.5, CCSL 140, p. 6.

58. Ibid., p. 5: "Alta enim quietis meae gaudia perdidi . . . Unde me a conditoris mei facie longe expulsum deploro."

59. Ibid.: "Videbar mihi in quodam rerum vertice stare."

me."⁶⁰ The whole passage, written on Gregory's accession to the papacy in 590, suggests that the monastery had been his "quiet place," while his new office brought nothing but tumult.

Yet the world was not so utterly painful nor the monastery so totally joyful as Gregory claimed. In the world was the compensation of affection, something that Gregory both despised and prized. In the monastery were moments of bitter sorrow and confusion (we have already seen one in the case of Justus), which Gregory viewed with considerable ambivalence.⁶¹ Let us take up each of these venues in turn.

Affection in the world

Gregory was tenderhearted. When he wrote to "ex-monk Venantius" he nevertheless addressed him as "dearest son" (*carissime fili*).⁶² When he heard that Venantius was ill, he wrote to John, bishop of Syracuse, about his "very sweet son lord Venantius."⁶³ He kept the whole family in mind. To Venantius's daughters, Barbara and Antonina, he wrote letters of consolation and reassurance.⁶⁴ He was in fact exquisitely sensitive to family feeling.

In one of his *Homilies on the Gospels*, given at the basilica of Saint Felicity in Rome on the saint's natal day, Gregory told the story of Felicity and her seven sons. They were all brought before Roman magistrates, made professions of their Christian faith, refused to sacrifice to the emperor, and were condemned to death. Gregory commented, "We read in the more correct accounts of her deeds that [Felicity] feared [*timuit*] leaving her seven sons alive after her in the flesh."⁶⁵ A review of the extant versions of the story suggests that there are no such accounts.⁶⁶ But Gregory was not a text editor.

---

60. Ibid., pp. 5–6: "ad timores pavoresque corrui, quia, etsi mihi nil timeo, eis tamen qui mihi commissi sunt multum formido."

61. On Gregory's ambivalence, see Straw, *Gregory: Perfection*, esp. pp. 22–24.

62. Gregory I, *Registrum* 6.42, CCSL 140, p. 415.

63. Ibid., 11.25, CCSL 140A, p. 895: "de dulcissimi filii mei domni Venantii aegritudine."

64. Ibid., 11.23, CCSL 140A, pp. 893–94; ibid., 11.59, pp. 965–66.

65. Gregory I, *Homiliae in Evangelia* 3.3, ed. Raymond Étaix, CCSL 141 (Turnhout, 1999), p. 21: "Septem quippe filios sicut in gestis eius emendatioribus legitur, sic post se timuit vivos in carne relinquere."

66. See Barbara H. Rosenwein, "*In gestis emendatioribus:* Gregory the Great and the *Gesta martyrum*," in *Retour aux sources. Textes, études et documents d'histoire médiévale offerts à Michel Parisse*, ed. Sylvain Gouguenheim et al. (Paris, 2004), pp. 843–48.

He meant simply to drive home the point that Felicity was no ordinary mother. Ordinary mothers, as he went on to say, would fear that their sons might die; Felicity feared that hers would survive her and be lost to God. In Gregory's view, Felicity's love for her sons, which reversed the expected order of feelings, was heroic. Because of it, she was "more than a martyr."[67] She had overcome "her sex along with the world."[68] In the emotional community that Gregory knew and invoked here, mothers loved their sons and wanted them to live. Even as he expressed admiration for Felicity, he could not repress his astonishment at her unnaturalness. Indeed, he had to reassure his audience by saying, "Let none among you, dearest brethren, think that her carnal heart beat with little emotion [*affectus*] as her sons died. Nor could she see her sons dying, whom she knew to be her flesh, without pain [*sine dolore*]. But it was the interior strength of her love [*vis amoris interior*] that conquered the pain [*dolorem*] of the flesh."[69]

Gregory turned even the Gospel reading of the homily into a disquisition on mothers and sons. He chose Matthew 12:46–50, where Jesus speaks to the crowd while his mother and brother stand outside (*foris*) trying to get his attention. Jesus snubs them: "Who is my mother and who are my brothers?" he asks, and then, stretching his hand toward his disciples, he says, "Here is my mother; here are my brothers." Gregory pretended puzzlement: clearly a man should know his own mother. Then Gregory explained: Jesus's meaning is hidden. The disjunction between what we expect and what Jesus actually does suggests that we must read the passage allegorically: Mary signifies the synagogue, condemned to stand outside (*foris*). A true mother is a preacher and that sort of mother is normally male. Thus Jesus's disciples become his mother. Then, turning to the main topic of his homily, Gregory linked Felicity to Jesus's disciples. Felicity, too, was a preacher, precisely because of her fear for her sons. For, because she feared,

---

67. Gregory I, *Homiliae in Evangelia* 3.3, p. 22: "Non ergo hanc feminam martyram, sed plus quam martyram dixerim."

68. Ibid., 3.4, p. 24: "quae cum saeculo sexum vicit." See 2 Macc. 7:21: "femineae cogitationi masculinum animum inserens, dixit ad eos . . ." (joining a man's heart to a woman's thought, she said to [her sons] . . .).

69. Gregory I, *Homiliae in Evangelia* 3.3, p. 22: "Nemo ergo ex vobis, fratres carissimi, existimet quod eius cor morientibus filiis etiam carnalis affectus minime pulsavit. Neque enim filios, quos carnem suam esse noverat, sine dolore poterat morientes videre, sed erat vis amoris interior, quae dolorem vinceret carnis."

she "strengthened the hearts of her sons in their love for the heavenly fatherland through preaching [*praedicando*]."[70]

At this point in the homily, Gregory turned to the men of his audience, metaphorically ousting the women. "Brothers," he said, "consider this woman" (he meant Felicity), "we who are men in our bodily members."[71] We men have plenty of problems: "if we hear one slight word of ridicule from the mouth of another, we instantly retreat," weak (*fracti*) and confounded (*confusi*).[72] We're supposed to love God, but instead we love worldly honor. Gregory accused men, himself included, not only of weakness but more precisely of mourning lost children inconsolably (*sine consolatione lugemus*).[73]

Thus men were soft on children. In the *Moralia* Gregory pointed out the difference between caring for the poor as an obligation and caring for them "like a father." In the latter case, one acted "out of love" (*per amorem*).[74] In his *Dialogues* Gregory recalled a father who loved his five-year-old son too much in the flesh (*nimis carnaliter diligens*).[75] He was so easy on the boy that he let him blaspheme. When the plague hit, and the child was near death, his father held him close. But, Gregory said,

> the boy, with trembling eyes saw evil spirits coming after him and began to cry out, "Hold them back, father; hold them back, father." And while shouting, he bent his face to hide himself from them in his father's bosom. When his father asked the trembling child what he saw, the boy explained, "There are black men here who want to take me away." And when he had said this, he immediately blasphemed the name of the [Divine] Majesty and gave up his soul.[76]

---

70. Ibid., p. 21: "filiorum corda in amorem supernae patriae praedicando roboravit."

71. Ibid., 3.4, p. 24: "Consideremus, fratres, hanc feminam, consideremus nos qui membris corporis viri sumus." I do not follow Felice Lifshitz, "Gender and Exemplarity East of the Middle Rhine: Jesus, Mary and the Saints in Manuscript Context," *Early Medieval Europe* 9 (2000): 333, when she argues that age, not gender, was Gregory's focus in a similar passage (Gregory I, *Homiliae in Evangelia* 11.3, p. 75): "Quid inter haec nos barbati et debiles dicimus?" (What do we say to these things, we who are bearded and weak?)

72. Gregory I, *Homiliae in Evangelia* 11.3, p. 75: "si unus contra nos levissimus sermo ab ore irridentis eruperit, ab intentione actionis nostrae fracti protinus et confusi resilimus."

73. Ibid.

74. Gregory I, *Moralia* 19.24.41, CCSL 143A, p. 989.

75. Gregory I, *Dialogues* 4.19.2, SC 265, p. 72.

76. Ibid., 4.19.3–4, SC 265, pp. 72–74: "malignos ad se venisse spiritus trementibus oculis puer aspiciens, coepit clamare: 'Obsta, pater. Obsta, pater.' Qui clamans declinabat faciem, ut

At this point Gregory was moved. "But putting aside this sad subject [*hoc triste*], let us return to those happy things [*laeta*] that I started to talk about."⁷⁷

Misery and Pain in the Monastery

The "happy things" that Gregory had just previously been talking about were the reunion of little Musa with the Virgin Mary. Warned in a dream to cease doing light and childish things and to abstain from "laughter and jokes" (*risu et iocis*) if she wished to serve Mary, Musa followed the admonition, fell ill, and soon "exited her virginal body to live with holy virgins."⁷⁸ In Gregory's emotional world, joy was tied to misery. When he spoke, as in his letter to Theoctista, about the profound joys (*gaudia*) of his monastic retreat, they were wrung, as it were, out of unhappiness itself.

This point is clearest in the monastic context. The "fruitless tumults of thoughts" that assailed men outside its walls crept in as well through its very confines. Consider Eleutherius, originally abbot of San Marco at Spoleto but later a monk at Gregory's monastery on the Caelian Hill. He told Gregory about a miracle. He had brought a boy to his monastery who, in his original home—a monastery of women—had been tormented by an evil spirit. Under Eleutherius's tutelage, the child was cured. But, as Gregory put it, "the old man's soul was touched overmuch by happiness [*inmoderatius per laetitiam*] regarding the health of the boy."⁷⁹ Eleutherius boasted to the brethren that the Devil might have been able to do his dirty work among a few nuns but dared not do so among true "servants of God." As soon as these words were uttered, the boy fell under the Devil's spell. Gregory recounted the scene:

> When he saw what happened, the old man [Eleutherius] immediately gave himself over to lamentation [*in lamentum dedit*]; and after he had mourned [*lugentem*] for a long time and the brethren had wanted to console him [*consolari*], he responded by saying, "Believe me, no bread is en-

---

se ab eis in sinu patris absconderet. Quem cum ille trementem requireret quid videret, puer adiunxit, dicens: 'Mauri homines venerunt, qui me tollere volunt.' Qui cum hoc dixisset, maiestatis nomen protinus blasphemavit et animam reddidit."

77. Ibid., 4.19.5, *SC* 265, p. 74: "Sed interim hoc triste seponentes, ad ea quae narrare coeperam laeta redeamus."

78. Ibid., 4.18.1–3, *SC* 265, pp. 70–72.

79. Ibid., 3.33.4, *SC* 260, p. 394: "senis animus de salute pueri inmoderatius per laetitiam tactus est."

tering anyone's mouth today unless that boy is snatched from the demon." Then he prostrated himself in prayer with all the brothers and they all prayed until the moment that the boy was healed from his torment.[80]

The tale is precisely about an unwanted thought—the tickle of happiness (*laetitia*)—that gave pleasure and commanded assent. Eleutherius felt immediate remorse. He lamented and mourned, as was right to do. His brethren felt compassion, but they took no action. It was only when they too fasted and prayed—entering into his agony—that the misfortune was put right. Sacrifice and sorrow, not joy, was valorized in the monastery. But that very reversal was itself understood as joyous.

That Gregory experienced the whole tenor of life in his monastery as painful is made clear in a story Gregory told about himself. He suffered excruciating stomach pains throughout his life, and his time in the monastery was no exception.[81] When these attacks came on, he was too weak to fast. On one Holy Saturday, shamed by the fact that even the young boys were carrying out a fast while he could not, Gregory was bitterly unhappy: "I became enfeebled," he says "more out of sorrow [*moerore*] than out of weakness [*infirmitate*]."[82] His very soul was sad (*tristis*). The solution that he alighted upon was to ask Eleutherius—the same man who had rejoiced too much—to go into the oratory and "to obtain by his prayers to the omnipotent Lord that the strength to fast be given me on this day."[83] Eleutherius did so, with warmth and conviction—that is, with tears—and when he was finished, Gregory reported a startling turn of events: "my stomach received such strength that I forgot about both food and pain entirely."[84] It was an

---

80. Ibid., 3.33.5, *SC* 260, p. 396: "Quo viso senex se protinus in lamentum dedit. Quem dum lugentem diu fratres consolari voluissent, respondit dicens: 'Credite mihi, quia in nullius vestrum ore hodie panis ingreditur, nisi puer iste a daemonio fuerit ereptus.' Tunc se in orationem cum cunctis fratribus stravit, et eo usque oratum est, quousque puer a vexatione sanaretur."

81. Gregory complained about these pains in *Moralia, ad Leandrum* 5, CCSL 143, p. 6.

82. Gregory I, *Dialogues* 3.33.7, *SC* 260, p. 398: "coepi plus moerore quam infirmitate deficere."

83. Ibid., 3.33.8, *SC* 260, p. 398: "eumque peterem, quatenus mihi, ut die illo ad jejunandum virtus daretur, suis apud omnipotentem Dominum precibus obtineret."

84. Ibid.: "Sed ad vocem benedictionis illius virtutem tantam meus stomachus accepit, ut mihi funditus a memoria tolleretur cibus et aegritudo."

Augustinian moment: "Who am I, who was I?" Gregory asked himself.[85] Without pain, he was bereft of his own identity.

Gregory reveals to us the importance of Christian doctrine in shaping at least one—his—emotional community. Looking forward to the life to come, devaluing the present, seeing true happiness in pain, and pain in pleasure, he continually reevaluated and second-guessed his emotions and those of others. While all those around him were mourning the impact of the plague on little ones, Gregory was excoriating them—and himself—for their feelings, reminding them that true Christians should be more concerned about blasphemy than death, should care more about eternal life than life in the world.

The values and goals of ascetic Christianity, first articulated by the Desert Fathers, shaped both what Gregory thought of his emotions (and those of others) and the very feelings themselves. They played a role analogous to the modern "emotionology" that interested Peter and Carol Stearns: "the attitude or standards that a society, or a definable group within a society, maintains toward basic emotions and their appropriate expression [and] ways that institutions reflect and encourage these attitudes in human conduct."[86] The social constructionist theory maintains that all feelings are shaped by such attitudes, since assessments of well-being rely on internalized standards of good and bad, weal and woe, that are socially determined. But when the ideal is "internal quiet," then even the joys of heaven are potentially suspect.

At the same time, however, Gregory gingerly welcomed emotions if they aided the machinery of salvation. No lover could have sworn truer affection than Gregory did in his exhortations to the wavering Venantius. No mourner could have lamented more bitterly than Eleutherius when trying to rid the boy once again of the demon. *Tristitia,* one of the deadly sins, was also a salvific force, helping the hapless Justus to repent and eventually achieve salvation. Felicity's fear was a lesson to all. Thus Gregory's emotional sensibilities helped shape the way in which he understood and wrote about the Christian religion.

Above all, Gregory privileged the feelings of a religious elite, mainly but not entirely male. He imagined Felicity trembling for her sons' salvation,

---

85. Ibid., 3.33.9, *SC* 260, p. 398: "Coepi mirari quis essem, quis fuerim."
86. Stearns and Stearns, "Emotionology," p. 813.

the *vir Dei* struck by compunction at the *paupercula*'s dilemma, Eleutherius in deep mourning. There were others who shared these ideals. Gregory certainly thought Theoctista a kindred spirit. Peter, Gregory's interlocutor in the *Dialogues,* was as well. He was depicted as hanging on Gregory's every word and agreeing with all of Gregory's sentiments. Peter was a real person—a member of Gregory's monastery and later an overseer of papal property in Italy. Most of the monks at St. Andrew's had been Gregory's childhood friends; many accompanied him to Constantinople and stayed on with him when he became pope.[87] In the *Moralia* they become his "anchored cable," holding on to the sea-tossed Gregory "by brotherly affection" (*germana caritate*).[88] They formed the core of the discussion group that importuned Gregory to expound his views on the Book of Job. These people constituted the emotional community of which Gregory was a part. They were keen on both virtue and authority, dual goals that helped shape both their feelings and their attitudes toward their feelings.

To be in this emotional community was to be constantly struggling against feelings that were no less keenly felt for being repudiated. As Augustine had long before argued, the City of God (which lives by faith) and the City of Man (which lives according to the world) were inextricably commingled on earth. This had emotional implications. Even the citizens of the City of God were mired in earthly feelings. Yet this was not all bad. As we have seen, such feelings were the hooks to which holy men tied their salvific ropes to haul up fallen men. Furthermore, as Gregory's discussion of Felicity shows, feelings directed toward worldly things had merit as long as they were, at the same time, counterbalanced. Felicity would have been a hardhearted monster had she not felt pain about her sons' deaths. Gregory could not imagine any good mother contemplating the deaths of her sons without sorrow. The constraints to virtue in Gregory's emotional community were mitigated by such concessions. What was wonderful about Felicity was not that she wanted her sons to die but that she felt as she did in spite of *not* wanting them to die.

If we were to try to match Gregory's community with any of those we have seen composing epitaphs in Gaul, it would come closest to that of the bereaved at Vienne, for whom Christian goals were paramount. But we know that at the same time as men and women at Vienne were sponsoring

---

87. See the quick review of the most important men in this group in Leyser, *Authority and Asceticism,* p. 131 n. 4; on Gregory's social world, Markus, *Gregory,* pp. 8–12.

88. Gregory I, *Moralia,* ad Leandrum 1, CCSL, 143, p. 2.

epitaphs emphasizing virtues, people at Trier were paying for inscriptions that reminded them of family affection. Let us now return to Gaul to explore its emotional communities more closely. We begin with one that was contemporary with Gregory.

4
THE POET AND THE BISHOP

In 573, around the time that Gregory the Great meant to retire for good to his monastery on the Caelian Hill (but was tapped for a mission to Constantinople instead), another Gregory was installed as bishop of Tours. His friend Venantius Fortunatus wrote a congratulatory poem to the citizens there: "Applaud, you happy [*felices*] people. . . . For here comes the hope [*spes*] of the flock, the father [*pater*] of the people, the lover [*amator*] of the city. Let the sheep rejoice [*laetificentur*] over the gift of this pastor."[1] The new bishop of Tours approved the effusiveness: he encouraged Fortunatus to publish his collected poems, this one included. Fortunatus complied, dedicating the volume to Gregory.

Venantius Fortunatus (ca. 535–ca. 605), trained in rhetoric at Ravenna, came to Gaul from Italy to earn his living by writing flattering poems to aristocrats and royalty in return for their largesse.[2] Gregory of Tours (ca. 538–ca. 594) spent his childhood at saints' shrines and learned his letters in the households of bishops at Lyon and Clermont.[3] If the two are mentioned together, it is normally to contrast them.[4] Yet they were good friends. For-

---

1. Fortunatus, *Poems* 5.3, ll. 1–6, ed. Reydellet, 2:16–17: "Plaudite, felices populi. . . . Spes gregis ecce venit, plebis pater, urbis amator: munere pastoris laetificentur oves." I use Reydellet's edition where possible, but it ends with book 8 of the poems, and for the poems of the later books and appendices, I use the edition of Leo (see note 11 below).

2. For biographical background, see Judith George, *Venantius Fortunatus: A Latin Poet in Merovingian Gaul* (Oxford, 1992), pp. 18–34; and Reydellet's introductory remarks in Fortunatus, *Poems,* 1:vii–xxviii. Regarding the date of death, Reydellet notes (p. xxvii) that Fortunatus became bishop of Poitiers ca. 600 and "died shortly thereafter." Yvonne Labande-Mailfert gives the date of death as "before 610"; Labande-Mailfert, "Les débuts de Sainte-Croix," in *Histoire de l'abbaye Sainte-Croix de Poitiers. Quatorze siècles de vie monastique = Mémoires de la Société des Antiquaires de l'Ouest,* 4th ser., 19 (1986–87): 112 n. 70.

3. For the basic facts of Gregory's early life, see Ian Wood, *Gregory of Tours,* Headstart History Papers (Bangor, 1994); and Martin Heinzelmann, *Gregory of Tours: History and Society in the Sixth Century,* trans. Christopher Carroll (Cambridge, 2001), pp. 29–35.

4. In Richard Koebner, *Venantius Fortunatus. Seine Persönlichkeit und seine Stellung in der*

tunatus wrote poems to or on behalf of Gregory during the nearly quarter-century of his poetic career; these paeans are sprinkled throughout the eleven books of poems he wrote between about 565 and 592.[5] The "second Orpheus" (as he called himself) depended on Gregory's patronage: in one poem he spoke of a villa that Gregory had given him; in another he asked him for some land; in a third he thanked Gregory for some shoe leather.[6] At the same time, Gregory needed Fortunatus's eloquence to go to work for him. He requested a panegyric from Fortunatus to laud Avitus of Clermont when the latter forcibly converted the Jews in his city; he had Fortunatus write inscriptions for St. Martin's refurbished cell at Tours; and he expressed the wish that Fortunatus, not he, had written the *Miracles of St. Martin*.[7]

---

geistigen Kulture des Merowingerreiches (Leipzig, 1915), p. 102, Fortunatus is "a conscious liar," while Gregory is "naive" and "sincere." In Samuel Dill, *Roman Society in Gaul in the Merovingian Age* (1926; repr., London, 1966), p. 281, Fortunatus is "vain, needy, and self-indulgent," but Gregory is "the grave Bishop of Tours." In Erich Auerbach, *Mimesis: The Representation of Reality in Western Literature,* trans. Willard Trask (1946; repr. Garden City, N.J., 1957), pp. 75, 78–79, Fortunatus is an artificial writer, while Gregory creates a new mimetic strategy of "visual vividness" and "sensory participation." Recent scholarship has tended to reverse the judgments, but this simply transposes the two men's position on the see-saw. Gregory is no longer naive and possibly not even sincere. For Walter Goffart, *The Narrators of Barbarian History: Jordanes, Gregory of Tours, Bede, and Paul the Deacon* (A.D. 550–800) (Princeton, 1988), p. 231, Gregory is a satirist: juxtaposing the worst with the best, his writings produce the "realism of caricature." In the hands of Ian Wood, "The Individuality of Gregory of Tours," in *The World of Gregory of Tours,* ed. Kathleen Mitchell and Ian Wood (Leiden, 2002), pp. 29–46, Gregory is a crafty writer, deftly forwarding his highly personal agenda. The "grave bishop" turns out to have been a skilled manipulator in depicting reality as he wished it to be. Meanwhile Fortunatus, rising in stature, has become the "new-style" writer, inventing (according to Godman, *Poets and Emperors,* chap. 1) a novel form of public declamatory verse: brief, pithy, and perfectly suited to its audience. In George, *Venantius Fortunatus,* esp. pp. 16–17, Fortunatus is the contrary of "vain and needy"; he is, instead, ever sensitive to others, giving an unconfident elite the identity it craves. This is also the verdict of Reydellet in Fortunatus, *Poems,* 1:lii–liii.

5. The final collection consisted of 218 poems and 12 works of prose. In addition, 31 poems by Fortunatus not included in the collection have been discovered. See George, *Venantius Fortunatus,* app. 2; and Fortunatus, *Poems,* ed. Reydellet, 1:xxviii–xxxiii. Two early poems were written while Fortunatus was still in Italy, prior to his departure from there at the end of the summer or in the fall of 565; the rest were written in Francia. See Fortunatus, *Poems,* ed. Reydellet, p. viii.

6. Fortunatus, *Poems* 8.19–21, ed. Reydellet, 2:159–61.

7. Fortunatus, *Poems* 5.5a and 1.5, ed. Reydellet, 2:19–20, 1:24–25. Gregory expresses the wish that Fortunatus, not he, had written the miracles in Gregory of Tours, *Libri I–IV de vir-*

The correspondence between the two men seems to have been easygoing and even (in Judith George's words) "affectionate and gently teasing."[8] The two shared a particular veneration for St. Martin, whose *Vita* Fortunatus versified and dedicated to Gregory, and they both had a special and close relationship with the nuns of the convent of the Holy Cross at Poitiers.

They were also part of the same court community at Reims/Metz, the center of one of the Merovingian kingdoms. The Frankish King Clovis (481–511), who famously converted early to Roman Catholicism, created the Merovingian kingdom in Gaul and bequeathed it to his four surviving sons (three by one mother, Clotild; one by a different woman) (see table 7). Though at loggerheads at times, the brothers successfully plotted together to keep their nephews from inheriting a throne. In 558, with the death of Childebert I, Clothar I became sole king. When he died, in 561, his kingdom was divided among his four sons, whose "civil wars" were bewailed in the pages of Gregory of Tours's *Histories*. Nevertheless, the idea of a single Merovingian kingdom ruled by blood brothers was not lost.

Sigibert's kingdom centered on Reims and Metz. Charibert's kingdom was associated with Paris, Guntram's with Orléans, and Chilperic's with Soissons. Later these kingdoms would be conceptualized more territorially, with Sigibert's called Austrasia, Charibert's Neustria, and Guntram's Burgundy. But in 561 the kingdoms were still envisioned as clusters of cities and their outlying regions. Trier was part of Sigibert's kingdom—it was (and is) about fifty miles from Metz—but so too was the distant city of Clermont.

Fortunatus began his career at Metz, celebrating the wedding of Sigibert and Brunhild there. Gregory was appointed bishop at Tours by the same king and queen's fiat: Fortunatus said that Gregory obtained the post at Tours by their *judicio*—their judgment or approbation. Moreover it was their bishop, Egidius of Reims, who consecrated Gregory.[9]

When Charibert died without heirs in 567, Tours and Poitiers went to Sigibert, but this devolution was disputed by Chilperic, and fighting between the two kings commenced, ending only in 575 with Sigibert's death, probably by assassins sent by Fredegund, Chilperic's wife. Then, in 584, when Chilperic died, Guntram in turn claimed Tours and Poitiers. These conflicts over Tours and Poitiers created another area of common ground for Fortu-

---

tutibus beati Martini episcopi, praef., ed. Bruno Krusch, MGH SRM 1/2, p. 136 (hereafter Greg. Tur., *VM*).

8. George, *Venantius Fortunatus*, p. 128.

9. Fortunatus, *Poems* 5.3, ll. 13–16, ed. Reydellet, 2:17.

natus and Gregory. Tours was Gregory's episcopal see, while Fortunatus had settled at Poitiers by 568 at the latest. Both had to be extremely wary of Chilperic and his wife, Fredegund. In 580 Gregory was hauled before this king and his bishops at Berny-Rivière on charges of treason and slandering the queen. It was, in the words of Ian Wood, a moment of "real danger," during which Gregory came "within a whisker of death."[10] Fortunatus came to the trial and declaimed a panegyric before the assembled king and "fathers." He praised Chilperic for his power, heritage, fame, and goodness; he called the queen wise, clever, prudent, useful, generous, and intelligent. He asked the king to add to all this one thing: to "be the apex of the Catholic religion."[11] Gregory himself never mentioned Fortunatus's presence at the hearing.[12] But it was surely a factor in his eventual acquittal.

COMMUNITIES

Perhaps Gregory did not in this case entirely appreciate Fortunatus's hyperbole. Both men were masters of flattery, but Fortunatus's was more flamboyant.[13] After all, he lived on its effects. Fortunatus made his first public appearance in Gaul in 566, when Sigibert married the Visigothic princess Brunhild at Metz.[14] At the wedding he declaimed in lofty Latin an epithalamium that he had composed for the occasion. Soon Fortunatus was writing poems with classical pretensions and words of praise to and about various Austrasian bishops: Carentinus of Cologne, Ageric of Verdun, Vilicus of Metz, Nicetius of Trier, Egidius of Reims.[15] Gregory of Tours was a great admirer of Bishop Nicetius of Trier; word of Fortunatus's talent spread through clerical networks such as these.[16]

---

10. Wood, *Gregory of Tours,* pp. 15, 17.

11. Venantius Fortunatus, *Poems* 9.1, l. 144, in *Venanti Honori Clementiani Fortunati . . . Opera Poetica,* ed. Fridericus Leo, MGH AA 4/1, p. 205: "sis quoque catholicis religionis apex."

12. Gregory discusses the charges and the court proceedings in Gregory of Tours, *Historiarum libri X* 5.49, ed. Bruno Krusch and Wilhelm Levison, MGH SRM 1/1, pp. 258–63 (hereafter Greg. Tur., *Histories*).

13. For Gregory's flattery, see Greg. Tur., *Histories* 9.21, p. 441, where King Guntram is likened to a good bishop.

14. George, *Venantius Fortunatus,* pp. 25–26.

15. Fortunatus, *Poems* 3.11–12 (Nicetius), 3.13 (Vilicus), 3.14 (Carentinus), 3.15 (Igidius), 3.23 and 23a (Ageric), ed. Reydellet, 1:106–15, 121–23.

16. Greg. Tur., *VP* 17.5, pp. 282–83.

TABLE 7. *The Merovingians*

Clovis I (481–511) = Clotild

```
├── Theuderic I (511–33)
├── Chlodomer (511–24)
├── Childebert I (511–58)
└── Clothar I (511–61)
    = Radegund
```

Children of Clothar I:
- Charibert I (561–67)
- Guntram (561–93)
- Sigibert I (561–75) = Brunhild
- Chilperic I (561–84) = Fredegund
- Gundovald (?)

Charibert I (561–67):
- Bertha = Ethelbert, king of Kent (d. 616)

Sigibert I & Brunhild:
- Childebert II (575–96)
  - Theudebert II (596–612)
    A (596–612)
  - Theuderic II (596–613)
    B (596–613)
    A (612–13)

Chilperic I & Fredegund:
- Clothar II (584–629)
  N (584–629)
  B (613–29)
  A (613–23)
  - Dagobert I
    A (623–32)
    N&B (629–39)

```
                                    Sigibert III         Clovis II
                                    A (632–ca. 656)      N&B (639–57)
                                                         A (ca. 656–57)
                                                         = Balthild
                    ┌───────────────┬─────────────────┐
                    Dagobert II                        Childeric II
                    A (675–79)                         A (662–75)
                                                       N&B (673–75)
                    Theuderic III
                    N&B (673, 675–ca. 690)             Daniel/Chilperic II
                    A (687–ca. 690)                    (ca. 715–21)
   ┌────────────────┤
   Childebert III
   (694–711)

   Dagobert III
   (711–ca. 715)

   Theuderic IV
   (721–37)
   | ?
   Childeric III
   (743–ca. 751)

Clothar III
N&B (657–73)

Clovis III
(ca. 690–94)
```

Note: This is a simplified genealogy. Most Merovingian kings had more than one wife (Sigibert I was an exception), and most had more children than those noted here. *A*, king of Austrasia; *B*, king of Burgundy; *N*, king of Neustria; "=" stands for "married to."

It spread through lay routes as well. Right after Sigibert's marriage, Fortunatus was already writing to his Austrasian "friends"—often designated by the word *dulcedo* (literally "sweetness") and its variants.[17] He wrote four poems to Gogo, Sigibert's counselor and the escort of Brunhild from Spain to Gaul, thanking him for dinner and praising him.[18] He wrote to Bodegisl, Sigibert's *dux* (governor), and to Bodegisl's wife, Palatina.[19] To Lupus, another of Sigibert's governors, he wrote three very long poems, and he addressed another to Lupus's brother.[20] For Dynamius of Marseille, another aristocrat connected to the Reims/Metz court, he composed two poems.[21] And so on. Nor were these affiliations separate from episcopal circles. Gregory of Tours, for example, knew the father of Palatina: he was bishop Gallomagnus, and Gregory praised him for his devotion to Gregory's own great uncle, Bishop Nicetius of Lyon.[22]

Fortunatus stayed on for a time at Sigibert's court, accompanying the king down the Mosel River after the wedding.[23] But soon thereafter he left Austrasia, traveling first to Paris, where he found King Charibert and praised him in a poem, and then to Tours, where Gregory's cousin Eufronius held the episcopal see.[24] By the end of 567 or the beginning of 568 Fortunatus had settled at Poitiers, where he became a priest and established himself as a friend of—and poet for—two religious women: Radegund, formerly queen-consort of Clothar, who, having left her husband for the reli-

---

17. Verena Epp insists, by contrast, on Fortunatus's use of the word *amor* as synonym for *amicitia*; Epp, "Männerfreundschaft und Frauendienst bei Venantius Fortunatus," in *Variationen der Liebe. Historische Psychologie der Geschlechterbeziehung*, ed. Thomas Kornbichler and Wolfgang Maaz, Forum Psychohistorie 4 (Tübingen, 1995), p. 14. Certainly *amor* is important, and, as we have seen in chapters 1 and 2, it is closely tied to *dulcis*, which is a term of endearment for those who are loved. On the many meanings of Fortunatus's *dulcedo*, see Godman, *Poets and Emperors*, pp. 16–21.

18. Fortunatus, *Poems* 7.1–4, ed. Reydellet, 2:85–90.

19. Fortunatus, *Poems* 7.5–6, ed. Reydellet, 2:90–93.

20. Fortunatus, *Poems* 7.7–10, ed. Reydellet, 2:94–102.

21. Fortunatus, *Poems* 6.9–10, ed. Reydellet, 2:80–84. On Dynamius, see Reydellet's biographical note, ibid., pp. 180–81 and n. 104.

22. Greg. Tur., *VP* 8.8, p. 248. For Nicetius's relationship to Gregory, see Wood, *Gregory of Tours*, pp. 6–7.

23. Fortunatus, *Poems* 6.8, ed. Reydellet, 2:77–79; for the date, see ibid., p. 180 n. 93.

24. The poem praising Charibert is Fortunatus, *Poems* 6.2, ed. Reydellet, 2:53–57; Fortunatus wrote three poems to Eufronius, ibid., 3.1–3, 1:81–86.

gious life, became a nun at her own foundation of the Holy Cross at Poitiers; and Agnes, the abbess of Holy Cross.[25]

Although we might imagine that the convent of the Holy Cross brought Fortunatus into a religious, social, and emotional community at variance with those with which he was otherwise familiar, this does not seem to have been the case. In addition to Radegund, who had been a queen, a couple of the nuns at Holy Cross were Merovingian princesses. Institutionally as well, Holy Cross had close connections with the royal court, especially that of Reims/Metz.[26] When Radegund wanted the relic of the Holy Cross for her monastery, she applied to King Sigibert for permission and help. When the bishop of Poitiers refused to install the relic, Sigibert was the king who ordered Eufronius of Tours to place it in her monastery. Baudonivia, the nun from Holy Cross who wrote Radegund's *Life* circa 600, made clear that Radegund commended her monastery to the churches of the realm, its bishops, and its kings, but most specifically "to the very serene lady Queen Brunhild. She loved [*dilexit*] [the kings and queen] with dear affection [*caro affectu*]."[27] To be sure, when Baudonivia was writing, Brunhild was the main power on the scene. Nevertheless, the passage suggests that Fortunatus's close relationship with Holy Cross did not take him far from his usual courtly haunts.

While at Poitiers, Fortunatus kept in contact with his former patrons and developed new ones. His panegyric to Chilperic and Fredegund when Gregory was brought to trial at Berny-Rivière was not, for example, his only poem to that king and queen.[28] It was in Fortunatus's interest—and part of his ideology of *dulcedo*—to smooth over differences between brothers and half-brothers with words of soothing tranquillity. Yet when all is said and done, the main recipients of Fortunatus's poems were three in number: the nuns at Holy Cross, Gregory of Tours, and the members of the Reims/Metz court. The latter remained an important source of patronage for Fortunatus even after Sigibert's death in 575, for the kingdom came under Brunhild's control, and it remained largely hers even when her son and grandsons were

---

25. On Fortunatus's friendship with these women, see Epp, *Amicitia*, pp. 74–76.
26. Nelson suggests ("Gendering Courts," p. 176) that Holy Cross was a satellite (or, as she puts it, "an ancillary form") of the royal court.
27. Baudonivia, *Vita Sanctae Radegundis* 16, ed. Bruno Krusch, MGH SRM 2, p. 389.
28. Fortunatus, *Poems* 9.1–3, ed. Leo, pp. 201–10; ibid., 9.4, p. 210 is an epitaph for Chilperic and Fredegund's young son Chlodobert.

on the throne. (She outlasted both Gregory and Fortunatus.) After a trip in 587 to Metz, in the company of Gregory to negotiate the Treaty of Andelot between Guntram, Brunhild, and her son Childebert II, Fortunatus wrote five poems to the queen and her son, filled with lavish praise.[29]

As for Gregory: "the first thirty years or so of [his] life must largely be defined in terms of saints' cults," to borrow the words of Ian Wood.[30] There were three saints in particular to whom Gregory was devoted: Benignus, Julian, and Martin. The cult of Benignus was Burgundian. Its center was Dijon, and it had been promoted actively by Gregory of Langres, Gregory's great-grandfather. Thereafter Benignus became a family saint. At Clermont, Gregory's mother kept the vigils of Benignus, saving her household from the plague.[31] Gregory himself collected Benignus's relics, and, after building a new baptistery alongside the church of Saint Martin at Tours, he placed those relics in the old baptistery, in this way associating two of his favorite patrons.[32]

The cult of Julian had its center at Brioude, which Gregory visited early in his life on family pilgrimages.[33] On one of these journeys, he experienced a terrible headache, cured only by the waters of the stream near which Julian had been decapitated, about 1¼ miles from Brioude. "I depart healthy," Gregory reported, "and joyfully [*laetus*] I enter [Julian's church, going] right up to the tomb of the glorious martyr."[34] Gregory's brother, Peter, was cured of a fever at this same tomb.[35] Gregory called himself the "foster child" (*alumnus*) of Julian, and he brought some of the saint's relics to his episcopal see at Tours.[36]

Nevertheless, the main saintly presence at Tours was St. Martin, who had been bishop there in the fourth century. Gregory was deeply involved in honoring the saint both professionally and personally. "I found the walls of the holy church [of Martin] damaged by fire, which I ordered to be painted

---

29. Fortunatus, *Poems* 10.7–9, app. 5–6, ed. Leo, pp. 239–44, 279–80. For the dates and circumstances, see George, *Venantius Fortunatus,* pp. 33, 97, n. 1.

30. Wood, *Gregory of Tours,* p. 8. See also Van Dam, *Saints and Their Miracles,* chap. 2.

31. Gregory of Tours, *Liber in gloria martyrum* 50, ed. Bruno Krusch, MGH SRM 1/2, p. 74 (hereafter Greg. Tur., *GM*).

32. Greg. Tur., *Histories* 10.31.18, p. 535.

33. Gregory of Tours, *Liber de passione et virtutibus sancti Juliani martyris* 24–25, ed. Bruno Krusch, MGH SRM 1/2, pp. 124–25 (hereafter Greg. Tur., *VJ*).

34. Greg. Tur., *VJ* 25, p. 125.

35. Greg. Tur., *VJ* 24, p. 125.

36. Greg. Tur., *VJ* 34–35, pp. 128–29.

and decorated ... as brightly as they had been before."[37] We have already seen that he built a new baptistery for this church. Gregory's *Histories* were in part written to demonstrate Martin's patronage and protection of the Touraine, while the *Miracles of Saint Martin* was the first work that he composed as bishop of Tours—indeed, his first published work altogether.[38] And both Gregory and his mother found cures at Martin's tomb.[39] The emotions that he associated with Martin were far more complex and anguished than those connected with Julian.[40]

Thus both Fortunatus and Gregory had experienced a variety of communities (some overlapping) in their younger days. While in the 560s each became attached to one particular community—Fortunatus at Poitiers, Gregory at Tours—they nevertheless continued to correspond, make visits to one another at home, and meet in common "outside" venues, such as Berny-Rivière and Metz. They did not agree on all things: Gregory excoriated Bishop Felix of Nantes, while Fortunatus wrote admiring poems to Felix, affirming the "affection of an admirer" (*affectu fautoris*).[41] But people do not have to be in accord on all matters to be part of the same emotional community; they have merely to hold similar values and express them according to similar norms. In the rest of this chapter I propose to explore the common emotional community of Gregory and Fortunatus: its parameters, assumptions, and modes of expression. I hope to explain the two men's easy familiarity. But I do not claim that their common emotional community was the only one in which these men felt comfortable. Nor do I claim that it

---

37. Greg. Tur., *Histories* 10.31.18, p. 535.

38. See Van Dam, *Saints and Their Miracles,* esp. pp. 65–67.

39. For his mother's cure: Greg. Tur., *VM* 3.10, p. 185; for his own cures: ibid., 1.32, 2.1, 2.60, pp. 154, 159, 179–80.

40. See Barbara H. Rosenwein, "The Places and Spaces of Emotion," in *Uomo e Spazio nell'alto medioevo,* Settimane di studio del Centro Italiano di Studi Sull'alto medioevo 50 (Spoleto, 2003), pp. 505–36. On the different circumstances of the cults, nature of the miracles, and Gregory's personal stakes in the cases of St. Julian and St. Martin, see Danuta Shanzer, "So Many Saints—So Little Time ... the *Libri Miraculorum* of Gregory of Tours," *Journal of Medieval Latin* 13 (2003): esp. 27–37.

41. Greg. Tur., *Histories* 5.5, p. 200; Fortunatus, *Poems* 3.4–10, ed. Reydellet, 1:86–105, quote from 3.4, p. 88. William C. McDermott argues that "the relations between Felix and Gregory were at times quite friendly," but the suggestion largely relies on rehabilitating the character of Felix and then assuming that two dedicated bishops could not have been at loggerheads all the time; McDermott, "Felix of Nantes: A Merovingian Bishop," *Traditio* 31 (1975): 19.

was exclusive to them; we shall in due course see others who shared their emotional styles.

DULCEDO

Grouping Fortunatus and Gregory together in the same emotional community is almost counterintuitive. Fortunatus is known for *dulcedo* and flattery, Gregory for irony and satire.[42] Yet the flatterer must be attuned to social norms if his writings are to glamorize, and the ironist must play off of the same if his audience is to feel indignation. *Dulcedo* served both men.

Dear to Fortunatus for its ennobling meanings, *dulcedo* in his hands emphasized the virtues of eloquence, power, and morality, at the same time expressing Fortunatus's approval and affection.[43] To Lupus he wrote, "O name of Lupus, sweet [*dulce*] to me and always worth repeating, / . . . the man whom the indestructible arc of my breast guards, once [he is] included on the tablets of sweetness [*dulcedinis*] within."[44] He complimented King Charibert for his *dulcedo* because he protected and nurtured the widow and daughters of King Childebert, his uncle.[45] At Berny-Rivière he addressed King Chilperic as "sweet head" (*dulce caput*).[46] In all of this was some intentional hyperbole; Fortunatus was knowingly exaggerating—while at the same time reveling in—an ancient ideal of friendship. His audience understood this and played along.[47]

Dulcedo is not normally associated with Gregory but nevertheless comes up frequently in his writings.[48] In his *Histories* it often has a satirical quality. Thus Queen Clotild is shown inveigling her sons to avenge the death of her parents by saying to them: "Don't let me regret, dearest ones [*carissimi*],

---

42. Goffart, *Narrators*, pp. 175–225.

43. On the many meanings of Fortunatus's *dulcedo*, see Godman, *Poets and Emperors*, pp. 16–21.

44. Fortunatus, *Poems* 7.8, ll. 33–36, ed. Reydellet, 2:98: "O nomen mihi dulce Lupi replicabile semper / quodque mei scriptum pagina cordis habet, / quem semel inclusum tabulis dulcedinis intus non abolenda virum pectoris arca tenet."

45. Fortunatus, *Poems* 6.2, l. 23, ed. Reydellet, 2:54.

46. Fortunatus, *Poems* 9.1, l. 33, ed. Leo, p. 202.

47. For this ideal of friendship, see Jaeger, *Ennobling Love*; and Epp, *Amicitia*.

48. The *Concordance de l'*Historia Francorum *de Grégoire de Tours*, ed. Denise St.-Michel, 2 vols. (Montréal, [1979]), s.v. "dulcedo," reveals fifteen uses of *dulcedo* (and variants) in Greg. Tur., *Histories*. To this may be added, culled from the on-line *Patrologia Latina* data base: two instances in his *GM*, four in *GC*, four in *VM*, twelve in the *VP*, yielding a total of thirty-seven instances in those of his writings that have been digitized.

that I raised you so sweetly [*dulciter*]; Contend against the wrong done to me, I beg you, and with keen zeal avenge the death of my father and mother."⁴⁹ When Ingund wants her husband Clothar I to marry off her sister Aregund to a worthy groom, Clothar weds Aregund himself and then reports back to Ingund: "I thought about how to carry out the favor that your sweetness [*tua dulcitudo*] asked of me. And in seeking a man who was rich and wise to whom I should join your sister, I found no one better than myself."⁵⁰ In the case of two citizens of Tours, Sichar and Chramnesind, who patched up a deadly feud so well that they "ate together and slept in the same bed," Sichar is quoted as saying at one of their meals, "You ought to give me a lot of thanks, oh very sweet brother [*dulcissime frater*], for killing your relatives; ever since you received the composition for it, gold and silver abounds in your house." At these words, Chramnesind turned out the lights and killed his companion.⁵¹

In these instances Gregory contrasted the tenderness of the overt sentiments with the violence or violation that hid behind it. But none of these episodes would have had any shock value if people did not ordinarily express real love with words of sweetness. Thus Gregory, who surely was not present when Sichar spoke to his "brother" Chramnesind, nevertheless fabricated Sichar's fawning remark in order to complete his cozy scene, to which he might contrast Sichar's insensitive teasing and Chramnesind's revenge.

Thus the word *dulcedo* was a well-known shorthand for affection even in Gregory's works. Nor was this true only in ironic passages. When he tells us about the Auvergnat aristocrat Injuriosus, who wedded a girl who wished to remain a virgin, Gregory recounts how the young man listened sympathetically to her wedding-night pleas: she had thought to remain chaste forever; her tears will never end; she will be unfaithful to her real spouse in

---

49. Greg. Tur., *Histories* 3.6, pp. 101–2: "Non me paeneteat, carissimi, vos dulciter enutrisse; indignate, quaeso, injuriam meam et patris matrisque mortem sagaci studio vindecate."

50. Ibid., 4.3, pp. 136–37: "Tractavi mercidem illam inplere, quam me tua dulcitudo expetiit. Et requirens virum divitem atque sapientem, quem tuae sorori deberem adjungere, nihil melius quam me ipsum inveni." On this episode, see Danuta Shanzer, "History, Romance, Love, and Sex in Gregory of Tours' *Decem libri historiarum*," in *The World of Gregory of Tours,* ed. Kathleen Mitchell and Ian Wood (Leiden, 2002), p. 412.

51. Greg. Tur., *Histories* 9.19, p. 433: "Magnas mihi debes referre grates, o dulcissime frater, eo quod interfecerim parentes tuos, de quibus accepta compositione aurum argentumque superabundat in domum tuam."

heaven and thus lose eternal life. At last Injuriosus turns to her and says: "By your very sweet arguments [*dulcissimis eloquiis*] eternal life illuminates me like a great radiance. Therefore, if you wish to abstain from carnal intercourse, I shall become a partner in your plan."[52]

In Gregory's writings mothers often had the word *dulcis* on their lips as they spoke tenderly to their children. Gregory's own mother is depicted doing this. When Gregory was young, he contracted an illness and went to the tomb of St. Illidius at Clermont to be cured. But his fever, which abated at the tomb, mounted when he was home again, and his mother said, as Gregory reports, "I will consider this a day of mourning, my sweet son [*dulcis nate*], since such a fever lays you low."[53] In the event, to be sure, Gregory recovered. Similarly, the mother of an infant, despairing of his life, and fearing for his unbaptised state, brought the child to the same saint's tomb. He called out to his mother: "Come here." And she, startled both by the sign of life and by the infant's use of words, replied, "What do you want, my most sweet son [*dulcissime nate*]?"[54] Saint Patroclus's mother addressed him in the same way when he returned home upon the death of his father: "Behold, your father, my very sweet son [*o dulcissime nate*], has died; I live without consolation."[55] This is clearly the way mothers were expected to address their sons.[56] But *dulcis* was not exclusive to that relationship. Gregory's great-grandmother told her husband not to accept the bishopric of Geneva: "My very sweet husband [*dulcissime conjux*], I ask you to desist from that cause and not seek the episcopacy of the city because I carry in my womb a bishop conceived by you."[57] And, as in the case of Fortunatus's friendship network, so too in Gregory's: the priest Aridius called Gregory his "very sweet [*dulcissime*] brother" even though they were not blood relations.[58]

---

52. Ibid., 1.47, p 31: "'Dulcissimis,' inquid, 'eloquiis tuis aeterna mihi vita tamquam magnum jubar inluxit, et ideo, si vis a carnali abstinere concupiscentiam, particeps tuae mentis efficiar.'"

53. Greg. Tur., *VP* 2.2, p. 220: "Maestum hodie, dulcis nate, sum habitura diem, cum te talis attenet febris."

54. Ibid., 2.4, p. 221: "'Accede huc.' . . . 'Quid vis,' inquit, 'dulcissime nate?'"

55. Ibid., 9.1, p. 253: "Ecce genitor tuus, o dulcissime nate, obiit; ego vero absque solatio degeo."

56. On terms of endearment and words of affection expressed by parents toward their children during the Merovingian period, see Réal, *Vies de saints*, pp. 430–54.

57. Greg. Tur., *VP,* 8.1, p. 241: "Desine, quaeso, dulcissime conjux, ab hac causa, et ne quaesieris episcopatum urbis, quia ego ex concepto a te sumpto episcopum gero in utero."

58. Ibid., 17 praef., p. 278.

Let us note the parallels between Gregory and Fortunatus's easy use of *dulcis/dulcedo* as terms of affection and the practices of some mourners at Trier (in chapter 2). Gregory was more restrained than his friend, reminding us of the reticence of families at Trier, who often used no emotion word whatever on a tombstone. But those who were more effusive were also very likely to use *dulcissimus* to express their affection, often, though not exclusively, when they commemorated a child. Gregory, too, makes clear the connection between that word and parental feeling. We may thus raise here the possibility that Gregory and Fortunatus were part of—or, in any event, comfortable with—the emotional community that can be only barely glimpsed at Trier through its inscriptions. Gregory and Fortunatus's close relations with the nearby Metz/Reims court gives some ballast to the argument.[59]

BEYOND SWEETNESS

Fortunatus's and Gregory's emphasis on sweetness alerts us to a key element in the complex of feelings that they privileged together: an intense sentimentality regarding the love that family members—parents and children, brothers and sisters, husbands and wives—felt for one another. Both men imagined these bonds to exist, and this suggests that they *did* exist or, at any rate, were normative and expected in the social circles with which poet and bishop were familiar. They also imagined close ties between friends. These ties were precious but fragile, needing constantly to be recalled and massaged. "Love"—already long hallowed in the pantheon of emotions—helped make that possible. This is not the place to explore the role of love in ancient notions of friendship.[60] But it is important to know that when, for example, Fortunatus spoke of being a "lover" (*amans*) of Bodegisl, he was

---

59. The inscriptions for Metz itself are too few and too mutilated to be useful. See *RICG I*, nos. 242–57. However, no. 242 is suggestive, mentioning "innocens Aspasius dulcissimmus."

60. Pierre Macherey argues that the ancient world usually associated love and friendship, but Plato dissociated the two, a dissociation which, according to Macherey, was then made normative by Christianity; Macherey, "Le 'Lysis' de Platon: dilemme de l'amitié et de l'amour," in *L'Amitié. Dans son harmonie, dans ses dissonances,* ed. Sophie Jankélévitch and Bertrand Ogilvie (Paris, 1995), pp. 58–75. By contrast, David Konstan sees love—variously defined—as an element in friendships throughout antiquity and into the Patristic period; Konstan, *Friendship in the Classical World* (Cambridge, 1997). Peter Dinzelbacher rightly argues that love in the Early Middle Ages was not the same as that of the twelfth century, but because he seeks a love that is like "our own"—companionate, focused on one other person—he overlooks the importance of affection in the earlier period, postulating that the care of in-

drawing upon a well-worn rhetorical and emotional tradition. As C. Stephen Jaeger has shown, this sort of love language—and the feeling behind it—was understood to ennoble both the lover and the beloved.[61]

Passionate family feeling accompanied by grief was the main theme of "The Destruction of Thuringia," a poem that Fortunatus wrote on behalf of Radegund. It was probably meant to form part of her petition to the Byzantine emperor Justin II to grant fragments of the Holy Cross to her convent at Poitiers.[62] All the members of Radegund's family had been killed, dispersed, or taken into custody by the Frankish conquest of Thuringia; she herself as well as her brother had been prizes of war. Married to King Clothar I, she left him when the king "afterward unjustly had her brother killed by wicked men," as Gregory tells the story.[63] She "turned to God" and was consecrated to the religious life by Bishop Medard of Soissons.

Written in the form of a plea to her cousin Amalfrid, who had escaped the Thuringian war and found refuge in Byzantium, the poem casts Radegund as a tragic heroine modeled on the fictional Heroides on whose behalf Ovid wrote reproachful letters to absent loved ones.[64] Here the tragedy of Thuringia is explicitly linked to that of Troy.[65] The poem is full of Radegund's tears: "I alone survive to weep for all the rest. / Nor am I compelled to mourn only my dead relatives. / I weep for those too whom kind life spares."[66] She recalls the artless love that once bound her and Amalfrid. "Remember, Amalfrid, how in those early years of yours / when I was your Radegund? / How much you as a sweet child once loved [*dilexeris*] me! / . . . What my dead father could have been, or my mother, or sister or

---

fants during this early period was lacking in affectivity ("di carenze affettive"), itself the result of impoverishment and the harshness of daily life; Dinzelbacher, "La donna," p. 234.

61. Jaeger, *Ennobling Love*; for the poem to Bodegisl, see note 91 below.

62. Baudonivia, *Vita Sanctae Radegundis* 16, p. 388.

63. Greg. Tur., *Histories* 3.7, p. 105: "cuius fratrem postea injuste per homines iniquos occidit." But as Fortunatus tells it, at the same time that Clothar ordered the brother to be killed, Radegund was "directed" (*directa*) by him to ask Bishop Medard of Soissons "to consecrate her to the Lord." It was his *proceres* (leading men) who tried to hold her back. See Fortunatus, *Vita Sanctae Radegundis* 12, ed. Bruno Krusch, MGH SRM 2, p. 368.

64. Fortunatus, *Poems* app. 1, ed. Leo, pp. 271–75 (hereafter "Destruction of Thuringia"). For the literary models, see Walther Bulst, "Radegundis an Amalafred," in *Bibliotheca Docet. Festgabe für Carl Wehmer* (Amsterdam, 1963), pp. 369–80.

65. Fortunatus, "Destruction of Thuringia," l. 19, p. 271.

66. Ibid., ll. 36–38, p. 272: "ut flerem cunctis una superstes ago. / Nec solum extinctos cogor lugere propinquos: / hos quoque, quos retinet vita benigna, fleo."

brother, you alone were to me."⁶⁷ Turning then to mourn her brother and accuse herself, the Radegund of the poem presents herself as another Canace, guilty of an unspeakable crime, unable to carry out even the rites of mourning: "The youth, with a beard still of tender down, is overcome. / I, his sister, was not there and did not see the awful funeral. / Not only did I lose him, but I did not close his pious eyes / nor, lying over him, say the last words. / I did not make his cold flesh warm by my hot tears / nor take away kisses from his dying flesh. / Nor did I tearfully cling to his neck in a heart-rending embrace / or, sobbing, caress his body on my unhappy bosom."⁶⁸

Love for Amalfrid is thus the love of family; he takes the place of father, mother, sister, and brother. But let us move for a moment from the high-flown rhetoric of Radegund's lament to the writings of others whose emotional worlds intersected with that of Gregory and Fortunatus. "The Destruction of Thuringia" may be compared to Queen Brunhild's letter to Emperor Maurice, written a few years later. There she speaks of her little grandson Athanagild, who was at Constantinople. He is, she says, all she has now that her daughter Ingund has died, victim of the civil wars in Spain. "I do not lose a daughter entirely," writes Brunhild, "if my exalted progeny [namely Athanagild] is preserved." She calls on him as her "very dear grandson" (*nepus carissime*). She can see in his eyes her own "sweet daughter" (*dulcis filia*)—though in fact she has never seen the child at all.⁶⁹

---

67. Ibid., ll. 47–52, p. 272: "vel memor esto, tuis primaevis qualis ab annis, / Hamalafrede, tibi tunc Radegundis eram, quantum me quondam dulcis dilexeris infans / et de fratre patris nate, benigne parens. / Quod pater extinctus poterat, quod mater haberi, quod soror aut frater tu mihi solus eras."

68. Ibid., ll. 133–40, p. 274: "percutitur juvenis tenera lanugine barbae, / absens nec vidi funera dira soror. / Non solum amisi, sed nec pia lumina clausi / nec superincumbens ultima verba dedi, / frigida non calido tepefeci viscera fletu, / oscula nec caro de moriente tuli, / amplexu in misero neque collo flebilis haesi / aut fovi infausto corpus anhela sinu." As Bulst points out ("Radegundis an Amalafred," p. 377), the passage has striking parallels to Ovid, *Heroides* 11, l. 115, trans. Grant Showerman, rev. G. P. Goold, Loeb Classical Library (Cambridge, Mass., 1986), p. 140, which is the lament of Canace to her brother, whose child she has borne, that she could not carry out the proper rites on behalf of her child, who was thrown to wild beasts by her father.

69. *Epistolae Austrasicae*, 27, ed. Wilhelm Gundlach, MGH Epistolae 3: Epistolae merowingici et karolini aevii (1892; repr. Munich, 1994), p. 139: "Accessit mihi, nepus carissime, votiva magne felicitatis occasio, per quam, cuius aspectum frequenter desidero vel pro parte relevor, cum directis epistulis amabilibus illis oculis repraesentor, in quo mihi, quam peccata subduxerunt, dulcis filia revocatur; nec perdo natam ex integro, si, praestante Domino, mihi proles edita conservatur."

The mother-child bond is paramount as well in Baudonivia's *Life of Radegund*. Radegund had no biological children, but she told the nuns at Holy Cross: "I have chosen you to be my daughters. You are my light, my life, my respite, and my entire happiness [*felicitas*]."[70]

We have already seen that Gregory's writings assume that families were bound by strong and loving emotions. His own uncle Gallus, he tells us, used to visit him as a child when he was gravely ill, showing him a "unique affection" (*dilectione unica*). This was the context for his mother's loving and anxious words: "I will consider this a day of mourning." Gregory responded tenderly in turn, recognizing her feelings: "Don't, I truly beg of you, be sad [*contristeris*], but take me back to the tomb of blessed bishop Illidius. For I believe, and it is my faith, that his power will bring happiness [*laetitiam*] to you and health to me."[71]

When Fortunatus wrote to Gregory about walking a path that St. Martin trod, he dwelt long on a chance meeting on the road. He came across a father and mother who, he said, "mourn [*lugent*] their daughter with weeping [*fletibus*], filling the air with their cries and covering their cheeks with tears [*lacrimando*]." Through their sobs and sighs they barely managed to explain to Fortunatus that their daughter had been sold into slavery. "Investigate, follow up," Fortunatus wrote to Gregory, "and if it be otherwise than it should be, sweet one and father, deliver her and join her to your flock. Return her also to her father."[72] Like Gregory the Great's *vir Dei*, Fortunatus was clearly moved by tears and extremely concerned about the salvation of souls. But Fortunatus's motive was not quite the same as Gregory's "condescension of emotion"; he was most concerned about the family separation.

Baudonivia voiced the same concern about the metaphorical family of nuns at the convent of the Holy Cross when Radegund died. The nuns stood around her body, "weeping and wailing [*flentes et heiulantes*], beating their chests with hard fists and stones."[73] At her funeral the congregation

70. Baudonivia, *Vita Radegundis* 8, p. 383: "Vos elegi filias, vos, mea lumina, vos, mea vita, vos, mea requies totaque felicitas."

71. Greg. Tur., *VP* 1.2, p. 220: "'Nihil,' inquid, 'prorsus, obsecro, contristeris, sed ad sepulchrum [tu] me remitte beati Illidii pontificis. Credo enim, et fides mea est, quod virtus eius et tibi laetitiam et mihi tribuat sospitatem.'"

72. Fortunatus, *Poems* 5.14, ll. 7–8, 21–22, ed. Reydellet, 2:39: "fletibus huc lugent genitor genetrixque puellam / voce inplendo auras et lacrimando genas.... Discute, distringe ac, si sit secus, eripe dulcis et pater adde gregi: hanc quoque redde patri."

73. Baudonivia, *Vita Radegundis* 21, p. 392: "luctuosa circa eius thorum flentes et heiulantes, pectora duris pugnis et lapidibus ferientes."

was so affected that their "mourning (*planctus*) took over the very psalmody." Baudonivia explained: "They rendered tears (*lacrimas*) for the psalms, a groan (*mugitum*) for the canticle, and a sigh (*gemitum*) for the alleluia."[74] Similarly, one of Fortunatus's patrons, Dynamius, wrote a *Life of St. Maximius* in which the parents of a boy killed by the bite of a rabid dog "beat their breasts with their fists" and watered the body with their tears.[75]

Gregory of Tours was equally willing to talk about the gestures of family feeling. Consider the way in which he depicted the anguish of Queen Fredegund confronted with the illness of her sons: striking her breast with her fists, clearly a topos of grief, as we have seen, Fredegund repented her sinfulness.[76] Gregory's dislike of Fredegund is well known, but when he came to describing her feelings as a mother, he imagined them to be fiercely loving. We need not assume that Gregory was reporting facts: he was reporting what he considered appropriate for mothers—even wicked mothers—to feel.

Gregory also tells us—again, coloring his account with his own emotional expectations—about the public mourning that took place at Paris when Fredegund's son died: "Great indeed was the lamentation [*planctus*] of all the people; for the men were mourning [*lugentes*] and the women were dressed in the mourning apparel that was normally worn for following husbands to the grave."[77] This was the counterpart to Fortunatus's evocation of public joy in his poems. We began this chapter with his celebration of Gregory's consecration: "Applaud, you happy [*felices*] people.... For here comes the hope [*spes*] of the flock, the father [*pater*] of the people."

Gregory's model for the funeral cortege at Paris was not, however, that of mourning blood relations; it was of marital feeling. The women following Fredegund wore widows' weeds. For both Gregory and Fortunatus, the

---

74. Ibid., 24, p. 393: "Dum sub muro cum psallentio sanctum eius corpus portaretur, quia instituerat, ut nulla vivens foras monasterio januam egrederetur, tota congregatio supra murum lamentans, ita ut planctus eorum superaret ipsum psallentium, pro psalmo lacrimas, pro cantico mugitum et gemitum pro alleluia reddebant."

75. Dynamius, *Vita Sancti Maximii* 10, PL 80, col. 38: "Adsunt parentes, pugnis sua verberant pectora, ora lacrymis usque adeo rigant super filio."

76. Greg. Tur., *Histories* 5.34, p. 240; the image recalls Vergil, *Aeneas* 4, l. 673, where Dido's sister beats her breast when she understands the real reason for the pyres, altars, and fires at Carthage.

77. Greg. Tur., *Histories* 5.34, p. 241: "Magnus quoque hic planctus omni populo fuit; nam viri lugentes mulieresque lucubribus vestimentis induit, ut solet in conjugum exsequiis fieri, ita hoc funus sunt prosecuti."

love and affection between spouses was no less great than that between parents and children. This expectation was very clear, for example, in Fortunatus's poem praising virginity, written on the occasion of Agnes's consecration as abbess of Holy Cross. The poem speaks of motherly and wifely love in precisely parallel terms. Both are intense, passionate, and—because of human mortality—bound to be disappointed. First Fortunatus invokes the feelings of the mother of a stillborn child: she is sad (*tristis*); she bewails (*dolens*) her double loss: her motherhood and her maidenhood. Unlike most mothers, whose own tears are comforted by the crying of the newborn, the mother of a stillborn can find no solace at all.[78] And what if her child lives, but not for long? Then the distraught mother, hair disheveled (*flagellatis . . . capillis*) "presses her dry breasts against the lips of her dead [child]. / Pouring out tears, she passionately revives her laments, / and she washes the cold body with a warm fountain [of tears]."[79] Like Radegund's nuns, like Fredegund, the bereaved mother clutches at her face, pulls her hair, beats her breast.

Tellingly, in the same poem by Fortunatus, this is not much different from the grieving gestures of the wife when her husband dies, though here sexual love adds additional pathos, as the new widow "holds the cold members for which she once glowed." She laments (*miserando*) before his tomb; she presses his bones; she mourns him (*luget*) with wet weeping (*fletibus inriguis*).[80]

With Fortunatus's easy blurring of the lines between this world and the next, consecrated virginity itself is envisioned as a passionate—and (happily) uniquely eternal—marriage. Christ the spouse speaks in this same poem on virginity, describing how Agnes waited for him: "She lay as though in vigil, in case I came from somewhere, / pressing her cold limbs on the now tepid marble. / She, turned to ice, preserved my fire in her bones. / While her inward parts are frozen, her breast glows with love [*amore*]. / Despising her body, she would sink down to the bare ground and, as she lay in

---

78. Fortunatus, *Poems* 8.3, ll. 342, 346, 348, ed. Reydellet, 2:144.

79. Fortunatus, *Poems* 8.3, ll. 359–62, ed. Reydellet, 2:145: "Triste flagellatis genetrix orbata capillis / defuncti in labiis ubera sicca premit; / infundens lacrimas lamenta resuscitat ardens / et gelidum corpus fonte tepente lavat."

80. Fortunatus, *Poems* 8.3, ll. 373–74, 377–78, 381, ed. Reydellet, 2:145: "De thalamo ad tumulum, modo candida, tam cito nigra / ante quibus caluit frigida membra tenet, / . . . Saepe maritalem repetit miserando sepulchrum / contemptaque domo funus amata colit. / . . . Fletibus inriguis, perituro carmine, luget."

self-forgetfulness, she remembered me. The humor of her cheeks exhausted by her continuous tears, / the earth swam with the waters from her [now] parched eyes. / And because living she was unable to see me by her carnal eyes, she lovingly [*amata*] sent up prayers."[81]

And there are more tears still when, in the middle of the poem, we read Agnes's purported "letter" to Christ, a sort of spousal counterpart to Radegund's plea to Amalfrid. Responding to the letter, Christ says: "When she lay on the ground, resting but not overcome by sleep, / I often lay down with her to take care of her. / I shared her grief [*condolui*]; I wiped away her river of tears [*lacrimarum flumina*], / giving her kisses [*oscula*] sweetened by shining honeycombs."[82] She is then elected into heaven and as queen joins Christ in the nuptial chamber.

We see the privileging of the same sort of emotional expression at Holy Cross itself. With less hyperbole than Fortunatus, but much the same approval, Baudonivia describes Radegund's love for Christ. The queen applied herself to her prayers, despised the throne of the fatherland, conquered the sweetness (*dulcedinem*) of marriage, and shut out worldly love (*caritatem mundialem*). If the king were to want her back, as she feared, she would prefer to end her life, because now she was in the embrace (*amplexus*) of the celestial King.[83] She "handed herself over to her celestial Spouse with such complete love [*toto amore*] that . . . she felt Christ to be an inhabitant within her."[84]

Similar sentiments, albeit expressed with still greater restraint, appear in Gregory's writings as well. Recall his depiction of the wedding night of Injuriosus and his bride. *Dulcis* is not the only emotion word in the tale. When the two lie down on the marriage bed together, she is very sad (*contristata*). Sighing, weeping copiously, she reveals that she had made marriage to

---

81. Fortunatus, *Poems* 8.3, ll. 211–20, ed. Reydellet, 2:138–39: "pervigil incubuit, si forte alicunde venirem, / marmore iam tepido frigida membra premens. / Haec gelifacta meum servavit in ossibus ignem: / visceribus rigidis pectus amore calet. / Corpore despecto recubabat in aggere nudo / seque oblita jacens me memor ipsa fuit. / Fletibus adsiduis exhausto humore genarum / siccatis oculis terra natabat aquis. / Et quia me vivens carnali lumine quondam / cernere non potuit, misit amata precem."

82. Fortunatus, *Poems* 8.3, ll. 253–56, ed. Reydellet, 2:140: "Cum recubaret humo neque victa sopore quievit, / consiliturus ei saepe simul jacui, / condolui pariter, lacrimarum flumina tersi, / oscula dans rutilis mellificata favis."

83. Baudonivia, *Vita Radegundis* 4, p. 381.

84. Ibid., 5, p. 382: "ita se toto amore caelesti tradidit Sponso, ut Deum mundo corde conplectens, Christum in se habitatorem esse sentiret."

Christ the centerpiece of her life.[85] Repudiating the vanities of the world with passion—they "horrify" (*horrent*) her; she "spits on" (*respuo*) the vast lands her husband holds—she makes the misery of her worldly marriage bed the inverse of the felicity of the marriage that counts. Marriage is a passionate affair; hers happens to be with Christ.[86]

Thus far we have looked only at celestial marriages. Brunhild's, however, is frankly of this world. Fortunatus considers how Sigibert and Brunhild must feel about one another before their wedding. The king is in love (*amans*), seized by fire (*igne*) for his bride. She desires (*cupit*) him as well, though modesty (*verecundia*) holds her back.[87] Cupid hovers over all, letting loose his "love-bearing" (*amoriferas*) arrows; he "inflames" (*perurit*) all creatures on earth, the commoners quickly, the king more slowly. At night, waiting for his Brunhild, Sigibert lies in the embraces (*per amplexum*) of the image of his wife-to-be.[88]

Did Sigibert really love Brunhild? It is impossible to know. But with William Reddy we may admit that in any case all emotions statements are approximations of the truth. Certainly we can be sure that Sigibert liked to hear that he loved his bride, that he was glad to have those assembled at his wedding imagine that he did, and that Fortunatus's poem evoked an emotional scenario pleasing to all. His epithalamium tells us about the image of married love prized at Sigibert's court.[89] That is information enough for the historian. Indeed, it is more valuable than knowing whether Sigibert loved Brunhild.

---

85. Greg. Tur., *Histories* 1.47, pp. 30–31.

86. Nevertheless even her worldly marriage is one of great tenderness—at least as Gregory tells it in Greg. Tur., *GC* 31, p. 317. Here the emphasis is on the end of the relationship. Even while lying dead in an open tomb, the wife gently teases her husband about their secret life of chastity. Not much later, the husband dies as well, and the two tombs, originally placed in different parts of a church, move together of their own accord. Thereafter the couple is known as "the two lovers" (*duos amantes*).

87. Fortunatus, *Poems* 6.1, ll. 51, 56–57, ed. Reydellet, 2:45–46: "Sigibertus amans Brunichilde carpitur igne; / . . . Hoc quoque virgo cupit, quamvis verecundia sexus / obstet . . ."

88. Fortunatus, *Poems* 6.1, ll. 37–46, ed. Reydellet, 2:45. Marital love was normative for Fortunatus: see ibid., 7.6, l. 27, p. 93, where the poet speaks of Duke Bodegisl's feelings for his wife Palatina: "Eligit e multis quam carus amaret amantem" (He [Bodegisl] chose from among many a loving [wife] whom the dear man might love).

89. On the importance of expressions of conjugal love in the sixth century (and their decline in the seventh) see Réal, *Vies de saints,* pp. 348–60.

Similarly we can never know if friends loved one another passionately. But we can be sure that they esteemed such bonds. They patronized Fortunatus because he expressed and celebrated such feelings in a most pleasing style.[90] When Fortunatus wrote about Duke Bodegisl, he said, "By your sweet speech you have satisfied the heart of a lover [*amantis*]: / For your words give food to me, your devoted one."[91] To *dux* Lupus he wrote: "What father and mother, brother, sister, the line of nephews— / what a locality could do—you fulfill by your dutiful love [*amore pio*]."[92] What exactly was fulfilled by this dutiful love? In a letter to Gogo, Fortunatus wrote: "You root out the groans [*gemitus*] of the afflicted and plant joys [*gaudia*]."[93] In the context, it was Fortunatus himself who had been "afflicted" and then made joyful. In a poem to Agnes, love was clearly desexualized through the evocation of family feeling: "Mother to me in honor, but sweet sister in love [*amore*] / whom I cherish [*colo*] with piety, faith, heart, and soul, / with celestial affection [*caelesti affectu*], not any sin of the body."[94] That love could tip into the sexual realm, however, everyone knew; hence the whispers that followed Fortunatus and Agnes.[95] Hence too the care Bishop Nicetius took not to allow his naked body to touch his grandnephew Gregory of Tours when he took the boy into bed with him to embrace him "with the sweetness of paternal affection" (*paternae dilectionis dulcedine*).[96]

---

90. On the aesthetic appeal of this kind of writing, see Michael Roberts, *The Jeweled Style: Poetry and Poetics in Late Antiquity* (Ithaca, N.Y., 1989). I am grateful to David Nirenberg for the reference.

91. Fortunatus, *Poems* 7.5, ll. 7–8, ed. Reydellet, 2:91: "Colloquio dulci satiasti pectus amantis: / nam mihi devoto dant tua verba cibum."

92. Fortunatus, *Poems* 7.9, ll. 11–12, ed. Reydellet, 2:101: "Quod pater ac genetrix, frater, soror, ordo nepotum, / quod poterat regio, solvis amore pio."

93. Fortunatus, *Poems* 7.1, l. 17, ed. Reydellet, 2:86: "Eruis adflictis gemitus et gaudia plantas."

94. Fortunatus, *Poems* 11.6, ll. 1–3, ed. Leo, p. 260: "Mater honore mihi, soror autem dulcis amore, / quam pietate fide pectore corde colo, / caelesti affectu, non crimine corporis ullo." Nevertheless, Franca Ela Consolino shows that Fortunatus borrowed without blushing the erotic vocabulary of pagan lyrical poetry to speak of the nuns at Holy Cross and his relationship to them; Consolino, "*Amor spiritualis* e linguaggio elegiaco nei *Carmina* di Venanzio Fortunato," *Annali della Scuola normale superiore di Pisa, classe di lettere e filosofia* 7 (1977): 1351–68.

95. It is alluded to precisely by Fortunatus's declaration that his love for Agnes is as if for a mother or sister. See George, *Venantius Fortunatus*, p. 173.

96. Greg. Tur., *VP* 8.2, p. 242. For more on the dangers and diversions of sexuality, see Shanzer, "History, Romance, Love, and Sex."

Relationships were understood to be fragile, whether due to sexual danger (as in the case of Agnes and Fortunatus) or distance (as in the case of most of Fortunatus's other literary recipients). The solution was not to forgo love; to the contrary, it was to reaffirm it continually. Fortunatus did not break off with Agnes nor suggest prudence: rather he ended his poem by vowing to live as he always had—that is, as close to Agnes as before—"as long as you wish me to be cherished with sweet love [*dulci amore*]."[97] To Gregory he wrote a poem full of feeling: Gregory "is light for my love [*lumen amore meo*]" and holds "the pledge of my friendship [*amicitiae meae*]" in his heart. "I pray," Fortunatus concludes, "that you be mindful I am yours [*me memor esse tuum*]."[98] Yet this entire poem was also sent to a Bishop Baudoaldus.[99] Keeping old fires burning was extremely important.[100] This had nothing to do with spontaneity or sincerity.[101]

It was thus a rather small step to go from passionate friendships to public forms of love. We have already seen that Gregory's idea of the funeral cortege for Fredegund's son was modeled on that of grieving widows. On a happier note, Fortunatus imagined Gogo residing at court with his "school of acolytes gathered before him, applauding [him] out of love [*amore*]."[102] Many of Fortunatus's poems evoked regional leaders—whether episcopal or

---

97. Fortunatus, *Poems* 11.6, ll. 15–16, ed. Leo, p. 261: "sed tamen est animus simili me vivere voto, / si vos me dulci vultis amore coli."

98. Fortunatus, *Poems* 5.12, ed. Reydellet, 2:38.

99. Fortunatus, *Poems* 9.8, ed. Leo, p. 215. Nothing certain is known about Baudoaldus: see Louis Duchesne, *Fastes épiscopaux de l'ancienne Gaule,* vol. 2, *L'Aquitaine et les Lyonnaises,* 2d ed. (Paris, 1910), p. 477 n. 3.

100. Michael Roberts calls attention to the role of letters as substitutes for physical contact in "Venantius Fortunatus; Elegy on the 'The Death of Galswintha' (*Carm.* 6.5)," in *Society and Culture in Late Antique Gaul,* ed. Mathisen and Shanzer, p. 308. See Fortunatus, *Poems* 6.5, l. 227, ed. Reydellet, 2:69: "Saepe tamen missis dulci sibi dulcis adhaesit" (Often Radegund sweetly clung to her [Galswintha's] sweet self in letters). On the association of friendship with warmth, see Epp, *Amicitia,* pp. 60–61, and on the importance of letter writing to stoke the fires, pp. 62–64. See also Ian Wood, "Letters and Letter-Collections from Antiquity to the Early Middle Ages: The Prose Works of Avitus of Vienne," in *The Culture of Christendom: Essays in Medieval History in Commemoration of Denis L. T. Bethell,* ed. Marc Anthony Meyer (London, 1993), pp. 29–43.

101. On this point, consider the observation in Reddy, *Navigation of Feeling,* p. 109, that sincerity is a "specialized skill" cultivated among certain groups only under particular historical conditions.

102. Fortunatus, *Poems* 7.4, l. 26, ed. Reydellet, 2:90: "cui scola congrediens plaudit amore sequax."

lay—loving and being loved by their people, along the lines of his poem on Gregory's consecration. In a poem about Lupus, Fortunatus claimed that "if anyone carried sorrow [*maestitiam*] in his troubled breast, / after he sees you he persists in better hope."[103] On behalf of King Charibert, he called on the people of Paris to "love [*dilige*] him who reigns in your high citadel / and cherish the protector who offers aid to you. / Embrace [*amplectere*] him now with eager hands, joyfully cherishing [*favens*] him / who is your lord by right but your father by loving kindness [*pietate*]."[104] Bishops were regularly invoked as fathers beloved by their children. To Bishop Carentinus of Cologne Fortunatus wrote, "You comfort the hearts of all with sweet words. / You make sad hearts happy by your visage. / You are food to the poor, drink to the thirsty. / Rightly you are father of the people [*pater populi*], because you give the treasure of salvation."[105]

TURNING LOVE TO HATE

The effusions of love in the work of Fortunatus are difficult to reconcile with the rapacity, odiousness, and fury that pepper the pages of Gregory's *Histories*. But that is because Gregory tended to emphasize the subversion of loving norms and expectations rather than celebrate them.[106] He concentrated on the moments in which the familial model broke down. Thus we read in the *Histories* a whole series of incidents that illustrate hatred rather than love, starting right with biblical times, when Joseph's visions caused his brothers to feel envy (*invidia*) and hatred (*odium*) against him.[107] More recently, Queen Marcatrude, the second wife of King Guntram, was jealous (*aemula*) of his son by his first wife and poisoned the boy. She deserved to lose her own child and incur the hatred (*odium*) of the king.[108] King Alboin

---

103. Fortunatus, *Poems* 7.7, ll. 9–10, ed. Reydellet, 2:94: "Maestitiam si quis confuso in pectore gessit, / postquam te vidit spe meliore manet."

104. Fortunatus, *Poems* 6.2, ll. 9–12, ed. Reydellet, 2:53: "Dilige regnantem celsa, Parisius, arce / et cole tutorem qui tibi praebet opem. / Hunc modo laeta favens avidis amplectere palmis / qui iure est dominus, sed pietate pater."

105. Fortunatus, *Poems* 3.14, ll. 17–20, ed. Reydellet, 1:113: "Pectora cunctorum reficis dulcedine verbi, / laetificas vultu tristia corda tuo. / Pauperibus cibus es, sed et esurientibus esca, / rite pater populi dando salutis opem."

106. This is rather close to what Godman, *Poets and Emperors*, p. 29, argues in his analysis of Fortunatus's poem praising Chilperic, where he suggests that Fortunatus gives the ideal, Gregory the reality, based on precisely the same criteria.

107. Greg. Tur., *Histories* 1.9, p. 10.

108. Ibid., 4.25, p. 156.

of the Lombards married a woman "whose father he had killed a little while before. Thus the woman always hated her husband [*in odio habens*] and was waiting for the moment when she could avenge the wrong done to her father."[109] Even public love could turn to hate: thus Bishop Quintianus of Rodez was expelled from his city "out of hatred [*odium*]" because the people feared he favored a Frankish takeover.[110]

Odium is far from exhausting Gregory's thesaurus of unloving emotion words. Consider an episode involving King Sigismund of Burgundy. His second wife was "strongly against" (*valide contra*) Sigeric, the son of his first wife. When she put on the very clothes of Sigeric's mother, the boy was "moved by gall" (*commotus felle*) and told her she was "not worthy" (*non digna*) to wear them. Then the woman, "raging with fury" (*furore succensa*) went to Sigismund to accuse Sigeric of treason. She incited the king by her words (*instigat verbis*) to kill his son. The family drama here was written up as a crescendo-decrescendo of resentment, beginning with the relatively pale *contra*, coming to a climax with *furor*, and dying out with *instigo*. In the very next sentence the emotional tone was entirely different as Sigismund repented (*paenetens*) and, falling over the dead body, began to weep (*flere*) bitterly.[111]

The very core of Gregory's emotional stance in the *Histories*, the anguish (*dolor animo*) that he records feeling about the civil wars of his day, is above all the pain of seeing brother fighting brother.[112] The first mention of civil war comes in the third book of the *Histories*, when Childebert and Theudebert, sons of Clovis, unite against their brother Clothar. As soon as Queen Clotild heard about it, Gregory tells us, "she went to the tomb of the blessed Martin . . . praying that civil war not arise between her sons."[113] Only once in the ten times that Gregory uses the term "civil war" does he *not* tie it to fraternal discord: in the instance of Sichar and Chramnesind, the both loving and feuding citizens of Tours whom we met above.[114] But here

---

109. Ibid., 4.41, p. 174: "[Alboenus] duxit conjugem, cuius patrem ante paucum tempus interfecerat. Qua de causa mulier in odio semper virum habens, locum opperiebat, in quo possit injurias patris ulcisci."

110. Ibid., 2.36, p. 84.

111. Ibid., 3.5, pp. 100–101.

112. Ibid., 4.50, p. 187.

113. Ibid., 3.28, p. 124: "beati Martini sepulchrum adiit, ibique in oratione prosternitur et tota nocte vigilat, orans, ne inter filios suos bellum civile consurgeret."

114. Ibid., 7.47, p. 366. See note 51 above.

too Gregory assimilated the events to a family drama. Initially unable to get the two sides to agree on terms (this was before the two men became good friends), Gregory preached: "We have lost sons of the church [*aeclesiae filios*].... Be peaceful sons [*filii pacifici*]."[115] We have seen how he conceived of their subsequent "fraternal" relationship and its breakup.

Both Gregory and Fortunatus were aware that love and hatred could be manipulated. Gregory's irony was based on just this fact. When he quoted King Clovis as complaining, "Woe is me who remain like a pilgrim among foreigners and have no relatives to help me if adversity comes," he thought the sentiments were pure pretense: "But he said this not sorrowing [*condolens*] about the death [of his relatives] but with deceit, [to see] if he could find anyone left to kill."[116] Less cynically but no less surely, Fortunatus knew that he was creating a dreamworld, an idyll, which his patrons willingly entered with a bit of good humor on all sides. But the norms were there, ready to be felt, or they could not have been exaggerated and celebrated by Fortunatus, ironized and unmasked by Gregory.

EMOTIONAL REFUGES

Thus Fortunatus and Gregory belonged to the same emotional community—or, rather, the same Christian, Gallic "subordinate" community in the sense discussed in this book's introduction. They exploited its possibilities in different ways. Because of his episcopal duties, his own self-interest, and perhaps, indeed, his character, Gregory focused on love gone sour. It is not by accident that the original sin that *he* emphasized was Cain's envy (*invidia*), which led to fratricide. "Then," Gregory said, "the whole human race fell to ruin in execrable crimes."[117] Fortunatus played the same strings more sweetly. His civil wars were due to too much love, mismanaged love. Thus Chilperic's warmongering was delicately blamed on his father's favoritism: "On you, sweet head, hung every solicitude of your father; / among so many brothers, you were in this way his one love [*amor unus*]."[118] It was fate

---

115. Ibid., 7.47, p. 367.
116. Ibid., 2.42, p. 93: "'Vae mihi, qui tamquam peregrinus inter extraneus remansi et non habeo de parentibus, qui mihi si venerit adversitas, possit aliquid adiuvare.' Sed hoc non de morte horum condolens, sed dolo dicebat, si forte potuisset adhuc aliquem repperire, ut interficeret."
117. Ibid., 1.3, p. 6: "Exhinc cunctum genus in facinus exsecrabile ruit."
118. Fortunatus, *Poems* 9.1, ll. 33–34, ed. Leo, p. 202: "in te, dulce caput, patris omnis cura perpendit; /inter tot fratres sic amor unus eras."

that was envious (*sors invida*), "shattering the spirits of the people and the treaties of the brothers."[119] It is perfectly possible to talk about Merovingian politics as a matter of interest and power rather than family.[120] That no one at the time did so is evidence of the dominance of the particular emotional assumptions that they lived by.

Fortunatus's poems seem designed to present in extreme form the expressive possibilities of his emotional community. If we consider Dynamius's *Life of Maximius,* for example, we see hugs and kisses, fear, love, tears, sorrow, and joy, but not so great a range of vocabulary or richness of imagery as in, for example, Fortunatus's versified *Life of St. Martin*.[121] Fortunatus too could write in a more restrained manner, as he did his in his own *Life of Radegund,* written before Baudonivia's version. Here there are kisses and tears, but no hugs; there are words for love, sorrow, happiness, fear, and anger (on the part of the king), but not for anxiety, laughter, sighs, blushing, furor, or shame, as we find in his larger corpus.[122] Recall Ekman's basic emotions, discussed in chapter 1; we are not far from his short list in Fortunatus's *Life of Radegund*.

Rather than postulate, with Reddy, emotional regimes separate from emotional refuges, we may thus imagine that one emotional community is capable of creating refuges within itself—at its extremes. On one end were Fortunatus's poems, which allowed men and women to sink momentarily and with pleasure into a welter of "classicized" feelings, passionately evoked, brilliantly expressed. On the other were the *Histories* of the cynical bishop of Tours, reminding all how emotions could be—and had been—dissembled and managed for effect, but also deeply felt. We can easily see how Fortunatus could serve as a "refuge"—in Reddy's sense—for Gregory. In Fortunatus's emotion-laden account of Avitus of Clermont's "conversion" of the Jews, written, as we saw above, at Gregory's request, the Jews were stinking (*iudaeus odor amarus*) and pricked by fury (*stimulante furore*).

---

119. Fortunatus, *Poems* 9.1, l. 41, 43, ed. Leo, p. 202: "concutiens animos populorum et foedera fratrum."

120. This is precisely the argument in Stephen D. White, "Clothild's Revenge: Politics, Kinship, and Ideology in the Merovingian Blood Feud," in *Portraits of Medieval and Renaissance Living: Essays in Memory of David Herlihy,* ed. Samuel K. Cohn Jr. and Steven A. Epstein (Ann Arbor, 1996), pp. 107–30.

121. Venantius Fortunatus, *Vita Sancti Martini,* in *Venance Fortunat, Oeuvres,* vol. 4, *Vie de saint Martin,* ed. and trans. Solange Quesnel (Paris, 1996). It is, to be sure, a very substantial work, and thus perhaps unfairly compared to Dynamius's short *Vita*.

122. Fortunatus, *Vita Sanctae Radegundis,* pp. 364–77.

The bishop, out of "love of God" (*in amore Dei*) admonished them to convert, speaking gently (*blande*), overcome by pity (*miserando*). In the end, he gave them the choice of conversion or expulsion, and the Jewish odor was washed away in the waters of baptism.[123] Gregory wrote about the same event in the *Histories*, but he reserved emotions for the end, where the bishop "cried for joy" and the people rejoiced.[124] It is thus easy to understand that Fortunatus's expressive powers added to the pleasures of the bishop.

There is evidence that Gregory served as a refuge for his friend in turn, though a refuge perhaps more practical than emotional. When Fortunatus was sick with fever, he asked "Doctor Gregory" to bring him aid.[125] After Agnes died and a rebellion broke out at Holy Cross under the new abbess, the anguished poet wrote to Gregory to intervene, invoking their shared love of Radegund, "your daughter and now your mother" (*filiae vel iam matris vestrae*), and looking to the bishop to act like another Martin.[126] We have already seen how Fortunatus turned to Gregory when he met parents mourning over their enslaved daughter.

Gregory, Fortunatus, Baudonivia, and others of their cohort were far more at ease with emotions—all sorts of emotions—than was Gregory the Great. Although they all belonged to a common Christian culture—anticipating the joys of heaven, demoting the pleasures of the world—nevertheless the differences in their emotional assumptions and styles, and thus their religious expression as well, are striking. To be sure, all saw the family as the locus of powerful emotions, but Gregory the Great wanted those feelings to be countered and reversed. The pope had one emotional template—he prized the emotional community of the City of God alone—and wanted all to be assimilated into it. Fortunatus and Gregory of Tours had a broader emotional palette.

One reason for this may have been their easygoing assumption about the closeness of the earthly and heavenly kingdoms.[127] The two friends saw

---

123. Fortunatus, *Poems* 5.5b, ll. 19, 23, 34, 73, 85, 104, ed. Reydellet, 2:21–24.
124. Greg. Tur., *Histories* 5.11, p. 206.
125. Fortunatus, *Poems* 8.11, l. 1, ed. Reydellet, 2:153.
126. Fortunatus, *Poems* 8.12 and 8.12a, ed. Reydellet, 2:154–55.
127. Giselle de Nie argues forcefully for the "continuum between physical and spiritual reality" in the writings of Gregory; de Nie, *Views from a Many-Windowed Tower: Studies of Imagination in the Works of Gregory of Tours* (Amsterdam, 1987), p. 158.

worldly emotions slide easily into precisely similar feelings about God. Fortunatus reveled in the passions of an Agnes for Christ, and of Christ for Agnes. His lovers burned with ardor, whether they were marrying at the court of Metz or awaiting one another after death at the convent of the Holy Cross. While Gregory the Great spoke of the plague carrying off little children as a temptation for overmuch love, Gregory of Tours lamented in a famous passage about an epidemic of dysentery: "And indeed, when this disease first began in the month of August, it snatched our young ones and sent them to their bed. We lost our sweet and dear little children, whom we caressed in our laps and carried in our arms and fed with our own hands.... But, wiping away our tears, we say with blessed Job, 'The Lord gave; the Lord hath taken away'" (Job 1:21).[128] He did not upbraid himself and his contemporaries for weeping.

The emotional community of Fortunatus and Gregory did not worry about "annoying" thoughts. That idea came from the ascetic tradition of the Desert Fathers, and neither Fortunatus nor Gregory were ascetics.[129] But Baudonivia, whose convent of the Holy Cross followed the strict rule of Caesarius of Arles, was potentially heir to that tradition.[130] Yet she showed no signs of its influence in her writing. While in Gregory the Great's world feelings were acceptable only when they were put to proper use—to achieve salvation for oneself or another—in Baudonivia's world all sorts of emotions that were "useless" for the pope were recognized and, if not celebrated, nevertheless unabashedly memorialized. Yet for all their differences, one could "move" easily between the emotional communities of the aristocrats of Austrasia and papal Romans: Dynamius of Marseille, for example, patron of Fortunatus and writer of at least one saint's *Life*, also corre-

---

128. Greg. Tur., *Histories* 5.34, p. 239: "Et quidem primum haec infirmetas a mense Augusto initiata, parvulus aduliscentes arripuit lectoque subegit. Perdedemus dulcis et caros nobis infantulos, quos aut gremiis fovimus aut ulnis baiolavimus aut propria manu, ministratis cibis, ipsos studio sagatiore nutrivimus. Sed, abstersis lacrimis, cum beato Job dicimus: 'Dominus dedit, Dominus abstulit.'"

129. Though, on occasion Gregory adopted some of the rhetorical strategies of the ascetics; see Conrad Leyser, "'Divine Power Flowed from this Book': Ascetic Language and Episcopal Authority in Gregory of Tours' *Life of the Fathers*," in *The World of Gregory of Tours*, ed. Kathleen Mitchell and Ian Wood (Leiden, 2002), pp. 283–94.

130. For Caesarius's asceticism see, most conveniently, William Klingshirn, *Caesarius of Arles: The Making of a Christian Community in Late Antique Gaul* (Cambridge, 1994); and Leyser, *Authority and Asceticism*, chap. 4.

sponded with Pope Gregory the Great.[131] The same was true of Queen Brunhild and her grandsons.[132]

The emotional community of men like Fortunatus and Gregory of Tours may be related to the royal family structure and its fragility in the second half of the sixth century. Brothers and half-brothers shared a kingdom whose theoretical unity is suggested by Baudonivia's frequent use of the word *patria,* fatherland. However fragmented it may have been in reality, it was understood to be a whole.[133] Its rulers, governors, and rectors needed the tools and metaphors of family bonding to keep this myth in place. Sigibert and Brunhild, with their imperial pretensions and their monogamous union, required this emotional reinforcement the most keenly. At the same time, they would not have felt the need had not the emotional assumptions privileging family feeling already been in place. Families are social constructions, and the Merovingian family was more manufactured than most, with its multiple royal partners and children.[134] Merovingians were quite adept at recognizing family relations when it suited them and forgetting them when they did not.[135] But they could not have wanted to invoke those relations at all, nor would they have been effective in doing so, if family feeling were not already a normative sentiment.

Thus the emotional community represented by Fortunatus and his patrons reinforced the goals of the ruling elite while itself helping to determine those goals. But in 613 the old regime came to an end when Austrasia was taken over by the Neustrian king Clothar II, son of Fredegund. The emotional community that next came to the fore was strikingly new.

---

131. Gregory I, *Registrum* 3.33, CCSL 140, p. 179.

132. For Brunhild, see, e.g., ibid., 8.4, CCSL 140A, pp. 518–21, referring (on p. 519) to letters that he had received from the queen in turn; for Theudebert II and Theuderic II, see, e.g., ibid., 6.51, CCSL 140, pp. 423–24.

133. Baudonivia, *Vita Radegundis* 4 and 10, p. 381: "despexit sedem patriae" (she despised the throne of the fatherland); p. 384: "et patria ne periret" (and the fatherland not perish). Gregory of Tours always used the singular *regnum* to refer to the Merovingian realm, even though we rightly see that it was divided into plural *regna*: on this point see de Nie, *Views from a Many-Windowed Tower,* p. 63, and compare with the title of Wood, *Merovingian Kingdoms.*

134. Ian Wood, "Deconstructing the Merovingian Family," in *The Construction of Communities in the Early Middle Ages: Texts, Resources and Artifacts,* ed. Richard Corradini, Max Diesenberger, and Helmut Reimitz (Leiden, 2002), pp. 149–71.

135. See White, "Clothild's Revenge."

5
COURTLY DISCIPLINE

When in 613 Clothar II defeated the dowager queen of Austrasia, Brunhild, and her remaining grandson—uniting the Merovingian kingdoms under his aegis—he had the old woman tortured, paraded on the back of a camel, and kicked to pieces by a wild horse.[1] It was a graphic signal of regime change. With political displacement came a transformation in emotional tenor. Gone were the effusive affirmations of family feeling, love, and sweetness, so characteristic of the Austrasian court's emotional style. Gone, indeed, was much of the old emotional vocabulary. There must have been people who still used the old words in the same old way. But they remain below the historians' radar. What we see, rather, is a new—and reticent—emotional community connected to the Neustrian court.

MONKS, KINGS, AND COURTIERS

We must begin with Columbanus (d. 615), the fierce Irish monk who came to the Continent circa 591.[2] This is because Columbanus's enmities became the enmities of the new regime, while his friends, followers, and disciples included most members of the royal court, including the kings and queens. As we shall see, a rich cluster of texts was produced by the social community connected to the courts of Clothar (d. 629), his son Dagobert I (d. 639), and the latter's two sons, Sigibert III (d. ca. 656) and Clovis II (d. 657). Key to this community's values—and even, to some extent, its emotional norms—was the inspiration of Columbanus.

Much of Columbanus's youth was spent under the tutelage of Irish monks. Inspired by the Desert Fathers, Irish monasticism nevertheless had its own peculiarities. Like earlier ascetics, Irish monks put emphasis on penance and prayer. But they also cultivated booklearning, elaborated the

---

1. Fredegar, *Chronicle* 4:42, in *The Fourth Book of the Chronicle of Fredegar with Its Continuations,* ed. and trans. J. M. Wallace-Hadrill (London, 1960), p. 35.
2. On Columbanus's life see Donald Bullough, "The Career of Columbanus," in *Columbanus: Studies on the Latin Writings,* ed. Michael Lapidge (Woodbridge, 1997), pp. 1–28.

practice of exile, and fostered a system of private penance. Columbanus's trip to the Continent was his version of exile, and for his newly founded continental houses of Annegray, Luxeuil, Fontaines, and Bobbio he wrote rules that included private penance.[3] What was most peculiar about these monasteries in the Gallic context was their emplacement in the countryside rather than in or near urban centers. This gave them a special role in royal networks of power, one eventually institutionalized by "immunities," which recognized a monastery's privilege from interference by royal officials and local bishops.[4]

Once in Gaul, Columbanus made himself well known at royal courts. Indeed, when he first arrived he was welcomed by a king who begged him to stay: "Do not cross over to our neighbors, leaving the soil of our jurisdiction."[5] Jonas, author of the *Life of Columbanus,* had his reasons for pretending that the king speaking these words was Sigibert I, but in fact that cannot be right, since Columbanus arrived on the Continent fifteen years after Sigibert's death.[6] Rather, the speaker must have been Sigibert's brother Guntram or, possibly, Sigibert's son, Childebert II, who took over Austrasia and Burgundy after Guntram's death in 593.[7] In any event, Columbanus did remain, as the king had begged him, and founded Annegray. Later he founded Luxeuil with the support of Childebert II.[8] But after he refused to bless the children of one of Childebert's sons, Theuderic II—they were brought out to him for that express purpose by their great-grandmother,

---

3. For an overview, see Jane Barbara Stevenson, "The Monastic Rules of Columbanus," in *Columbanus,* ed. Lapidge, pp. 203–16.

4. Barbara H. Rosenwein, *Negotiating Space: Power, Restraint, and Privileges of Immunity in Early Medieval Europe* (Ithaca, N.Y., 1999).

5. Jonas, *Vitae Columbani abbatis discipulorumque eius* (hereafter *Vita Columbani*) 1.6, ed. Bruno Krusch, MGH SRM 4:72: "ne, nostrae ditionis solo relicto, ad vicinas pertranseas nationes."

6. The reasons have to do with Jonas's partisanship on behalf of Clothar II, as Ian Wood makes clear in "Jonas, the Merovingians, and Pope Honorius: *Diplomata* and the *Vita Columbani,*" in *After Rome's Fall: Narrators and Sources of Early Medieval History: Essays Presented to Walter Goffart,* ed. Alexander Callander Murray (Toronto, 1998), pp. 111–12. On the structure and purposes of the *Vita Columbani,* see Clare Stancliffe, "Jonas's *Life of Columbanus and his Disciples,*" in *Studies in Irish Hagiography: Saints and Scholars,* ed. Máire Herbert, John Carey, and Pádraig Ó Riain (Dublin, 2001), pp. 189–220.

7. See Wood, "Jonas, the Merovingians, and Pope Honorius," pp. 105–6.

8. For royal involvement in the foundation of Luxeuil, see Wood, "Jonas, the Merovingians, and Pope Honorius," pp. 107–8.

Brunhild—he was expelled, as Jonas put it, from that "jurisdiction."⁹ From then on, Brunhild and Theuderic were vilified in the sources connected to the Neustrian court and to Columbanus.

Before making his way to Italy to found the monastery of Bobbio in 613, Columbanus visited Clothar II. This was just prior to the Neustrian king's triumph over Brunhild. Clothar immediately became Columbanus's partisan. Jonas stressed the importance of the meeting: "When [the king] saw him, he received him as a gift from heaven, and, rejoicing, he begged Columbanus to reside within the boundaries of his kingdom if he liked, and [the king said that] he himself, as he wished to do, would wait upon [the monk]."¹⁰ Columbanus refused to stay for long, but he did not depart before putting his stamp on the court: "Castigated by Columbanus on account of certain failings—in which hardly any royal court is lacking—Clothar responded that he would emend everything in accordance with [the monk's] command."¹¹ The court became a nursery for Columbanian supporters. Its restrained emotional character—the feelings and modes of expression that it privileged and the many that it did not—contrasts with the exuberance of Gregory of Tours and his associates.

Clothar asked Columbanus to return to Francia, but the reformer was now committed to Bobbio. The king nevertheless became the protector of Luxeuil, the most important of Columbanus's Gallic monasteries.¹² Clothar's son and grandsons went on to support, among other Columbanian foundations, Solignac, Rebais, Stablo-Malmedy, Lagny, and Nant.¹³

---

9. Jonas, *Vita Columbani* 1.20, p. 91.

10. Ibid., 1.24, p. 98: "Quem cum vidisset, velut caelestem munus recepit, ovansque precatur, ut, si velit, intra sui regni terminos resedeat, seque ei, prout voluerit, famulaturum."

11. Ibid.: "castigatusque ab eo ob quibusdam erroribus, quos vix aula regia caret, spondit se Chlotharius iuxta eius imperium omnia emendaturum."

12. For Clothar's support of Luxeuil, see Jonas, *Vita Columbani* 1.30, p. 108, where Columbanus asks the king "regali adminiculo ac presidio foveret" (to favor it with royal support and protection), which the king fulfills: "Omni presidio supradictum monasterium munire studet, annuis censibus ditat, terminos undique, prout voluntas venerabilis Eusthasii erat, auget omnique conatu ad auxilium inibi habitantium ob viri Dei amorem intendit." (He was zealous to defend the monastery with every protection, endowed it with an annual tax, expanded its boundaries everywhere—as was the wish of the venerable [Abbot] Eustasius—and made every effort to help those living within on account of his love for the man of God.)

13. For Solignac, see *Vita Eligii episcopi Noviomagensis* 1.15, ed. Bruno Krusch, MGH SRM 4:680–81; its foundation charter is printed on pp. 746–49; for Rebais, see *Diplomata, Chartae, Epistolae, Leges,* ed. Jean Marie Pardessus, 2 vols. (1843; repr., Aalen, 1969), 2:39–41, no.

But it would be wrong to see these as purely royal foundations; rather, they were group projects, created by the kings and their courtiers. Who were these courtiers? Consider the brothers Rado, Ado, and Dado (the latter also known as Audoenus, the future St. Ouen). As boys, all three—unlike the great-grandchildren of Brunhild—were blessed by Columbanus. They went on to propagate Columbanian monasticism. Ado founded Jouarre, Rado founded "Radolium," and Dado founded Rebais.[14] But they were also important men at court: Rado was treasurer under Dagobert and very likely referendary (a sort of proto-chancellor) under Clovis II.[15] Dado was a man-at-arms under Dagobert, later becoming the king's referendary.[16] Thus kings and courtiers worked together to support Columbanus and his monasteries. They formed a tight network that we can dimly see in witness lists: Dado and Rado, for example, appeared together as signatories of the foundation charter for Solignac, drawn up in the name of Eligius.[17] Eligius himself served as goldsmith and minter for Clothar, diplomat for Dagobert, and royal adviser at the court of Clovis II's wife, Balthild, even as he presided as bishop over the see of Noyon.[18]

Eligius's career well illustrates the fact that although many of the courtiers became bishops, they remained the king's men.[19] Episcopal appointments

---

275 (Burgundofaro's exemption, which mentions the king); and Rosenwein, *Negotiating Space*, p. 69; for Stablo-Malmedy and Lagny, see Friedrich Prinz, *Frühes Mönchtum im Frankenreich: Kultur und Gesellschaft in Gallien, den Rheinlanden und Bayern am Beispiel der monastischen Entwicklung (4. bis 8. Jahrhundert)*, 2d ed. (Munich, 1988), p. 149; for Nant see *Vita Amandi* 1.23, ed. Bruno Krusch, MGH SRM 5:445. For more on royal patronage of Columbanian monasticism, see Ian Wood, "The *Vita Columbani* and Merovingian Hagiography," *Peritia* 1 (1982): 63–80; idem, "Jonas, the Merovingians, and Pope Honorius"; Prinz, *Frühes Mönchtum*.

14. For Jouarre and Rebais, see Jonas, *Vita Columbani* 1.26, p. 100; for "Radolium," see *Vita Agili* 6 [recte 4], AASS August VI, p. 582.

15. Horst Ebling, *Prosopographie der Amtsträger des Merowingerreiches von Chlothar II. (613) bis Karl Martell (741)* (Munich, 1974), pp. 201–2, no. 258.

16. Richard A. Gerberding, *The Rise of the Carolingians and the "Liber Historiae Francorum"* (Oxford, 1987), p. 85, and for Dado's social network, pp. 86–87.

17. For the charter, see note 13 above.

18. See Hayo Vierck, "L'oeuvre de saint Eloi, orfèvre, et son rayonnement," in *La Neustrie. Les pays au nord de la Loire, de Dagobert à Charles le Chauve (VIIe–IXe siècle)*, ed. Patrick Périn and Laure-Charlotte Feffer (Rouen, 1985), pp. 403–9; *Vita Eligii* 1.9, p. 676; 2.32, p. 717; Wood, *Merovingian Kingdoms*, pp. 150–51.

19. For a list of the bishops who were originally courtiers at the Neustrian court, see Carlo Servatius, "'Per ordinationem principis ordinetur.' Zum Modus der Bishofsernennung im

were almost always made by royal fiat. Consider Desiderius, treasurer under both Clothar and Dagobert. We have two charters from Dagobert ("reworked" but probably essentially authentic) appointing him bishop of Cahors and asking Sulpicius, the bishop of Bourges and former *elemosinarius* (royal alms-giver) of the palace, to perform his consecration.[20] Another bishop, Amandus, may serve as a particularly striking example of royal and episcopal coordination. A man with missionary ambitions, he was "forced [*coactus*] by the king"—in this case Clothar II—to become a bishop of no particular see.[21] Determined to preach to the pagans living along the Scheldt River, he petitioned for—and received—letters from Dagobert demanding that "if anyone did not willingly consent [*sponte . . . voluisset*] to be born again through the waters of baptism," he was to be compelled (*coactus*) by the king to submit to it.[22] Amandus was so successful a missionary that the people of the region destroyed their sanctuaries "with their own hands." In their place Amandus, supported by "the munificence of the king," built monasteries and churches.[23] Although he was subsequently exiled by Dagobert for upbraiding the king about the latter's "capital crimes," he was soon forgiven and recalled to baptize and serve as godfather to Dagobert's son Sigibert. When at first Amandus hesitated to take on this role, Dagobert had his courtiers Eligius and Dado importune him. The mission of these, his cocourtiers, succeeded.[24] Later, when the bishopric of Maastricht came open, Amandus was yet again "forced [*coactus*] by the king" to take the position.[25]

Jonas, the author of the *Life of Columbanus* and other important hagiographical texts, was a member of this courtier-ecclesiastical group. Born in Susa, he became a monk at Bobbio a few years after Columbanus's death

---

Edikt Chlothars II vom Jahre 614," *Zeitschrift für Kirchengeschichte* 84 (1973): 1–29, with list on pp. 16–17.

20. The charters are MGH D Merov., ed. Theo Kölzer (Hannover, 2001), pt. 1, nos. 37, 38; for Desiderius, see Ebling, *Prosopographie,* pp. 126–27, no. 142; for Sulpicius, see *Vita Sulpicii episcopi Biturigi,* ed. Bruno Krusch, MGH SRM 4: 371–80. He was at Clothar's court in 620 and, appointed bishop of Bourges in 624, remained in that position until his death in 646/7.

21. *Vita Amandi* 1.8, p. 434. On Amandus see Ian Wood, *The Missionary Life: Saints and the Evangelisation of Europe 400–1050* (Harlow, 2001), pp. 38–42.

22. *Vita Amandi* 1.13, p. 437: "vir sanctus . . . ad Aicharium episcopum . . . adiit eique humiliter postulavit, ut si quis se non sponte per baptismi lavacrum regenerare voluisset, coactus a rege sacro ablueretur baptismate. Quod ita factum est."

23. Ibid., 1.15, p. 439.

24. Ibid., 1.17, pp. 440–41.

25. Ibid., 1.18, p. 442.

there. In the late 630s, he joined Amandus in Maastricht, assisting him for three years.[26] Shortly thereafter, he published the *Life of Columbanus*, which, among many other things, was a clearly partisan piece on behalf of Clothar's dynasty, particularly through its denigration of Brunhild and her progeny. At the time that he wrote the *Life*, Jonas was important at the royal court as a supporter of Clovis's queen, Balthild. She was a well-known sponsor of monastic reform in what by then was considered to be the Columbanian "tradition."[27] Very likely Jonas himself became abbot of Marchiennes, one of Amandus's monasteries.[28]

We thus may dimly perceive a community of courtiers, former courtiers, and their hangers-on, lasting from about 614 to mid-century, with the bulk of their writings coming from the 630s and 640s. They formed a group that was evidently tightly bound by ties of affection but nevertheless wary of effusive emotional expression. The point may be illustrated by the letter collection of Desiderius, whom we have already met as royal treasurer and bishop of Cahors.[29]

A word, first, must be said about letters and letter collections.[30] The epistolary art had certain conventions—and much room for play.[31] A letter,

---

26. Jonas, *Vita Columbani* epist., p. 62.

27. Rosenwein, *Negotiating Space*. In Jonas, *Vita Johannis abbatis Reomaensis*, ed. Bruno Krusch, MGH SRM 3:505, the author speaks of a lengthy trip he took in the area of Chalon "at the order" (*ex jusso*) of prince Clothar III and his mother, Balthild.

28. On Jonas's career, see Adalbert de Vogüé's, introduction to Jonas de Bobbio, *Vie de Saint Colomban et de ses disciples*, trans. Adalbert de Vogüé (Bégrolles-en-Mauges, 1988), pp. 19–23.

29. Desiderius of Cahors, *Epistulae*, in *Epistulae S. Desiderii Cadurcensis*, ed. Dag Norberg, Studia Latina Stockholmiensia 6 (Stockholm, 1961) (hereafter Desiderius, *Ep.*). On the single late eighth- or early ninth-century manuscript in which we find this collection, see Ralph W. Mathisen, "The *Codex Sangallensis* 190 and the Transmission of the Classical Tradition during Late Antiquity and the Early Middle Ages," *International Journal of the Classical Tradition* 5 (1998): 163–94. See also his remarks on the manuscript in *Ruricius of Limoges and Friends: A Collection of Letters from Visigothic Gaul*, trans. Ralph W. Mathisen, Translated Texts for Historians 30 (Liverpool, 1999), pp. 63–76. A few other letters, not copied into *Sangallensis* 190, are contained in *Vita Desiderii Cadurcae urbis episcopi*, ed. Bruno Krusch, MGH SRM 4: 569–71. For help and bibliography I am grateful to Ralph Mathisen, who, with Danuta Shanzer, is preparing a translation of Desiderius's letters.

30. See Wood, "Letters and Letter-Collections" for a survey of late antique collections and their significance.

31. The rhetoricians tried to classify the various types of letters but were not entirely successful "because the letter-writing tradition was essentially independent of rhetoric." See

which was understood to be a kind of gift, began with an opening salutation, often quite elaborate.[32] This was followed by the text, which might invoke the importance of friendship; offer advice, condolence, or praise; make a request or plea; take up apologetic or doctrinal matters; and/or show off the writer's learning and wit, thus implicitly complementing the recipient for catching the allusions. A farewell salutation brought the letter to a close.[33] Correspondence was seen as an inexhaustible resource and limitless mediator: "it is written by me," ruminated Ruricius (d. 510), bishop of Limoges and avid letter writer, "and read by you, and yet even so it is not divided, . . . because it is handed on like the divine word and does not depart."[34] Letters were thought to give friends "a series of amiable fictions designed to preserve the illusion of an actual union: a letter is a symbol of the voice, a conversation, an embrace, a bond of union. It is also a token of remembrance, a consolation, a pledge of friendship."[35] The poetic letters of Fortunatus that we saw in the last chapter were but one variant of the genre.

Desiderius's prose letters were another. During his years as bishop, from 630 until 655, messengers crisscrossed the roads of Francia to bring his greetings and petitions to his many contacts (bishops, kings, mayors of the palace, a couple of monastics) and from his correspondents back to him.

Stanley K. Stowers, *Letter Writing in Greco-Roman Antiquity* (Philadelphia, 1986), p. 52. *Topoi* in letters included "reminders concerning the foundation of friendship in past shared experiences"; the "communication of affection and concern"; the assurance that "friends share in each other's minds through letters when they are physically separated"; and words of "longing to be with the loved one" (ibid., pp. 59–60). For further discussion of these and other *topoi*, see Klaus Thraede, *Grundzüge griechisch-römischer Brieftopik* (Munich, 1970), esp. pt. 3.

32. On letters as gifts, see M. Monica Wagner, "A Chapter in Byzantine Epistolography: The Letters of Theodoret of Cyrus," *Dumbarton Oaks Papers* 4 (1948): 119–81. The opening greetings of many of the letters in collections extant today are often very plain and simple, but this may well reflect the fact that their copyists did not have access to the actual, sent letter but rather to a file copy that abbreviated the salutation. See *Avitus of Vienne,* ed. and trans. Shanzer and Wood, pp. 56–57.

33. On the changes in letter form and content wrought by Christianity, see Michaela Zelzer, "Der Brief in der Spätantike. Überlegungen zu einem literarischen Genos am Beispiel der Briefsammlung des Sidonius Apollinaris," *Wiener Studien* 107–8 (1994–95): 541–51.

34. Ruricius, *Epistularum libri duo* 2.5, ed. R. Demeulenaere, CCSL 64 (Turnhout, 1985), p. 339; for a discussion of the implications of this letter, see *Avitus of Vienne,* ed. and trans. Shanzer and Wood, pp. 59–60.

35. Wagner, "A Chapter in Byzantine Epistolography," 132–33.

The *Life of Desiderius*, written circa 800, reports that "many of the bishops, dukes, and royal administrators [*domestici*] spent their time under his protective wing; many of the nobles rejoiced to do him favors; and Queen Nanthild loved him in particular."[36] Hyperbole, no doubt, and far more emotive than any of Desiderius's letters. Nevertheless, it correctly describes his dense network of contacts.

Desiderius's most enduring bonds were with Eligius, Dado, Sulpicius, and Paulus. We have already met the first three. Paulus's curriculum vitae was little different. He apparently spent time at the royal court before retiring to become a monk and then bishop of Verdun circa 638.[37] A letter written by Desiderius to Dado, harking back to the comradery of this group, raises most of the affective issues that shall concern us in the course of this chapter: an emphasis on deference; the expression of painful longing, assuaged primarily by two emotions—love and joy—connected to religious feeling; the importance of fraternity rather than mixed-sex bonds. It is useful to consider the letter in its entirety:

> To Pope [as bishops were called in this period] Dado, holy and preferred apostolic father, from Desiderius, servant of the servants of God
>
> While much time has slipped by without our being able to see you in person, immense joy [*gratulatio*] has now presented itself to my mind because in some measure, even after a long interval, the opportunity has arisen of my appearing before your eyes by means of a letter. Therefore, having humbly offered due obedience, I ask this more especially: that you grant and ever deign to be the one whose person you once showed me with a unique love [*unico amore*] in that flower of primeval youth, namely my Dado. Let the pristine love [*caritas*] between ourselves and your—or rather our—[friend] Eligius remain unaltered, as indivisible as our fraternity once was. Let us aid one another by mutual prayers so that we may merit to live together in the celestial palace of the high King in the same way as we were associates in the hall of the earthly prince. And

---

36. *Vita Desiderii* 5, p. 566: "Multi quoque episcoporum, ducum hac domesticorum sub ala tuitionis eius degebant, multi nobilium sibi eum gratificare gaudebant; regina autem Nanthildis unice ipsum diligebat."

37. *Vita Pauli Episcopi Virdunensis*, AASS Feb. II, pp. 175–78. See also Norberg's note in Desiderius, *Ep.*, p. 32.

although I have now lost two brothers from our college [Rusticus and Syagrius, Desiderius's blood brothers], we have in their place venerable Paulus and, no less praiseworthy in merits, Sulpicius. Therefore, whoever among us is the more successful, let him strive all the more to climb the rungs of progress. Moreover, I might add that I am sure that I can attain these things more by your prayers than by my own powers. It only needs you to deign to pray without ceasing, and I believe the piety of our Lord Jesus Christ will bestow what you request.

Farewell, man of God, and remember me.[38]

DEFERENCE AND HIERARCHY

"To Pope Dado holy and preferred apostolic father, from Desiderius, servant of the servants of God": this salutation is full of admiration and deference, accompanied by considerable self-abnegation, but it is not at all emotional. There is affection in the body of the letter itself, to be sure, and we shall return to that in a moment. Here, however, let us explore the ways in which relationships were announced in salutations in the letters of this group. There are thirty-seven letters in Desiderius's collection (seventeen from Desiderius to various recipients, nineteen to Desiderius, and one between two bishops about Desiderius), all written between about 630 and 655. Their salutations are effusive about status, not feeling. Bishops are

---

38. Desiderius, *Ep.* 1.11, p. 30: "Sancto ac preferendo apostolico patre Dadone papae Desiderius servus servorum dei. Dum plurima tempora elabuntur, quod praesentiam vestram videre nequimus, nunc inmensa se gratulatio menti objicit, dum aliquatenus, vel post diutina intervalla, sese opportunitas praehibuit, qua vel pagellari offitio me vestris conspectibus praesentarem. Igitur, debito obsequio humiliter exhibeto, illud peculiarius peroro ut, quem quondam in ipso flore primevae juventutis unico mihi amore prebuisti, semper concedere digneris illum meum Dadonem. Maneat pristina inter nos atque illum tuum, immo nostrum Elegium inconvulsa caritas, indisjuncta, ut fuit quondam, fraternitas. Mutuis nos jubemus praecibus, ut, quemadmodum in aula terreni principis socii fuimus, ita in illo superni regis caelesti palacio simul vivere mereamur. Et licet de nostro collegio duos iam amiserim germanos, habemus pro his venerabilem Paulum nec minus praedicabilem meretis Sulpicium. Quisquis igitur nostrum quantum plus praevalet, tanto amplius profectuum grados conscendere elaboret. Ad haec autem, predico, plus me vestris orationibus quam meis viribus adtingere posse confido. Tantum est ut indesinenter vos orare dignetis, et pietas Domini nostri Jesu Christi, credo, praestabit, quod rogatis. Vale, vir Dei, et memento mei."

"honorable" or "holy"; kings are "most glorious"; important court officials are "illustrious" and "honorable"; and nearly everyone is a "lord," often "my everlasting" one (*domino semper suo*), while the writer often qualifies himself a lowly sinner.[39] Here are some typical examples. "To the illustrious lord and more especially to be honored by us [*suspiciendo*], lord and son in Christ, Grimoald, mayor of the palace, from Desiderius, the sinner."[40] "To the most glorious lord, crowned with the triumphal palm, son of the holy Catholic church, King Sigibert, from your servant Desiderius, bishop of the city of Cahors."[41] "To his everlasting lord Pope Medoaldus, from Desiderius, the sinner."[42] More telling, perhaps, are the salutations between members of the close quintet of courtiers. We have already seen one greeting to Dado. To Paulus, Desiderius wrote: "To his everlasting lord Bishop Paulus, [from] Desiderius the sinner."[43] To Sulpicius: "To the holy patriarch Sulpicius, from Desiderius, servant of the servants of God."[44]

To be sure, Desiderius's opening flourish to Bishop Sallustius of Agen calls its recipient "lovable"; but this is unique. And in fact even this salutation is rather less emotional than it might seem, since the word expressing love is used in the gerundive form, which implies obligation: "to the most holy lord and the one *to be beloved* by me in Christ above all others."[45] As

---

39. In thirteen out of fifteen letters (counting Desiderius, *Ep.* 2.8, pp. 56–57, among the letters originating with Desiderius, though it appears in the section of his correspondents, and not counting either *Ep.* 1.10, pp. 28–29, which is missing its *intitulo*, or *Ep.* 1.15, p. 37, to Abbess Aspasia) the status term *dominus* is used in the salutation. The two greetings that do not use this term are to Dado (*Ep.* 1.11, p. 30) and to Sulpicius (*Ep.* 1.13, p. 33), members of the quintet referred to above. In six out of seventeen letters, Desiderius calls himself "the sinner," while in twelve out of twenty letters written *to* Desiderius, the writer designates himself "the sinner." Contrast this latter point with the letters pertaining to Ruricius of Limoges, which are contained in the same St. Gallen MS as Desiderius's letters (see note 29 above): in Ruricius's collection, the letter writer, while often expressing great deference toward the recipient, never demeans his own status. See Ruricius, *Epistularum*, pp. 313–415, and *Ruricius of Limoges and Friends*.

40. Desiderius, *Ep.* 1.2, p. 12: "Domino inlustri et a nobis peculiarius suspiciendo, domino et in Christo filio Grimoaldo maiorem domus Desiderius peccator."

41. Ibid., 1.3, p. 15: "Domino gloriosissimo, triumphali palma coronato, sanctae catholicae ecclesiae filio Sigeberto rege servus vester Desiderius Cadurcae urbis episcopus."

42. Ibid., 1.7, p. 22: "Domino semper suo Medoaldo papae Desiderius peccator."

43. Ibid., 1.12, p. 31: "Domino semper suo Paulo episcopo Desiderius peccator."

44. Ibid., 1.13, p. 33: "Sancto patriarchae Sulpicio Desiderius servus servorum dei."

45. Ibid., 1.1, p. 9 : "Domino sanctissimo atque prae omnibus mihi in Christo diligendo."

usual in medieval epistolary form, the opening flourishes of Desiderius's letters placed the recipient first, emphasizing hierarchy by showing deference.[46] Tellingly, in his letter to Abbess Aspasia, he put his own name first. The norms of male discourse, emotional and otherwise, did not (as we shall see) fully apply to women.

In turn, those who wrote to Desiderius—even the Merovingian kings—invariably referred to him as "lord" and put his name first in their opening flourish. Sulpicius, whom Desiderius called—in the letter to Dado quoted above—a "brother," wrote in the greeting of one letter: "To his everlasting lord and guardian of the apostolic seat, lord Desiderius, bishop of the city of Cahors, from Sulpicius, bishop of the city of Bourges."[47] In a second letter, Sulpicius's salutation was equally deferential: "To the lord always to be admired [*suspiciendo*] and to be spoken of venerably with every honor, Lord Pope Desiderius, from Sulpicius the sinner."[48] When Eligius, another member of the "court fraternity," wrote to Desiderius, he addressed him as "his enduring lord and apostolic father."[49] Paulus, yet another participant in the "indivisible" quintet, was still more terse: "To Pope Desiderius, ever our lord, from Paulus, the sinner."[50] The *Life of Columbanus,* written by Jonas circa 640, and thus in the midst of the flurry of Desiderius's letters, begins with a dedication to the abbots of Luxeuil and Bobbio that echoes the dry and status-conscious salutations of the letters we have been considering: "To the fathers Waldebert and Bobolenus, distinguished lords, adorned by the authority of the sacred summit and sustained by the power of religion, from Jonas the sinner."[51]

But why not assume that unemotional salutations were the norm in late antique letters? Sidonius Apollinaris, whose epitaph we saw in chapter 2 and who was noted as a letter writer both in his own day and our own, seems to bear this out. Here is a typical opening: "To his [*suo*] Eriphius,

---

46. Heinrich Fichtenau, "Adressen von Urkunden und Briefen," in *Beiträge zur Mediävistik: Ausgewählte Aufsätze,* vol. 3 (Stuttgart, 1986), pp. 149–66, esp. 153.

47. Desiderius, *Ep.* 2.1, p. 41: "Domno semper proprio atque apostolica sede colendo, domno Desiderio Cadurcae urbis pontifice Sulpicius Bitorige urbis episcopus."

48. Ibid., 2.10, p. 58: "Domno semper suspiciendo et cum omni honore venerabiliter nominando, domno Desiderio papae Sulpicius peccator."

49. Ibid., 2.6, p. 52: "Domno semper suo atque apostolico patre."

50. Ibid., 2.12, p. 61: "Domno semper suo Desiderio papae Paulus peccator."

51. Jonas, *Vita Columbani,* pref., p. 61: "Dominis eximiis et sacri culminis regimine decoratis religionisque copia fultis Waldeberto et Boboleno patribus Ionas peccator."

greeting."⁵² But Sidonius likely reduced and normalized his salutations when he edited his letters for publication.⁵³ Certainly Fortunatus's letters were effusive, as we have seen.⁵⁴ The letters of Ruricius of Limoges were less demonstrative but nevertheless unafraid of emotion words: "To Abbot Pomerius, the lord of my soul, to be honored with all the inward parts of love [*dilectionis visceribus*] in Christ the Lord, [from] Bishop Ruricius"; or, "To the holy and most blessed lord and pope, Bishop Sedatus, to be especially honored by me, Bishop Ruricius, with particular worship and affection [*affectu*]."⁵⁵ Indeed, love also entered the salutations of the correspondence of Desiderius—but only once, and tellingly it was in a letter *from* Abbot Bertegiselus *to* "the treasurer Desiderius"—thus the young and not yet episcopal Desiderius. He was called "illustrious lord and cherished by us with the greatest love [*summa dilectione colendo*] and named with all reverence."⁵⁶ Bertegiselus presided over the monastery of St. Victor at Marseille, whose norms—emotional and otherwise—may have been different from those prevailing at the Neustrian court.⁵⁷

Like the opening flourishes, the texts of Desiderius's letters also emphasized status and hierarchy. Although the letters were about many disparate issues, one theme ran through many of them: the importance of "commendation." A bit over one-third of the letters contain the word in its various forms.⁵⁸ As it appears in these materials, commendation is a kind of dependency that must be requested (by the person who is commended, or on that person's behalf) of another, superior, person. Properties may be "com-

---

52. Sidonius, *Letters* 5.17, p. 226.

53. See *Avitus of Vienne*, trans. Shanzer and Wood, p. 62; André Loyen, *Sidoine Apollinaire et l'esprit précieux en Gaule aux derniers jours de l'empire*, Les Belles Lettres (Paris, 1943), pp. 124–25.

54. See chap. 4 above.

55. Ruricius, *Ep.* 1.17, p. 327: "Domno animae suae et totis in Christo domino dilectionis visceribus excolendo Pomerio abbati Ruricius episcopus"; ibid., 2.18, p. 358: "Domino sancto ac beatissimo et mihi peculiari cultu affectuque specialiter excolendo papae Sedato episcopo Ruricius episcopus."

56. Desiderius, *Ep.* 2.2, p. 45: "Domino inlustri et a nobis summa dilectione colendo atque cum omni reverentia nominando."

57. See Bruno Krusch's introductory remarks to the *Vita Desiderii*, p. 548.

58. Desiderius, *Ep.* 1.2, p. 12; 1.4, p. 17; 1.6, p. 20; 1.7, p. 22; 1.8, p. 24; 1.9, p. 27; 1.10, p. 29; 2.7, p. 54; 2.8, p. 56; 2.11, p. 60; 2.14, p. 66; 2.18, p. 71. In fully half of these the word appears more than once.

mended" as well. Commendation is a gracious favor, to be granted by someone in the position to protect and help those commended.[59] Bishop Rauracius of Nevers, for example, began his letter to Desiderius by commending his messengers:

> With the most humble greeting, I commend to your Apostleship your servants Presbyter Mummolus and Garimundus, whom we have sent to your city and your small residence at Gregionnacus and at Albares to examine the register of serfs. We ask that you deign to receive those men I have commended and that they may merit to have your assistance in all matters when they have need of it. . . . At the same time we suggest with respect to that small farm and the people residing there that you deign to regard them as under your protection, received [by you] and commended as if they were your own dependents.[60]

No particular emotion is invoked as frequently as the nonemotional but very honorable "commendation" and its variants, a word that comes up twenty-two times in the correspondence. But emotion words and emotional expressions do appear, in measured and dignified manner, here as in other writings from this group.

LONGING, LOVE, JOY, AND ANXIETY

In this emotional culture, male emotions were largely expressed in the context of longing, particularly for the afterlife. Desiderius's letter to Dado hoped for his correspondent's affection not directly but by remembering a past love and invoking its future in the life to come. To repeat the passage:

> I ask this more especially: that you grant and ever deign to be the one whose person you once showed me with a unique love [*unico amore*] in that flower of primeval youth, namely my Dado. Let the pristine love

---

59. For a discussion of commendation during this period, which should not be confused with its "feudal" variant, see Mayke de Jong, *In Samuel's Image: Child Oblation in the Early Medieval West* (Leiden, 1996), pp. 198–204.

60. Desiderius, *Ep.* 2.7, p. 54: "Cum humillima salutationis officia commendo apostulatui vestro servellos vestros Mummolo presbytero et Garimundo, quos ad urbem vestram et ad hospiciolum vestrum Gregionnaco sive Albares descriptionem manicipiorum inquirenda direximus. Suplicamus ut commendatos ipsos recipere dignetis, et, ubi ipsis necessitas extiterit, vestro auxilio in omnibus mereantur haberę . . . Simulque suggerimus ut, de ipsa curtecella vel hominibus inibi consistentibus, sub vestra defensione tamquam propria familia dignetis haberae receptos et commendatos."

[*caritas*] between ourselves and your—or rather our—[friend] Eligius remain unaltered, as indivisible as our fraternity once was. Let us aid one another by mutual prayers so that we may merit to live together in the celestial palace of the high King in the same way as we were associates in the hall of the earthly prince.

The love (*amor*) is unique and past, and even though Desiderius hopes it will never change, he in fact uses a different word, *caritas,* when he repeats it, no doubt to emphasize its religious character. He also transforms the old court relationship into a mutual prayer society that will persist in heaven. Let us consider more closely professions of affection—whether by the words *affectus/affectio, amor* and its variants, *caritas,* or *diligo/dilectio*—for, taken together, they constitute the greatest part of the emotional vocabulary of the correspondence, appearing thirty-two times.

In his letter to Bishop Sallustius of Agen, Desiderius speaks of the very loving manner (*satis amabiliter*) in which the magnates and princes at court greeted him after his extended absence.[61] He and they once had a "cemented friendship" (*conglutinata amicitia*), he recalls, and "we to this day hold them in the name of God so that mutual love [*caritas mutua*] may never die but grow more and blossom as the days go by."[62] The term "cemented friendship" has some classical echoes,[63] but it also may have derived from 1 Kings 18:1: "The soul of Jonathan was knit with [*conglutinata est*] the soul of David, and Jonathan loved [*dilexit*] him as his own soul." In all of these cases, both classical and biblical, the friendship was very much of this

---

61. Ibid., 1.1, p. 9.

62. Ibid.: "Omnes obtimates et principes, iuxta quod antea cum ipsos habebamus conglutinata amicitia,—gratias Christo qui est bonorum omnium dispensator—satis amabiliter nos reciperunt, et nos eos eatenus in Dei nomine retenemus, ut caritas mutua nunquam decidat sed aucta magis in dies floriscat."

63. Cicero, *Laelius de amicitia* 9.32, trans. William Armistead Falconer, Loeb Classical Library (Cambridge, Mass., 1964), p. 144: "si utilitas amicitias conglutinaret eadem commutata dissolveret" (if expediency were what held together friendships, a change in this would break them up). There is also Cicero, *Epistulae ad Atticum* 7.8.1, in *Cicero's Letters to Atticus,* ed. D. R. Shackleton Bailey (Cambridge, 1968), 3:176–78: "tu soles conglutinare amicitias testimoniis tuis" (you are accustomed to cement friendships by your testimonials). Isidore of Seville, *Sententiarum libri tres* 3.29.6, PL 83, col. 703: "et quos ante conglutinatos charitate habuerunt, postquam ad culmen honoris venerint, amicos habere despiciunt" (and after achieving the pinnacle of honor, they despise having as their friends those whom they had previously held close out of love) was written not much before the time of Desiderius's letter. I am grateful to Danuta Shanzer for these references.

world. But in Desiderius's letter, it was part of a remembered past and a longed-for future under the aegis of a benevolent and generous Christ.

In a letter to Grimoald, the mayor of the palace, Desiderius spoke of the unique affection (*unicus affectus*) that the mayor's father, Pippin, had had for him; he hoped that Grimoald would have the same "grace [*gratiam*] as your father toward me."[64] This is tepid. Nor were direct expressions of affection, unusual in themselves, much stronger. To Sallustius, who had asked about Desiderius's reception at court, he wrote: "we thank you amply and with the fullest affection [*affectu*] for your inquiry, which was made with so much love [*dilectionem*]."[65] To Paulus, whom Desiderius had invited for the dedication of St. Amantius, the monastery he founded at Cahors, he urged: "Come, therefore, dearest [*carissime*], with a speed equal to your distance."[66] It was the first and last time Desiderius called anyone *carissimus*.

Love was, therefore, prized but also highly restrained, allowed vivid expression only when related to religious matters. In Jonas's *Life of Columbanus*, "love of Columbanus" is invoked as the reason why a bishop of Besançon and his brother founded two monasteries under the saint's Rule. Similarly, according to Jonas, King Clothar extended his protection over Luxeuil "on account of his love for the man of God."[67] Love, in the form of *caritas*, also helped constitute the paradisaical early community that Columbanus and his followers established in Gaul. It was a community which, like those of the Desert Fathers, cast out the vices—and emotions—of sloth, discord, arrogance, elation, anger, and envy, substituting in their stead a total harmony of will and renunciation that was animated by patience, "the emotion of love" (*caritatis affectus*), and mildness.[68] Love of Columbanus was much on display when he was expelled from his monastery by men sent by Brunhild and Theuderic. The thugs themselves, impelled by fear (*urguenti formidinae*)—on the one hand for their lives, on the other hand for their souls—begged him with tears (*cum lacrimis*) to leave voluntarily so that they might be spared committing "a crime of such great wickedness."

---

64. Desiderius, *Ep.* 1.6, pp. 20–21: "precor ut illam gratiam genetoris vestri erga me tenere dignetis."

65. Ibid., 1.1, p. 9: "satis et cum plenissimo affectu . . . pro tantam inquisicionis vestrae dilectionem gratias agimus."

66. Ibid., 1.12, p. 32: "Veni igitur, carissime, quantum longius tantum velocius."

67. For the founding of monasteries, Jonas, *Vita Columbani* 1.14, p. 79: "in amore beati Columbani"; for Clothar, ibid., 1.29, p. 108: "ob viri Dei amorem."

68. Ibid., 1.5, p. 71.

When Columbanus acceded, he departed amidst "the shrieks and grief of everyone," the monks following him "as if it were a funeral."[69] At Bobbio under Columbanus's successor, Athala, love and fear (*amor et timor*) overwhelmed the monks.[70]

One sermon probably by Eligius has survived; it is full of affection and emotion.[71] Drawing on a topos of sermon writing, he called his listeners his "dearest brothers" (*fratres karissimi*) and offered his advice in love (*caritate*). He asked them to listen to him, "so that I, with you, may merit to rejoice [*gaudere*] in the company of the angels in perpetual peace."[72] His exhortations were full of emotion words: "For you have become Christians so that you may always do the works of a Christian, namely, love chastity [*castitatem ametis*], flee lust and drunkenness, adhere to humility, detest pride [*superbiam detestemini*] . . . repudiate envy [*invidiam respuatis*], and have love [*caritatem*] for one another."[73]

Fear, expressed ordinarily by the word *timor* or *terror* (though *formido, metus,* and *pavor* were also used), was always associated with religious feeling. It was a good emotion, rightly felt, expressed, and contemplated. To Abbess Aspasia, Desiderius wrote:

> Moved by your tears to this point, I have prepared for you the story from the Gospel about the excellent woman [Mary Magdalene; see Luke 7:37–50]. You will certainly find in her divine consolation and fear [*timorem*]. Consolation, because the pious benignity of the Lord does not reject the soul that recovers from the burden of sin. Fear, because the soul that attends to the service of God may ready itself bravely to withstand tempta-

---

69. Ibid., 1.20, p. 91.

70. Ibid., 2.4, p. 117.

71. Auctor incertus [Eligius], *De rectitudine catholicae conversationis tractatus,* PL 40, cols. 1169–90 = PL 87, cols. 524–50. On its attribution to Eligius, see *Clavis patristica pseudepigraphorum medii aevi,* vol. 1, *Opera homiletica,* pt. A, ed. John Machielsen (Turnhout, 1990), no. 1113, p. 237. An abbreviated text is edited by Bruno Krusch in MGH SRM 4: 751–61. For the *topos* of *fratres carissimi* see Thomas N. Hall, "The Early Medieval Sermon," in *The Sermon,* ed. Beverly Mayne Kienzle, Typologie des sources du Moyen Age occidental 81–83 (Turnhout, 2000), pp. 206–7.

72. Eligius, *De rectitudine,* PL 40, col. 1169: "ut vobiscum pariter merear in Angelorum consortio perpetua pace gaudere."

73. Ibid., col. 1170: "Nam ideo christiani facti estis, ut semper opera christiani faciatis, id est, ut castitatem ametis, luxuriam et ebrietatem fugiatis, humilitatem teneatis, superbiam detestemini . . . invidiam etiam respuatis, charitatem invicem habeatis."

tions, as in the saying of Solomon: "Son, yield to the service of God; stand in fear [*timore*]; and prepare your soul for temptation" [Ecclus. 2.1.][74]

In the *Life of Columbanus,* two girls are "noble in the world and given over to the fear [*timore*] of Christ."[75] This is good. Similarly, two sinful nuns find no rest in death: lights and screaming voices hover over their graves, and after six months their bodies have turned to cinders. The punishment lasts three years "so that the terror [*terror*] of the damned might give fright [*timorem*] to the remaining sisters."[76] The father of Gibitrudis is struck with a fever when he opposes his daughter's religious vocation; the experience leads him to a change of heart: "Now he yearned for the fear of the divine cult [*ad timorem divini cultus aspirabat*] after the example of his daughter."[77]

In the last example, *timor* is nearly the equivalent of *amor*; in many other instances the association of these two emotions is explicit. We have already met Athala, who "poured out" love and fear together. Leudeberta saw St. Peter ready to take her to heaven, and she reported on the experience so that by her example "she could point to the great riches with which [the Creator of things] does not cease to endow those who leave this light in fear and love [*timore vel amore*] of Him."[78] Eligius exhorted believers to "fear [*timete*] Him over all things; adore [*adorate*] Him among all things; love [*amate*] Him beyond all things."[79] Even the legal writings of the court reflected the words' connectedness. An original charter of 654 issued by Clovis II to confirm a privilege by Bishop Landeric of Paris for the monastery of Saint-Denis is full of references to *timor* and *amor*. Toward the middle of the text, the terms are explicitly entwined as the charter observes that the holy shrine

---

74. Desiderius, *Ep.* 1.15, p. 37: "Lacrimis tuis hactenus motus, hanc tibi historiam de evangelio egregiae illius femine distinavi. In ipsam quippe divinam consolationem repperies et timorem. Consolationem quidem, quoniam, qui de peccati onere resipiscet, hanc animam pia Domini benignitas non refutat. Timorem ideo, quia anima, quae accedit ad servitutem Dei, continuo ad temptationes sustinendas se fortiter paret, dicente Salomone: 'Fili, accedens ad servitutem Dei, sta in timore et prepara animam tuam ad temptationem.'"

75. Jonas, *Vita Columbani* 1.14, p. 80.

76. Ibid., 2.19, p. 140: "ut terror damnatorum timorem praeberet sodalium remanentium."

77. Ibid., 2.12, p. 132: "ex filiae exemplo iam ad timorem divini cultus aspirabat."

78. Ibid., 2.18, p. 138: "et tantis munerum copiis superis demonstraret quibus [rerum sator] ab hac luce in suo timore vel amore migrantes ditare non desinit."

79. Eligius, *De rectitudine*, PL 40, col. 1173: "Illum ergo, fratres, super omnia timete, illum inter omnia adorate, illum ultra omnia amate."

was endowed with property "by princes themselves and other earlier kings and indeed God-fearing [*timentebus*] Christian people ... on account of their love [*amorem*] of God and the life eternal."[80] And again, near the end, the king prohibits bishops from taking any of the property given "by previous princes or our parents or by God-fearing [*timentebus*] people on account of their love [*amore*] of God."[81] It stands to reason that Clovis would issue charters of this sort; we have at least one letter written by a bishop to him at the time of his accession to the throne, exhorting him to "fear God, and love Him."[82] The association of these two emotions was part of royal schooling.[83]

Anxiety and other emotions of the troubled mind were also privileged in these texts, but generally in measured doses. Desiderius and his correspondents rarely talked about painful things directly (though letters to and from Felix of Limoges were, rather unusually, about hurts and apologies), but they were full of appreciation for consoling words.[84] "Because you have deigned to console [*consolare*] us with pious solicitude by letter, our mind is insufficient to offer the measure of thanks," Desiderius wrote to King Sigi-

---

80. *ChLA* 13, no. 558 = MGH D Merov, 1:218, no. 85: "ab ipsis principebus vel a citeris priscis regebus vel aeciam a Deo timentebus christianis hominebus ipse sanctus locus in rebus propter amorem Dei et vita aeterna videtur esse ditatus."

81. Ibid.: "a priscis principebus seo genetorebus nostris vel a Deum timentebus hominebus propter amorem Dei."

82. *Epistolae aevi Merowingici collectae*, 15, ed. Wilhelm Gundlach in MGH, Epistolae 3: Epistolae merowingici et karolini aevi (1892; repr., Berlin, 1994), 1: 460: "Time Deum, ama illum." For discussion of this letter and further bibliography, see Yitzhak Hen, "The Christianisation of Kingship," in *Der Dynastiewechsel von 751. Vorgeschichte, Legitimationsstrategien und Erinnerung*, ed. Matthias Becher and Jörg Jarnut (Münster, 2004), pp. 163–77.

83. The pairing was not automatic in Christian writings and appears to be particularly characteristic of the emotional community of the Neustrian court. To be sure, the association of the words may be found in Augustine, *City of God* 5.14, CCSL 47, p. 147. But in the Rule of St. Benedict, fear of God (*timor Dei; formido*) constitutes the first rung of the "ladder of humility," while love of God (*caritas Dei; amor*), "which, when perfect casts out fear" (*quae perfecta foris mittit timorem*), is the prize after the final rung. See *Regula Benedicti* 7 in *La règle de Saint Benoît*, ed. Adalbert de Vogüé, SC 181 (Paris, 1972), pp. 474, 488–90. This ranking of the two emotions is also found in Gregory the Great; see Italo Sciuto, "Le passioni e la tradizione monastica," *Doctor Seraphicus: Bolletino d'informazioni del Centro di studi bonaventuriani* 45 (1998): 14.

84. For letters to and from Felix, see Desiderius, *Ep.* 1.16, p. 39; 2.21, pp. 75–76. On Christian consolation literature see Peter von Moos, *Consolatio. Studien zur mittellateinischen Trostliteratur über den Tod und zum Problem der christlichen Trauer*, 4 vols. (Munich, 1971–72).

bert.⁸⁵ "I ask that the person whom you have thus consoled [*consolasti*] with benefits you may now aid with the benefit of prayer," he wrote to Bishop Medoaldus.⁸⁶ And in the same letter, "let us merit to be consoled [*consolari*] by regular replies about your health and that of the lord king and your brethren and sons."⁸⁷ These were polite anxieties. More telling were those expressed by Jonas, especially in his *Life of John of Réomé*, written perhaps in 660, where we can see emotional restraint take hold by degrees.⁸⁸ Jonas's John was an anxious young man. At twenty, the "anxious vow of his heart" (*anxia cordis vota*) was to build an oratory, but he changed his mind, "aflame with ardor of mind and desire for heaven," and sought out instead the "wilderness" of Burgundy.⁸⁹ However, after building a monastery there, he was prodded by the "anxious goad of his heart" (*anxio cordis stimulo*) to agonize about whether he ought to preside over monks or obey an abbot himself.⁹⁰ Arriving at the exemplary monastery of Lérins to learn true discipline, he was soon recalled to Burgundy by the bishop of Langres. His anxious heart stinging him once again, he weighed what he should do, eventually deciding to return.⁹¹ Yet as he took charge of his monastery, his anxieties diminished, and, on his deathbed, he admonished his brethren "with smiling face and joyful mien."⁹²

Most emotions in these materials were either weak or rejected. If Abbot

---

85. Desiderius, *Ep.* 1.4, p. 16: "Quod nos pia sollicitudine litteris dignati estis consolare, insufficiens est mens nostra gratiarum iura persolvere."

86. Ibid., 1.7, p. 22: "supplico ut quem tunc beneficiis consolasti, nunc orationis beneficio iubes."

87. Ibid.: "de vestra et domni regis vel fratrum ac filiorum vestrorum mereamur incolomitate rescripti seriae consolari."

88. For the date, Jonas, *Vita Johannis*, p. 505, where the author speaks of conceiving the project in the third year of the reign of Clothar III, i.e., 660.

89. Ibid., 2, p. 507: "intrepidus mentisque ardore et celesti desiderio accensus." Anxiety is a key emotion in this piece, appearing (in one form or another: *anxietas, anxio corde, anxius*) four times in the approximately 315 lines of its published edition (see citations here and below). This is, admittedly, only once every 79 lines or so, but compare it, for example, to the four uses of an anxiety word in the first book of Jonas, *Vita Columbani*: (1.4, p. 71; 1.7, p. 73; 1.13, p. 78; 1.19, p. 89; 1.20, p. 91): once every 279 lines.

90. Jonas, *Vita Johannis* 3, p. 508.

91. Ibid., 4, p. 509.

92. Ibid., 18, p. 515: "vultu hilaris et letus facie monebat." It is one of the younger monks who considers matters "anxio cordis animo" (with anxious spirit of heart) in ibid., 16, p. 514. Albrecht Diem points out that John becomes the model "of the responsibly-acting, non-ascetic monastic manager"; Diem, "Monks and Kings in the Early Middle Ages: Some

Athala exuded love and fear, nevertheless at his monastery "no one was worn down by grief [*merore*] nor uplifted by too much happiness [*letitia*]."[93] Love itself might need tamping down, as it did for Gregory the Great. Thus the wily devil tried to snare Columbanus "by arousing in him love [*amores*] for lascivious girls."[94] It was only bad people who "raged" (*furor* and its variants); good ones never did. Indeed, there was something almost inhuman about such passion, for the demons themselves tormented their victims "with savage fury" (*horrido furore*).[95] Brunhild, "raging" (*furens*) after Columbanus refused to bless her great-grandchildren, "ordered the little ones to go. The man of God was leaving the royal court, and when he leaped across the threshold, a noise arose that shook the whole house and inspired terror in all, yet did not restrain the fury [*furorem*] of that wretched woman."[96] Brunhild, as we know, was the bugaboo of the Neustrian dynasty. In another instance, when an oarsman struck one of the monks who chose to leave Gaul with Columbanus, the saint upbraided him: "Why, cruel one, do you add grief to grief? . . . Know that you will be struck by divine punishment in that place in which, raging [*furens*], you struck a member of Christ."[97] And this is indeed what happened.

OVERWROUGHT MOTHERS

Mothers often partook of these excesses and shared in their opprobrium. They were expected to be emotionally overwrought yet condemned for it.[98] Brunhild was the archetype of such a mother, and hatred for her may well

---

Thoughts on the End of the Holy Man" (unpublished). I am grateful to Dr. Diem for sending me a draft of his paper.

93. Jonas, *Vita Columbani* 2.4, p. 117: "nullus iuxta eum vel merore terebatur neque nimia letitia extollebatur."

94. Ibid., 1.3, p. 68: "lascivarum puellarum in eum suscitare amores."

95. Ibid., 1.21, p. 94.

96. Ibid., 1.19, p. 87: "Illa furens parvulus abire iubet. Egrediens vir Dei regiam aulam, dum limitem transiliret, fragor exorta totam domum quatiens omnibus terrorem incussit nec tamen misere feminae furorem conpescuit."

97. Ibid., 1.21, p. 93: " 'Quur,' inquid 'crudelis, addis merori merorem? . . . Memento te a divina ultione in hoc loco percussurum, in quo Christi membrum furens percussisti.' "

98. Already Augustine had spoken of his always-weeping mother, but he also rather admired her excessive tears; see, for example, *Confessions* 3.12, 1:63, where her weeping and begging on behalf of her son leads a bishop to say dryly: "Vade a me; ita vivas, fieri non potest, ut filius istarum lacrimarum pereat." (Leave me be: with you living this way, it's not possible that the son of those tears should perish.)

have helped pave the way for the jaundiced view of mothers in general. It is also likely that Clothar II, whose father was arguably not Chilperic but rather his mother's lover, found it politically important to downgrade mothers altogether as he took up the royal mantle of his putative father.[99] Even the mothers of saints were understood to be importuning, their demands dangerous. The best remedy was escape. We have already seen how Columbanus "leaped over" (*transileret*) Brunhild's threshold (*limitem*) with great noise. He was here, in Jonas's account, reprising an earlier scene with his own mother. When he announced to her that he was leaving home, her grief, like Brunhild's fury, knew no bounds:

> His mother, struck with sorrow [*dolore*], begs him not to leave her. But he replies, "Haven't you heard: 'He who loves his father and mother more than me is not worthy of me'?" [Matt. 10:37] He begs his mother, who is standing in his way and clinging to the threshold of the door, to let him go. She, wailing and prostrate on the pavement, denies she will permit it. He leaps over [*transilit*] both the threshold [*limitem*] and his mother and tells his mother to be happy [*se laetam habeat*]: she will never see him again in this life, but he will go wherever the path of salvation shows the way.[100]

The image of a parent restraining a child at the "threshold" may have come from Jerome, who admonished Heliodorus (in a well-known letter) to reject all family attachments in order to pursue the ascetic life: "although your father should lie on the threshold [*limine*], keep going by treading on your father."[101] If this is the source, it is telling that the Neustrian courtiers turned the father into a mother.

---

99. On Clothar's parentage, see Wood, "Deconstructing the Merovingian Family," pp. 163–64.

100. Jonas, *Vita Columbani* 3, p. 69: "Materque eius dolore stimulata, precatur, ut se non relinquat. At ille: 'Non,' inquid 'audisti: "Qui amat patrem aut matrem plus quam me, non est me dignus"?' Obstanti matri et limitem ostii inherenti postulat, ut se ire sinat. Illa eiulans et pavimento prostrata, denegat se permissuram; ille limitem matremque transilit poscitque matri, se laetam habeat: illum numquam deinceps in hac vita visurum, sed, quocumque salutis via iter pandat, se progressurum."

101. Jerome, *Epistola XIV ad Heliodorum* 2, PL 22, col. 348. Columbanus himself knew and quoted from this letter by Jerome: see Neil Wright, "Columbanus's *Epistulae*," in *Columbanus: Studies on the Latin Writings*, ed. Lapidge, p. 73. For more on the topos of the saint leaving his or her family against its wishes, see Lutz E. von Padberg, *Heilige und Familie. Studien zur Bedeutung familiengebundener Aspekte in den Viten des Verwandten- und Schülerkreises um Willibrord, Bonifatius, und Liudger*, 2d ed. (Mainz, 1997), pp. 86–91.

The mother of Jonas's John of Réomé was also importunate—and summarily rejected. She wanted to see her "long-desired" child upon his return from Lérins, but

> hearing this, he declined and excused himself from giving in to the emotion [*affectum*] of his mother, recalling that "He who does not leave his father and mother is not worthy of me" [Matt 10:37]. Nevertheless, lest he injure by rash condemnation the faith of the mother, which, he knew, was imbued with the love and fear of Christ [*in Christi amorem et timorem*], he walked past her [*transsiens ante aeam*], appearing for a moment to her eyes so that he might satisfy the desire of his mother yet not weaken the vigor of his religion on account of the flatteries [*blandimenta*] of his mother.[102]

Had Jonas wished to emphasize the pathos of the moment and the tender feelings of the son, he certainly had a number of possible models to choose from. When Augustine determined to leave Carthage, his mother was so upset that she followed him down to the coast. He had to lie to get away from her. But Augustine was not proud of himself: "You have mercifully forgiven me even this."[103] In the *Life of Fulgentius of Ruspe,* the saint's mother was exceptionally demanding, full of fury (*furibundus*) as she asked that her son return to her and leave the monastery. Her demands were rejected, but her son suffered deeply, for he "had always loved [*semper amaverat*] his mother."[104] In the *Life of Simeon Stylites,* the hero's mother weeps, shakes out her hair, and berates her son when she is not allowed to see him at his monastery.

> "Son, why have you done this? For the womb in which I bore you, you have overwhelmed me with mourning [*luctu*]; for the milk with which I suckled you, you have given me tears [*lacrymas*]; for the kisses with which I kissed you, you have given me bitter heart pangs; for the sorrow and labor that I suffered you have inflicted on me the cruelest

---

102. Jonas, *Vita Johannis* 6, p. 509: "Hoc ille auditu abnuit, matrisque affectum ut faveret, recusavit, reminiscens illud: 'Qui non reliquerit [note, not *amat*] patrem aut matrem, non est me dignus.' Sed tamen, ne fidem matris, quam in Christi amorem et timorem inditam noverat, temere contemnendo violaret, transsiens ante aeam, parumper obtutibus eius apparuit, ut et desiderium matris saciaret et vigorem relegionis ob matris blandimenta non molliret."

103. Augustine, *Confessions* 5.8.15, 1:104: "Et hoc dimisisti mihi misericorditer."

104. Ferrandus, *Vita beati Fulgentii pontificis* 4 in *Vie de Saint Fulgence de Ruspe,* ed. and trans., P. G.-G. Lapeyre (Paris, 1929), pp. 25–27.

blows." And she said such things as to make us all weep [*faceret flere*].¹⁰⁵

No monk wept in Jonas's accounts. Rather he made his own the flat affect that we see, for example, in the Latin *Life of St. Pachomius*.¹⁰⁶ Here a mother seeks out her son in a monastery, bringing with her episcopal writings to prove that her son should be returned home, and asking to see him. Pachomius tells the boy to leave, but the young man insists that he left his mother along with the world and cannot put her ahead of divine love. Like Jonas's Columbanus, he quotes Matthew 10:37.¹⁰⁷

Perhaps Jonas was influenced by Cassian, who warned that the temptations of "the feminine sex" originated in recalling, in seeming innocence, a mother or a sister.¹⁰⁸ But Jonas's deprecation of mother love was not just connected to fear of lust. Consider Jonas's story of Deurechild and her mother. The two entered a monastery together, but the daughter was more virtuous than her mother and was assured of eternal life. As Deurechild lay on her deathbed, her anxious (*anxia*) mother "amidst sobs and sighs begged her daughter that, should she have strength enough, she, Deurechild, should pray to be restored to the land of the living, or, should she actually be reaching her life's finish, she quickly take her mother from this world after her, for, said she, it was impossible for her to live after her daughter's departure." This sort of affection was belittled by the daughter, who attributed it to "carnal desires" (*carnalibus . . . desideriis*). And yet its importance

---

105. Antonius, *Vita sancti Simeonis stylitae* 9, PL 73, col. 329: "Fili, quare hoc fecisti? pro utero quo te portavi, satiasti me luctu; pro lactatione qua te lactavi, dedisti mihi lacrymas; pro osculo quo te osculata sum, dedisti mihi amaras cordis angustias; pro dolore et labore quem passa sum, imposuisti mihi saevissimas plagas. Et tantum locuta est, ut nos omnes faceret flere."

106. Denis the Little, *Vita Sancti Pachomii* 29–31, in *La vie latine de saint Pachome traduite du grec par Denys le Petit*, ed. H. van Cranenburgh (Brussels, 1969), 152–60.

107. Ibid., 31, p. 158: "parentes non debeo divinae praeponere caritati." The lack of affect is here all the more striking given that the rest of the episode with Theodore is full of expressions of emotion: when he had his conversion to the ascetic life, his mother found him with his eyes "full of tears" ("invenit oculos eius plenos lacrimis") (ibid., 29, p. 152); when he declared himself ready to follow Pachomius, he was "overcome by tears [*lacrimis vincebatur*] and utterly inebriated by divine love [*amore divino fortiter sauciatus*]" (ibid., 30, p. 156); when he saw Pachomius for the first time, he wept for joy (ibid.); and Pachomius soon came to love him ("satis eum dilexit et in corde suo conservit") (ibid., 31, p. 158).

108. John Cassian, *Institutes* 6.13 in Jean Cassian, *Institutions cénobitiques*, ed. and trans. Jean-Claude Guy, SC 109 (Paris, 1965), p. 276.

was not denied. After the daughter died—joyfully (*ovans*)—she obtained the favor of her mother's death in turn.[109]

It is true that Christian values at every period put a premium on death (and the afterlife), downgrading this world and its fleshy feelings. But different actors variously interpreted this script. Here we see emphasized the pettiness of particular feelings, the exaggeration of mother love, so that it seems out of proportion to the measured emotions of those virtuous beings—male virgins—around them.[110] This is worlds away from Gregory of Tours.

The only mother who showed restraint (in the ways that her feelings were depicted in a text, in any event) was Jonas's own, and that only after she learned a lesson about being too importunate. She had begged Jonas's abbot, Athala, to be allowed to see her son. Eventually, permission was granted, and Jonas set out with two companions. His mother's joy was short-lived and quickly suppressed for a higher good:

> When we arrived there, I was received graciously [*gratuite*] by my mother after the passage of so many years, but not for long did my mother enjoy [*fruitur*] the wished-for gift. For that same night I was struck by a fever and began to cry out amidst the burning heat that I was being tortured by the prayers of the man of God [Athala] not to remain there even a little while against his prohibition.[111] If [my companions] did not move me right away and if I did not return to the monastery with whatever strength I could muster, I would soon be overtaken by death. To this my mother said, "It is better for me, son, to know you are healthy there than to weep [*deflere*] for you dead here."[112]

---

109. Jonas, *Vita Columbani* 2.15, p. 135: "Videns anxia genetrix incumbentem unicae prolis exitum, inter singultus ac gemitus filiam poscit, ut si valeat impetrare, superis reddatur; aut si suae vitae metam suppleat, se cito de hac vita post se ducturam, nec posse se post eius vivere exitum."

110. For Christian traditions that downgraded mothers, though not especially for their emotionalism, see Clarissa W. Atkinson, *The Oldest Vocation: Christian Motherhood in the Middle Ages* (Ithaca, N.Y., 1991), esp. chaps. 1, 3.

111. Jonas had indeed obtained permission from his abbot, but in the meanwhile Athala found himself on his deathbed. Hence the new "prohibition": the abbot now wanted Jonas's return.

112. Jonas, *Vita Columbani* 2.5, p. 118: "Ubi ut pervenimus, gratuite a genetrice post tantorum intervallo annorum susceptus, sed non diu genetrix optatum fruitur donum. Nam eadem nocte febre correptus inter incendia clamare coepi, me Dei precibus viri torqueri, ne inibi contra interdictum quantisper morarer; si non me cito submoveant, quocumque po-

One mother has actually left us some writings: Herchenefreda, the mother of Desiderius. A few of her letters have been preserved, not in her son's letter collection but in the Carolingian *Life of Desiderius*.[113] If their authenticity may be granted (and nothing suggests the contrary), she was unambiguously affectionate: "To my sweetest [*dulcissimo*] and most beloved [*amantissimo*] son Desiderius, from Herchenefreda"; or, playing on her son's name, "To my sweetest [*dulcissimo*] and most desirable [*desiderantissimo*] son Desiderius, from Herchenefreda"; and again, contrasting her own emotional state to that of her son's, "To my always desirable [*desiderabili*] and sweetest [*dulcissimo*] son Desiderius, from Herchenefreda, your wretched [*misera*] mother."[114]

With such effusiveness, how did she retain her dignity in the world her son moved in? Perhaps she did not; after all, her letters were not saved in Desiderius's letter collection, and we have no evidence that he sent letters to *her*. Nevertheless, her letters have survived, presumably in Desiderius's keeping. I suggest that she carefully crafted her letters to follow the genre of the sermon, where (as we have seen in the case of Eligius) emotions were welcomed.[115] Like Dhuoda, whose *Handbook* for her son walked a fine line between pathos and pomposity, Herchenefreda advised her son on how to live at court: "I admonish you, my sweetest [*dulcissimum*] child [*pignus*: literally, a pledge of love], that you assiduously think of God, have God constantly on your mind, not consent to or act upon the bad works that God hates [*odit*]; be faithful [*sis fidelis*] to the king; love [*diligas*] your fellow courtiers [*contubernales*]; always love [*ames*] and fear [*timeas*] God."[116] Her instructions thus consisted in a string of emotional stances. But because she pro-

---

tuissem conamine ad monasterium repedare, me cito morte preventum. Mater ad haec: 'Melius mihi esse, fili, te inibi sanum scire, quam hic mortuum deflere.'"

113. *Vita Desiderii* 9–11, pp. 569–70. The vita dates from ca. 800 (see Krusch's remarks on p. 556), but the letters were presumably copied from authentic exemplars that the author had access to, perhaps in the archives of Saint-Géry (originally St. Amantius), the monastery that Desiderius founded at Cahors (ibid., p. 550; Desiderius, *Ep.*, 1.2, p. 12).

114. *Vita Desiderii* 9, p. 569; 10, p. 569; 11, p. 570.

115. I thank Julia Smith for discussions on this point. To be sure, St. Paul had already turned *paraenesis*, that is, exhortation, into an epistolary mode. The point here is that this mode appears to have been, for Desiderius and friends, the only acceptable vehicle for emotion talk.

116. *Vita Desiderii* 9, p. 569: "Te vero, dulcissimum mihi pignus, moneo, ut assidue Deum cogites, Deum jugiter in mente habeas, mala opera quae Deus odit nec consentias nec facias; regi sis fidelis, contubernales diligas, Deum semper ames et timeas."

nounced them, as Eligius did his, as a sort of "preacher," she perhaps evaded the opprobrium of an overwrought mother.

Thus, in a letter announcing the murder of her son Rusticus, she embedded her emotional turmoil within sermonizing admonitions:

> I, unhappy [*infelix*] mother, what should I do, now that your brothers are here no longer? If you should die, I would be bereft, childless. But you, my most pious *pignus*, my sweetest one [*dulcissime*], constantly take care that, though you have lost the solace [*solatia*] of your brothers, you do not lose yourself and, God forbid, go to your destruction. Beware always the wide and spacious road, which leads to perdition, and keep yourself in the path of God. As for me, grief on this great a scale (*prae nimio dolore*) is, I suspect, taking my life away. What you can do is pray that He in whose love I sigh day and night [*in cuius amore die noctuque suspiro*] will receive [my] soul as it departs [this life].[117]

THE EMOTIONAL WORLD OF COLUMBANUS

Whence an emotional community so wary of words of passion that they fit mainly in sermons and longing for another world? We might argue, in the tradition of Elias, that a court culture—even one in the seventh century—worked to restrain impulses. But, as the social constructionist theory has taught us, passionate emotional expressions are also products of social constraints. And, indeed, we saw a very different set of emotional norms at the Austrasian court of Brunhild and Sigibert in an earlier generation. Restraint is not a useful term, then, to explain or compass the emotional tenor at Neustria in the first half of the seventh century. Emotional shaping needs more than "tamping down." It needs norms, codes, models, articulated value-systems (such as aphorisms), and inarticulate ones (such as those implied by loving a charismatic leader). We have seen what the results of these were at the Neustrian court; but what explains them?

They came, to be sure, from the ascetic impulse. The models and writ-

---

117. Ibid., 11, p. 570: "Ego infelix mater quid agam, cum fratres tui iam non sunt? Si tu discesseris, ego orbata absque liberis ero. Sed tu, piissime pignus, mihi dulcissime, sic te jugiter praecave, ut dum solatia fratrum perdidisti, te non perdas, ut ne, quod absit, in interitum vadas. Cave semper latam et spatiosam viam, quae ducit ad perditionem, et temet ipsum in via Dei custodi. Ego prae nimio dolore vitam meam amittere suspicor. Tu ora, ut egredientem animam ille suscipiat, in cuius amore die noctuque suspiro."

ings of the Desert Fathers remained influential in seventh-century Gaul. Nor should we forget that a narrowing of the educational program—with classical literature largely falling by the wayside and the Psalter becoming the essential primer—was accompanied by an impoverishment of emotional vocabulary.[118] Education has much to do with values, which, in turn, determine the emotions that are privileged or downgraded.

To some degree, the change must have sprung as well from Clothar's hatred of Brunhild and her brood; he set himself against their culture and their modes of expression. If the values of the old regime privileged passion, then the new regime would favor the opposite. Already the earliest public pronouncements of the new dynasty set the tone. The Edict of Paris, promulgated in 614, suppressed Brunhild's entire line by the simple expedient of naming only Guntram, Chilperic I, and Sigibert I as Clothar's predecessors.[119] At about the same time, the Council of Paris set forth a series of rules delimiting the prerogatives of bishops, including their right to act on certain emotions: "If a bishop, either out of anger [*iracundia*] or for money ejects an abbot from his position uncanonically, let the abbot have recourse to a synod."[120] It was perfectly proper for a bishop to remove an unjust abbot, but here the assembly recognized anger and greed—both sins, both also emotions—as illegitimate motives.

The Neustrian court also had the example and the exhortations of Columbanus to guide it. We have seen that he spent some time with Clothar as both a "gift from heaven" and a "castigator." What emotional norms and expectations did he bring? We shall soon see. But we must not expect Columbanus's sensibilities to have been followed slavishly by the "next generation," the one represented by Desiderius and Jonas.[121] Few of them had known the reformer; they had mainly the memories of others and

---

118. See Pierre Riché, *Education and Culture in the Barbarian West Sixth through Eighth Centuries*, trans. John J. Contreni (Columbia, S.C., 1976), esp. pt. 3.

119. Edict of Paris 9, MGH Capitularia Regum Francorum, 1, ed. Alfred Boretius (Hannover, 1883), p. 22.

120. Council of Paris (614), 4, in *Concilia Galliae a. 511–a. 695*, ed. Charles de Clercq, CCSL 148A (Turnhout, 1963), p. 276.

121. T. M. Charles-Edwards makes the point with regard to the importance of penance: "the penitential regime was central to Columbanian monasticism in the generation after his death, whereas in his own writings such themes as the perception of human life as a *peregrinatio* alienated from a heavenly *patria* were more prominent"; Charles-Edwards, "The Penitential of Columbanus," in *Columbanus: Studies on the Latin Writings*, ed. Lapidge, p. 219.

their own imaginations to guide them. To be sure, Columbanus left sermons, poems, rules, and letters to posterity. There is little evidence, however, that the courtiers of Neustria read them. Jonas clearly knew the rules and penitentials of Columbanus, but he may have relied on oral traditions and his own lived experience at Bobbio for his knowledge. In his *Life of Columbanus,* he mentions some of Columbanus's writings, but he himself borrows only five short phrases directly from the extant writings of Columbanus.[122] In addition, the goals of the fiery reformer, a "holy man" of the old school, were quite different from the goals of the Neustrian court, which included institutionalizing Columbanian ideals in monasteries that would work for them as holy sites without any saintly presence at all.[123] It should thus not be surprising that the Neustrian emotional world was different from Columbanus's. Yet we will also find many commonalities.

While Columbanus's affective palette was large, he used only five emotion words (and their grammatical variants) thirty or more times in his works: *amor* (love), *caritas* (love), *diligo* (love), *laetitia* (joy), and *timor* (fear).[124] Love (via three different words), joy, and fear: these were the chief

---

122. Bruno Krusch identifies ten echoes of the writings of Columbanus in Jonas, *Vita Columbani*. Of these, only five directly use words from Columbanus's texts.

123. Diem, "Monks and Kings," argues for the institutionalization of charisma in the monastery; on the monastic space itself taking on sacred status, apart from any saint within, see Rosenwein, *Negotiating Space*.

124. The frequency of the most used emotion words in Columbanus, *Opera*, ed. and trans. G. S. M. Walker (Dublin, 1957), are as follows: *amor*: 60; *caritas*: 33; *diligo*: 63; *laetitia*: 38; *timor*: 31. (Verbal, noun, and adjectival forms of all these words are included in the count.) These numbers were calculated by using the Patrologia Latina Database published by ProQuest Information and Learning Company, taking care to eliminate all writings considered spurious or doubtful by Walker. Walker's assessment of Columbanus's writings has recently been largely affirmed by the discussions in *Columbanus: Studies on the Latin Writings*. It is likely, however, that the metrical poems titled in Walker "Ad Hunaldum," "Ad Sethum," and "Ad Fidolium" were not by Columbanus (see Michael Lapidge, "Epilogue: Did Columbanus Compose Metrical Verse?" in *Columbanus: Studies on the Latin Writings*, ed. Lapidge, pp. 274–85); and thus I have eliminated them from the word count here. On the other hand, I have included the short "Oratio S. Columbani" in Columbanus, *Opera*, p. 214, which Walker considered of dubious authorship but which Lapidge ("The *Oratio S. Columbani*," in *Columbanus: Studies on the Latin Writings*, pp. 271–73) sees as likely by Columbanus; and the hymn "Precamur patrem," which Lapidge ("'Precamur Patrem': An Easter Hymn by Columbanus?" in ibid., pp. 255–63) argues is Columbanian as well. For the text of this hymn, see *The Antiphonary of Bangor, an Early Irish Manuscript in the Ambrosian Library at Milan*, ed. F. E.

emotions that Columbanus expressed, almost always in the context of religious feeling.

Unlike the Neustrian courtiers, Columbanus was glad to express his affection lavishly, while he was less interested in hierarchy and deference. True, when writing to Pope Gregory I, he piled up honorifics in his salutation while demeaning himself: "To the holy Lord and Father in Christ, the most beautiful ornament of the Roman Church, to the most august person in the whole of parched Europe, to a kind of flower, as it were, to the illustrious Overseer who has mastered the contemplation of divine eloquence, I, Bar-Jona, a wretched dove [Columba/Columbanus means 'dove' in Latin], send greeting in Christ."[125] But Columbanus was ambivalent about commendation, a crucial difference from the Neustrian courtiers. He flouted his independence from the whole institution right in front of Pope Gregory himself: "I think it extremely superfluous to commend my own [people] to you since the Savior decrees that they are to be received as if walking in His name."[126] Yet this came directly after he wished peace to the pope and *his* dependents.

To his own monks, Columbanus was openly affectionate. Consider his greeting in a letter to them: "To his sweetest [*dulcissimis*] sons and dearest [*carissimis*] disciples."[127] He called Athala "most beloved" (*amantissime*).[128] Indeed, he used the word so freely that he termed the bishops who opposed his ideas about Easter "most beloved fathers and brothers" (*amantissimi patres ac fratres*).[129] It was a *topos,* indeed, and here no doubt used to sugar the otherwise hostile intent of the letter, but we have seen that *topoi* have mean-

---

Warren and William Griggs, 2 vols. (London, 1895), 2:5–7. On the authenticity of Columbanus's first letter, addressed to Pope Gregory the Great, see Robert Stanton, "Columbanus, Letter 1: Translation and Commentary," *Journal of Medieval Latin* 3 (1993): 149–68.

125. Columbanus, *Opera,* p. 2: "Domino Sancto et in Christo Patri, Romanae pulcherrimo Ecclesiae Decori, totius Europae flaccentis augustissimo quasi cuidam Flori, egregio Speculatori, Theoria utpote divinae Castalitatis potito, ego, Bar-Jona (vilis Columba), in Christo mitto Salutem." I borrow the translation of *flaccentis* as "parched" and the reading of *potito* (rather than *perito*) from Stanton, "Columbanus, Letter 1," pp. 152, 156–58. I am grateful to Laura Peelen, University of Utrecht, for pointing out to me that Columbanus was more interested in hierarchy than I had first imagined.

126. Columbanus, *Opera,* p. 10: "Persuperfluum puto commendare tibi meos, quos salvator quasi in suo nomine ambulantes recipiendos esse decernit."

127. Ibid., p. 26.
128. Ibid., p. 28.
129. Ibid., p. 16.

ing even when manipulated, and it is significant that, in the next generation, this easy use of *amor* gave way to reticence.[130]

If at ease with love, Columbanus was nevertheless profoundly ambivalent about it. As he pointed out to Athala, whom he left behind at Luxeuil because of his exile, "There is danger if [the monks] hate and danger if they love. Know that certain realities are involved in both hating and loving: peace perishes in hatred while integrity perishes in love."[131] Love was bad if aimed toward the world: "This world shall pass / . . . daily the present life they love [*amant*] fades away."[132] But it was good when directed at eternal life: "From earthly things lift up / The eyes of your heart. / Love [*ama*] the most beloved [*amantissimos*] host of angels."[133] Nor were these sentiments exclusive to *amor*; they applied to love in the guise of *dilectio* as well: "The love [*dilectio*] of God is the restoration of his image; he loves [*diligit*] God who keeps his commandments."[134] On the other hand: "How shall we flee the world, which we who are in the world ought not to love [*diligere*]?"[135] Only *caritas*, for Columbanus a consistently spiritualized form of love, was wholly good.

Happiness too was ambivalent. "Let the world laugh [*rideat*] with the devil; far be their happiness [*laetitia*] from us!"[136] This was the wrong sort of happiness. But there was a right one as well: "the end of the life of the just is eternal life, rest, perpetual peace, the heavenly fatherland, blessed eternity, infinite happiness [*laetitia*]."[137] Indeed, *laetitia* was one of the virtues; in

---

130. Gillian R. Knight, *The Correspondence between Peter the Venerable and Bernard of Clairvaux: A Semantic and Structural Analysis* (Aldershot, 1988), chap. 1, points out that affectionate words in letters may be ways to manipulate relationships, not to express affection per se. However, this caution is true of all emotions and is, indeed, one reason why Reddy coined the word "emotives."

131. Columbanus, *Opera*, p. 28: "periculum, si oderint, periculum, si amaverint. Scito utraque vera esse, inde vel odire vel amare; in odio pax, in amore integritas perit."

132. Ibid., p. 182: "Mundus iste transibit, / . . . Cottidie decrescit / Vita praesens quam amant."

133. Ibid., p. 184: "De terrenis eleva / Tui cordis oculos; / Ama amantissimos / Angelorum populos."

134. Ibid., p. 106: "Dei enim dilectio imaginis eius renovatio. Deum autem diligit qui eius mandata custodit."

135. Ibid., p. 74: "Nos quomodo fugiemus mundum, quem diligere non debemus, qui in mundo sumus."

136. Ibid., p. 82: "Rideat mundus cum diabolo, absit a nobis eorum laetitia."

137. Ibid., p. 96: "Justorum autem vitae finis est vita aeterna, requies, pax perennis, patria caelestis, aeternitas beata, laetitia infinita."

one of his Rules, Columbanus listed it between patience (*patientia*) and constancy (*stabilitas*).[138]

Fear alone was a uniformly positive emotion, as it was for the Neustrian courtiers. "Fear greatly [*expavescite*], I beg you, the weight of his words [referring to Matt 16:27, which threatens divine retribution], and with your mind uplifted in fear and trembling [*cum timore et tremore*], think constantly of the terrible advent of divine judgment."[139] Fear of the Last Judgment was its most frequent association, but fear was also useful in this world, as when Columbanus cautioned Athala to "fear" (*time*) the love of the monks at Luxeuil "because it will be dangerous to you."[140]

The general ambivalence toward emotions extended to how they should be expressed. Columbanus was uncomfortable with effusiveness. In his letter to his brethren he wrote:

> I wanted to write to you a tearful [*lacrimosam*] letter. But because I know your heart, therefore I have used another style, mentioning only necessary duties, harsh and arduous in themselves, and preferring to stop up [*obturare*] rather than call forth [*provocare*] tears. And so outwardly my words seem calm [*mitis*], [but] grief [*dolor*] is enclosed within. See: the tears rush forth; but it is better to stop up [*obturare*] the fountain, for it is not right for a brave soldier to weep [*plorare*] in battle.[141]

Columbanus here managed to condemn a demonstrative emotive style while nevertheless exploiting it to the hilt.

Did Columbanus think that the "brave soldier" was the antithesis of the "weak woman"? Did he, like the Neustrian fraternity, associate excessive emotionality with mothers? There is no evidence of it. He did not gender female those "happy people" who "laugh without reason" and "will weep

---

138. Ibid., p. 136.

139. Ibid., p. 98: "Expavescite, quaeso, dictorum pondus, et cum timore et tremore suspecta semper mente illum tremendum divini judicii adventum indesinenter cogitate."

140. Ibid., p. 28: "Sed tu et ipsum eorum time amorem, quia tibi periculosus erit."

141. Ibid., p. 30: "Lacrimosam tibi volui scribere epistolam; sed quia scio cor tuum, idcirco necessariis tantum allegatis, duris et ipsis arduisque, altero stilo usus sum, malens obturare quam provocare lacrimas. Foris itaque actus est sermo mitis, intus inclusus est dolor. En proruunt lacrimae, sed melius est obturare fontem; non enim fortis militis est in bello plorare."

[*flebunt*] bitterly" at the passing of the world.[142] Like all male ascetics, he fled women: "Beware, little son, / the forms of women / Through whom death enters."[143] But here he was upbraiding men for the sins of lust and desire, not women for their melodramatics.

Indeed, none of the other emotional communities that we have seen associated women so clearly with excessive emotions as did the Neustrian courtiers.[144] Gregory the Great thought parents of both sexes overprotected their children; St. Felicity was his one shining exception. Fortunatus celebrated rather than denigrated both male and female passion. Gregory of Tours considered mothers to be tender and had no qualms about such feelings in himself. I do not wish to argue that the Neustrian courtiers constituted the first emotional community to bring a jaundiced attitude toward women to the fore. That view was constructed out of shards left over from the repertory of words, phrases, and ideas of the ancient world. But an attitude need not be new to be important. Taken together with the same group's disparagement of emotions in general, it was a defining characteristic of their emotional community. That community was shaped by the regime's own dynastic interests, as we have noted. But it was also a byproduct of the intense comradery of the court, a quasi-monastic group that had to outdo real monks in its wariness of emotional involvement and expression if it were to gain the kingdom of heaven.

Columbanus's ascetic impulse and the emotional norms that went with it were absorbed as well as adapted and transformed by the courtiers of Neustria of the next generation. Like him, they privileged love. Happiness they expressed as well—we have seen their longing for it—and even a charter from the period, a confirmation for Saint-Denis issued by Dagobert circa 632, begins with the hope that transitory things may be transformed into "eternal joys" (*gaudia sempeterna*).[145] The emphasis on male-male bonds turned the court into a monastery manqué. Only their celebration of status showed the attraction of secular habits. The Neustrian courtiers incorporated hierarchy into the Columbanian model by making deference part of their male fraternity culture. There was a "cost," however: male-male bonds

---

142. Ibid., p. 184.
143. Ibid., p. 182: "Caveto, filiole, / Feminarum species, / Per quas mors ingreditur."
144. Though there is a hint of this in Plato; see chap. 1 above.
145. *ChLA* 13, no. 551, p. 10 = MGH D Merov, 1:41, p. 110.

were drained of effusive emotional expression. Since the deference was "of this world," it could not properly be accompanied by passionate vows of love, given the values and goals of the monklike group involved in such exchanges. But soon those values and goals would fall by the wayside, as a new and far less fraternal community came to the fore.

6
REVELING IN RANCOR

The last of Clothar's courtiers, the indefatigable Dado (St. Audoin), died in 684.¹ But even before that moment the moderated tones of the emotional community that had formed under Clothar II were dying away. Consider Fredegar, a historian who wrote between 659 and 714, probably circa 660.² His *Chronicle* is rightly associated with Jonas's *Life of Columbanus,* for he knew the text and happily borrowed its vilification of Queen Brunhild.³ But, except where he copied this source, his emotional palette was quite different. Hatred (*odium*), for example, was a word that the Neustrian courtiers almost never used. It came up only once in the *Life of Columbanus,* to speak of a food preference: a young nun's excessive hunger was punished by God's exciting in her "hatred [*odium*] of licit food," so that she could find solace only in "grain husks, leaves, and mixed wild herbs."⁴ Desiderius was still more circumspect, never using the word "hatred" or any of its variants at all. His

---

1. For the date, see *Vita Audoini episcopi Rotomagensis,* ed. Wilhelm Levison, MGH SRM 5:540 (hereafter *Vita Audoini*).

2. Roger Collins gives a wide range of possible dates for Fredegar (*Fredegar,* Authors of the Middle Ages, Historical and Religious Writers of the Latin West, vol. 4, no. 13 [Aldershot, 1996], p. 83), but on p. 111 he points out that "the balance of probability" has Fredegar a layman writing around 660. For a forceful presentation of the date "in or shortly after 659," and for Fredegar as a member of one faction of the Austrasian aristocracy, see Ian N. Wood, "Fredegar's Fables," in *Historiographie im frühen Mittelalter,* ed. Anton Scharer and Georg Scheibelreiter (Vienna, 1994), 359–66. For a review of the scholarship on Fredegar, see the introduction to *Frédégaire, Chronique des temps mérovingiens (Livre IV et Continuations),* trans. Olivier Devillers and Jean Meyers (Turnhout, 2001), pp. 5–53.

3. For example, chap. 36 of Fredegar's *Chronicle* is taken (as Wallace-Hadrill remarks) "verbatim, with very few additions, and some omissions that obscure the sense of the original, from the *Vita Columbani* of Jonas"; Fredegar, *Chronicle* 36, ed. Wallace-Hadrill, p. 23 n. 2. In particular, Fredegar follows Jonas, *Vita Columbani* 1.18–19 and part of 20, MGH SRM 4:86–91, precisely the segment that has to do with Columbanus's confrontation with Brunhild and its aftermath.

4. Jonas, *Vita Columbani* 2.22, p. 142: "excitavit odium liciti cibi, nec valebat turbata mens aliud quicquam quam furfures frondesque et herbarum agrestium mixturam edere."

mother used it once, draining it of worldly passion by attributing it to God: "Do not consent to or act upon the bad works that God hates [*odit*]."[5]

By contrast, Fredegar saw hatred everywhere. It (and other powerful emotions) explained human action. Thus "the Burgundian nobles, whether bishops or other lords, fearing [*timentis*] Brunhild and feeling hatred toward her [*odium in eam habentes*]," called on Clothar to take over their kingdom.[6] When he had done so, he spared Merovech, the son of Theuderic, and executed Brunhild, both motivated by his strong feelings:

> By order of Clothar, Merovech was secretly sent to Neustria, [since Clothar] cherished him with that love [*eodem amplectens amore*] with which he had raised him from the holy [baptismal] font.... [But] when Brunhild was presented to his sight, Clothar felt overwhelming hatred toward her [*odium contra ipsam nimium haberit*] ... and ordered that she be led through the entire army seated on a camel and afterward that the hair of her head, one foot, and an arm be tied to the tail of the most vicious horse. And then she was torn apart limb by limb by its hooves and the speed of its pace.[7]

It is tempting to imagine that Fredegar was a harbinger of the new emotional community of the late seventh century which we shall soon discuss. Certainly that community privileged strong emotions, vehemently expressed. But because Fredegar was writing (it would seem) a decade earlier, he cannot securely be brought into rapprochement with any other writers. It is not until the last two or three decades of the seventh century that a cluster of sources emerge that may be associated—though uncertainly—with one another.

A COMMUNITY OF ANONYMOUS AUTHORS?

The late seventh-century community that this chapter embraces is the most tenuous of all we have dealt with. The communities of those who commissioned epitaphs at Vienne, Trier, and Clermont, for example, were at least members of the same locality, defined and circumscribed by place. Even if

---

5. *Vita Desiderii* 9, MGH SRM 4:56; see chap. 5, note 116 above.

6. Fredegar, *Chronicle*, p. 34: "Burgundaefaronis vero tam episcopi quam citeri leudis timentis Brunechildem et odium in eam habentes."

7. Ibid., p. 35: "Meroeus secrecius iusso Chlothariae in Neptrico perducetur, eodem amplectens amore quod ipso de sancto excepisset lavacrum ... Chlotharius, cum Brunechildis suum presentatur conspectum et odium contra ipsam nimium haberit, ... iobetque eam prius camillum per omne exercito sedentem perducere, post haec comam capitis, unum pedem et brachium ad veciosissemum aequum caudam legare: ibique calcibus et velocitate cursus membratim disrumpetur."

they did not know one another, even if they lived generations apart, they still had a city and its ongoing traditions in common. The "community" of Gregory of Great was problematic in a different way: it was approached by exploring one individual's ideas and modes of expression as if they constituted a window onto the emotional norms of a larger social cadre. But the extension seemed warranted, given Gregory's sensitivity as a observer of his flock and his own participation in a particular clerical group. Gregory of Tours and Fortunatus were more promising. Admittedly a small community of two, they nevertheless represented a real social entity, one that reached beyond themselves to the many people, particularly at the Austrasian court, with whom they maintained contact over a long period of time. The Neustrian courtiers assembled by and around Clothar II and his progeny had a similar social reality, and happily we had more evidence for their relationships and their emotional norms. We were thus able to call upon the writings not of just two men, but of Desiderius, his mother, Eligius, Jonas, and a few others.

By contrast, the late seventh-century writings to be discussed in this chapter can boast no common city or court. Nor can we demonstrate that the authors knew one another, though they certainly read one another (as various literary borrowings indicate), and their audiences must have overlapped. What allows us to bring them together here as representative of an emotional community? The answer is that in the period circa 670–700, when these sources were written, the elites of Francia were less tied than previously to particular regions. Those of Burgundy were absorbed into the political life of Neustria already in the time of Dagobert; they no longer wanted a king of their own. The elites of Austrasia were moving in the same direction in the 670s, when one faction there joined Ebroin, the former Neustrian mayor of the palace, in his bid to regain power in Neustria.[8] Later, in the 680s, the Austrasians ceased to have a king altogether, while one faction of its magnates, under the leadership of Pippin II, began to cannibalize Neustria. The process began with war (at Bois-du Fays in 679; at Tertry in 687) and continued with the Pippinids and their followers marrying into Neustrian families, becoming Neustrian landowners, and slowly taking over patronage of the Neustrian church.[9] Elsewhere, the same sort of

---

8. *Passiones Leudegarii episcopi et martyris Augustodunensis I* (hereafter *Passio Leudegarii*) 18, 19, 25, 26, ed. Bruno Krusch, MGH SRM 5:300–301, 306–7.

9. I do not mean to suggest the inevitability of this process nor that its end result—the Carolingian takeover—would have been clear to people in the last decades of the seventh century. See the discussion in Gerberding, *The Rise of the Carolingians,* chap. 6.

homogenization was taking place: the *Martyrdom of Praejectus* shows that even the elites of the Auvergne were drawn into the political orbits of the northern kings.[10]

The much-noted violence of the late seventh century was due not to regionalism or separatism but to a common desire for access to an increasingly centralized court and its powers.[11] We are no longer in Gregory's and Fortunatus's world of fraternal civil wars. The aristocracy was more powerful now, and its competition was key to the fighting of the period—and to our sources, which reflect the interests of the elites. Several of these texts are *passiones,* accounts of the deaths—interpreted as "martyrdoms"—of men, now called "saints," who led particular elite factions. We might think that such factions would imply different—perhaps even polarized—emotional communities. But this does not appear to have been the case. The important point—from the emotional point of view—is the sharing of common values and goals, even if such "sharing" engenders competition. Let us recall the very definition of emotions: they have to do with appraisals of things *affecting me.* The sources that we shall be looking at, no matter their place of origin, were obsessed by the motives behind power holding, power grabbing, and power sharing. That they often found these motives in strong and usually rancorous emotions betrays the hold that these feelings had on their authors' imagination and modes of presentation. From their writings we can glimpse the emotions that they privileged or downgraded, their frequency of expression, and the contexts in which they arose. Like all shaped materials, these sources had not only purely "expressive" purpose but also rhetorical ends; they were meant to interpret the past for the interests of the present. The sources from circa 670 to 700 are nostalgic, though not a bit sentimental: they look back on a violent period and claim the virtuous high

---

10. *Passio Praejecti episcopi et martyris Arverni,* ed. Bruno Krusch, MGH SRM 5:225–48 (hereafter *Passio Praejecti*); see the comments on how this text shows the integration of the Auvergne in the politics of the north in *Late Merovingian France,* ed. and trans. Fouracre and Gerberding, pp. 269–70.

11. See Paul Fouracre, "Attitudes towards Violence in Seventh- and Eighth-Century Francia," in *Violence and Society in the Early Medieval West,* ed. Guy Halsall (Woodbridge, 1998), pp. 60–75; and, assessing the importance of regional variations, idem, "The Nature of Frankish Political Institutions in the Seventh Century," in *Franks and Alemanni in the Merovingian Period: An Ethnographic Perspective,* ed. Ian Wood (Woodbridge, 1998), pp. 285–301. See also the excellent interpretive sections in *Late Merovingian France,* ed. and trans. Fouracre and Gerberding.

ground of their own day in part by means of a highly charged emotional and moral vocabulary.

It will be convenient for the reader to have a brief list of these materials, here organized (where possible) alphabetically by the name of their hero or heroine:[12]

1. *The Life of Bishop Audoin*.[13] This is the life of Dado (Audoin), whom we have met as a member of Desiderius's "indivisible" quintet. The author is anonymous, but he knew Audoin's disciples, who told him about the saint's miracles.[14] It is thus likely that he wrote between 684 (Audoin's date of death) and around 704. Because he uses the word *Franci* to mean "the Neustrians," he was likely writing to the Neustrian elites.[15]

2. *The Life of Lady Balthild*.[16] This is the life of Queen Balthild, whom we met in the previous chapter as a patron of Eligius and Jonas. The author is anonymous; the fact that the prologue addresses "*dilectissimi fratres*" (most beloved brethren) does not seem decisive for his or her identification as male.[17] The author wrote the *Life* after Balthild's

---

12. Here I have not considered the *Acta S. Annemundi* [i.e., *Aunemundi*], AASS, Sept. VII, pp. 694–96, because, although "rehabilitated" as a source of the seventh century by Fouracre and Gerberding in *Late Merovingian France*, pp. 170–71, "descriptive passages" are likely interpolated (p. 171). Since the emotions are precisely in these passages, it seems prudent to eliminate this text for our purposes.

13. *Vita Audoini*, pp. 553–67.

14. Ibid., 7, p. 558; see *Late Merovingian France*, ed. and trans. Fouracre and Gerberding, p. 133.

15. Ibid., 13, p. 562. On the significance of the term *Franci*, see Gerberding, *The Rise of the Carolingians*, p. 76.

16. *Vita Sanctae* [i.e., *Domnae*] *Balthildis A* (hereafter *Vita Balthildis*), ed. Bruno Krusch, MGH SRM 2:482–508.

17. *Vita Balthildis* prol., p. 482: "Michi quidem, ut imperatum est, dilectissimi fratres, ad tam subtile piumque opus peragendum." (To me indeed, most beloved brothers, it was commanded to complete so fine and pious a work.) A male author is proposed by Fouracre and Gerberding in *Late Merovingian France*, p. 115, because "the first line of the preface . . . expressly dedicates the work to the author's *dilectissimi fratres*." However, the author does not say he or she is a member of the fraternity, and it seems equally plausible to argue, with Janet L. Nelson, that "the 'A' *Vita* was evidently written by a nun at Chelles, and commissioned by some monks—perhaps those of Corbie?" See Nelson, "Queens as Jezebels: The Careers of Brunhild and Balthild in Merovingian History," in eadem, *Politics and Ritual in Early Medieval Europe* (London, 1986), p. 17 n. 83.

death, circa 680, perhaps quite shortly thereafter.[18] Because the *Franci* here meant the Neustrians, the author was, again, probably writing to Neustrians.[19]

3. *The Vision of Barontus.*[20] Barontus was a nobleman, recently converted to the religious life at the monastery of Saint Peter in Longoret, near Bourges. His near-death and out-of-body experience first in heaven and then in hell is recounted here. The author, probably a monk at Longoret or nearby Méobecq, presumably wrote his account shortly after the vision, which took place in 678 or 679.[21] Although the immediate audience was no doubt the monks of Longoret and Méobecq, the fact that the *Vision* places Bishops Dido of Poitiers (d. ca. 677) and Vulfoleodus of Bourges (d. ca. 672) in hell suggests that the author had in mind a larger public as well.[22] Dido appears in the *Martyrdom of Leudegar* (below) not only as the saint's uncle but as a man "filled with an extraordinary abundance of prudence."[23] If, as it seems, the author of Leudegar's life was speaking to one faction of the Frankish aristocracy, the author of the *Vision* clearly spoke for and to a different group.[24]

4. *The Life of Germanus, Abbot of Grandval.* Germanus was a monk in

---

18. On the date of the *Vita Balthildis* see *Late Merovingian France*, ed. and trans. Fouracre and Gerberding, pp. 114–15.

19. *Vita Balthildis* 10, p. 495, where the *Franci*, i.e., the Neustrians, kill Bishop Sigobrandus of Paris.

20. *Visio Baronti monachi Longoretensis*, ed. Wilhelm Levison, MGH SRM 5:377–94. See also Maria Pia Ciccarese, *Visioni dell'Aldilà in occidente. Fonti, modelli, testi* (Florence, 1987), pp. 231–75 (giving the text of the *Visio* and annotated Italian translation); Claude Carozzi, *Le voyage de l'âme dans l'au-delà, d'après la littérature latine: V^e–XIIIe siècle* (Rome, 1994), chap. 3.

21. For the date, see Carozzi, *Voyage de l'âme*, p. 140, and John J. Contreni, "'Building Mansions in Heaven': The *Visio Baronti*, Archangel Raphael, and a Carolingian King," *Speculum* 78 (2003): 673 n. 2.

22. On the local nature of the *Visio*'s audience, see Yitzhak Hen, "The Structure and Aims of the *Visio Baronti*," *Journal of Theological Studies*, n.s., 47 (1996): 477–97; and Isabel Moreira, *Dreams, Visions, and Spiritual Authority in Merovingian Gaul* (Ithaca, N.Y., 2000), p. 159. Michelle L. Roper argues that the vision may have been a "repository of the monastic rule" and thus mainly (though not entirely) addressed to the community itself; Roper, "Uniting the Community of the Living with the Dead: The Use of Other-World Visions in the Early Middle Ages," in *Authority and Community in the Middle Ages*, ed. Donald Mowbray, Rhiannon Purdie, and Ian P. Wei (Stroud, 1999), p. 29.

23. *Passio Leudegarii* 1, p. 283: "prudentia divitiarumque opibus insigne copia erat repletus."

24. But here I part with Carozzi, *Voyage de l'âme*, pp. 143–44, who sees the factions as having "national" origins, with Barontus a "son or relative of an Aquitainian in the service of the

the Columbanian tradition, first at Remiremont, then at Luxeuil, and finally at Grandval (in Alsace), which he founded. The author of his *Life* was a priest named Bobolenus.[25] He wrote after Germanus's martyrdom in about 675, probably quite soon thereafter.[26] Although he dedicated the *Life* to Ingofrid, abbot of Luxeuil, the connection to Luxeuil does not necessarily link him to the Neustrian court, since Luxeuil had supporters in Austrasia as well. Thus, it is not surprising to read that Germanus was part of the Austrasian court of Sigibert III, and Bobolenus too seems best understood in an Austrasian context.[27]

5. *The Life of St. Gertrude.*[28] This is the life of the sister of Grimoald (a Pippinid mayor in Austrasia who was executed by Clovis II) and daughter of Pippin I (an earlier mayor of the palace) and his wife, Itta. Gertrude was abbess of Nivelles, one of several monasteries founded by her mother. She died in 653, and her *Life* was composed circa 670.[29] The author was a monk, probably connected to Nivelles.

6. *The Martyrdom of St. Leudegar.*[30] This recounts the martyrdom of Bishop Leudegar. A member of the supra-regional elite mentioned above, Leudegar, whose brother was count of Paris, was appointed bishop of the Burgundian city of Autun by Queen Balthild.[31] The author of his *Life*, whose name is not known, was a monk at Saint-

---

Neustrian court" and thus a natural enemy of the "Burgundian" Leudegar, the "Austrasian" Dido, and perhaps even of the "Neustrian" Vulfoleodus.

25. Bobolenus, *Vita Germani abbatis Grandivallensis,* ed. Bruno Krusch, MGH SRM 5:33 (hereafter *Vita Germani*), where the author calls himself "Bobolenus exiguus omnium presbyterorum" (Bobolenus, least of all priests).

26. Following the argument of Hans J. Hummer, *Politics and Power in Early Medieval Europe: Alsace and the Frankish Realm, 600–1000* (Cambridge, 2005), chap. 1.

27. Bobolenus, *Vita Germani* 1, p. 33, where Germanus's brother is said to have been educated "under King Sigibert." Germanus's family came from Trier, and Germanus was portrayed by Bobolenus as a disciple of Arnulf of Metz (see ibid., 4, pp. 34–35), a key Austrasian figure, while his murderer, the Alsatian *dux* Adalricus Eticho (see ibid., 11, p. 38, where he is termed Chaticus) was deeply involved in Austrasian political factionalism. On Luxeuil's close relations with both the Neustrian and Austrasian courts, see Wood, *Merovingian Kingdoms,* p. 192.

28. *Vita Sanctae Geretrudis A,* ed. Bruno Krusch, MGH SRM 2:453–64 (hereafter *Vita Geretrudis*).

29. *Late Merovingian France,* ed. and trans. Fouracre and Gerberding, p. 303 n. 10.

30. *Passio Leudegarii,* pp. 282–324.

31. See *Late Merovingian France,* ed. and trans. Fouracre and Gerberding, p. 198.

Symphorien in Leudegar's episcopal city. He was commissioned to write by Hermenar, who was his former abbot, counterclaimant to Leudegar's see, and eventually Leudegar's successor at Autun. Writing after Leudegar's death circa 678 but likely before Leudegar's relics were transferred to Poitiers in 684, the writer represents the Neustrian/Burgundian faction that once opposed Leudegar but now wished to claim his fame for themselves.[32]

7. *The Martyrdom of St. Praejectus.*[33] This is the account of the life and death of Praejectus, bishop of Clermont. He was a member of an Auvergnat family of the lesser nobility. The author was perhaps a nun from the monastery of Chamalières, a house founded at Praejectus's urging and presided over by an abbess who was probably a member of Praejectus's family. Alternatively the author may have been male and a monk, perhaps at Volvic or Saint-Amarin. The *Martyrdom* was written shortly after Praejectus's murder in 676 at the hands of a faction loosely aligned with St. Leudegar and at loggerheads with the Austrasians. It must have been completed by 690, the date of the death of Bishop Avitus of Clermont, during whose lifetime the piece was written.

8. *The Life of St. Sadalberga.*[34] This is the tale of Sadalberga, of noble birth, who was healed of blindness by the Columbanian abbot Eustasius of Luxeuil. After two marriages (both against her will) and many children, she converted to the religious life. She first founded a monastery at Langres, but, anticipating the wars between Theuderic III and Dagobert II in the 670s, she established a more permanent foundation at Laon and became its abbess. She died circa 670. The author of her *Life* says that he or she wrote at the request of Sadalberga's daughter and successor at Laon. Dismissed as a ninth-century forgery by Bruno Krusch, the *Life*'s authenticity and a seventh-century date (ca. 680) have recently been forcefully argued by Hans Hummer.[35]

9. *The Life of St. Wandregisil.*[36] Wandregisil (d. 668), a noble turned

---

32. On the date, ibid., p. 201; on the circumstances of its writing, pp. 201–6 and Joseph-Claude Poulin, "Saint Léger d'Autun et ses premiers biographes (fin VIIe–milieu IXe siècle)," *Bulletin de la Société des Antiquaires de l'Ouest,* 4th ser., 16 (1977): 167–200, esp. 176–78.

33. For the information below, I follow Fouracre and Gerberding in *Late Merovingian France,* pp. 254–70.

34. *Vita Sadalbergae abbatissae Laudunensis,* ed. Bruno Krusch, MGH SRM 5:40–66.

35. Hans Hummer, "Die merowingische Herkunft der Vita Sadalbergae," *Deutsches Archiv für Erforschung des Mittelalters* 59 (2003): 459–93.

36. *Vita Wandregiseli abbatis Fontanellensis,* ed. Bruno Krusch, MGH SRM 5:13–24.

ascetic, lived briefly at the monasteries of Bobbio and Romainmôtier before becoming abbot of his own foundation, Fontanelle, near Rouen. His anonymous *Life,* written after 684 (i.e., after Audoin's death), probably circa 700,[37] puts its hero in close touch with both the Neustrian and Austrasian elites.[38]

10. Original Latin charters of seventh-century Francia. These are legal documents drawn up by kings, bishops, and very wealthy magnates. They have been published in facsimile and transcription by Hartmut Atsma and Jean Vezin.[39] Including wills, judgments (*placita*), privileges, and confirmations, those extant today represent a tiny fraction of the charters that must have been written during the period. But because there is no doubt about their authenticity, they may be mined for the emotional vocabulary that they use—and do not use.

Many of these writings were haunted by the ghosts of Ebroin, mayor of the Neustrian palace, and Leudegar, Balthild's Burgundian episcopal appointee. Onto these wraiths our mainly anonymous authors projected emotional lives very different from those of the Neustrian courtiers in the first part of the same century. They used emotion words liberally and with verve. They expected people—both men and women—to be passionate: to love, hate, exult in joy, and break down in tears. Above all, they foregrounded rancorous and fearful feelings. Even the Devil was accorded a complex emotional life in these writings. The emotional community of the elites of late seventh-century Francia saw emotions as animating elements of thought, behavior, and human (and inhuman) interaction.

FREQUENCIES

Let us begin to explore this new emotional community via its charters. This may at first appear foolhardy: formulaic in the extreme, charters are a rela-

---

37. See the remarks of Bruno Krusch, MGH SRM 5:3.

38. *Vita Wandregiseli* 3, p. 14, where he serves as a royal tax collector (i.e., for Dagobert, who was king of Austrasia); ibid., 7, p. 16, where he is brought to court by Dagobert II for taking the tonsure without royal permission (but ultimately reconciles with the king); ibid., 14, p. 19, where his monastery at Fontanelle is described as "ex fisco quem adsumpsit regale munere" (on fiscal land which he received by royal generosity), and ibid., p. 20, where he is "carus Dadone pontefice" (dear to Bishop Dado, i.e., Audoin).

39. *ChLA* 13–14 concern the seventh century.

tively unemotional genre. Yet precisely because of their resistance to even minor verbal changes, documents such as these can be telling when they do betray something new. Moreover, they bear comparison because they are fairly equal in length, containing between about ten and a hundred lines of text.

Consider, then, the first (datable) ten charters drawn up before 670.[40] We have already briefly mentioned the only two that used emotion words: the charter of Dagobert on behalf of Saint-Denis circa 632 and the charter of Clovis II confirming a privilege by Bishop Landeric of Paris in 654.[41] The first spoke of "eternal joys," the second repeatedly spoke of love and fear. Doubtless the emotions could not have been "deeply felt" in the modern sense. Nevertheless, the words are significant. Just as the royal confirmation of Landeric's privilege listed the sorts of properties that Saint-Denis had been given (estates, slaves, gold and silver), so it needed to describe the motives for those gifts—religious, righteous, and (the implication is there) deeply held—which justified the provisions of the exemption itself. The exemption prohibited the bishop—Landeric himself—from taking any of the properties belonging to the monastery.[42] This was a major sacrifice on Landeric's part, and the royal confirmation's reiterated emotion words justified it. The words were not formulaic, however routine they may sound. Indeed, they were not formulaic because they appeared in only two out of ten charters.

However—and this is the key point—the largely unemotional tenor of

---

40. From the end of the sixth century to a charter dated 660–73 there are thirteen charters, but one (*ChLA* 13, no. 549 [619/20]) is too fragmentary to be useful, and two of them (nos. 557 [658/59–678/79] and 560 [657–88]) straddle the 670 divide by too wide a margin to be counted here. The ten that remain were all issued by kings. The documents (with their corresponding number in MGH D Merov in parenthesis, and dates etc. in brackets) are: *ChLA* 13, nos. 550 (22) [584–628; confirmation of Clothar II]; 552 (28) [625; confirmation of Clothar II]; 554 (32) [629–37; confirmation of Dagobert I]; 551 (41) [632–33; confirmation of Dagobert I]; 556 (72) [639; confirmation of Clovis II]; 555 (74) [639–49/50; charter of protection by Clovis II]; 559 (75) [639–49/50; confirmation of Clovis II]; 558 (85) [654; confirmation of Clovis II]; 561 (93) [659–60; placitum (court hearing) of Clothar III]; 553 (94) [660–73; placitum of Clothar III].

41. *ChLA* 13, no. 551, p. 10 = MGH D Merov, 1:108–10, no. 41; *ChLA* 13, no. 558, pp. 36–37 = MGH D Merov, 1:218, no. 85. See chap. 5, notes 80 and 145.

42. On Merovingian immunities and exemptions in general, see Rosenwein, *Negotiating Space*, chaps. 2–4, and on this royal confirmation in particular, pp. 74–77.

the charters prior to 670 changed thereafter. Five, rather than two, of the first datable ten charters from that later period contain emotion words.[43] Moreover, the emotion words in those charters are more wide ranging, more daring than those of the earlier sample. When, in 673, a lady named Clotild, *Deo devota* (dedicated to God), endowed the monastery of Bruyères-le-Châtel and installed her niece Mummola as abbess there, she included a curse clause at the end that called down the wrath (*iram*) of the Holy Trinity on anyone who might dare to oppose the provisions of her charter.[44] After a council deposed Chramlinus from the bishopric of Embrun, Theuderic III, "moved by mercy" (*mesericordia muti*), lifted the sentence of exile and allowed the man to convert to the monastic life at Saint-Denis.[45] When Wademir and Ercamberta gave their properties to various churches and monasteries, Wademir referred to his wife as "sweetest" (*dulcissema*).[46]

Moving beyond the first ten charters extant after 670, we see—in an exemption granted by Agerad, the bishop of Chartres, to Notre-Dame de Bourgmoyen in 696—all the emotions of the confirmation for Landeric's exemption, plus some telling new ones.[47] Here the "fear of God," which is certainly mentioned, is joined by the worldly fear (even stronger, if the intensifier *per-* is taken into account) that the monks felt about being deprived of their property. Thus the privilege is granted "so that it may be allowed to the holy congregation of the servants of God . . . to live in peace, such that they need not fear [*pertimiscant*] having to give anyone meals [*convivia*],

---

43. There are eleven documents between 673 and 693, but *ChLA* 13, no. 569 (= Pardessus, no. 413) cannot be dated with precision. All but three of the remainder were issued by a king. The documents are: *ChLA* 13, nos. 564 (= Pardessus, no. 361) [673; monastic foundation]; 566 (121) [679; gift of Theuderic III]; 565 (122) [679; judgment by Theuderic III]; 568 (123) [679–90; privilege of Theuderic III]; 567 (126) [682; placitum of Theuderic III]; 570 (131) [690; gift of Theuderic III]; 571 (= Pardessus, no. 412) [690–91; gifts to churches]; 563 (= Pardessus, no. 421) [691?; exchange of land]; *ChLA* 14, nos. 572 (135) [692; placitum of Clovis III]; 573 (137) [693; placitum of Clovis III].

44. *ChLA* 13, no. 564, p. 66 = Pardessus 2:148–50, no. 361. On this charter see Léon Levillain, "Études mérovingienne. La charte de Clotilde (10 mars 673)," *Bibliothèque de l'École des chartes* 105 (1944): 5–63, at p. 20. On the history and significance of maledictory curses, see Little, *Benedictine Maledictions*.

45. *ChLA* 13, no. 565, p. 69. The charter is dated 679 in MGH D Merov 122, p. 310.

46. *ChLA* 13, no. 571, p. 95 = Pardessus 2:210, no. 412.

47. *ChLA* 14, no. 580, pp. 26–27.

lodging [*mansiones*], supplies [*paratas*], and gifts [*munera*]."⁴⁸ The person most likely to demand the meals, lodging, supplies, and gifts was the very bishop handing out the exemption—the local diocesan bishop—along with his imagined successors. The document continues by questioning the intentions of such bishops: if the local diocesan is invited to do the various blessings (of the altar and so on) that the monastery needs, let him not do so for the sake of "wicked desire" (*pravae cupiditatis*). Meanwhile, the monks should govern themselves with an abbot whom they choose for his "honest way of life, . . . vigilant and wise in the love [*amore*] of God."⁴⁹ But if they fail, and the monastery becomes troubled, the bishop should intervene, "like a father [*paterno more*]," to restore peace. He must beware, however, not to dominate the monastery—here follows a list of all the rights he and others might not have over it. Malice (*malicia*), sent by the Devil, has a way of obstructing good intentions; hence a curse is placed on any bishop who might violate the provisions of the privilege. Finally, Agerad speaks of the virtues of the monks: "We have seen them desire with the highest desire [*summo desiderio desiderare*]" to praise God according to the Rule. He implores Christ that they may continue to advance "in love [*amore*] of God."⁵⁰ The timid evocation of the love and fear of God, the most acceptable Christian emotions and ones used frequently by the Neustrian courtiers (as we have seen), has here given way to a wider spectrum: there is love and fear of God, to be sure, but also malice, fear of worldly destitution, and desires both good—*desiderium*—and bad—*cupiditas*.

The increasing emotionalism of the charters is echoed in other texts of the period. In the *Martyrdom of Leudegar*, a representative narrative from the period, I count a very large number of different emotion words (twenty-seven) along with six other words that indicate an emotional state—tears, trembling, and so on.⁵¹ Love is astonishingly absent: it occurs only eight

---

48. Ibid., p. 26: "ut liciat sancta congregacioni servorum dei in ipso monastirio constitutum, . . . quieti vivere, ut a nullos convivia nec mansionis nec paratas nec munera expedenda non pertimiscant."

49. Ibid.: "qui honestis moribus sit, non generositatis nobilium, sed in dei amore expergencius atque sagacius inbutum."

50. *ChLA* 14, no. 580, p. 27.

51. The emotion words in the *Passio Leudegarii* (I here list one form, but I have counted them in whatever form or part of speech) and their frequency in the text (in parentheses) are: *amor* (4), *caritas* (3), *cupiditas* (5), *dispereo* (1), *despicio* (1), *dilectio* (1), *doleo* (4), *formido* (2), *furor* (6), *gaudeo* (9), *invideo* (10), *ira* (5), *laetor* (3), *livor* (3), *lugeo* (3), *malitia* (3), *miseratio* (1), *metus* (12), *moleste* (2), *odium* (4), *pavor* (1), *p(a)eniteo* (4), *superbia* (5), *timor* (9), *terror/perteri-*

times, with *amor* and *caritas* preferred over *dilectio*. Compare this with the frequency of rancorous words, which come up thirty-four times in the text, envy being by far the commonest.[52] Nearly as frequent are words of fear, which appear twenty-nine times, with *metus* and *timor* most recurrent. If trembling (*tremens*) is added to the list (as it ought to be), then fear is evoked thirty-two times. Like Agerad, the Leudegar author saw strong passions at work in the world. Agerad tried to set up a system that would impede their effects; the Leudegar author created a saint who was their victim. Like an exempt monastery, Leudegar was portrayed as the calm pole around which the malice, envy, and desire of others raged ineffectually. Thus, though Leudegar was blinded, he did not utter one groan; when his lips and tongue were cut off, he nevertheless "brought forth the sounds of words"; as he was led off to his death, he was happy (*laetabatur*), and when his head was chopped off, a chorus of angels rejoiced (*gaudens*).[53] Of course, these are the *topoi* of martyrs, but they are particularly impressive here because of the strongly rancorous and fearful emotion words swirling around them.

CODED DISPLAYS

In these materials people expressed their feelings—or were so portrayed—graphically and (seemingly) unabashedly. (I say "seemingly" because all emotional expression is shaped.) We see for the first time the widespread use of some of those gestures that Huizinga considered the hallmarks of the medieval mentality—"uninhibited" expressions of grief and joy. We also once again find—we saw it previously in Gregory of Tours—some of the public uses of emotion that Gerd Althoff has dubbed the "rules of the game."[54]

Thus in the *Life of Audoin*, when the hero returned from Rome to his diocese, "the citizens outside the walls and the common people, exulting for

---

tus (4), *turbatus* (mental) (1), *vereor* (1). The emotion markers are: *commotus* (mental) (2), *fleo/defleo* (4), *jemitus* (i.e., *gemitus*) (1), *inrisio* (1), *lacrima* (1), *tremens* (3). The frequencies were obtained by using the on-line text provided by the PL database.

52. The other words of rancor: *despicio, furor, ira, livor, malitia, moleste, odium*.

53. *Passio Leudegarii* 24, p. 306; 30, p. 312; 33, p. 315; 35, p. 317.

54. See the introduction, note 51. It is true that such emotional demonstrations are not entirely lacking in the Neustrian materials discussed in chapter 5; the shrieks and grief of Columbanus's followers (see chap. 5 at note 69) are evidence of that. But this is a rare instance, and even then it is brief compared to the effusions of the later seventh century.

joy [*exultantes prae gaudio*] and weeping [*merentes*] at the same time, rolled out in throngs.... Then a lucky messenger notified the royal court of [Audoin's] advent, and the king together with his queen and the nobles of the palace rejoiced [*laetantes*] [and] clapped their hands."[55]

Similarly ecstatic was the joy of Arnulf of Metz when he saw the young Germanus: "rejoicing in his heart [*ovans animo*], he gave thanks to the Creator of all [and] received him happily [*laetus*] and merrily [*hilaris*]."[56] And again, when Germanus came to Luxeuil, "all with equally merry faces [*unanimiter hilari vultu*] received him joyfully [*ovantes*] within the monastic enclosure."[57] The author of the *Life of Wandregisil* did not hesitate to exhort every group to cheer Wandregisil's entry into heaven: "Let the old exult; let young people be happy; let adolescents rejoice; let monks be glad!"[58]

Expressions of sorrow tended to be similarly dramatic. If Wandregisil's eternal redemption prompted joy, his preparations for death moved his monks to lament noisily: "The brothers ... were very sad [*contristati*], saying 'What will become of us if you leave us so quickly, father? We want to hear your usual words; we all desire to go on being corrected by your admonition!' And they prostrated themselves in prayer with groans and tears [*gemito et lacrimis*]."[59] In the *Life of Germanus* the monks found the martyr's body and bore it back to church "with great wailing" (*cum eiulatu magno*).[60] The *Vision of Barontus* had the brethren "weep [*lacrimare*] for sorrow [*dolore*] very violently" when they saw his inert body.[61] No wonder that the

---

55. *Vita Audoini* 11, p. 560: "Cum autem pervenisset ad fines diocesis suae, suburbani cives et vulgi populus, exultantes prae gaudio simulque merentes, catervatim provolvuntur ... Exinde felix nuntius ad aulam regalem eius adventum innotuit, et una pariter rex et regina cum proceribus palatii laetantes simulque plaudentes manibus et benedicentes Christum, qui talem virum tantumque pastorem remeare fecit in eorum regnum."

56. *Vita Germani* 4, pp. 34–35: "At vero beatus Arnulfus cernens eum, ovans animo, gratias agens omnium conditori, excoepit laetus et hilaris."

57. Ibid., 6, p. 35: "omnes unanimiter hilari vultu infra monasterii septa recipiunt ovantes."

58. *Vita Wandregiseli* 21, p. 24: "Exultent senes, letentur jovenes, gaudeant aduliscentes, alacri sint monachi."

59. Ibid., 18, p. 22: "Fratres ... contristati sunt valde, dicentes: 'Quid facturi sumus, ut nobis tam cito relinques, pater? Verba tua audire vellemus, adsueta admonicionem tuam omnes desideramus corregi!' Et prostraverunt se cum gemito et lacrimis in oracione."

60. *Vita Germani* 13, p. 39: "Illi vero cum eiulato magno deferunt eum in basilicam sancti Petri."

61. *Visio Baronti* 2, p. 378: "Qui ut viderunt nullum membrum agitare, lacrimare prae dolore vehementer nimis coeperunt."

damned in hell in this story had no compunction about expressing their unhappiness graphically: when those who "had done no good in the world" saw others receiving a snack of manna, "they groaned [*gementes*], closed their eyes, and beat their breasts [*pectora sua percutiebant*], and in a loud voice said, 'Woe to us, wretched ones [*miseris*], who did nothing good when we could have.'"[62] It is more surprising, given the general sway of Stoicism in Christianity, that people in heaven were nearly as effusive. Among the saved were some of Barontus's fellow monks; when they saw his soul (*anima*) (tiny as a newborn chick) and realized that his redemption was in jeopardy, "they were inwardly touched by great sorrow [*dolore*] . . . and they began to groan [*gemere*]."[63] They found consolation only after the archangel Raphael, Barontus's guide, assured them that he had some hope in the outcome.

In the *Life of Audoin*, where (as we have seen) the crowds were elated by the hero's advent, his death prompted equal, if opposite, sorrow. "There was a great wailing [*planctus*]; the whole royal entourage was shaken to its foundation; all of high rank were brought low; all joy turned into lamentation [*gaudium in lamento vertitur*]; all laughter was silenced [*risus quiescitur*], acute bitterness [*amaritudo*] grew greater. The royal house mourned [*plangitur*] its very prudent counselor, and all the people rose up openly in lamentation [*lamentum*]."[64] At his funeral there was even the complexity of ambivalent feeling: "Therefore the king with the queen and the assembly of bishops and the mayor of the palace and the nobles of the palace came together, carrying the holy man on the bier and celebrating the holy funeral obsequies with grief [*merore*]; and whoever merited to carry the body of the blessed man on his shoulders rejoiced [*gaudebat*] and considered himself most highly rewarded."[65]

---

62. Ibid., 17, p. 392: "sed gementes oculos suos claudebant et pectora sua percutiebant et alta voce dicebant: 'Vae nobis miseris, qui nullum bonum, quando potuimus, fecimus!'"

63. Ibid., 8, pp. 383–84: "Ad illi, intrinsecus tacti nimio dolore . . . gemere coeperunt."

64. *Vita Audoini* 15, p. 564: "Fit planctus magnus, omnis regalis dignitas concutitur, omnis altitudo humiliatur, omne gaudium in lamento vertitur, omnis risus quiescitur, amaritudo magna adcrescitur. Domus regia plangitur prudentissimum consiliarium; sed plane universus populus in lamentum adsurgit." I owe the translation of "regalis dignitas" as "royal entourage" to Fouracre and Gerberding in *Late Merovingian France*, p. 167.

65. *Vita Audoini* 16, p. 564: "Igitur rex cum regina et episcoporum conventum atque maiorum domus seu priores palatii una pariter conglobati, sanctum virum in feretrum deportantes, sancta exsequia cum merore celebrantes, gaudebat se quisque et in maximo lucro deputabat, qui mereretur beati viri corpus in suis humeris deportasse."

Even when, as here, people are depicted as feeling contradictory emotions, it is possible to speak, as do Althoff and Stephen D. White, of emotions' signaling functions. In this case, both grief and joy reflected the dignity of the hero; the emotions gave him his due. The passage is comparable to those evoking the tears that often, in these materials, accompanied prayer. Such tears were not understood as a gift of grace but rather served to communicate (to all who saw or learned about them) the overwhelming charity and devotion of the weeper.[66] Wandregisil built a cell for himself, and there he fasted and observed vigils "with daily groans [*gemitus*] and daily tears [*lacrimas*]."[67] Lady Balthild took on demeaning services in her monastery "with a joyful [*gaudio*] and happy [*leto*] heart, . . . and she applied herself ceaselessly to devout prayer with tears [*cum lacrimis*]."[68] When a wall fell and Praejectus thought it had crushed a bystander, he "poured forth a shower of tears [*lacrimarum inbrem*], shouting out prayers to the God of Saboath."[69] To be sure, we have seen tears intimately connected to prayer before this: Gregory the Great's Eleutherius wept as he prayed for his friend, for example.[70] But in these late seventh-century materials, the tears are particularly noisy and abundant.

These sources also portray some blatantly "political" emotions. Thus, when Leudegar was appointed bishop of Autun, "at his coming all the enemies of his church and city were terrified [*territi sunt*], as were those who continually fought one another with hatreds [*odiis*] and murders. . . . For those whom preaching had failed to lead to peace were now constrained by the terror [*terror*] of [his] justice."[71] The passage is reminiscent of the portrayal in the *Chronicle* of Fredegar, written (probably) a generation earlier, of Dagobert's royal entry into Burgundy: "the coming of Dagobert struck the bishops and magnates with such great fear [*timore*]—not to mention the

---

66. On the gift of tears, see Piroska Nagy, *Le don des larmes au Moyen Âge. Un instrument spirituel en quête d'institution (V*^{e}*–XIII*^{e} *siècle)* (Paris, 2000).

67. *Vita Wandregiseli* 8, p. 16: "Ibi se jejuniis et vigiliis adfligebat, cotidiae gemitus, cotidiae lacrimas . . ."

68. *Vita Balthildis* 11, pp. 496–97: "Et hoc totum cum gaudio ac leto perficiebat animo. . . . Insistebatque assidue orationi devota cum lacrimis."

69. *Passio Praejecti* 11, p. 232: "Lacrimarum inbrem profundens, Dei Sabaoth proclamat preces."

70. See chap. 3, note 84.

71. *Passio Leudegarii* 2, pp. 284–85: "ita in adventum eius territi sunt omnes ecclesiae vel urbes illius adversarii, necnon et hii qui inter se odiis et homicidiis incessanter certabant . . . quia quos praedicatio ad concordiam non adduxerat, justitiae terror cogebat."

other great men living there—that it was wondered at by all; but since the poor received justice, it brought great joy [*gaudium*]."[72]

The emotions here signal the immense power of the king or—in the case of Leudegar—the bishop. They are the people's counterpart—their reaction—to "royal anger," the *ira regis* that some historians have argued functioned as an institution of government.[73] Thus in the *Life of Sadalberga*, the saint's father, "fearing [*metuens*] lest he incur the anger and ferocity of the king [*iram regis saevitiamque*] on account of his daughter," who was unmarried, forced her to wed a courtier of the palace.[74] There is also the anger of Saint Peter in the *Vision of Barontus:* he had been happy enough to use the demons clutching Barontus's soul as informants, but when they resisted his verdict—finding Barontus's good deeds to overcome his sins—he "was moved against them in anger [*in ira*] and began to say twice and three times, 'Begone, evil spirits; begone, enemies of God and ever contrary to Him, release Barontus.'" When they refused, he tried to hit them on the head with the three keys he held in his hand, but the demons flew off before he could strike.[75]

EMOTIONAL INTERACTION

Nevertheless, it is wrong to isolate these "political" uses of emotions from their less spectacular—more private and intimate—communicative and interactive functions. For, to return to psychological theory for a moment, emotions are not *just* about "appraisals of things affecting me" but about appraisals that both signal and lead to change. Their expression transforms our relations with ourselves and others.[76] This, I think, is the basis for the observation (which is, however, wrongly globalized to the *entire* Middle Ages) that certain public emotions had well-understood meanings. The materials from late seventh-century Francia exploit this communicative and in-

---

72. Fredegar, *Chronicle* 58, ed. Wallace-Hadrill, p. 48: "Tanta timore ponteficibus et procerebus in regnum Burgundiae consistentibus seo et citeris leudibus adventus Dagoberti concusserat ut a cunctis esset mirandum; pauperibus justitiam habentibus gaudium vehementer inrogaverat."

73. See the introduction at notes 41–51.

74. *Vita Sadalbergae* 10, p. 55: "Metuens autem praefatus Gundoinus, ne ob filiam iram regis saevitiamque incurreret . . ."

75. *Visio Barontii* 12, p. 387: "Tunc sanctus Petrus in ira contra eos commotus, eis bis terque dicere coepit: 'Recedite, spiritus nequam; recedite, inimici Dei eique semper contrarii, dimittite illum!'" An illustration of the keys *qua* weapon is featured in several manuscripts.

76. This is argued most forcefully in Reddy, *Navigation of Feeling*, pp. 100–107.

teractive potential in ways both old and new. We have already seen that Gregory the Great gave the pastor the right, authority, and capacity to feel with—and transform the emotions of—his flock. Rather differently, Gregory of Tours and Fortunatus saw family feeling and the interactions that they engendered—whether loving or (in dysfunctional families) hating—as the key elements of emotional life. (By contrast, the Neustrian courtiers around Clothar II and Dagobert saw deference rather than emotional expression as the foundation of human interaction.)

These are all ways to understand when and why people have emotions. In the case of Gregory the Great, in addition to the cogitations of the mind sent by the Devil, there was a kind of emotional vibration that one person picked up from another, leading (in the most favorable instances) to conversion. In the late seventh-century materials that we are discussing here, however, there is rather little emotional "echoing." Although Queen Balthild "sorrowed with the sorrowful . . . and rejoiced with the joyful" (*dolebat enim cum dolentibus . . . et cum gaudentibus gaudebat*), her biographer did not suggest that some people could calibrate their emotions to lead others to salvation.[77] In the case of Gregory of Tours and Fortunatus, family feeling was a substrate on which other emotions were founded. In the late seventh century this sensibility had almost disappeared, though, to be sure, "[Lady Balthild] loved her sister [nuns] with the most pious affection [*affectu diligebat*], as if they were her own daughters."[78] Mainly, however— and the *emphasis* was new in the late seventh century, though the idea was certainly present in Cassian and Gregory the Great—emotions were understood to be aroused or transformed by the manipulation and persuasion of external events.

Sometimes virtuous emotions were stirred, consonant with the values of the authors. When his enemies were camped outside his city, Leudegar's biographer showed him mobilizing his clergy and townspeople with high-flown sentiments: "'An earthly man,'" he preached. "'should he receive such power from God, is liable to persecute, seize, loot, burn, and kill: we cannot escape these things by turning away. And if here we are handed over to punishment in transitory matters, let us not despair [*disperemus*] but rather rejoice [*gaudeamus*] in the pardon to come.' . . . And so, rousing [*commovens*] the whole population of this city, with a three-day fast, with the sign of the

---

77. *Vita Balthildis* 11, p. 497.
78. Ibid., p. 496: "Ipsa vero piissimo affectu diligebat sorores ut proprias filias."

cross, and making a circuit of the walls with saints' relics, clinging to the ground at each and every entryway, he prayed to the Lord with tears [*cum lacrimis*] that He would not allow the people entrusted to him to be captured."[79] But this sort of conversion was very rare, and in the *Visio Baronti*, which was written as a cautionary tale for monks, we see why: "Who is there, I ask, dearest brothers [*karissimi*] with so ironclad a mind that these announced punishments [that Barontus has seen in hell] would not terrify [*terreant*] him? . . . But many do not believe, because the love [*amor*] of the world and earthly things delights [*delectat*] them more than the love [*amor*] of God and the society of angels and the saints."[80] Thus bad emotions get in the way of good ones, and people do not change course. Consider Leudegar's unsuccessful intervention with the drunken and angry Childeric II: "Undaunted, he went to the irate king [*regem iratum*] and asked with soothing words [*verbis mitibus*] why he had not come before vigils and persisted full of anger [*ira*] in the solemnity of such a holy night [before Easter]. The other, while distressed [*turbatus*] by Leudegar's ineffable wisdom, could answer only by saying said that he held Leudegar in suspicion for a certain reason."[81]

But if people were hard to convert to virtuous feelings, they were, by contrast, easy targets for those who urged on them anger, fear, and envy. Because the young Praejectus was preferred by his patron, Bishop Genesius

---

79. *Passio Leudegarii* 22, pp. 303–4: "Terrenus homo si talem a Deo acceperit potestatem, persequatur, conprehendat, praedit, incendat, interfitiat: haec nullatenus possumus declinantes effugire. Et si hic tradimur de rebus transitoriis ad disciplinam, non disperemus, immo potius gaudeamus in futuro de venia. Muniamus ergo virtutibus animam simul et civitatis custodiam, ne inveniant utrique hostes aditum, per quod inferre possunt periculum. Commovens igitur universum urbis illius populum, cum triduano jejunio, cum signo crucis et reliquias sanctorum murorum circumiens ambitum, per singulos etenim aditos portarum terrae adherens, Dominum praecabatur cum lacrimis, ut si illum vocabat ad passionem, plebem sibi creditam non permitterit captivari, et ita praestatum est evenisse."

80. *Visio Baronti* 20, p. 393: "Quisnam ille est, fratres karissimi, rogo, tam ferream mentem habet, quem non terreant ista denuntiata supplicia? . . . Sed ideo multi non credunt, quia plus eos delectat amor saeculi et quomoda terrena, quam delectat amor Dei et societas angelorum adque sanctorum."

81. *Passio Leudegarii* 10, p. 293: "intrepidus adiit regem iratum eumque verbis mitibus requisivit, cur ante vigilias non venisset, vel in tam sacrae noctis sollemnia repletus ira persisteret. Nam dum illius ineffabili sapientiae aliud turbatus non valuisset respondere, suspectum se eum quadam de causa dixit habere."

of Clermont, other clerics, competing for the same favors, were envious. "And as it is the custom that clerics denigrate the knowledge of many because they cannot fill their own storehouses [with wisdom], they desired to pour out evil hatreds [*odia maligna*] on others endowed with wisdom. Therefore the poison of the clerics aroused envy [*invidiam*] against Praejectus in a certain Martin," the cantor who sounded the tones of the chants. This Martin forced the boy to sing a particularly difficult tune, a challenge that Praejectus met only with the intercession of a saint.[82] Note that the envy did not originally come from Martin himself; it was the poisonous fruit of human suggestion.

But this is a singular example. The prime mover to rancorous emotion in these late seventh-century materials was not human at all: it was the Devil. Evil thoughts did not come from within; they were roused up by a Devil who knew how to manipulate people with finesse and sophistication.

In this regard the emotional community of the late seventh-century elite was building upon older notions of the Devil's role and personality. Always potentially the instigator of bad deeds, the Devil and his minions (the demons) were, in the writings of the Desert Fathers, closely linked to the emotions. For Evagrius, they were equivalent to the prickings and tinglings of evil thoughts: there was a "demon" of vainglory and a "demon" of fornication, for example.[83] Cassian, while sometimes internalizing the sources of vice, noted that Adam would not have been tempted by the emotion (*passio*) of fornication had he not been baited by the Devil.[84] At the same time, the Devil himself was an emotional being in Cassian's world. In his seventh and eighth *Conferences,* both devoted to demonology, Cassian associated him with two emotional vices above all: pride (*superbia*) and envy (*invidia*).[85] But the Devil also had feelings which, in other people and under other circumstances, might be considered positive: he rejoiced (*gaudet*), for ex-

---

82. *Passio Praejecti* 4, p. 228: "Et ut mos est clerum multorum scientiam praegravare, quod in suas non valent replere cellas, ceteros sapientie datos odia maligna desiderant perfundere. Unde Martinum quendam, qui cantilene vocis pro decorem sanctarum ecclesiarum in multismodis meditationibus insonantem, concitat clericorum venena in Prejecti invidiam, prefundunt in aure, ut fatiat puerum inter ceteros meditum cuiusdam soni, unde ipse inscius erat, vix tandem, ut ita dicam, puncto ore meditum personasse, quem sui aemuli longo iam evo sonitum vocibus decantabant."

83. See chap. 1, note 49.

84. Cassian, *Conlationes* 5.6, CSEL 13:125.

85. Ibid., 8.10, p. 226.

ample, when he or his demons introduced a vice into the human heart, and he felt a certain anxiety and sadness (*quandam anxietatem et tristitiam*) when struggling in vain with virtuous souls.[86] Sorrow (*dolor*) and distress (*confusio*) followed upon his defeat.[87]

While the elites of the late seventh century drew little inspiration from the asceticism of the Desert Fathers, they did make use of some elements of their writings. Certainly these were readily available. Cassian's *Conferences*, in particular, was recommended reading in the Rule of St. Benedict and other monastic rules.[88] But, as we have seen with the vocabulary of emotions, different groups drew on traditions variously and for their own purposes. While Gregory the Great explained how Job managed to be virtuous despite the "bad thoughts" of the Devil, the writers of the late seventh century focused on the Devil as a key actor in a complex process of emotional incitement.[89] Consider the Devil's role in the *Martyrdom of Leudegar*:

> But because malice [*malitia*] is always opposed to good will, and the ancient serpent, who is envious [*invidus*], always finds those through whom he may sow temptation, some high-ranking men, ignorant of spiritual things but rather holding secular power, seeing Leudegar to be the inflexible pinnacle of justice, began to twist with spiteful envy [*invido livore*] and determined, if possible, to get in the way of his progress. Now at that time the majordomo (as we call him) was Ebroin; he ruled the palace under King Clothar, for the queen . . . was now living in the monastery which she had prepared for herself beforehand. The aforementioned envious men [*invidi*] went to Ebroin and aroused his heart to fury [*furore*] against the man of God.[90]

---

86. Ibid., 7.17, p. 196; 7.21, p. 198.

87. Ibid., 7.21, p. 198.

88. Adalbert de Vogüé, "Les mentions des oeuvres de Cassien chez Benoît et ses contemporains," *Studia Monastica* 20 (1978): 275–85.

89. The exceptions are a "certain old man" in the *Vita Wandregiseli* 6, pp. 15–16, who was attacked by the envious (*invidiosus*) devil but who managed to resist, and, more ambiguously, Gertrude in the *Vita Geretrudis* 2, p. 456, who "non parvam sustinuit temptationem" (sustained not a few temptations) of the Devil. For Gregory the Great, see chap. 2.

90. *Passio Leudegarii* 3–4, p. 286: "Sed quia bona voluntate semper discordat malitia et antiquus serpens invidus semper invenit, per quos scandalum seminet, aliquid honorati spiritalia nescientes, set potius potentiam secularem timentes [*recte?* tenentes], videntes hunc virum inflexibilem per justitiae culmen existere, invido coeperunt livore torquere et statuunt, si sit aditus eius obviare profectibus. Erat enim in illis temporibus Ebroinus, ut dicimus, ma-

Thus working by proxy, not at all automatically but by divining the interests of various groups, the Devil orchestrated an emotional transformation. First, the "ancient serpent" incited a faction of the Neustrian magnates to envy the privileges and power of Leudegar, Queen Balthild's appointee. With the queen's retirement, which perhaps they engineered, they saw their opportunity.[91] But the key to *their* power was Ebroin, mayor of the palace, who controlled access to the king. And thus they worked on his feelings, rousing him to anger. Although the emotions are simple and straightforward, the ways in which they are elicited are not. There is an implicit acknowledgment here of the cognitive view of emotions as assessments made on the basis of one's interests.

Most striking in these materials are the feelings of the demons, rivaling those in Cassian's writings. Indeed, the fact that the *Vision of Barontus* stars two demons tells us that they were now "personalities." Envy was, to be sure, their primary emotion. We have seen how it was first the "envious" Devil who stirred up the magnates who would, in turn, move Ebroin's heart to fury.[92] Another example is in the *Life of Wandregisil,* where the Devil felt "the greatest envy" (*maximam invidiam*) when he saw God call a saintly old man to eternal life.[93] But envy was not the whole story. Anger came next: one of the demons in Barontus's vision gave him a kick and, "full of anger" (*iracundia*), declared: "'I had you in my power once already and hurt you badly; now you will be tormented forever in hell.'"[94] And rancor was only the beginning. Listen to Wandregisil speaking to his monks and parsing the emotions of the Devil: "[Act virtuously so that] the devil may fall low and lament [*lugeat*], because he has the greatest grief [*maximam merorem*] when

---

jordomus, qui sub rege Chlothario tunc regebat palatium; nam regina . . . iam in monasterio, quod sibi antea praeparaverat, resedebat. Praeterea memorati invidi adeunt Ebroinum et contra Dei virum eius in furore suscitant animum." For the emendation of *timentes* to *tenentes,* see *Late Merovingian France,* ed. and trans. Fouracre and Gerberding, p. 220 n. 98.

91. The *Vita Balthildis* 10, p. 495, admits that a faction of nobles "counseled" Balthild to retire from the court: "sed ipsa domna Dei voluntatem considerans, ut hoc non tam eorum consilium, quam Dei fuisset dispensatio" (but that lady considered it the will of God that it had been not so much their counsel as the dispensation of God).

92. See note 90 above.

93. The same phrase occurs twice: *Vita Wandregiseli* 6 and 19, pp. 16, 23. Another example is in the *Vita Geretrudis* 2, p. 455, where the "enemy of the human race" is "envious" (*invidus*) of good works.

94. *Visio Baronti* 4, p. 381: "te habui in potestatem et nocui valde, nunc autem in infernum cruciabis perpetualiter."

he sees someone very carefully obeying the commandments of God."[95] At Balthild's tomb, a raging demon was "terrified by divine fear" (*conterritus divino pavore*). Turning stiff (*obriguit*) and falling silent (*conticuit*), he fled the body of the man he had possessed.[96] Envy, anger, grief, fear: Ekman and Friesen's modern list of "universal emotions" differs little from the Devil's emotional capacity in the late seventh century.[97]

FEELING BEINGS

Projecting emotions onto the Devil may seem, from a modern point of view, an abnegation of self-knowledge. In fact, to the contrary, it allowed late seventh-century authors the latitude to explore inner psychologies more fully than we have seen hitherto and even to expand the semantic field of one word, *furor*, whose meaning had hitherto been circumscribed by rigid moral categories. In the first half of the seventh century the Neustrian courtiers had used the term to mean anger out of control. Thus in Jonas's *Life of John of Réomé* a servant named Clarus, incensed by a letter, turned in fury (*furore*), spat on the letter, and, cursing (*ferocia redens responsa*), kicked out (*exprevit*) the letter carrier.[98] *Furor* meant much the same thing in the passage from the *Martyrdom of Leudegar* quoted above, where envious men incited Ebroin to fury, though, unlike Clarus, Ebroin knew how to bide his time. But in another late seventh-century source, the *Life of Gertrude*, the word suddenly was allowed new, expanded, and virtuous meaning. Confronted with a suitor after she had pledged herself to Christ, Gertrude, "as if filled with fury [*furore*], rejected him with an oath."[99] Here, as Catherine Peyroux has shown, fury had come to mean righteous anger.[100] Nor did the *quasi* ("as if") that preceded *furor* signify that the author hesitated to use the word. *Quasi* seems to have simply been a rhetorical tic; the same author used it for the emotion of fear, whose meaning was entirely traditional: Gertrude, "as if utterly terrified by fear" (*quasi pavore perterrita*), announced

---

95. *Vita Wandregiseli* 15, p. 21: "diabulus ut decidat et lugeat, quia maximam merorem habet, quando quemquam viderit prumtissimum a mandatis Dei custodiendum."

96. *Vita Balthildis* 17, p. 505: "conterritusque divino pavore, ilico sevissimus demon obriguit atque conticuit."

97. For Ekman and Friesen, see chap. 1, note 82.

98. Jonas, *Vita Johannis* 10, p. 511: "Cumque Clarus nomen audisset, in furore versus, beati viri epistolam salibo inlitam abjecit, et ferocia redens responsa, gerolum exprevit."

99. *Vita Geretrudis* 1, p. 454: "at illa quasi furore repleta, respuit illum cum juramento."

100. Catherine Peyroux, "Gertrude's *furor*: Reading Anger in an Early Medieval Saint's Life," in *Anger's Past*, ed. Rosenwein, chap. 2.

that she had seen a flaming sphere.[101] With the Devil absorbing and containing the evil side of things, a word such as *furor*, which formerly had been linked to sin, could now become virtuous if dissociated from him.

Moreover, with the Devil incarnating evil, even bad men gained psychological complexity. Ebroin is the best example. When we first meet him he is, as we have seen, burning with fury (*furor*) against Leudegar. But that is not all. He is also "fired up with the torch of desire" (*cupiditatis face succensus*) for money and power.[102] Fearing (*de metu*) Leudegar and his faction, he begins an initial round of persecutions.[103] When Clothar III dies, Ebroin, "puffed up by the spirit of pride" (*superbiae spiritu tumidus*), strikes fear in turn into the hearts of the nobles by refusing to call them together.[104] The ploy backfires, however, because the nobles, including Leudegar's faction, call in King Childeric and exile Ebroin to Luxeuil. Soon, however, Leudegar has a falling out with Childeric, and he too is banished to Luxeuil. With both men out of favor and inhabiting the same monastery, Ebroin feigns (*simulans*) friendship with Leudegar.[105] Presumably he still "really" feels enmity, but short-term goals now take precedence when it comes to emotional expression. Soon the faction loyal to Childeric is disillusioned and kills the king. Now Ebroin pretends (*simulans*) to be the *fidelis*—the faithful adherent—of Theuderic, whom, indeed, he had once supported.[106] Once reinstated as mayor under Theuderic, he feigns sorrow (*simulans se dolere*) about Childeric's death as a cover to persecute those he hates (*odisset*).[107] And so on. He is not far from an Iago in emotional range.

Similarly, the men who conspire against Ebroin have complicated feelings. They fear him (*timoris causa*); their hearts are touched by grief (*dolore*) as they see him despoil them of their wealth; they are roused against him (*commoti*).[108] And there are other complex beings in some of the other

---

101. *Vita Geretrudis* 4, p. 458.

102. *Passio Leudegarii* 4, p. 286.

103. Ibid., p. 287. It is not entirely clear whose fear the phrase "de metu" refers to, but Fouracre and Gerberding, *Late Merovingian France*, p. 221 n. 104, point out that elsewhere (*Passio Leudegarii* 28, p. 309) Ebroin's persecutions are clearly the result of his own fear.

104. *Passio Leudegarii* 5, p. 287: "Ideo magis coeperunt metuere" (therefore they began to be more fearful).

105. Ibid., 13, p. 296: "Ebroinus . . . simulatam gerens concordiam" (Ebroin, manifesting simulated harmony).

106. Ibid., 16, p. 298.
107. Ibid., 29, p. 310.
108. Ibid., 4, pp. 286–87.

sources. Queen Balthild, who shows no emotion while at court (at least, not in the hands of her biographer), becomes a more passionate being in her monastery. There, as we have seen, "she loved [*diligebat*] her sisters with the most pious affection [*affectu*], as if they were her own daughters,"[109] and she entered into the emotional lives of others by mirroring their feelings. She visited the sick, "sorrowing [*dolebat*] with the sorrowful [*dolentibus*] through her zeal for charity [*caritatis*]; and she rejoiced [*gaudebat*] with the joyful [*gaudentibus*]; and for the healthy ones [or, possibly, the slaves], she often humbly asked the lady abbess that they might be consoled."[110]

VARIETIES OF EMOTIONAL LIFE

Thus far, I have discussed these materials as if they constituted the products of one emotional community. Certainly there is much to recommend this procedure. All were about members of an increasingly homogeneous elite, written by members of that elite for other members' delectation. They used a similar emotional vocabulary, and they expressed the same presuppositions about the nature and use of emotions.

Nevertheless, one of them—the *Life of Sadalberga*—seems a bit odd. Above all, it uses—uniquely within this set of materials, and with some frequency—the word *anxius* (anxious). Sadalberga was anxious (*anxia*) when she had no children and so she prayed at the tomb of St. Remigius for them.[111] And "that which she had petitioned for faithfully and anxiously [*anxie*] was given to her."[112] Later in the story, nuns at Sadalberga's monastery were anxious (*anxiae*) because they could not do their assigned task.[113] (Happily, a miracle solved the problem.) The word is thus used three times in this short text; only *amor* equals its frequency, and *caritas* exceeds it by just one other use. But that too is strange. We have seen that in the *Martyrdom of Leudegar,* a representative work for the emotional community we

---

109. *Vita Balthildis* 11, p. 496: "Ipsa vero piissimo affectu diligebat sorores ut proprias filias."

110. Ibid., p. 497: "Dolebat enim cum dolentibus per studium caritatis et cum gaudentibus gaudebat et pro sanis, ut consolarentur, domna abbatissa humiliter sepius suggerebat." Most manuscripts read *sanis* (for the healthy), but one reads *tribulatis* (for the troubled), while Krusch himself suggests *servis* (for the slaves) or *saniosis* (for the healthier ones). Fouracre and Gerberding, *Late Merovingian France*, p. 127 n. 198, choose *servis*. On the monastery as a substitute family in hagiography, see Padberg, *Heilige und Familie,* esp. 88–89, 121–22, 147–50.

111. *Vita Sadalbergae* 11, p. 55, where she is characterized as "christianissima femina anxia."
112. Ibid.: "hoc quod fideliter et anxie petierat a Domino est ei collatum."
113. Ibid., 21, p. 62.

have been exploring, words of love were quite infrequent. Conversely, the words that are most frequent in the hands of the Leudegar author, fear and rancor, are of little importance in the *Life of Sadalberga*. Anger comes up once, in the form of *ira regis*, the anger of the king; fear occurs once as well, as *pavor* in response to the work of the Devil.[114] Finally, although there is a long discussion of the Devil and his evil doings in chapters 15 and 16 of the *Life of Sadalberga*, not once does he betray an emotion, nor is he said to motivate people to feel in any particular way.

Until recently, the *Life of Sadalberga* was considered a Carolingian confection. Were Hummer's recent defense of its seventh-century authorship not so convincing, it would be convenient to drop it from our present dossier. But its late seventh-century authorship is now quite certain. What, then, explains its anomalous understanding and expression of emotions? Is it the visible tip of an otherwise hidden emotional community—or, rather, subcommunity, since the *Life of Sadalberga* is, as we have seen, in some ways very much part of the late seventh-century mainstream?

I think that this may be so. I shall also very tentatively suggest that we may know something, though not much, about this emotional community already. There are some resemblances between the emotional vocabulary and sensibility of the *Life of Sadalberga* and Jonas's *Life of John of Réomé*. Bruno Krusch, the editor of the *Life of Sadalberga*, long ago noted the correspondences therein to Jonas's *Life of Columbanus*. But Krusch was not looking at the expression of emotion. The *Life of John* and the *Life of Sadalberga* share the free use of *anxius*,[115] the privileging of loving words, and the avoidance of rancorous emotions.[116]

It is just possible that in the *Life of Sadalberga* we have the traces of a community in Alsace that was touched in its own way by Columbanus or, more precisely, his disciples. Sadalberga is mentioned in Jonas's *Life of Columbanus:* as a young girl, her blindness was cured by Eustasius, Columbanus's follower and abbot of Luxeuil.[117] The *Life of Sadalberga* repeats the

---

114. For *ira regis*, ibid., 10, p. 55; for *pavor*, ibid., 15, p. 58.

115. Compare the *Vita Sadalbergae*, with three uses of an anxiety word, to the *Vita Johannis*, with four uses. The former is about 280 lines; the latter 315, so the frequency is roughly comparable.

116. In the *Vita Sadalbergae*, the emotion words are *affectus, amor, anxius, caritas, diligo, ira, metuo, ovo, pavor,* and *spem*, with *dulcedo* and *hilaris* as emotion markers. In the *Vita Johannes* they are *affectus, amor, anxius, ardor, desiderium, diligo, furor, gaudium, l(a)etus, metus, m(a)estus, ovo, pavefactus (pavor),* and *timor*, with emotion markers *gemo* and *hilaris*.

117. Jonas, *Vita Columbani* 8, p. 122.

story and tells us that Waldebert, also a disciple of Columbanus and abbot of Luxeuil after Eustasius, was Sadalberga's advisor when she decided to found a monastery, which she first did near Langres.[118] This was in the vicinity of Réomé, which was already in Jonas's day a "Columbanian" monastery, reformed by Luxeuil.[119] There may thus have been a Luxeuil/Langres emotional community whose norms, always evolving, may nevertheless be glimpsed (just barely) as they were interpreted by Jonas in 559—when he visited Réomé and wrote the *Life* of John—and by Sadalberga's anonymous hagiographer circa 680 when he wrote at the request of Sadalberga's daughter.

Drawing on a vast repertory of emotion words, ideas, and gestures, the writers of the late seventh century turned the factional fighting of the previous decades into martyr stories about passionate men and women. Emotions were key to their conception of the past: the elites of late seventh-century Francia explained recent history by seeing everywhere rancorous and envious but also passionate and loving feelings. Kings and queens mourned the death of a saint; bishops offered exemptions to monasteries to counteract their own greed; envious men, fired up by the Devil, carried out nefarious deeds. The turmoil of the "age of Ebroin"—about 660 to 680—no doubt lies behind the emotional styles of the later period.[120] But it is equally likely that the emotional styles of the elite played a role both in fostering the political events and in shaping our conception of them. I shall consider both of these points more fully in the final part of my concluding chapter.

118. *Vita Sadalbergae* 4 and 12, pp. 53, 56–57.
119. See Prinz, *Frühes Mönchtum*, p. 297.
120. See Paul Fouracre, "Merovingian History and Merovingian Hagiography," *Past and Present*, no. 127 (1990): 35–36.

CONCLUSION

While emotions may be expressed more or less dramatically, they are never pure and unmediated drives or energies. They are always mediated because they are "upheavals of thoughts"—as Nussbaum has put it—that involve judgments about whether something is good or bad for us. These assessments depend, in turn, upon our values, goals, and presuppositions—products of our society, community, and individual experience, mediators all.

Society, community, and individual experience are always changing. This book challenges the idea that we may speak of any one emotional stance, structure, or set of norms as characteristic of the "Middle Ages." It insists that the history of emotions must be traced in relatively small increments of transformation and change. In this final chapter I wish to sum up the argument of this book. I shall then problematize the methods that I have used to read the sources and query what, exactly, they can tell us about emotions. Finally, I shall suggest a theory of how and why emotional norms change and what makes them important.

THE ARGUMENT

The capacious English word "emotions" elides many differences between what English speakers once called—with fairly clear distinctions—appetites, passions, affections, and sentiments. While the ancient world also had many words for what we call emotions, the Stoics in rejecting them dubbed the whole lot as *pathē*. This was accepted by Cicero in the first century B.C.E., who translated the Greek word by the Latin *perturbationes* and then listed some of the terms that belonged in the category. His inventory, which, as he himself noted, was open-ended, is strikingly close to modern lists of emotions. That fact—and the fact that different groups emphasized and/or ignored various words on this and similar lists—makes it possible to begin to write a history of the emotions, or, more precisely, of the *perturbationes, motus animi, passiones, affectus,* and so on which, at least until the thirteenth century, were overlapping if not precisely synonymous categories of feeling.[1]

---

1. On the precision that began in the twelfth century and was quite marked in the thirteenth, see Sciuto, "Le passioni," and Peter King, "Aquinas on the Passions," in *Aquinas's*

Most of this book concerns a relatively short period, just over a century, from the papacy of Gregory the Great (590–604) to about 700. The inscriptions for the dead commissioned by mourners at Trier, Vienne, and Clermont cover a slightly longer period because they start earlier. They introduce three emotional communities: the epitaphs of each place are different enough from one another to suggest that local traditions had a good deal of say in how and which emotions would be expressed or not expressed. The disparate norms at Trier, Vienne, and Clermont, uniformly Christian, were overlapping, and no doubt any mobile individual could have bridged them; nevertheless they were recognizably distinct.

The reaction to death's toll is only a small part of the life of any community. To get at the norms for all—or more—facets of life, it is necessary to turn to fuller sources. Gregory the Great and Gregory of Tours provide our first examples of emotional communities "in the round." Contemporaries, they lived far from one another, the first in Italy, the second in Gaul. Sharing in the by then widespread assumptions of Catholic Christianity—demeaning the love of earthly things, fearing God, and valorizing the joys of heaven—they nevertheless navigated these principles very differently when they conceived of and expressed emotions, whether speaking of themselves or others. Gregory the Great distrusted emotions, but he thought that they were "useful" as hooks for lifting sinners to virtue when properly managed—by the saints and rectors of the church. In Gaul around the same time, however, Gregory of Tours and his friend Fortunatus found comfort in family feeling, an idiom and metaphor that suffused the way they understood and expressed emotions of every sort.

The overturning of Austrasian hegemony at the beginning of the seventh century brought an end to the ascendancy of the emotive style typified by Fortunatus and Gregory of Tours. A new emotional sensibility came to the fore at the court of Clothar II and his progeny. It was wary of passion, tethered to restraint and deference. Mothers, whose emotional expression was rather warmer (perhaps a residue of the old emphasis on family feeling?), were presented as temptresses threatening the religious life. Negative emotions such as envy, hatred, and greed were largely unmentioned; the emphasis was on love, joy, and fear of God. This was surely in part a by-product of the king and courtiers' engagement in the monasticism of St. Columbanus.

The late seventh century saw an end to this set of emotional norms. A

Moral Theory: Essays in Honor of Norman Kretzmann, ed. Scott MacDonald and Eleonore Stump (Ithaca, N.Y., 1999), pp. 101–32.

new emotional community came to the fore, that of a pan-Frankish elite. It seethed with passions, both positive and negative. The new sensibility celebrated public displays of emotion, attributed complex sentiments to the devil, made much of "feigned" feelings, and appreciated the role of emotions in interpersonal interactions.

READING THE SOURCES

A history of emotions should be about how people felt. Yet this book speaks of norms, codes, and modes of expression rather than feelings. Is it, then, a history of emotions? The answer requires first a discussion of what we can know from our sources.

The sources tell us at least what people thought other people would like to hear (or expected to hear). Most do not pretend to be expressions of emotion; they are accounts or descriptions—imagined and otherwise—about human behavior, and that includes the ways in which emotions must be (and to some degree were) expressed. A few sources are exceptional. Epitaphs and letters reveal—in however commonplace a fashion—the feelings (or simulated feelings) of those who composed them. Then, too, there is the occasional flash of autobiography: Gregory the Great tells us about his experience with stomach pangs; Gregory of Tours narrates his cure at the tomb of St. Illidius; Jonas takes us on an abortive trip to see his mother.

Yet even these less oblique sources are problematic, though not because the sentiments that they express are formulaic. As I noted in the introduction, commonplaces are socially true even if they may not be individually sincere. To look at the matter in another way, they are emotives: a first draft. That they exist at all is significant. The real problem in these sources is to evaluate the emotions properly. Is it right to discuss in the same way, as I do in this book, a word of affection, such as *carissimus* (dearest); a metaphorical use of an emotion word, such as *Tartarus furens* (hell raging); and an outright declaration of emotion, such as Desiderius's to Aspasia: "Moved by your tears . . ."? I once thought of eliminating metaphors on the grounds that they are purely literary devices. But what makes them more or less literary than terms of endearment? Doesn't the metaphor gain its force precisely because of its use of an emotion word? "Hell raging" is not just a metaphor; it also reveals a sensibility that appreciates the power of fury.[2]

Would it not be best—as I do not do—to "map" emotion words in ac-

---

2. However, the difficulties in interpreting the metaphors of cultures long past is well described in Pelliccia, *Mind, Body, and Speech*, pp. 32–39.

cordance with whether they are "good" (*caritas,* for example) or "bad" (*furor,* for example)? This is the sort of thing that Thomas Dixon wishes to do with Augustine, in order to argue that even in the early Middle Ages people made a clear distinction between affections (which were Godly) and passions (which were not).[3] However, while this sort of understanding of the emotions may fit Patristic definitions and scholastic arguments, it is quite inapplicable to local practice, when even *furor,* as we have seen in the case of Gertrude, could have godly meaning, and *caritas* could signify, as in the hands of Baudonivia, worldly love (*caritatem mundialem*) ripe for repudiation.

The examples of *furor* and *caritas* show that emotions cannot be decontextualized; they come in clusters of words. Their meaning has everything to do with the phrases around them and the way that those phrases were taken (ironically, metaphorically, literally) both by the writer and his or her audience. Additionally, like the colors of a palette, emotions blend; that is why historians can speak of a "romantic era" or an "age of anxiety," referring to a synergistic picture.[4] It is necessary for the historian to see not only what emotion words were used by an emotional community, but also to understand how they worked together and within a context.

From time to time I have counted emotion words, suggesting that frequency is of some importance. Is this justified? Admittedly, the method is rough-and-ready. But at least it allows us to check our assumptions, both those that infer emotions where they are not and those that suppose the predominance of particular emotions where the words themselves do not warrant it. Consider a passage from Gregory of Tours: "Waddo . . . complained that his horses had been taken by the son-in-law of Beretrudis, and he decided to go to one of the villas she had left to her daughter . . . saying, 'This man . . . took my horses and I shall take his villa.'"[5] In her discussion of this passage, Nira Pancer assumes emotion. "Outraged [*outragé*]," she writes, "by the theft of horses perpetrated by the son-in-law of Beretrudis, Waddo considered it a point of honor to react."[6] Pancer may be right. But

---

3. Dixon, *From Passions to Emotions,* chap. 2.

4. Some psychologists take seriously the likeness of emotions to colors. See Plutchik, "Emotions," pp. 204–5, and the survey in Reddy, *Navigation of Feeling,* chap. 1.

5. Greg. Tur., *Histories* 9.35, pp. 455–56: "Waddo . . . quaerebatur, a genero eius [sc. Beretrudis] equos suos fuisse direptus."

6. Nira Pancer, *Sans peur et sans vergogne: De l'honneur et des femmes aux premiers temps mérovingiens* (Paris, 2001) p. 123.

the text says nothing about outrage or honor. I have preferred to assume that if an emotion word does not appear, the silence itself is significant. Similarly, if an emotion word appears frequently, I assume it has particular importance to the writer. This cannot be entirely wrong, though I expect and hope that other scholars of emotions will refine the method.

This sort of reading allows poems to be assessed together with charters, narratives with saints' lives. A whole tradition of literary studies would say that this is wrong, that placing Fortunatus's poems alongside Gregory of Tours's *Histories* is a fundamental misunderstanding of genre. I quite agree. But by considering these writings as social products, their lowest common denominator, I am able to get at what is normative about their emotional expression. I do not deny the soundness of many other sorts of readings. But I maintain that this one, too, has validity, especially if it is done with *some* sensitivity to literary artifice and genre. It is essential, for example, to pay attention to Gregory of Tours's satirical intent in order not to be deceived by his use of *dulcedo*. Nevertheless, it is useful to recall that satire works only when it is playing with social mores, and those mores are precisely the point of this book.

But doesn't genre determine emotional expression? It is not for nothing that Aristotle chose the topic of rhetoric as the place to discuss emotions. Rules of rhetoric and their mastery allowed medieval writers to heap praise on someone one day, excoriate him or her the next.[7] Robert Levin, a modern composer, is able to write a convincing new ending for Mozart's *Requiem* without becoming a member of Mozart's world.[8] While not denying the validity of these observations, one might also point out that Aristotle had a particular—a Greek—notion of emotions; that invective and praise, however different in intent, *both* constitute aspects of an emotional community; and that Mozart, as currently played, is part of *our* world.

Moreover, it should be clear from this book that genres are flexible. Funerary inscriptions, while formulaic, were by no means uniform across Gaul. Literary genres, such as letters and saints' Lives could be tweaked. Even charters, perhaps the most prone to boilerplate, nevertheless could add a word of affection here, a word of terror there. It is by just such tiny

---

7. See Conrad Leyser's assessment of Eugenius Vulgaris's "change of sides," in "Charisma in the Archive: Roman Monasteries and the Memory of Gregory the Great, c. 870–c. 940," in *Le Scritture dai monasteri*, ed. Flavia De Rubeis and Walter Pohl (Rome, 2003), p. 220.

8. Wolfgang Amadeus Mozart, *Requiem in D Minor, K.626,* New Completion by Robert Levin. Telarc Digital CD-80410, 1995.

things that emotions are expressed. In addition, it would seem that the need or desire to express emotions might sometimes nudge a genre. In the case of Herchenefreda, the mother of Desiderius, we see how the letter, so dry in her son's hands, could be transformed into a sort of sermon, and thereby gracefully contain all sorts of sentiments that ordinary letters of the Neustrian court did not.

Closely tied to the issue of genre is that of purpose. Many early medieval sources are didactic, meant to teach rather to describe or express. Gregory the Great sometimes revealed—I use the word cautiously—how he and others felt, but above all he was interested in the theory of "cogitations," a subject that seems at first glance to belong more to the history of ideas *about* emotions than to the history of emotions per se. Yet the two cannot be so easily disentangled. Linguists have shown that our folk theories about anger, for example, have much to do with way in which we experience anger.[9] Peter Stearns's work strongly suggests that when emotional standards change, emotional styles—the way feelings are expressed and, surely, to some degree, felt—change to follow suit. Belief has much to do with feeling. If I believe that my anger should be "let out," I cultivate it. The Stoics believed that anger was no part of the wise man, and so they encouraged tranquillity. The valuation of the anger is entirely opposite in these instances. Thus, while it is impossible to prove that anger is felt variously by a Stoic and a ranter, nevertheless the *full* experience, with its dismay at or enjoyment of the emotion itself, is certainly different. People train themselves to have feelings that are based on their beliefs. At the same time, feelings help to create, validate, and maintain belief systems.[10]

We may now return to the question: is this book a history of emotions? The answer is affirmative as long as we recognize the limitations of any such inquiry, especially regarding the Early Middle Ages. We cannot know how all people felt, but we can begin to know how some members of certain ascendant elites thought they and others felt or, at least, thought they ought to feel. That is all we can know. But it is quite a lot. How much more do we know about the feelings of the people around us?

---

9. Lakoff, *Women, Fire, and Dangerous Things*, pp. 380–416, a discussion of the metaphors that we use to speak of anger—e.g., "I blew my stack!"—that reflect our conception of the feeling, and thus the way that we feel it. While Lakoff thinks the experience of the emotion produces the metaphor, a social constructionist argument would make the metaphor shape the way the emotion is experienced.

10. On this, see Reddy, *Navigation of Feeling*, esp. p. 258.

EMOTIONAL DEPENDENCY, EMOTIONAL AGENCY

To the extent that historians have thought about it at all, they have given two very different explanations for why emotional norms have changed over time.[11] The first proposes that emotions respond to outside social, economic, religious, political, and other pressures. The second makes emotions themselves the causes of their own transformation.

State formation is the event that transformed the emotional life of the West for Norbert Elias. The absolutist court created the conditions for emotional transformations, from coarse, simple, and direct to delicate, complex, and oblique. Economic developments aided the process, with the expanding bourgeois class aping the norms of those above. Confronted by an increasingly fastidious middle class, the aristocracy responded by valuing still greater refinement. Meanwhile, the various demands made "by bourgeois professional and commercial functions" on members of the middle class worked in the same direction as the strictures of the court, inhibiting drives.[12] In this sense the history of emotions depended secondarily on the rise of capitalism.

Peter Stearns, while agreeing that outside forces cause change, places emphasis on different factors. Industrialization, for him, was the "cause" of the emotional style of the Victorian era, which emphasized loving mothers at home and angry but courageous men in the public sphere: "People began to realize that the same industrial world that required the family as emotional haven also required new emotional motivations for competitive work. . . . The resultant response explains why Victorianism introduced its most distinctive emotional emphases in arguing for channeled anger and courageous encounters with fear."[13] And just as industrialization determined Victorian emotional culture, so too a new mix of factors—among them the ideal of "companionate marriage," the reality of smaller families, and the development of consumerism—led to a repudiation of that culture and an emphasis on muted emotions, the so-called "cool" style.

Stearns's theory thus has emotional standards (his focus) responding to

---

11. The ascendency of the *Annales* school until recently has meant that there has been greater emphasis on structures (which tend to persist) than on change.

12. Elias, *Civilizing Process*, p. 426; on the relationship between the courtiers and the "bourgeois strata" in general see pp. 422–27.

13. Peter N. Stearns, *American Cool: Constructing a Twentieth-Century Emotional Style* (New York, 1994), p. 63.

external forces. Emotions change because other things change; they are "caused" by more traditional historical factors. "New economic forms redefined functional emotions."[14] For Stearns, emotions rarely cause anything; rather, they react and adapt.[15]

William Reddy, in contrast to both Elias and Stearns, seeks "a dynamic, a vector of alteration" in the nature of emotions themselves.[16] He proposes "emotives" as the engine of change that needs no outside push because, by definition, emotives are "self-altering." We have already seen in the introduction to this book how Reddy traced the processes of emotional transformation around the time of the French Revolution. Let me summarize his argument here. The emotives of the pre-Revolutionary court were highly restricted, for emotions were of no interest to the king. At the salons and other "emotional refuges" of the period, however, "sentimentalism" flourished. Celebrating passion as the font of morality, the salon style overcame the court style, and the French Revolution was born. But the emotives of sentimentalism induced their own constriction and emotional suffering. The revolutionaries could not tolerate that goals might change or that passions might lead people down different paths. A new emotional regime emerged to ease the suffering. It relegated feelings to the private sphere, where they could flourish in luxuriant and contradictory abundance, while leaving the public sphere to "reason."

The mechanisms that Reddy argues for these two transformations are not precisely parallel. The emotional suffering of the court was ameliorated by the "refuges"—so in this case, the change to the new emotional regime of the French Revolution was the triumph of the salon and the theater. The emotional suffering of the Terror was ameliorated by nothing at all—suggesting that the new emotional regime of Romanticism grew out of sheer desperation. Nevertheless, in both cases emotional styles changed because of emotional suffering. Suffering, or rather its relative lack, also explains the resilience of Romanticism.[17]

Not only does Reddy's theory largely deny agency to external factors, but it makes such factors depend on emotions themselves: "The power of emotives to shape feeling had a decisive impact on the opening and the outcome

---

14. Ibid., p. 193.

15. Ibid., p. 66. But Stearns and Stearns, *Emotionology*, p. 820, suggests that it is possible that "emotional changes *cause* other fundamental changes" (emphasis in original).

16. Reddy, "Against Constructionism," p. 327.

17. On the stability of the new emotional regime, see Reddy, *Navigation of Feeling*, chap. 7.

of the Revolution. The eighteenth-century rise of sentimentalism gave the Revolution both its initial impetus and a strong bias toward extremism."[18]

EMOTIONAL COMMUNITIES AS AGENTS OF CHANGE

Stearns and Elias must be at least partly right. If emotions are involved in assessments of weal and woe, then they must respond to social, political, and economic changes, because those are the things that create the stimuli that both require and shape judgment and action. Nevertheless, Reddy is surely correct in asserting that emotions have a dynamic of their own and real historical force. The Neustrian courtiers around Clothar II and Dagobert competed for favor and power not by fomenting factions (that would be a later development) but by drawing together in a tight fraternity dedicated to patronage and commendation. The nature of their emotional style—one inspired, I have argued, by Columbanian monasticism—helped determine the ways in which the Neustrians responded to the cares, duties, and goals of kings, courtiers, and bishops. They *could* have been highly competitive, but they were not. Later, however, the elites of Francia saw and appreciated the role of envy. This was not only because they were confronted with feuding factions but also because they had their own expectations and assumptions about human and demonic behavior, which *led* them to see envy in such instances. I am arguing that the norms of their emotional community helped fan the flames of factional feuding. There is not one emotional response to events or situations but rather many possible ones. Emotional communities help determine which responses win out—and which ones are never tried.

If we sought emotional codes and norms in the aggregate—within the entire European West, for example—we would see *no* difference between the emotional world of the Neustrian courtiers and that of the late seventh-century elite, since foremost would be the emotional presuppositions of Christianity, which were intrinsic to both. If, to the contrary, we sought emotional norms at the level of the family, we would be even more hard put to get our bearings. It is only when we look at the norms of groups smaller than universal Christendom and larger than nuclear families that we are able to see how the general Christian stance was variously interpreted, expressed, and, indeed, contested. Contestation means that different emotional com-

---

18. Ibid., p. 258. It is true that Reddy mentions in passing factors other than sentimentalism that led to the Terror (p. 210), and that, in his *H-France Review* reply to Popkin (p. 3), he regrets not "underscor[ing] this point more carefully."

munities coexisted. This is easiest to see in the example of Gallic funeral epitaphs, where the bereaved of different cities expressed emotions—if at all—very differently. While at the end of the sixth century the pope at Rome, Gregory the Great, distrusted most emotions, in Gaul at about the same time Bishop Gregory of Tours and his friend Fortunatus luxuriated in emotions of every sort. In place of Reddy's "emotional regime" I suggest we speak of ascendant emotional communities. When the Neustrian court, chastised and reformed by Columbanus, came to the fore, it displaced the group adhering to Brunhild and Sigibert (patrons of Gregory and Fortunatus) not only politically but also with regard to the production of texts. The Neustrians became an ascendant emotional community.

But it seems reasonable to suppose that the emotional style that had once characterized the Austrasian court of Brunhild continued to be cultivated among some aristocratic groups, changing over time, to be sure (just as we have seen that epitaphs even in one place changed over time). Other communities, too—with different norms and largely invisible to us—no doubt persisted even under Neustrian hegemony. One such "subordinate" emotional community, for example, may have existed at Langres; it emphasized anxiety. More important for the future, some of the groups coexisting under the Neustrians were already cultivating the rancorous, Devil-filled styles of emotional expression which came to the fore in the late seventh century. Fredegar, the chronicler with whom chapter 6 begins, may represent one such a group.[19] It was only in the last two or three decades of that century, however, that members of such communities gained sufficient influence to claim, through their near monopoly on writing, their own interpretation of the past. Thus the group in power, by dominating the instruments of communication, setting the parameters for preferment, and locking out those who do not share their views, has a mighty influence on the emotional norms of a period—at least, on the norms that the historian is able to see.

SECULAR SPHERES / RELIGIOUS SPHERES

Elias, Stearns, and Reddy are the most important theorists of the history of emotion to date. It is striking that all three situate emotions and their transformations—whether imposed at court, liberated in refuges, or discussed in

---

19. Marina Mangiameli argues that Fredegar's work reflects the interests of the aristocracy, keen to gain new concessions and convinced that these were best guaranteed through the palace mayors; Mangiameli, "Rileggendo 'Fredegario': Appunti per una analisi del *Chronicon*," *Romanobarbarica* 14 (1996–97): 307–57, esp. 342, 348–57.

advice books—in the secular sphere. None concerns himself with religion in the slightest degree.[20] Is the Middle Ages—that "Age of Faith"—still to be set apart from the "secular" modern age in emotions history as in all other areas of inquiry? In the light of the role of religion in our own day, this seems a blinkered view. Rather, the example of the Middle Ages suggests that religious values, ideas, and teachings powerfully influence the expression of emotion. Further, the effects go the other way as well: habits of emotional expression shape the ways in which religion is experienced and understood.

With regard to the Early Middle Ages, the first of these statements—that religion, in this instance Christianity, helped shape emotional communities—is probably sufficiently clear from the forgoing chapters. Like the notes of a scale, the building blocks of Christianity were both varied and finite; and like notes, they could be arranged, drawn upon, omitted, and emphasized in nearly infinite ways. Thus the late seventh-century community of Gallic elites embraced teachings about the demons that had originally been embedded in the ascetic program of the Church Fathers, but the goals of that particular program itself—the extirpation of passions—they nearly left out. The early seventh-century Neustrian courtiers, potential heirs to the enormous range of emotional vocabulary of a Gregory of Tours (itself based on the legacy of Late Antiquity), privileged a few words, letting the others lapse.[21] Christianity may be said to have informed emotional styles, but there was no "one" Christianity.[22]

This leads to the other side of the coin, that emotional communities in turn helped shape religious expression. The community of Gregory the Great, so ascetic and full of feeling at the same time, expressed its religious ideas quite differently from that of its contemporary Gregory of Tours, whose *Histories* have rightly been interpreted as the bishop's attempt to "edify the church"—to show the "establishment of the kingdom of God

---

20. In his review of *Navigation of Feeling* in *H-France Review*, Jeremy Popkin notes (p. 6): "Reddy's account says nothing about religion, despite its large role in inculcating styles of emotional management and the powerful emotions unleashed by anything affecting it."

21. Manuscripts of Gregory's works were produced in the seventh century, as a glance at those collated for the MGH edition of Gregory's *Histories* shows (e.g., MSS B1 and B2, MGH SRM 1/1, p. xxv). However, I am assuming that people who wrote (such as Gregory) also spoke and trained others to speak; in this way, among others, emotional communities that no longer show up in the extant sources may have nevertheless perpetuated themselves.

22. See Brown, *Rise of Western Christendom*.

through word and deed."[23] The *Histories* were a form of religious expression, but because they recognized such porous borders between the divine and worldly, they might be (and have been) taken to concern the world alone. In effect I am arguing a very basic and general point: that emotional styles have much to do with modes of religious expression. This has implications beyond a general sort of "feel" in religious writings. It means that new words—and their attached ideas—may enter the religious vocabulary as their emotional valence changes. It was a commonplace in Christianity that virtuous women dedicated to God not lose their chastity: consider the bride of Injuriosus in Gregory of Tours's account, weeping and sighing on her wedding night. But in the late seventh century, which privileged rancorous emotions, a saint could become "furious" at a would-be suitor to show her love of God: religious expression here depended on the norms of a particular emotional community.

To be sure, secular factors are also crucial for emotional communities; this was true in the Early Middle Ages as well as now. The Austrasian community of which Gregory of Tours was a part had good political reasons to stress fraternal love; the Neustrian community of Desiderius needed to think a lot about patronage and deference; and the elites of the late seventh century were obliged to worry about the causes and consequences of internecine warfare. The point is not to make religion the sole source of cause and effect but rather to recognize its synergistic role alongside politics, family structure, education, and social norms and obligations. Emotional communities did not become ascendant simply because they gained political power but because their emotional styles suited certain forms of power and lifestyles at certain times.

STAGNATION AND CHANGE

The term *longue durée* was coined by the historian Fernand Braudel to refer to structures of the landscape, material culture, and attitudes that have lasted over the long haul. Few notions fit the idea as well as Western emotions, which has been a category of mind—however variously understood—since the time of Plato.

But this fact should not imply that the history of emotions has changed with the glacial slowness of the *longue durée*. Historians have tended to periodize emotional transformations within the broad eras reminiscent of Western civilization courses: there are "Greek" emotions or even "Greek and

---

23. Heinzelmann, *Gregory of Tours*, p. 172.

Roman" emotions; then come the emotions of the Middle Ages; finally the emotions of the modern period appear.[24]

William Reddy and Peter Stearns have already made clear the enormous transformations in emotional standards, norms, and styles within the modern period. The present book hopes to do the same for a period of the Middle Ages that has rarely been known for its variety and dynamism.[25] By looking at emotional communities, we have seen not just that this or that emotion changed its meaning and valuation but more importantly that whole systems of emotion—integrally related to the traditions, values, needs, and goals of different groups—could come to the fore or fade away within a short span of time. The study of emotional communities alerts us to transformations at the core of human societies once considered invariable and offers new ways to think about the perennial historical issues of stasis and change.

24. I am thinking here above all of Elias, *Civilizing Process* and works beholden to it, but also of such excellent recent studies as Konstan, *Emotions of the Ancient Greeks* and Robert A. Kaster, *Emotion, Restraint, and Community in Ancient Rome* (Oxford, 2005).

25. But see Julia M. H. Smith, *Europe after Rome: A New Cultural History 500–1000* (Oxford, 2005).

SELECTED BIBLIOGRAPHY

PRIMARY SOURCES

Antonius, *Vita sancti Simeonis stylitae*. PL 73. Cols. 325–34.

Aristotle, *The "Art" of Rhetoric*. Translated by John Henry Freese. Loeb Classical Library. London, 1926.

———. *Nicomachean Ethics*. Translated by A. Rackham. Loeb Classical Library. Cambridge, Mass., 1932.

Augustine. *City of God*. Edited by Bernardus Dombart and Alphonsus Kalb. CCSL 47–48. Turnhout, 1955.

———. *Confessions*. Edited by Pierre de Labriolle. Les Belles Lettres. 2 vols. Paris, 1969, 1977.

Avitus of Vienne: Letters and Selected Prose. Edited and translated by Danuta Shanzer and Ian Wood. Liverpool, 2002.

Baudonivia. *Vita Sanctae Radegundis*. Edited by Bruno Krusch. MGH SRM 2. Pp. 377–95. 1888. Reprint, Hannover, 1984.

Bobolenus. *Vita Germani abbatis Grandivallensis*. Edited by Bruno Krusch. MGH SRM 5. Pp. 33–40. 1910. Reprint, Hannover, 1997.

Cassian, John. *Conlationes XXIIII*. Edited by Michael Petschenig. CSEL 13. Pt. 2. Vienna, 1886.

Chartae Latinae Antiquiores. Facsimile Edition of the Latin Charters Prior to the Ninth Century. Edited by Albert Bruckner and Robert Marichal. 46 vols. Lausanne and Dietikon-Zurich, 1954–96.

Cicero. *Laelius de amicitia* 9.32. Translated by William Armistead Falconer. Loeb Classical Library. Cambridge, Mass., 1964.

———. *Cicero on the Emotions: Tusculan Disputations 3 and 4*. Translated by Margaret Graver. Chicago, 2002.

———. *Tusculan Disputations*. Translated by J. E. King. Loeb Classical Library. Cambridge, Mass., 1945.

Columbanus. *Opera*. Edited and translated by G. S. M. Walker. Dublin, 1957.

Desiderius of Cahors. *Epistulae*. In *Epistulae S. Desiderii Cadurcendsis,* edited by Dag Norberg. Studia Latina Stockholmiensia 6. Stockholm, 1961.

Diplomata, Chartae, Epistolae, Leges. Edited by Jean Marie Pardessus. 2 vols. 1843. Reprint, Aalen, 1969.

Dynamius. *Vita Sancti Maximii*. PL 80. Cols. 31–40.

Eligius. *De rectitudine catholicae conversationis tractatus*. PL 40. Cols. 1169–90.

Epistolae aevi Merowingici collectae. Edited by Wilhelm Gundlach. MGH Epistolae 3. Epistolae merowingici et karolini aevi 1. Pp. 110–53. 1892. Reprint, Berlin, 1994.

Epistolae Austrasicae. Edited by Wilhelm Gundlach. MGH Epistolae 3. Epistolae merowingici et karolini aevi 1. Pp. 434–68. 1892. Reprint, Munich, 1994.

Evagrius of Pontus. *Practical Treatise*. In *Évagre de Pontique. Traité pratique ou Le moine,* edited and translated by Antoine Guillaumont and Claire Guillaumont. *SC* 170–71. Paris, 1971.

Ferrandus. *Vita beati Fulgentii pontificis.* In *Vie de Saint Fulgence de Ruspe,* edited and translated by P. G.-G. Lapeyre. Paris, 1929.

Fortunatus, Venantius. *Poems.* In *Venance Fortunat, Poèmes,* edited and translated by Marc Reydellet. Les Belles Lettres. 2 vols. Paris, 1994, 1998.

———. *Poems.* In *Venanti Honori Clementiani Fortunati . . . Opera Poetica,* edited by Fridericus Leo, MGH AA 4/1. Berlin, 1881. Repr. 1981.

———. *Vita Sancti Martini.* In *Venance Fortunat, Oeuvres,* vol. 4, *Vie de saint Martin,* edited and translated by Solange Quesnel. Paris, 1996.

———. *Vita Sanctae Radegundis.* Edited by Bruno Krusch. MGH SRM 2. Pp. 364–77. 1888. Reprint, Hannover, 1984.

Frédégaire, Chronique des temps mérovingiens (Livre IV et Continuations). Edited by Olivier Devillers and Jean Meyers. Turnhout, 2001.

Fredegar. *Chronicle.* In *The Fourth Book of the Chronicle of Fredegar with Its Continuations,* edited and translated by J. M. Wallace-Hadrill. London, 1960.

Galen. *De propriorum animi cuiuslibet affectuum dignotione et curatione.* Edited by Wilko de Boer. Leipzig, 1937.

———. *On the Doctrines of Hippocrates and Plato.* Edited and translated by Phillip de Lacy. Berlin, 1980–84.

———. *On the Passions and Errors of the Soul.* Translated by Paul W. Harkins. [Athens, Ohio], 1963.

Gregory I the Great. *Dialogues.* In *Grégoire le Grand, Dialogues,* edited by Adalbert de Vogüé, translated by Paul Antin. *SC* 251, 260, 265. Paris, 1978–80.

———. *Homiliae in Evangelia.* Edited by Raymond Étaix. CCSL 141. Turnhout, 1999.

———. *Moralia in Job.* Edited by Marcus Adriaen. CCSL 143, 143A, 143B. Turnhout, 1979, 1985.

———. *Registrum Epistularum.* Edited by Dag Norberg. CCSL 140, 140A. Turnhout, 1982.

Gregory of Tours. *Historiarum libri X.* Edited by Bruno Krusch and Wilhelm Levison. MGH SRM 1/1. 1961. Reprint, Hannover, 1993.

———. *Liber de passione et virtutibus sancti Juliani martyris.* Edited by Bruno Krusch. MGH SRM 1/2. Pp. 112–33. Rev. ed. Hannover, 1969.

———. *Liber in gloria confessorum.* Edited by Bruno Krusch. MGH SRM 1/2. Pp. 294–370. Rev. ed. Hannover, 1969.

———. *Liber in gloria martyrum.* Edited by Bruno Krusch. MGH SRM 1/2. Pp. 34–111. Rev. ed. Hannover, 1969.

———. *Liber Vitae Patrum.* Edited by Bruno Krusch. MGH SRM 1/2. Pp. 211–93. Rev. ed. Hannover, 1969.

———. *Libri I–IV de virtutibus beati Martini episcopi.* Edited by Bruno Krusch. Pp. 132–210. MGH SRM 1/2. Rev. ed. Hannover, 1969.

Inscriptions chrétiennes de la Gaule antérieures au VIIIe siècle. 2 vols. Edited by Edmond Le Blant. Paris, 1856, 1865.

Jonas. *Vitae Columbani abbatis discipulorumque eius.* Edited by Bruno Krusch. MGH SRM 4. Pp. 61–152. 1902. Reprint, Hannover, 1997.

———. *Vita Johannis abbatis Reomaensis*. Edited by Bruno Krusch. MGH SRM 3. Pp. 502–17. 1896. Reprint, Hannover, 1995.

Lactantius. *On the Anger of God*. In *Lactance. La colère de dieu*, edited by Christiane Ingremeau. SC 289. Paris, 1982.

Late Merovingian France: History and Hagiography, 640–720. Edited and translated by Paul Fouracre and Richard A. Gerberding. Manchester, 1996.

Nouveau receuil des inscriptions chrétiennes de la Gaule antérieures au VIIIe siècle. Edited by Edmond Le Blant. Paris, 1892.

Ovid. *Heroides*. Translated by Grant Showerman. Revised by G. P. Goold. Loeb Classical Library. Cambridge, Mass., 1986.

Passio Praejecti episcopi et martyris Arverni. Edited by Bruno Krusch. MGH SRM 5. Pp. 225–48. 1910. Reprint, Hannover, 1997.

Passiones Leudegarii episcopi et martyris Augustodunensis I [*Passio Leudegarii*]. Edited by Bruno Krusch. MGH SRM 5. Pp. 282–324. 1910. Reprint, Hannover, 1997.

Plato. *Phaedo*. Translated by Harold N. Fowler. Loeb Classical Library. Cambridge, Mass., 1966.

———. *Phaedrus*. Translated by Harold N. Fowler. Loeb Classical Library. Cambridge, Mass., 1982.

———. *Philebus*. Translated by Harold N. Fowler. Loeb Classical Library. Cambridge, Mass., 1942.

———. *The Republic*. Translated by Paul Shorey. Loeb Classical Library. Cambridge, Mass., 1963.

———. *Timaeus*. In *The Timaeus of Plato*. Edited and translated by R. D. Archer-Hind. London, 1888.

Prudentius. *Psychomachia*. Translated by H. J. Thomson. Loeb Classical Library. London, 1949.

Recueil des inscriptions chrétiennes de la Gaule antérieures à la Renaissance carolingienne. Vol. 8, *Aquitaine première*. Edited by Françoise Prévot. Paris, 1997.

Recueil des inscriptions chrétiennes de la Gaule antérieures à la Renaissance carolingienne. Vol. 1, *Première Belgique*. Edited by Nancy Gauthier. Paris, 1975.

Recueil des inscriptions chrétiennes de la Gaule antérieures à la Renaissance carolingienne. Vol. 15, *Viennoise du Nord*. Edited by Henri I. Marrou and Françoise Descombes. Paris, 1985.

Regula Benedicti. In *La règle de Saint Benoît*, edited by Adalbert de Vogüé. SC 181–86. Paris, 1972–77.

Ruricius. *Epistularum libri duo*. Edited by R. Demeulenaere. CCSL 64. Turnhout, 1985.

Saint-Simon, Louis de. *Mémoires complets et authentiques de Louis de Saint-Simon*. Edited by Adolphe Chéruel. Vol. 1. Paris, 1965.

Seneca. *On Anger*. Translated by John W. Basore. Loeb Classical Library. Cambridge, Mass., 1963.

Sidonius. *Letters, Books III–IX*. Translated by W. B. Anderson. Loeb Classical Library. Cambridge, 1965.

Tacitus, *The Histories*. Translated by Clifford H. Moore. Loeb Classical Library. London, 1925.

Die Urkunden der Merowinger = MGH Diplomata regum francorum e stirpe merovingica.

Edited by Theo Kölzer with Martina Hartmann and Andrea Stieldorf. 2 parts. Hannover, 2001.

Visio Baronti monachi Longoretensis. Edited by Wilhelm Levison. MGH SRM 5. Pp. 377–94. 1910. Reprint, Hannover, 1997.

Vita Agili. AASS August VI. Pp. 575–87.

Vita Amandi. Edited by Bruno Krusch. MGH SRM 5. Pp. 428–49. 1910. Reprint, Hannover, 1997.

Vita Audoini episcopi Rotomagensis. Edited by Wilhelm Levison. MGH SRM 5. Pp. 553–67. 1910. Reprint, Hannover, 1997.

Vita Desiderii Cadurcae urbis episcopi. Edited by Bruno Krusch. MGH SRM 4. Pp. 547–602. 1902. Reprint, Hannover, 1997.

Vita Eligii episcopi Noviomagensis. Edited by Bruno Krusch. MGH SRM 4. Pp. 663–741. 1902. Reprint, Hannover, 1997.

Vita Pauli episcopi Virdunensis. AASS February II. Pp. 175–78.

Vita Sadalbergae abbatissae Laudunensis. Edited by Bruno Krusch. MGH SRM 5. Pp. 49–66. 1910. Reprint, Hannover, 1997.

Vita Sanctae [Domnae] Balthildis A. Edited by Bruno Krusch. MGH SRM 2. Pp. 482–508. 1888. Reprint, Hannover, 1984.

Vita Sanctae Geretrudis A. Edited by Bruno Krusch. MGH SRM 2. Pp. 453–64. 1888. Reprint, Hannover, 1984.

Vita Sulpicii episcopi Biturigi. Edited by Bruno Krusch. MGH SRM 4. Pp. 371–80. 1902. Reprint, Hannover, 1997.

Vita Wandregiseli abbatis Fontanellensis. Edited by Bruno Krusch, MGH SRM 5. Pp. 13–24. 1910. Reprint, Hannover, 1997.

SECONDARY SOURCES

Abu-Lughod, Lila. *Veiled Sentiments: Honor and Poetry in a Bedouin Society.* Berkeley, 1986.

Althoff, Gerd. "Empörung, Tränen, Zerknirschung. 'Emotionen' in der öffentlichen Kommunikation des Mittelalters." *Frühmittelalterliche Studien* 30 (1996): 60–79.

———. "*Ira Regis:* Prolegomena to a History of Royal Anger." In *Anger's Past,* chap. 3.

———. "Demonstration und Inszenierung. Spielregeln der Kommunikation in mittelalterlicher Öffentlichkeit." *Frühmittelalterliche Studien* 27 (1993): 27–50.

———. *Otto III.* Translated by Phyllis G. Jestice. University Park, Pa., 2003.

Ancient Anger: Perspectives from Homer to Galen. Edited by Susanna Braund and Glenn W. Most. Yale Classical Studies, vol. 32. Cambridge, 2003.

Anger's Past: The Social Uses of an Emotion in the Middle Ages. Edited by Barbara H. Rosenwein. Ithaca, N.Y., 1998.

Annas, Julia. "Epicurean Emotions." *Greek, Roman, and Byzantine Studies* 30 (1989): 145–64.

Approaches to Emotion. Edited by Klaus R. Scherer and Paul Ekman. Hillsdale, N.J., 1984.

Ariès, Philippe. *Centuries of Childhood.* Translated by Robert Baldick. New York, 1962.

Arnold, Magda B. *Emotion and Personality.* 2 vols. New York, 1960.

Atkinson, Clarissa W. *The Oldest Vocation: Christian Motherhood in the Middle Ages.* Ithaca, N.Y., 1991.

Auerbach, Erich. *Mimesis: The Representation of Reality in Western Literature.* Translated by Willard Trask. Garden City, N.J., 1957.
Bailey, Lisa. "Building Urban Christian Communities: Sermons on Local Saints in the Eusebius Gallicanus Collection." *Early Medieval Europe* 12 (2003): 1–24.
Baldwin, John W. *The Language of Sex: Five Voices from Northern France around 1200.* Chicago, 1994.
Barton, Richard E. "'Zealous Anger' and the Renegotiation of Aristocratic Relationships in Eleventh- and Twelfth-Century France." In *Anger's Past,* chap. 7.
Becher, Matthias. "'*Cum lacrimis et gemitu*': Vom Weinen der Sieger und der Besiegten im frühen und hohen Mittelalter." In *Formen und Funktionen öffentlicher Kommunikation im Mittelalter,* edited by Gerd Althoff and Verena Epp, pp. 25–52. Stuttgart, 2001.
Bloch, Marc. *Feudal Society.* Translated by L. A. Manyon. Chicago, 1961.
Boesch Gajano, Sofia. *Gregorio Magno. Alle origini del Medioevo.* Rome, 2004.
———. "La proposta agiografica dei 'Dialogi' di Gregorio Magno." *Studi Medievali,* ser. terza, 21 (1980): 623–64.
Boquet, Damien. *L'ordre de l'affect au Moyen Âge. Autour de l'anthropologie affective d'Aelred de Rievaulx.* Caen, 2005.
Bowlby, John. *Attachment and Loss.* Vol. 1, *Attachment.* New York, 1969.
The Broken Body: Passion Devotion in Late-Medieval Culture. Edited by Alasdair A. MacDonald, H. N. B. Ridderbos, and R. M Schlusemann. Groningen, 1998.
Brown, Peter. *The Rise of Western Christendom: Triumph and Diversity A.D. 200–1000.* Oxford, 1996.
Bullough, Donald. "The Career of Columbanus." In *Columbanus: Studies on the Latin Writings,* pp. 1–28.
Bulst, Walther. "Radegundis an Amalafred." In *Bibliotheca Docet. Festgabe für Carl Wehmer,* pp. 369–80. Amsterdam, 1963.
Byers, Sarah C. "Augustine and the Cognitive Cause of Stoic 'Preliminary Passions' (*Propatheiae*)." *Journal of the History of Philosophy* 41 (2003): 433–48.
Carozzi, Claude. *Le voyage de l'âme dans l'au-delà, d'après la littérature latine: V^e–XIIIe siècle.* Rome, 1994.
Caswell, Caroline P. *A Study of "Thumos" in Early Greek Epic.* Leiden, 1990.
Charles-Edwards, T. M. "The Penitential of Columbanus." In *Columbanus: Studies on the Latin Writings,* pp. 217–39.
Cheyette, Fredric L. "Giving Each His Due." In *Debating the Middle Ages. Issues and Readings,* edited by Lester K. Little and Barbara H. Rosenwein, pp. 170–79. Oxford, 1998.
Ciccarese, Maria Pia. *Visioni dell'Aldilà in occidente. Fonti, modelli, testi.* Florence, 1987.
Cicero on the Emotions: Tusculan Disputations 3 and 4. Translated by Margaret Graver. Chicago, 2002.
Clanchy, Michael. "Law and Love in the Middle Ages." In *Disputes and Settlements,* pp. 47–67.
Clark, Stuart. "French Historians and Early Modern Popular Culture." *Past and Present,* no. 100 (1983): 62–99.
Cohen, Esther. "The Animated Pain of the Body." *AHR* 105 (2000): 36–68.

Colish, Marcia L. *The Stoic Tradition from Antiquity to the Early Middle Ages.* Vol. 1, *Stoicism in Classical Latin Literature.* Rev. ed. Leiden, 1990.

Collins, Roger. *Fredegar.* Authors of the Middle Ages. Historical and Religious Writers of the Latin West, vol. 4, no. 13. Aldershot, 1996.

Columbanus: Studies on the Latin Writings. Edited by Michael Lapidge. Woodbridge, 1997.

*Concordance de l'*Historia Francorum *de Grégoire de Tours.* Edited by Denise St.-Michel. 2 vols. Montréal, [1979].

Consolino, Franca Ela. "*Amor spiritualis* e linguaggio elegiaco nei *Carmina* di Venanzio Fortunato." *Annali della Scuola normale superiore di Pisa, classe di lettere e filosofia* 7 (1977): 1351–68.

Contreni, John J. "'Building Mansions in Heaven': The *Visio Baronti,* Archangel Raphael, and a Carolingian King." *Speculum* 78 (2003): 673–706.

Cornelius, Randolph R. *The Science of Emotion: Research and Tradition in the Psychology of Emotion.* Upper Saddle River, N.J., 1996.

Curtius, Ernst Robert. *European Literature and the Latin Middle Ages.* Translated by Willard R. Trask. New York, 1953.

Damasio, Antonio R. *The Feeling of What Happens: Body and Emotion in the Making of Consciousness.* New York, 1999.

Darwin, Charles. *The Expression of the Emotions in Man and Animals.* Edited by Paul Ekman. 3d ed. New York 1998.

de Jong, Mayke. *In Samuel's Image: Child Oblation in the Early Medieval West.* Leiden, 1996.

de Nie, Giselle. "Images of Invisible Dynamics: Self and Non-Self in Sixth-Century Saints' Lives." *Studia Patristica* 35 (2001): 52–64.

———. *Views from a Many-Windowed Tower: Studies of Imagination in the Works of Gregory of Tours.* Amsterdam, 1987.

Delumeau, Jean. *La Peur en Occident, XIVe-XVIIIe siècle. Une cité assiégée.* Paris, 1978.

———. *Rassurer et protéger. Le sentiment de sécurité dans l'Occident d'autrefois.* Paris, 1989.

de Vogüé, Adalbert. "Grégoire le Grand est-il l'auteur des *Dialogues*?" *Revue d'histoire ecclésiastique* 99 (2004): 158–61.

———. "Les mentions des oeuvres de Cassien chez Benoît et ses contemporains." *Studia Monastica* 20 (1978): 275–85.

Dill, Samuel. *Roman Society in Gaul in the Merovingian Age.* London, 1926.

Dinzelbacher, Peter. *Angst im Mittelalter. Teufels-, Todes- und Gotteserfahrung; Mentalitätsgeschichte und Ikonographie.* Paderborn, 1996.

———. "La donna, il figlio e l'amore. La nuova emozionalità del XII secolo." In *Il secolo XII: la «renovatio» dell'Europa cristiana,* edited by Giles Constable et al., pp. 207–52. Bologna, 2003.

Disputes and Settlements: Law and Human Relations in the West. Edited by John Bossy. Cambridge, 1983.

The Disputing Process: Law in Ten Societies. Edited by Laura Nader and Harry F. Todd. New York, 1978.

Dixon, Thomas. *From Passions to Emotions: The Creation of a Secular Psychological Category.* Cambridge, 2003.

Doi, Takeo. *The Anatomy of Dependence.* Translated by John Bester. Tokyo, 1973.

Dror, Otniel E. "The Scientific Image of Emotion: Experience and Technologies of Inscription." *Configurations* 7 (1999): 355–401.

———. "Techniques of the Brain and the Paradox of Emotions, 1880–1930." *Science in Context* 14 (2001): 643–60.

Duindam, Jeroen. *Myths of Power: Norbert Elias and the Modern European Court.* Amsterdam, [1994].

Ebling, Horst. *Prosopographie der Amtsträger des Merowingerreiches von Chlothar II. (613) bis Karl Martell (741).* Munich, 1974.

Effros, Bonnie. *Caring for Body and Soul: Burial and the Afterlife in the Merovingian World.* University Park, Pa., 2002.

Ekman, Paul. "All Emotions Are Basic." In *The Nature of Emotion: Fundamental Questions.* edited by Paul Ekman and Richard J. Davidson. New York, 1994.

Ekman, Paul, and Wallace V. Friesen. "Constants across Cultures in the Face and Emotion." *Journal of Personality and Social Psychology* 17 (1971): 124–29.

Elias, Norbert. *The Civilizing Process.* Translated by Edmund Jephcott. Rev. ed. Oxford, 1994.

———. *The Germans: Power Struggles and the Development of Habitus in the Nineteenth and Twentieth Centuries.* Edited by Michael Schröter. Translated by Eric Dunning and Stephen Mennell. New York, 1996.

Eliasoph, Nina, and Paul Lichterman. "Culture in Interaction." *American Journal of Sociology* 108 (2003): 735–94.

Ellsworth, Phoebe C. "Some Implications of Cognitive Appraisal Theories of Emotion." In *International Review of Studies on Emotion.* Vol. 1. Pp. 143–61.

Elm, Susanna. *"Virgins of God": The Making of Asceticism in Late Antiquity.* Oxford, 1994.

Emotions: Syllabi and Instructional Materials. Edited by Catherine G. Valentine, Steve Derné, and Beverley Cuthbertson Johnson. New York, 1999.

Epp, Verena. *Amicitia. Zur Geschichte personaler, sozialer, politischer und geistlicher Beziehungen im frühen Mittelalter.* Stuttgart, 1999.

———. "Männerfreundschaft und Frauendienst bei Venantius Fortunatus." In *Variationen der Liebe. Historische Psychologie der Geschlechterbeziehung,* edited by Thomas Kornbichler and Wolfgang Maaz. Forum Psychohistorie 4. Tübingen, 1995.

The Ethnography of Law. Edited by Laura Nader. Menasha, Wisc., 1965.

Evans, Dylan. *Emotion: The Science of Sentiment.* Oxford, 2001.

Ewig, Eugen. *Trier im Merowingerreich. Civitas, Stadt, Bistum.* Trier, 1954.

Fichtenau, Heinrich. "Adressen von Urkunden und Briefen." In *Beiträge zur Mediävistik: Ausgewählte Aufsätze,* 3:149–66. Stuttgart, 1986.

Fillion-Lahille, Janine. *Le "De ira" de Sénèque et la philosophie stoïcienne des passions.* Paris, 1984.

Fouracre, Paul. "Attitudes towards Violence in Seventh- and Eighth-Century Francia." In *Violence and Society in the Early Medieval West,* edited by Guy Halsall, pp. 60–75. Woodbridge, 1998.

———. "Merovingian History and Merovingian Hagiography." *Past and Present,* no. 127 (1990): 3–38.

———. "The Nature of Frankish Political Institutions in the Seventh Century." In *Franks and*

Alemanni in the Merovingian Period: An Ethnographic Perspective, edited by Ian Wood, pp. 285–301. Woodbridge, 1998.

Fournier, P.-F. "Clermont-Ferrand au VIe siècle. Recherches sur la topographie de la ville." *Bibliothèque de l'École des Chartes* 128 (1970): 273–344.

Franks, David D. "The Bias against Emotions in Western Civilization." In *Sociology of Emotions: Syllabi and Instructional Materials,* ed. Catherine G. Valentine, Steve Derné, and Beverley Cuthbertson Johnson. New York, 1999.

Freud, Sigmund. *The Complete Introductory Lectures on Psychoanalysis.* Translated and edited by James Strachey. New York, 1966.

Gallant, Thomas W. "Honor, Masculinity, and Ritual Knife Fighting in Nineteenth-Century Greece." *AHR* 105 (2000): 358–82.

Gauthier, Nancy. *L'Évangélisation des pays de la Moselle. La province romaine de Première Belgique entre Antiquité et Moyen âge, IIIe–VIIIe siècles.* Paris, 1980.

Gauvard, Claude. *"De Grace Especial." Crime, état et société en France à la fin du Moyen Age.* 2 vols. Paris, 1991.

George, Judith. *Venantius Fortunatus: A Latin Poet in Merovingian Gaul.* Oxford, 1992.

Gerberding, Richard A. *The Rise of the Carolingians and the "Liber Historiae Francorum."* Oxford, 1987.

Godman, Peter. *Poets and Emperors: Frankish Politics and Carolingian Poetry.* Oxford, 1987.

Goffart, Walter. *The Narrators of Barbarian History: Jordanes, Gregory of Tours, Bede, and Paul the Deacon (A.D. 550–800).* Princeton, 1988.

Grima, Benedicte. *The Performance of Emotion among Paxtun Women: "The Misfortunes Which Have Befallen Me."* Austin, 1992.

Guerreau-Jalabert, Anita. "*Caritas* y don en la sociedad medieval occidental." *Hispania* 60 (2000): 27–62.

——. "*Spiritus* et *caritas.* Le baptême dans la société médiévale." In *La parenté spirituelle. Textes rassemblés et présentés,* edited by Françoise Héritier-Augé and Elisabeth Copet-Rougier. Paris, 1995.

Hanawalt, Barbara A. "Medievalists and the Study of Childhood." *Speculum* 77 (2002): 440–60.

Handley, Mark A. "Beyond Hagiography: Epigraphic Commemoration and the Cult of Saints in Late Antique Trier." In *Society and Culture in Late Antique Gaul: Revisiting the Sources,* edited by Ralph W. Mathisen and Danuta Shanzer, pp. 187–200. Aldershot, 2001.

——. *Death, Society and Culture: Inscriptions and Epitaphs in Gaul and Spain, AD 300–750.* BAR International Series 1135. Oxford, 2003.

——. "Inscribing Time and Identity in the Kingdom of Burgundy." In *Ethnicity and Culture in Late Antiquity,* edited by Stephen Mitchell and Geoffrey Greatrex, pp. 83–102. London, 2000.

Hankinson, James. "Actions and Passions: Affection, Emotion and Moral Self-Management in Galen's Philosophical Psychology." In *Passions and Perceptions,* pp. 184–222.

Harris, William V. *Restraining Rage: The Ideology of Anger Control in Classical Antiquity.* Cambridge, Mass., 2001.

Heinzelmann, Martin. *Gregory of Tours: History and Society in the Sixth Century.* Translated by Christopher Carroll. Cambridge, 2001.

Hen, Yitzhak. "The Christianisation of Kingship." In *Der Dynastiewechsel von 751. Vorgeschichte, Legitimationsstrategien und Erinnerung,* edited by Matthias Becher and Jörg Jarnut, pp. 163–77. Münster, 2004.

———. *Culture and Religion in Merovingian Gaul, A.D. 481–751.* Leiden, 1995.

———. "The Structure and Aims of the *Visio Baronti*." *Journal of Theological Studies,* n.s. 47 (1996): 477–97.

Hochschild, Arlie Russell. *The Managed Heart: Commercialization of Human Feeling.* Berkeley, 1983.

Huizinga, Johan. *The Autumn of the Middle Ages.* Translated by Rodney J. Payton and Ulrich Mammitzsch. Chicago, 1996.

Hummer, Hans. "Die merowingische Herkunft der Vita Sadalbergae." *Deutsches Archiv für Erforschung des Mittelalters* 60 (2004): 1–35.

———. *Politics and Power in Early Medieval Europe: Alsace and the Frankish Realm, 600–1000.* Cambridge, 2005.

Hyams, Paul. *Rancor and Reconciliation in Medieval England.* Ithaca, N.Y., 2003.

International Review of Studies on Emotion. Vol. 1. Edited by Ken T. Strongman. Chichester, 1991.

Inwood, Brad. "Seneca and Psychological Dualism." In *Passions and Perceptions,* pp. 150–83.

Isen, Alice M. and Gregory Andrade Diamond. "Affect and Automaticity." In *Unintended Thought,* edited by James S. Uleman and John A. Bargh, pp. 124–52. New York, 1989.

Jaeger, C. Stephen. *Ennobling Love: In Search of a Lost Sensibility.* Philadelphia, 1999.

Jannet-Vallat, Monique. "L'organisation spatiale des cimetières Saint-Pierre et Saint-Georges de Vienne (IVᵉ–XVIIIᵉ siècle)." In *Archéologie du cimetière chrétien,* Actes du 2ᵉ colloque A.R.C.H.E.A. (Association en Région Centre pour l'Histoire et l'Archéologie), edited by Henri Galinié and Elisabeth Zadora-Rio, pp. 125–37. Tours, 1996.

Jolliffe, J. E. A. *Angevin Kingship.* 2d ed. London, 1963.

Kaster, Robert A. *Emotion, Restraint, and Community in Ancient Rome.* Oxford, 2005.

King, Margaret. "Commemoration of Infants on Roman Funerary Inscriptions." In *The Epigraphy of Death: Studies in the History and Society of Greece and Rome,* edited by G. J. Oliver, pp. 117–54. Liverpool, 2000.

King, Peter. "Aquinas on the Passions." In *Aquinas's Moral Theory: Essays in Honor of Norman Kretzmann,* edited by Scott MacDonald and Eleonore Stump, pp. 101–32. Ithaca, N.Y., 1999.

Klingshirn, William. *Caesarius of Arles: The Making of a Christian Community in Late Antique Gaul.* Cambridge, 1994.

Knight, Gillian R. *The Correspondence between Peter the Venerable and Bernard of Clairvaux: A Semantic and Structural Analysis.* Aldershot, 1988.

Knuuttila, Simo. "Medieval Theories of the Passions of the Soul." In *Emotions and Choice from Boethius to Descartes,* edited by Henrik Lagerlund and Mikko Yrjönsuuri, pp. 49–83. Dordrecht, 2002.

Koebner, Richard. *Venantius Fortunatus. Seine Persönlichkeit und seine Stellung in der geistigen Kulture des Merowingerreiches.* Leipzig, 1915.

Konstan, David. "Aristotle on Anger and the Emotions: The Strategies of Status." In

Ancient Anger: Perspectives from Homer to Galen, Yale Classical Studies, vol. 32, edited by Susanna Braund and Glenn W. Most, pp. 99–120. Cambridge, 2003.

———. *The Emotions of the Ancient Greeks: Studies in Aristotle and Classical Literature.* Toronto, forthcoming.

———. *Friendship in the Classical World.* Cambridge, 1997.

———. *Pity Transformed.* London, 2001.

Labande-Mailfert, Yvonne. "Les débuts de Sainte-Croix." In *Histoire de l'abbaye Sainte-Croix de Poitiers. Quatorze siècles de vie monastique = Mémoires de la Société des Antiquaires de l'Ouest,* 4th ser., 19 (1986–87): 21–116.

Lakoff, George. *Women, Fire, and Dangerous Things: What Categories Reveal about the Mind.* Chicago, 1986.

Lapidge, Michael. "Epilogue: Did Columbanus Compose Metrical Verse?" In *Columbanus: Studies on the Latin Writings,* pp. 274–85.

Leclercq, Jean. *The Love of Learning and the Desire for God.* Translated by Catherine Misrahi. New York, 1961.

———. *Monks and Love in Twelfth-Century France.* Oxford, 1979.

LeDoux, Joseph. *The Emotional Brain: The Mysterious Underpinnings of Emotional Life.* New York, 1996.

Leighton, Stephen R. "Aristotle and the Emotions." In *Essays on Aristotle's Rhetoric,* edited by Amélie Oksenberg Rorty. Berkeley, 1996.

Le Jan, Régine. *La société du haut Moyen Âge, VIe–IXe siècle.* Paris, 2003.

Levillain, Léon. "Études mérovingienne. La charte de Clotilde (10 mars 673)." *Bibliothèque de l'École des chartes* 105 (1944): 5–63.

Leyser, Conrad. *Authority and Asceticism from Augustine to Gregory the Great.* Oxford, 2000.

———. "Charisma in the Archive: Roman Monasteries and the Memory of Gregory the Great, c. 870–c. 940." In *Le Scritture dai monasteri,* edited by Flavia De Rubeis and Walter Pohl. Rome, 2003.

———. "'Divine Power Flowed from this Book': Ascetic Language and Episcopal Authority in Gregory of Tours' *Life of the Fathers.*" In *The World of Gregory of Tours,* pp. 283–94.

Lifshitz, Felice. "Gender and Exemplarity East of the Middle Rhine: Jesus, Mary and the Saints in Manuscript Context." *Early Medieval Europe* 9 (2000): 325–44.

Little, Lester K. *Benedictine Maledictions: Liturgical Cursing in Romanesque France.* Ithaca, N.Y. 1993.

Loyen, André. *Sidoine Apollinaire et l'esprit précieux en Gaule aux derniers jours de l'empire.* Les Belles Lettres. Paris, 1943.

Macherey, P. "Le Lysis de Platon: dilemme de l'amitié et de l'amour." In *L'Amitié. Dans son harmonie, dans ses dissonances,* edited by Sophie Jankélévitch and Bertrand Ogilvie, pp. 58–75. Paris, 1995.

MacMullen, Ramsay. *Feelings in History, Ancient and Modern.* Claremont, Calif., 2003.

Mandler, George. *Mind and Emotion.* New York, 1975.

Mangiameli, Marina. "Rileggendo 'Fredegario': Appunti per una analisi del *Chronicon.*" *Romanobarbarica* 14 (1996–97): 307–57.

Markus, Robert A. *Gregory the Great and His World.* Cambridge, 1997.

Mathisen, Ralph W. "The *Codex Sangallensis* 190 and the Transmission of the Classical

Tradition during Late Antiquity and the Early Middle Ages." *International Journal of the Classical Tradition* 5 (1998): 163–94.

McDermott, William C. "Felix of Nantes: A Merovingian Bishop." *Traditio* 31 (1975): 1–24.

Medieval Conduct. Edited by Kathleen Ashley and Robert L. A. Clark. Minneapolis, 2001.

Metts, Sandra, Susan Sprecher, and Pamela C. Regan. "Communication and Sexual Desire." In *Handbook of Communication and Emotion: Research, Theory, Applications, and Contexts,* edited by Peter A. Andersen and Laura K. Guerrero, pp. 353–77. San Diego, 1998.

Meyvaert, Paul. "The Date of Gregory the Great's Commentaries on the Canticle of Canticles and on 1 Kings." *Sacris Erudiri* 23 (1979): 191–216.

Miller, William Ian. *Humiliation: And Other Essays on Honor, Social Discomfort, and Violence.* Ithaca, N.Y., 1993.

Monsacré, Hélène. *Les larmes d'Achille. Le héros, la femme et la souffrance dans la poésie d'Homère.* Paris, 1984.

Montanari, Massimo. "Uomini e orsi nelle fonti agiografiche dell'alto Medioevo." In *Il Bosco nel medioevo,* edited by Bruno Andreolli and Massimo Montanari, pp. 57–72. Bologna, 1988.

Moos, Peter von. *Consolatio. Studien zur mittellateinischen Trostliteratur über den Tod und zum Problem der christlichen Trauer.* 4 vols. Munich, 1971–72.

Moreira, Isabel. *Dreams, Visions, and Spiritual Authority in Merovingian Gaul.* Ithaca, N.Y., 2000.

Morsbach, H., and W. J. Tyler. "A Japanese Emotion: *Amae.*" In *The Social Construction of Emotions,* edited by Rom Harré, chap. 15. Oxford, 1986.

Nagy, Piroska. *Le don des larmes au Moyen Âge. Un instrument spirituel en quête d'institution (V^e–XIIIe siècle).* Paris, 2000.

Nelson, Janet L. "Gendering Courts in the Early Medieval West." In *Gender in the Early Medieval World: East and West, 300–900,* edited by Leslie Brubaker and Julia M. H. Smith, pp. 185–97. Cambridge, 2004.

———. "Queens as Jezebels: The Careers of Brunhild and Balthild in Merovingian History." Chap. 1 in *Politics and Ritual in Early Medieval Europe.* London, 1986.

Newhauser, Richard. *The Treatise on Vices and Virtues in Latin and the Vernacular.* Turnhout, 1993.

Nielsen, Hanne Sigismund. "Interpreting Epithets in Roman Epitaphs." In *The Roman Family in Italy: Status, Sentiment, Space,* edited by Beryl Rawson and Paul Weaver, pp. 169–204. Canberra, 1997.

Nussbaum, Martha C. *The Therapy of Desire: Theory and Practice in Hellenistic Ethics.* Princeton, 1994.

———. *Upheavals of Thought: The Intelligence of Emotions.* Cambridge, 2001.

Oatley, Keith. *Best Laid Schemes: The Psychology of Emotions.* Cambridge, 1992.

Padberg, Lutz E. von. *Heilige und Familie. Studien zur Bedeutung familiengebundener Aspekte in den Viten des Verwandten- and Schülerkreises um Willibrord, Bonifatius, und Liudger.* 2d ed. Mainz, 1997.

Pancer, Nira. *Sans peur et sans vergogne. De l'honneur et des femmes aux premiers temps mérovingiens.* Paris, 2001.

Passions and Perceptions: Studies in Hellenistic Philosophy of Mind. Proceedings of the Fifth

Symposium Hellenisticum. Edited by Jacques Brunschwig and Martha C. Nussbaum. Cambridge, 1993.

The Passions in Roman Thought and Literature. Edited by Susanna Morton Braund and Christopher Gill. Cambridge, 1997.

Pelletier, André. "Vienne et la réorganisation provinciale de la Gaule au Bas-Empire." *Latomus* 26 (1967): 491–99.

Pelliccia, Hayden. *Mind, Body, and Speech in Homer and Pindar.* Göttingen, 1995.

Pétré, Hélène. *Caritas. Étude sur le vocabulaire latin de la charité chrétienne.* Louvain, 1948.

Peyroux, Catherine. "Gertrude's *furor*: Reading Anger in an Early Medieval Saint's *Life*." In *Anger's Past,* chap. 2.

Pinker, Steven. *How the Mind Works.* 2d ed. New York, 1999.

Plutchik, Robert. "Emotions: A General Psychoevolutionary Theory." In *Approaches to Emotion,* pp. 197–220.

Popkin, Jeremy D. Review of *Navigation of Feeling,* by William M. Reddy. *H-France Review* 2 (November 2002), no. 118. www3.uakron.edu/hfrance/vol2reviews/popkin4.html.

Poulin, Joseph-Claude. "Saint Léger d'Autun et ses premiers biographes (fin VIIe–milieu IXe siècle)." *Bulletin de la Société des Antiquaires de l'Ouest,* 4th ser., 16 (1977): 167–200.

Prinz, Friedrich. *Frühes Mönchtum im Frankenreich: Kultur und Gesellschaft in Gallien, den Rheinlanden und Bayern am Beispiel der monastischen Entwicklung (4. bis 8. Jahrhundert).* 2d. ed. Munich, 1988.

The Prosopography of the Later Roman Empire. Vol. 3, A.D. 527–641. Edited by John Robert Martindale. Cambridge, 1992.

Réal, Isabelle. *Vies de saints, vie de famille. Représentation et système de la parenté dans le Royaume mérovingien (481–751) d'après les sources hagiographiques.* Turnhout, 2001.

Rebillard, Éric. *"In hora mortis." Évolution de la pastorale chrétienne de la mort aux IVe et Ve siècles dans l'occident Latin.* Rome, 1994.

Reddy, William M. "Against Constructionism: The Historical Ethnography of Emotions." *Current Anthropology* 38 (1997): 327–51.

———. "Emotional Liberty: Politics and History in the Anthropology of Emotions." *Cultural Anthropology* 14 (1999): 256–88.

———. *The Navigation of Feeling: A Framework for the History of Emotions.* Cambridge, 2001.

———. Reply to Jeremy D. Popkin's review of *Navigation of Feeling. H-France Review* 2 (November 2002), no. 119. www3.uakron.edu/hfrance/vol2reviews/reddy2.html.

Reynaud, Jean-François. "Les églises Saint-Pierre et Saint-Georges de Vienne. Documents du XIXe siècle et études archéologiques récentes." *Bulletin archéologique du Comité des Travaux Historique et Scientifiques.* Nouv. sér., 10–11 A (1977): 7–32.

———. "'Vienne la Sainte' au moyen-âge." *Archeologia* 88 (1975): 44–54.

Richards, Jeffrey. *Consul of God: The Life and Times of Gregory the Great.* London, 1980.

Riché, Pierre. *Education and Culture in the Barbarian West Sixth through Eighth Centuries.* Translated by John J. Contreni. Columbia, S.C., 1976.

Roberts, Michael. *The Jeweled Style: Poetry and Poetics in Late Antiquity.* Ithaca, N.Y., 1989.

———. "Venantius Fortunatus; Elegy on the 'The Death of Galswintha' (*Carm.* 6.5)." In *Society and Culture in Late Antique Gaul: Revisiting the Sources,* edited by Ralph W. Mathisen and Danuta Shanzer, pp. 298–312. Aldershot, 2001.

Roberts, Simon. *Order and Dispute: An Introduction to Legal Anthropology.* Harmondsworth, England, 1979.
Romagnoli, Daniela. "La courtoisie dans la ville: un modèle complexe." In *La ville et la cour. Des bonnes et des mauvaises manières,* edited by Daniela Romagnoli, chap. 1. Paris, 1995.
Roper, Michelle L. "Uniting the Community of the Living with the Dead: The Use of Other-World Visions in the Early Middle Ages." In *Authority and Community in the Middle Ages,* edited by Donald Mowbray, Rhiannon Purdie, and Ian P. Wei, pp. 19–42. Gloucestershire, 1999.
Rosaldo, Renato. *Culture and Truth: The Remaking of Social Analysis.* 2d ed. Boston, 1993.
———. *Ilongot Headhunting: A Social History, 1883–1974.* Stanford, 1980.
Rosenwein, Barbara H. "Emotional Space." In *Codierungen von Emotionen im Mittelalter,* edited by C. Stephen Jaeger and Ingrid Kasten, pp. 289–93. Berlin, 2003.
———. "*In gestis emendatioribus:* Gregory the Great and the *Gesta martyrum.*" In *Retour aux sources. Textes, études et documents d'histoire médiévale offerts à Michel Parisse,* edited by Sylvain Gouguenheim et al., pp. 843–48. Paris, 2004.
———. *Negotiating Space: Power, Restraint, and Privileges of Immunity in Early Medieval Europe.* Ithaca, N.Y., 1999.
———. "The Places and Spaces of Emotion." In *Uomo e Spazio nell'alto medioevo,* Settimane di studio del Centro Italiano di Studi Sull'alto medioevo 50, pp. 505–36. Spoleto, 2003.
———. "Worrying about Emotions in History." *AHR* 107 (2002): 921–45.
Ruricius of Limoges and Friends: A Collection of Letters from Visigothic Gaul. Translated by Ralph W. Mathisen. Translated Texts for Historians 30. Liverpool, 1999.
Schmidt-Wiegand, Ruth. "Gebärdensprache im mittelalterlichen Recht." *Frühmittelalterliche Studien* 16 (1982): 363–79.
Schmitt, Emile. *Le mariage chrétien dans l'oeuvre de Saint Augustin. Une théologie baptismale de la vie conjugale.* Paris, 1983.
Schubert, Martin J. *Zur Theorie des Gebarens im Mittelalter. Analyse von nichtsprachlicher Äußerung in mittelhochdeutscher Epik: Rolandslied, Eneasroman, Tristan.* Cologne, 1991.
Schwerhoff, Gerd. "Zivilisationsprozeß und Geschichtswissenschaft. Norbert Elias' Forschungsparadigma in historischer Sicht." *Historische Zeitschrift* 266 (1998): 561–606.
Sciuto, Italo. "Le passioni e la tradizione monastica." *Doctor Seraphicus: Bolletino d'informazioni del Centro di studi bonaventuriani* 45 (1998): 5–39.
Servatius, Carlo. "'Per ordinationem principis ordinetur.' Zum Modus der Bishofsernennung im Edikt Chlothars II vom Jahre 614." *Zeitschrift für Kirchengeschichte* 84 (1973): 1–29.
Shanzer, Danuta. "History, Romance, Love, and Sex in Gregory of Tours' *Decem libri historiarum.*" In *The World of Gregory of Tours,* pp. 395–418.
———. "So Many Saints—So Little Time . . . the *Libri Miraculorum* of Gregory of Tours." *Journal of Medieval Latin* 13 (2003): 19–60.
Shaver, Phillip, Judith Schwartz, Donald Kirson, and Cary O'Connor. "Emotion Knowledge: Further Exploration of a Prototype Approach." *Journal of Personality and Social Psychology* 52 (1987): 1061–86.
Smail, Daniel Lord. "Hatred as a Social Institution in Late-Medieval Society." *Speculum* 76 (2001): 90–126.

Smith, Craig. A. and Richard S. Lazarus. "Appraisal Components, Core Relational Themes, and the Emotions." *Cognition and Emotion* 7 (1993): 233–69.
Smith, Julia M. H. *Europe after Rome: A New Cultural History 500–1000*. Oxford, 2005.
Sorabji, Richard. *Emotion and Peace of Mind: From Stoic Agitation to Christian Temptation*. The Gifford Lectures. Oxford, 2000.
Soulet, Marie-Hélène. "L'image de l'amour conjugal et de l'épouse dans l'épigraphie chrétienne lyonnaise aux VIe et VIIe siècles." In *La Femme au Moyen Âge*, edited by Michel Rouche and Jean Heuclin, pp. 139–45. Maubeuge, 1990.
Stafford, Pauline. "Parents and Children in the Early Middle Ages." *Early Medieval Europe* 10 (2001): 257–71.
Stancliffe, Clare. "Jonas's *Life of Columbanus and his Disciples*." In *Studies in Irish Hagiography: Saints and Scholars*, edited by Máire Herbert, John Carey, and Pádraig Ó Riain, pp. 189–220. Dublin, 2001.
Stanton, Robert. "Columbanus, *Letter* 1: Translation and Commentary," *Journal of Medieval Latin* 3 (1993): 149–68.
Stearns, Carol Zisowitz, and Peter N. Stearns. *Anger: The Struggle for Emotional Control in America's History*. Chicago, 1986.
Stearns, Peter N. *American Cool: Constructing a Twentieth-Century Emotional Style*. New York, 1994.
Stearns, Peter N., with Carol Z. Stearns. "Emotionology: Clarifying the History of Emotions and Emotional Standards." *AHR* 90 (1985): 813–36.
Stevenson, Jane Barbara. "The Monastic Rules of Columbanus." In *Columbanus: Studies on the Latin Writings*, pp. 203–16.
Storia delle Passioni. Edited by Silvia Vegetti Finzi. Rome, 1995.
Stowers, Stanley K. *Letter Writing in Greco-Roman Antiquity*. Philadelphia, 1986.
Straw, Carole. *Gregory the Great*. Authors of the Middle Ages. Historical and Religious Writers of the Latin West, vol. 4, no. 12. Aldershot, 1996.
———. *Gregory the Great: Perfection in Imperfection*. Berkeley, 1988.
Strongman, Ken T. *The Psychology of Emotion*. 3rd ed. Chichester, 1987.
Sullivan, Shirley Darcus. *Aeschylus' Use of Psychological Terminology: Traditional and New*. Montreal, 1997.
———. *Psychological and Ethical Ideas: What Early Greeks Say*. Leiden, 1995.
———. *Sophocles' Use of Psychological Terminology: Old and New*. Ottawa, 1999.
Tavris, Carol. *Anger: The Misunderstood Emotion*. Rev. ed. New York, 1989.
Thacker, Alan. "Memorializing Gregory the Great: The Origin and Transmission of a Papal Cult in the Seventh and Early Eighth Centuries." *Early Medieval Europe* 7 (1998): 59–84.
Thraede, Klaus. *Grundzüge griechisch-römischer Brieftopik*. Munich, 1970.
Toch, Michael. "Ethics, Emotion and Self-interest: Rural Bavaria in the Later Middle Ages." *Journal of Medieval History* 17 (1991): 135–47.
Topographie chrétienne des cités de la Gaule des origines au milieu du VIIIe siècle. Edited by Nancy Gauthier and J.-Ch. Picard. Vol. 6, *Province ecclésiastique de Bourges (Aquitania Prima)*, edited by François Prevot and Xavier Barral i Altet. Paris, 1989.

Topographie chrétienne des cités de la Gaule des origines au milieu du VIIIe siècle. Edited by Nancy Gauthier and J.-Ch. Picard. Vol. 1, *Province ecclésiastique de Trèves (Belgica Prima)*, edited by Nancy Gauthier. Paris, 1986.

Topographie chrétienne des cités de la Gaule des origines au milieu du VIIIe siècle. Edited by Nancy Gauthier and J.-Ch. Picard. Vol. 3, *Provinces ecclésiastiques de Vienne et d'Arles*, edited by Jacques Biarne. Paris, 1986.

Van Dam, Raymond. *Saints and Their Miracles in Late Antique Gaul*. Princeton, 1993.

Vegetti, Mario. *La medicina in Platone*. Venice, 1995.

Viano, Cristina. "Competitive Emotions and *Thumos* in Aristotle's *Rhetoric*." In *Envy, Spite and Jealousy: The Rivalrous Emotions in Ancient Greece*, Edinburgh Leventis Studies 2, edited by David Konstan and N. Keith Rutter, pp. 85–97. Edinburgh, 2003.

Vierck, Hayo. "L'oeuvre de saint Eloi, orfèvre, et son rayonnement." In *La Neustrie. Les pays au nord de la Loire, de Dagobert à Charles le Chauve (VIIe–IXe siècle)*, edited by Patrick Périn and Laure-Charlotte Feffer, pp. 403–9. Rouen, 1985.

Wagner, M. Monica. "A Chapter in Byzantine Epistolography: The Letters of Theodoret of Cyrus," *Dumbarton Oaks Papers* 4 (1948): 119–81.

White, Stephen D. "Clothild's Revenge: Politics, Kinship, and Ideology in the Merovingian Blood Feud." In *Portraits of Medieval and Renaissance Living: Essays in Memory of David Herlihy*, edited by Samuel K. Cohn Jr. and Steven A. Epstein, pp. 107–30. Ann Arbor, 1996.

———. "The Politics of Anger." In *Anger's Past*, chap. 6.

Wood, Ian. "Constructing Cults in Early Medieval France: Local Saints and Churches in Burgundy and the Auvergne, 400–1000." In *Local Saints and Local Churches in the Early Medieval West*, edited by Alan Thacker and Richard Sharpe, pp. 155–87. Oxford, 2002.

———. "Deconstructing the Merovingian Family." In *The Construction of Communities in the Early Middle Ages: Texts, Resources and Artifacts*, edited by Richard Corradini, Max Diesenberger, and Helmut Reimitz, pp. 149–71. Leiden, 2002.

———. "The Ecclesiastical Politics of Merovingian Clermont." In *Ideal and Reality in Frankish and Anglo-Saxon Society: Studies Presented to J. M. Wallace-Hadrill*, edited by Patrick Wormald, Donald Bullough, and Roger Collins, pp. 34–57. Oxford, 1983.

———. "Fredegar's Fables." In *Historiographie im frühen Mittelalter*, edited by Anton Scharer and Georg Scheibelreiter, pp. 359–66. Vienna, 1994.

———. *Gregory of Tours*. Headstart History Papers. Bangor, Gwynedd, 1994.

———. "The Individuality of Gregory of Tours." In *The World of Gregory of Tours*, pp. 29–46.

———. "Jonas, the Merovingians, and Pope Honorius: *Diplomata* and the *Vita Columbani*." In *After Rome's Fall: Narrators and Sources of Early Medieval History: Essays Presented to Walter Goffart*, edited by Alexander Callander Murray. Toronto, 1998.

———. "Letters and Letter-Collections from Antiquity to the Early Middle Ages: The Prose Works of Avitus of Vienne." In *The Culture of Christendom: Essays in Medieval History in Commemoration of Denis L. T. Bethell*, edited by Marc Anthony Meyer, pp. 29–43. London, 1993.

———. *The Merovingian Kingdoms, 450–751*. London, 1994.

———. *The Missionary Life: Saints and the Evangelisation of Europe 400–1050*. Harlow, England, 2001.

———. "The Vita Columbani and Merovingian Hagiography." *Peritia* 1 (1982): 63–80.

The World of Gregory of Tours. Edited by Kathleen Mitchell and Ian Wood. Leiden, 2002.
Wright, Neil. "Columbanus's *Epistulae.*" In *Columbanus: Studies on the Latin Writings,* pp. 29–92.
Zaborowski, Robert. *La crainte et le courage dans l'Iliade et l'Odyssee: contribution lexicographique à la psychologie homérique des sentiments.* Warsaw, 2002.
Zelzer, Michaela. "Der Brief in der Spätantike. Überlegungen zu einem literarischen Genos am Beispiel der Briefsammlung des Sidonius Apollinaris." *Wiener Studien* 107–8 (1994–95): 541–51.
Zivilisations-Prozesse. Zu Erziehungsschriften in der Vormoderne. Edited by Rüdiger Schnell. Cologne, 2004.

INDEX

Abu-Lughod, Lila, 21, 24
Ado, 133. *See also* Neustrian court and courtiers
affectus, 39, 93, 191
Agen. *See* Sallustius, bishop
Agerad, bishop, 173–75
Ageric, bishop, 103
Agnes, abbess 107, 118–19, 121–22, 127–28. *See also* Holy Cross convent
Alboin, king, 123
Alsace, 188
Althoff, Gerd, 12–13, 175, 178
amae, 15
Amalfrid, 114–15
Amandus, bishop, 134–35
amor. *See* love words
Andelot, Treaty of, 108
anger words, 39, 41–42, 44–48, 50, 81–83, 149, 151, 156, 173, 179, 181, 184, 188, 194, 196. *See also* envy words; malice
Annales school, 6
Annegray, 131
anxiety words, 90, 147–48, 152, 187–88, 200
Apollinaris, Sidonius, 60, 72, 140–41
Arian heresy, 68, 73
Aristotle, 35–37, 195
Arles. *See* Caesarius, bishop
Arnold, Magda, 13–14
Arnulf of Metz, 176
Aspasia, abbess, 140, 145, 193
Athala, abbot, 145–46, 149, 153, 158–60
Athanagild, 115
Atsma, Harmut, 171
Auden, W. H., 11
Audoenus. *See* Dado
Augustine, Saint, 41–42, 50–51, 98, 151, 194
Austrasia, 62, 69, 102, 129–30, 165, 169, 200. *See also* Brunhild, queen; Dagobert I, king; Sigibert I, king; Reims/Metz court

Autun, 169–70. *See also* Martyrdom of Leudegar
Auvergne, 166, 170. *See also* Clermont
avarice words, 42, 46, 81, 156
avaritia. *See* avarice words
Avitus, bishop of Vienne, 73, 75
Avitus I, bishop of Clermont, 101, 126–27
Avitus II, bishop of Clermont, 170

Balthild, queen, 133, 135, 169, 171, 184. *See also Life of Balthild; Martyrdom of Leudegar*
banality. *See* topoi
Barontus. *See Vision of Barontus*
Baudoaldus, bishop, 122
Baudonivia, 107, 116, 119, 126, 128–29, 194
Berny-Rivière, 103, 107, 110
Bertegiselus, abbot, 141
biblical exegesis, and emotions, 28
Bobbio, 131–32, 134, 140, 145. *See also* Athala, abbot; Columbanus; Waldebert, abbot; Wandregisil
Bobolenus. *See Life of Germanus*
Bobolenus, abbot, 140
Bodegisl, 106, 113, 121
Bourdieu, Pierre, 25
Bourges. *See* Sulpicius, bishop; Vulfoleodus, bishop
Bowlby, John, 6
Braudel, Fernand, 202
Brioude, 108
Brunhild, queen, 102–8, 115, 120, 129, 132–33, 144, 149–50, 155–56, 163–64, 200
Bruyères-le-Châtel, 173
Burgundy and Burgundians, 73, 102, 124, 148, 165, 178

Caesarius, bishop, 128
Cahors. *See* Desiderius
Canace, 115
Carentinus, bishop, 123
caritas. *See* love words
carus/carissimus. *See* terms of endearment
Cassian, John, 47, 152, 180, 182–84
Cassiodorus, 86
Chamalières, 170
Charibert, king, 102, 106, 110, 123
charters, 146–47, 161, 171–74, 195
Chartres. *See* Agerad, bishop
Cheyette, Fredric, 11–12
Childebert I, king, 110, 124
Childebert II, king, 108, 131
Childeric II, king, 181, 186
Chilperic, king, 102–3, 110, 150, 156
Chramlinus, bishop, 173
Chramnesind. *See* Sichar and Chramnesind
Chronicle of Fredegar. *See* Fredegar
Cicero, 38–40, 48–49
Civilizing Process. *See* Elias, Norbert: *Civilizing Process*
Clanchy, Michael, 12
Clarus, 185
Clermont: city of, 68–72, 100, 102. *See also* Avitus I, bishop of Clermont; Avitus II, bishop of Clermont; *Martyrdom of Praejectus*
Clothar I, king, 102, 106, 111, 114, 124
Clothar II, king, 129–30, 132–35, 144, 150, 156, 163–64
Clothar III, king, 183, 186
Clotild, *Deo devota*, 173
Clotild, queen, 102, 110
Clovis I, king, 102, 124
Clovis II, king, 130, 133, 146–47, 169, 172
Cologne. *See* Carentinus, bishop
Columbanus, 130–35, 192, 200; emotions in writings of, 131, 157–61. *See also* Jonas: *Life of Columbanus*
commendation, 141–42
compassion: in Gregory the Great, 86–89
compunction: in Gregory the Great, 86–89

condescension of emotion: in Gregory the Great, 85–91
consolation words, 65, 68, 145, 147–48, 155
Cornelius, Randolph, 15
Council of Paris, 156
cupiditas. *See* desire words
Curtius, Ernst, 29

Dado, 133–34, 137–40, 142, 163. *See also Life of Audoin*; Neustrian court and courtiers
Dagobert I, king, 130, 133–34, 172, 178
Dagobert II, king, 170
deference and hierarchy, 138–42, 158, 161–62, 180
Delumeau, Jean, 6
demons and Devil, 47, 81–82, 95, 171, 174, 179, 182–85, 188, 200
Desert Fathers, 42–43, 46–50, 97, 128, 130, 144, 156, 182–83. *See also* Cassian, John; Evagrius
Desiderius: career, 134, 156; letters of, 135–48, 163, 193. *See also Life of Desiderius*; Neustrian court and courtiers
desire words, 38, 174, 186
"Destruction of Thuringia, The," 114–15. *See also* Fortunatus, Venantius
Deurechild, 152–53
Devil. *See* demons and Devil
Dhuoda, 154
Dialogues, 79–80, 86–89. *See also* Gregory the Great: theory of emotions of
Diamond, Gregory Andrade. *See* Isen, Alice M.
Dido, bishop, 168
dilectio/diligo. *See* love words; terms of endearment
dilectus/dilectissimus. *See* love words; terms of endearment
Dinzelbacher, Peter, 6
Disticha Catonis, 8
Dixon, Thomas, 3, 194
dolor. *See* grief words; sadness words
dulcedo, 29, 66, 106–7, 110–113, 195. *See also*

Fortunatus, Venantius; Gregory of Tours; terms of endearment
dulcis/dulcissimus. See dulcedo; family feeling; love words; terms of endearment
Dynamius of Marseille, 106, 126, 128

Ebroin, mayor, 165, 171, 183–86
Edict of Paris, 156
Egidius, bishop, 102–3
Ekman, Paul: lists of emotions of, 54, 126, 185
Eleutherius, 95–96, 178
Elias, Norbert: *Civilizing Process*, 7–10, 155, 197, 200; historians' responses to, 9–13
Eligius, bishop, 133–34, 137, 140, 143, 145–46, 154–55. *See also* Neustrian court and courtiers; sermons
elite, 196. *See also* pan-Frankish elite
Embrun. *See* Chramlinus, bishop
emotional communities: ascendant, 200; defined, 2, 23–27, 109, 164–67, 188–89; overarching and subordinate, 24, 61–62, 125, 199–200. *See also entries for particular emotional communities*
emotional refuges and regimes, 19–23, 125–27, 198–200
emotional suffering. *See* emotional refuges and regimes
emotionology, 6–7, 97, 197–98
emotions: as agents of change, 196–200, 202–3; ancient words for, 38–40, 47, 191; automatic and habitual nature of, 18, 27, 29, 82; cognitive and social constructionist theories of, 13–15, 18, 155, 179, 191; gestures and, 12–13, 27, 117; gendering of, 8, 149–55, 161; historical sources and, 26–29, 193–96; historiography of, 9–13, 17–23, 196–99; hydraulic theory of, 13, 33; modern lists of, 53–55; modern words for, 3–5, 191; political uses of, 11–13, 117, 122–23, 175–79; religious sensibilities and, 127–28, 200–202; Stoic theory of, 37–42, 55, 196; vices and, 39, 46–49, 81–91, 156, 182–83. *See also affectus*; *motus/motus animi*; *pas-*

sio/passiones; *perturbatio/perturbationes*; pre-emotions; *entries for individual emotion words; emotions markers and gestures; texts; vices; and writers*
emotives, Reddy's theory of, 18–22, 25, 27, 198–99
envy words, 42, 45, 48, 72, 81, 123, 125–26, 175, 182–84
epitaphs, 61, 193, 195, 200; models for, 59–61; number of, in Gaul, 57; physical appearance of, 57; at Clermont, 60, 68–72; at Trier, 60, 62–68; at Vienne, 61, 73–77
Ercamberta, 173
Eufronius, bishop, 106–7
eupatheiai, 42
Eustasius, abbot, 170, 188
Evagrius, 46–47, 182
evil thoughts. *See* pre-emotions

family feeling: at Trier, 66–68, 99; in Gregory the Great, 92–95; in Gregory of Tours and Fortunatus, 113–22, 180. *See also* love; friendship
fathers and other men, 94, 123, 150
fear words, 38, 41–42, 50, 76, 84, 92, 97, 145–47, 157, 160, 172–73, 175, 178, 185–86, 188
feigning emotion. *See* sincerity
Felicity, Saint: *Homily* on, 92–94, 98
felix. See happiness words
first movements. *See* pre-emotions
Fontaines, 131
Fontanelle, 171. *See also Life of Wandregisil*
Fortunatus, Venantius: friendship with Gregory of Tours, 100–102, 109; life and background, 100, 102–8; *Life of Radegund*, 126; poem in praise of virginity, 118–19; sincerity of, 29, 100–101 n. 4, 122; *See also* "The Destruction of Thuringia"; *dulcedo*; Gregory of Tours; letters and letter collections
Foucault, Michel, 25
Franci, 167–68

Fredegar, 163–64, 178
Fredegund, queen, 103, 117, 129, 150
French Revolution, 19–21, 198–99
Freud, Sigmund, 7
friendship, 11, 113–14, 122, 136, 143–44. See also Fortunatus, Venantius; Gregory of Tours; letters and letter collections; love words
Friesen, Wallace. See Ekman, Paul
Fulgentius of Ruspe, 151
furor, 185–86, 202. See also anger words

Galen, 41, 49
Gallomagnus, bishop, 106
Gallus, uncle of Gregory of Tours, 70 n. 52, 116
gastrimargia. See gluttony
gaudium. See joy words
gemitus. See groans and sighs
gender. See fathers and other men; mothers and other women
Genesius, bishop, 181
genre: constraints of, 27–29, 195–96. See also emotions: historical sources and; *topoi*; *entries for individual genres*
Germanus, abbot. See *Life of Germanus*
Gertrude. See *Life of Gertrude*
gestures. See emotions: and gestures
gluttony, 35, 46–48, 81
Gogo, 106, 121–22
Grandval, 168–69. See also *Life of Germanus*
greed. See avarice words
Gregory of Tours: and Clermont, 100; and cult of saints Julian and Martin, 108–9; emotional sensibility of, 28, 119–20, 124–25, 127–29, 132, 153, 192, 194–95, 200–202; episcopal appointment of, 102; irony in, 110–11, 125, 195; and Vienne, 69–70; use of *dulcedo*, 110–13. See also Fortunatus, Venantius
Gregory the Great: community of, 81, 129, 158, 201; life and works, 79–80; seven deadly sins in, 48, 81; theory of emotions of, 81–91, 116, 127–28, 149, 180, 183, 192, 196, 200. See also *Dialogues*; letters and letter collections; *Moralia in Job*
grief words, 42, 44, 65–66, 75, 89, 116–17, 155, 177–78, 184. See also tears; emotions: gestures and; sadness words
Grima, Benedicte, 22
Grimoald, mayor, 139, 144, 169
groans and sighs, 44, 49, 75, 90, 177. See also emotions: political uses of; grief words; sadness words
Guntram, king, 102, 123, 131, 156

Habermas, Jürgen, 19 n. 75
hagiography: constraints of genre of, 151–52, 195; defined, 25; and emotions, 28
Hanawalt, Barbara, 9
Handley, Mark A., 63, 67
happiness words, 38, 44, 50, 64, 71, 95–96, 157, 159–60. See also joy words
Harré, Rom, 53
hate words, 41–42, 45, 123–25, 163–64
hēdonē. See happiness words
Heliodorus, 150
Herchenefreda, 154–55, 164, 196
Hermenar, bishop, 170
Heroides, 114
hierarchy. See deference and hierarchy
Hochschild, Arlie, 23–24
Holy Cross convent, 102, 106–7, 116–17, 127–28
Homer, 32–33
Homilies on the Book of Ezechiel, 79
Homilies on the Gospel, 79. See also Felicity, Saint: *Homily* on
Huizinga, Johan, 5–6, 8, 175; historians' responses to, 9–13
Hummer, Hans, 170, 188
Hyams, Paul, 12
hydraulic theory. See emotions: hydraulic theory of

Illidius, Saint, 112, 116
imitatio Christi, 22
immunities, 131

Ingund, daughter of Brunhild, 115
Ingund, queen of Clothar I, 111
Injuriosus, 111, 119–20, 202
inscriptions, funerary. *See* epitaphs
invidia. See envy words
ira. See anger words
Irish monasticism, 130–31. *See also* Columbanus
Isen, Alice M., 18, 21, 27, 29
Itta, wife of Pippin I, 169

Jaeger, C. Stephen, 10–11, 114
James-Lange theory, 27
jealousy. *See* envy words
Jerome, Saint, 43–46, 150
John of Réomé. *See* Jonas: *Life of John of Réomé*
Jolliffe, J. E. A., 11
Jonas: life, 134–35, 156; *Life of Columbanus*, 131–32, 140, 144, 146, 149, 152–53, 157, 163, 188; *Life of John of Réomé*, 148, 151, 185, 188–89. *See also* Neustrian court and courtiers
Jouarre, 133
joy words, 44, 64–65, 68, 75, 77, 95, 117, 137, 153, 161, 175–78. *See also* happiness words; tears
Julian, Saint, 108
Justin II, emperor, 114
Justus, monk, 89–90

kissing, 44
Krusch, Bruno, 170, 188

Lactantius, 42, 46
laetitia. See happiness words; joy words
Lagny, 132
Landeric, bishop, 146, 172–73
Langres, 148, 170, 189, 200. *See also* Jonas: *Life of John of Réomé*; *Life of Sadalberga*
Laon, 170
laughter and smiles, 44, 76, 95, 148, 159. *See also* happiness words; joy words
Lazarus, Richard, 14

Leclercq, Jean, 10
Lérins, 148
letters and letter collections, 28, 90–92, 135–36, 140–41, 196. *See also* Desiderius: letters of
Leudeberta, 146
Leudegar, 169–71. *See also Martyrdom of Leudegar*
Levin, Robert, 195
libido, 38, 41–42
Life of Audoin, 167, 175–78
Life of Balthild, 167–68, 178, 180, 185, 187. *See also* Balthild, queen
Life of Columbanus. See Jonas: *Life of Columbanus*
Life of Desiderius, 137, 154. *See also* Desiderius
Life of Fulgentius of Ruspe, 151
Life of Germanus, 168–69, 176
Life of Gertrude, 169, 185–86, 194
Life of John of Réomé. See Jonas: *Life of John of Réomé*
Life of Pachomius, 152
Life of Sadalberga, 170, 179, 187–89
Life of Simeon Stylites, 151
Life of Wandregisil, 170–71, 176, 178, 184
Limoges. *See* Ruricius, bishop
Longoret, monastery of Saint Peter at, 168
longue durée, 202
Louis XIV, court of, 21–22
love words, 41, 45, 64–65, 76–77, 83, 85, 90–91, 93–95, 113–23, 125, 137–39, 142–47, 151, 157–59, 175, 194. *See also* family feeling; fathers and other men; friendship; mothers and other women
luctus. See grief words
Lupus, 106, 110, 121, 123
lust, 48, 81
Luxeuil, 131–32, 140, 144, 169, 176, 186, 188–89. *See also* Athala, abbot; Columbanus; Eustasius, abbot
luxuria. See lust

Maastricht. *See* Amandus, bishop
maeror. See grief words

Index { 225

malice, 174, 183. *See also* anger words
Mandler, George, 14
Marcatrude, queen, 123
Marchiennes, 135
Martin, cantor, 182
Martin, Saint, 102, 108–9, 116, 126
Martyrdom of Leudegar, 168–70, 174–75, 178–81, 183–87
Martyrdom of Praejectus, 166, 178, 181–82
Maurice, emperor, 115
Medard, bishop, 114
Medoaldus, bishop, 139, 148
melancholy. *See* sadness words
Méobecq, monastery at, 168
Merovech, son of Theuderic II, 164
metaphors, 193, 196 n. 9
metus. *See* fear words
Metz. *See* Reims/Metz court; Vilicus, bishop
Miller, William Ian, 12
Moore, John C., 10
Moralia in Job, 79, 81–85. *See also* Gregory the Great: theory of emotions of
mothers and other women, 93–94, 98, 112, 124, 149–55, 160–61, 192. *See also* family feeling
motus/motus animi, 5, 50, 191
mourning. *See* grief words
Mozart, Amadeus, 195
Mummola, abbess, 173

Nant, 132
Nanthild, queen, 137
Neustria, 102, 130, 165. *See also* Ebroin, mayor; *Franci*; Neustrian court and courtiers
Neustrian court and courtiers: 130, 132–35, 137, 143, 151, 155, 157–58, 161–62, 180, 185, 192, 199–200, 202. *See also entries for individual members of the court*
Nevers. *See* Rauracius, bishop
Nicetius, bishop of Lyon, 106, 121
Nicetius, bishop of Trier, 69, 103
Nivelles, 169. *See also Life of Gertrude*

Notre-Dame de Bourgmoyen, 173
Noyen. *See* Eligius, bishop
Nussbaum, Martha C., 3, 16–17, 191

Oatley, Keith, 14, 55
odium. *See* hate words
Ouen, Saint. *See* Dado
Ovid, 114

Pachomius, Saint, 152
pain. *See* grief words; sadness words
Palatina, 106
Pancer, Nira, 194
pan-Frankish elite, 165–67, 189, 193, 200–202. *See also entries for the writings of members of this elite*
pan-Gallic elite. *See* pan-Frankish elite
Paris. *See* Charibert, king; Council of Paris; Landeric, bishop
passio/passiones: as martyrdom accounts, 166; as word for "emotion," 47, 85, 182, 191
Pastoral Rule, 79
pathos/pathē, 33–39, 47, 191
Patroclus, 112
Paul, Saint, 86
Paulus, bishop, 137–40, 144
pavor. *See* fear words
perturbatio/perturbationes, 38, 40, 83
Peter, Saint, 146, 179
Pippin I, 144, 169
Pippin II, 165
planctus. *See* grief words
Plato, 33–35
pleasure. *See* happiness words
Plutchik, Robert, 54–55
Poitiers, 170. *See also* Dido, bishop; Holy Cross convent
Praejectus, bishop. *See Martyrdom of Praejectus*
pre-emotions, 39, 41, 46–47, 50, 82, 85, 96, 182
pride, 46–48, 81
Psalter, 156
psuchē, 33–34

Quadragesimus, 87
Quintianus, bishop, 124

Radegund, 106–7, 114, 116–17, 119. *See also* Baudonivia; "The Destruction of Thuringia"; Fortunatus, Venantius: *Life of Radegund*; Holy Cross convent
Rado, 133. *See also* Neustrian court and courtiers
"Radolium," 133
Rauracius, bishop, 142
Rebais, 132–33
Reddy, William M., 16–23, 120, 126, 198–200, 203
Reims/Metz court, 102, 107, 113, 128, 155, 165. *See also* Austrasia; Brunhild, queen; Fortunatus, Venantius; Gregory of Tours; Sigibert I, king
Remiremont, 169
risus. See laughter and smiles
Rodez. *See* Quintianus, bishop
Romainmôtier, 171
Rosaldo, Renato, 22, 24
Rouen. *See* Dado
Rule of St. Benedict, 183
Ruricius, bishop, 136, 141
Rusticus, brother of Desiderius, 138, 155

Sadalberga. *See Life of Sadalberga*
sadness words, 43, 47–48, 50, 65, 71, 77, 81, 84, 89–91, 93, 97, 119–20, 176–78. *See also* grief words
Saint Amantius monastery, 144
Saint-Amarin, 170
Saint-Denis, 146–47, 172–73
Saint-Symphorien, Autun, 170
Sallustius, bishop, 139, 143–44
salutations. *See* letters and letter collections
satire. *See* Gregory of Tours: irony in
Seneca, 39, 41
sermons: and emotions 28, 145, 154–55
Shaver, Philip, 54–55
Sichar and Chramnesind, 111, 124–25
Sigeric, son of Sigismund, 124

sighs. *See* groans and sighs
Sigibert I, king, 102–7, 120, 129, 131, 155–56, 200
Sigibert III, king, 130–34, 139, 147–48, 169
Sigismund, king, 124
Simeon Stylites, 151
sincerity, 19, 26, 28–29, 122, 172, 186, 193
sins. *See* emotions: vices and
Smail, Daniel Lord, 12
smiles. See laughter and smiles
Smith, Craig, 14
Soissons. *See* Medard, bishop
solamen. See consolation words
Solignac, 132–33
Stablo-Malmedy, 132
Stearns, Carol, 7, 97
Stearns, Peter, 7, 97, 196–98, 200, 202
Stoics. *See* emotions: Stoic theory of
Strongman, Ken T., 53
Sullivan, Shirley Darcus, 33
Sulpicius, bishop, 134, 137–40
superbia. *See* pride
sweetness. *See dulcedo*
Syagrius, brother of Desiderius, 138

tears, 43, 45, 49–50, 65, 75, 77, 84, 88, 96, 116, 128, 144–45, 152–53, 160
terms of endearment: in St. Augustine, 51; in charters, 173; in Columbanus's writings, 158; in Desiderius's letter collection, 144; in Herchenefreda's letters, 154–55; at Trier, 64, 66–68, 113; at Vienne, 76. *See also dulcedo*; family feeling
textual communities, 25
Theoctista, Byzantine princess, 91, 95, 98
Theudebert, king, 124
Theuderic I, king, 69
Theuderic II, king, 131–32, 144, 164
Theuderic III, king, 170, 173, 186
thumos, 32–33, 35
timor. *See* fear words
topoi, 27–30, 61, 193. *See also* emotions: historical sources and; sincerity

Tours, 102–3. *See also* Eufronius, bishop; Gregory of Tours
Trier, 62–68, 99, 102, 113
tristitia. *See* sadness words
Tusculan Disputations. *See* Cicero

Venantius, *patricius Italiae*, 90–92
Verdun. *See* Ageric, bishop; Paulus, bishop
Vetus Latina, 43
Vezin, Jean, 171
vices. *See* emotions: vices and; pre-emotions; *entries for individual vices*
Vienne, 72–78, 98–99
Vilicus, bishop, 103
vir Dei, 86–89, 116
virtues, 49, 160
Visigoths: in southern Gaul, 68

Vision of Barontus, 168, 176, 179, 181, 184
voluntas, 39, 50
Volvic, 170
Vulfoleodus, bishop, 168
Vulgate bible: emotion words in, 43–46

Wademir, 173
Waldebert, abbot, 140, 189
Wandregisil, 170–71. *See also Life of Wandregisil*
weeping. *See* tears
White, Stephen D., 12, 178
will. *See voluntas*
women. *See* mothers and other women
Wood, Ian, 103

zelus. *See* envy words

www.ingramcontent.com/pod-product-compliance
Lightning Source LLC
Chambersburg PA
CBHW030135240426
43672CB00005B/131